The Art of Poetry

The Art of Poetry

·THE OXFORD LECTURES 1984–1989·

Peter Levi

·YALE UNIVERSITY PRESS·NEW HAVEN AND LONDON·

For Deirdre

Set in Sabon by Excel Typesetters Co., Hong Kong
Printed and bound in Great Britain by Billing & Sons Ltd, Worcester

Library of Congress Cataloging-in-Publication Data

Levi, Peter.
The art of poetry: the Oxford lectures, 1984–1989/Peter Levi.
p. cm.
Includes bibliographical references and index.
ISBN 0-300-04847-5
1. Poetics. 2. Poetry – History and criticism. I. Title.
PN1042.L37 1991
809.1 – dc20   90-43665
                                                CIP

Contents

Acknowledgements

Thanks are due to the following for permission to quote copyright material from the sources indicated:

Ardis Publishers, Ann Arbor, Michigan:

Boris Pasternak, *My Sister — Life* and *A Sublime Malady* (trans. Mark Rudman with Bohdan Boychuk, 1983).

Boosey & Hawkes Ltd:

The extract from the libretto by W.H. Auden and Chester Kallman for *The Rake's Progress* by Igor Stravinsky © Copyright 1951 by Boosey & Hawkes, Inc. is reprinted by permission of Boosey & Hawkes Music Publishers Ltd.

Faber & Faber Ltd:

W.H. Auden, *Collected Poems* (ed. Edward Mendelson, 1976) and *The English Auden, Poems, Essays and Dramatic Writings 1927–1939* (ed. Edward Mendelson, 1977).

Lawrence Durrell, *Collected Poems* (1966, 1980).

Philip Larkin, *Collected Poems* (ed. Anthony Thwaite, 1988).

Robert Lowell, *Poems 1938–1949* (1950): *Life Studies* (1950); *Imitations* (1962); *For the Union Dead* (1965); *Near the Ocean* (1967); *The Dolphin* (1973); *History* (1973); *Day by Day* (1978).

Ezra Pound, *The Cantos of Ezra Pound* (1964).

Macmillan Publishers Ltd:

Charles Causley, *A Field of Vision* (1988).

W.B. Yeats, *The Poems of W.B. Yeats* (ed. Richard Finneran, 1983).

The Marvell Press:

Philip Larkin, *The Less Deceived* (1955).

Methuen London:

Dom Moraes, *Poems* (Eyre & Spottiswoode, 1960).

Oxford University Press:

David Gascoyne © Oxford University Press. Reprinted from *Collected Verse Translations* by David Gascoyne, edited by Alan Clodd and Robin Skelton (1970) by permission of Oxford University Press.

Penguin Books Ltd:

James Michie, *The Odes of Horace* (Hart-Davis, 1964; Penguin, 1967).

Boris Pasternak, *Selected Poems* (trans. Jon Stallworthy and Peter France, 1983).

Michael Hamburger:

Friedrich Hölderlin, *Poems & Fragments*, ed. and trans. Michael Hamburger (Cambridge University Press, 1980; paperback reprint 1986).

The Salamander Press, Edinburgh:

James Fenton, *The Memory of War* (1982).

Secker & Warburg Ltd:

James Fenton, *Terminal Moraine* (1972).

University of Michigan Press, Ann Arbor, Michigan:

Boris Pasternak, *Poems* (trans. Eugene M. Kayden, 1959).

Unwin Hyman Ltd:

Extract taken from Boris Pasternak, *Poems of Boris Pasternak*, chosen and translated by Lydia Pasternak Slater © George Allen & Unwin, 1963 & 1984. Reproduced by kind permission of Unwin Hyman Ltd.

The Oxford Lectures

The following list gives the order in which the lectures were originally delivered, together with (in parentheses) their date of composition.

Introduction

To introduce this volume of lectures it is necessary to explain the Chair of Poetry at Oxford, which gives its holder a five-year term of office. He or she is appointed by an archaic process of election by the Masters of Arts, but he is not an ordinary professor, because he has no syllabus to follow, and no lectures to support him, and his pupils are not submitted to any examination. This makes him appear amateur, but that impression is mistaken: the point is that poetry is in the end too important and too closely involves freedom of spirit to be systematized or tyrannized over, or tidied away and examined, even though the study of it draws on ordinary academic sources. It depends on libraries, and its professors are distinctly bookish. The Chair of Poetry is a little like a bishop's throne, the *cathedra* or chair from which cathedrals take their name. I make this claim in view of Louis Gernet's *Droit et institutions en Grèce antique*: 'Dans le culte des morts, le terme *cathedra* est un terme technique. Par cette attitude, les vivants s'associent et s'assimilent aux morts: les morts sont représentés comme assis....'[1] I like the idea that the Professor of Poetry is by his office seated among the dead, among the ancestors of the art.

This book was planned six years ago in 1984, when I was elected to the Chair of Poetry at Oxford, but was finished only in 1989, when the five years of my term of office came to an end. I have chosen to print the fifteen lectures that I gave, with only a little necessary editing and revision, because there is something to be said for spontaneity. Modest references have been added at this stage, as an aid to the reader.

Once I was elected, I found my opinions about how best to proceed were already altering. I stuck to a determination to read long passages aloud, to face central subjects, and treat them in a direct way. I was always conscious that I might be speaking to some young poet I had never met, and was anxious to advise and encourage. But I rapidly saw that even in Oxford we have almost no culture in common; a professor of poetry must not assume that his whole audience knows foreign or dead languages or much about modern or very ancient poetry. So I took a long time to work up the courage to discuss Horace and Aeschylus, and even then I always planned lectures of that kind in terms of translations. When the Chair was founded around 1700, there were no schools of modern languages or of English: the subjects were studied, but privately and unofficially. Today the Professor has trouble picking on subjects not dealt with better by other professors. His subject is poetry itself, poetry as poetry, and he normally speaks as a poet.

During his five years of office, he is usually expected to lecture once a term. The original statute governing his behaviour probably represents arguments about whether to accept that poetry should be officially studied, but it is still unrepealed: it commands him to lecture on Latin, Greek and Hebrew poetry, so that a sense of that poetry will aid our understanding of the ancient world. The statute assumes he will lecture in Latin. Many of the lectures of many of the professors seem to have perished, but we have an early Latin lecture by Thomas Tickell, not a great poet, though surely underestimated. He talked about pastoral poetry, a controversial subject at the time; his Latin is elegant but his criticism is jejune. A number of distinguished men occupied the Chair in the eighteenth century, including Louth, whose views on Hebrew prosody appear to have had an influence on Christopher Smart and even on William Blake. They also included Thomas Warton, who combined the positions of Professor of Poetry at Oxford and Poet Laureate to King George III. There was little he could do for his Chair, since the lectures were still in Latin, but he did a great deal for the study of English poetry, and something for Latin; he was an antiquarian, almost an archaeologist, and a fine poet.

Keble's influence as Professor was in its day very great, but the first Professor to speak in English was Matthew Arnold. He was elected young, at the age of thirty-six, and held the Chair for two terms. His intellectual energy was dazzling, and he made this Chair seem central to the University and to English culture. The interest he attracted was not wholly desirable, since the Chair then became a kind of football for political and other such parties. Many of the elections since Arnold's day have been ridiculous or disgraceful, starting with the one at which Arnold himself refused to stand, and persuaded Walter Pater and J. A. Symonds the Renaissance historian not to stand, because they were not respectable enough to win; he jobbed in his friend

Principal Shairp, the head of a college in St Andrews, an old Balliol man and a very bad poet indeed who lectured against Shelley.

In this century the holders of the Chair have usually been academic and not undistinguished until Sir Maurice Bowra gave it his formidable attention. As Professor of Poetry he produced the most brilliant books on the subject since Arnold, and when he lectured on Boris Pasternak he got a letter from that poet saying his dearest ambition had been to be lectured on by Bowra, but the result exceeded his wildest expectations. From about this time onwards, under the influence of Bowra and of Enid Starkie, another remarkable aesthete, Oxford began to elect poets, at first mostly Oxford poets like Auden and Graves and Day Lewis and John Wain. Today one does not need to have been at Oxford to be a candidate, though the voters are still Oxford Masters of Arts, so a local candidate has a head start. I believe the field was widened to allow William Empson to stand, but he never did so. The first non-Oxford Professor was a highly distinguished one, Roy Fuller. The energy I have associated with Sir Maurice Bowra has now subsided.

The whole idea of a professor of poetry is a curious one. It makes sense as an aesthetic gesture in 1700, and at least in retrospect it makes good sense as an expression of romantic high-mindedness in the age of Matthew Arnold. It was a delight and a privilege for my generation to listen to Day Lewis reading Hardy and Valéry, and thrilling to encounter Auden, but the Professor is not now quite like a writer in residence: the University has grown too big for that to be possible. He sees young poets and corresponds with them, he may go to student societies, and he judges occasional competitions, but he has also to make his living, because although his salary is generous as a price per lecture, it is not a living wage: it is more like an enormous tip. The academic world feels awkward about poets unless they are safely dead, and that is that.

Different professors have intended different functions for themselves and I am sure they will continue to do so. I decided to concentrate on these lectures. Their tactics will be seen to vary, but at a deeper level I think their message is very much the same. The light they try to throw on poetry is usually of the same kind. Meanwhile, I earned my living by writing *The Life and Times of William Shakespeare*, and then a book about Boris Pasternak. But I intended these lectures very seriously indeed. I felt and still feel that, whatever I had thought out about the technique and art of poetry, here was my chance to express it. It is a chance given to few poets, and I am more grateful than I can express to those who twice proposed me, those who voted for me and those who listened to me. After my wife, I owe an unpayable debt of gratitude to Fram Dinshaw and to several other fellows of my College, and another to Peter Jay and Anvil Press, who with small resources have been publishing my poems for twenty-five years, and published both my first and my last lectures on the day they were given. I am particularly grateful to John Wain, whose opinions I have often silently absorbed, and to Michael Hamburger, for permission to print his letter (p. 104).

Finally I should add a brief statement about my approach to poetry, which is evident and implicit in all the lectures but nowhere fully and clearly stated. I found it very hard to do this: but I think my approach mostly comes from taking the poems perfectly seriously as human statements, murmuring with pleasure over their technique, and casting a beady glance at history and at literary history. The basic devices of poetry are extremely simple and not intellectual inventions; but on a number of occasions I have tried to show how learning and libraries can illuminate even quite simple poetry. All the same I have dealt only with poems that move me now or once moved me in the past. I tried to bring in obscure or minor writers and queer corners of literary history only on the margin of great and central writers. I have little respect for most of what is normally called literary criticism, much more for history and the knowledge of languages and peoples.

For the purposes of publication, I have altered the order of the lectures except the first and last to a chronological series, though I am not clear that the resulting order makes much more sense than the order in which they were given. It hardly needs saying that the neglect of a particular poet or even of a period will usually be fortuitous: for example, I had already written elsewhere about John Clare, Thomas Hardy and Alexander Pope, I had written a book about ancient Greek literature and now I am writing one about Tennyson; it was chance (and perhaps a fear of the minutiae of criticism proper to them) that kept me away from Donne and Yeats and Marvell, whom of course I esteem quite as highly as the others. My most alarming gap is from Milton to Edward Lear, unless 'Dryden's Virgil' fills it, but 'Visionary Poets' includes Henry Vaughan and William Blake. I wish I had found time for Gower and for William Barnes, but they are not quite the central figures I sometimes imagine they are, and I was afraid they would draw too thin an audience. The important thing is to witness that the art of poetry itself is alive and vigorous.

The Lamentation of the Dead

Today is the feast of Crispinus and Crispianus; it is Agincourt day. When England was still a small, victorious kingdom, at the time when Oxford had recently contributed the word 'quadrangle' to the English language, Shakespeare in his *Henry V* commemorated the dead of Agincourt. The amazing figure of the Chorus in that play, with his inspired voice and his thrilling rhetoric, has a function unique in Shakespeare's works. He summons up reality, and yet he creates an exalted atmosphere. That was how Shakespeare's audience would like to think of history, and of the heroic dead.

> Can this cockpit hold
> the vasty fields of France? or may we cram
> within this wooden O the very casques
> that did affright the air at Agincourt?
> (Prologue, ll. 11–14)

The helmet of Henry V, a battered metal object which Shakespeare tells us the King in modesty refused to have paraded through London, is still displayed above his tomb in Westminster Abbey, and Shakespeare knew it. This play is not so much a lament as a commemoration, a summoning up of the dead. The tiny knot of actors of the Elizabethan stage stand well in their inadequacy for the tiny crowd of the English at Agincourt.

> Then shall our names,
> familiar in his mouth as household words,
> Harry the King, Bedford and Exeter,
> Warwick and Talbot, Salisbury and Gloucester,
> be in their flowing cups freshly remembered.
> This story shall the good man teach his son;
> and Crispin Crispian shall ne'er go by

5

> from this day to the ending of the world,
> but we in it shall be remembered.
> (Act Four, scene 3, ll. 51–9)

This is the assurance of eternal praise. But the burial, even the lamentation of the dead, is also an important theme that runs through the play from the first act until the chorus of the last.

> I Richard's body have interred new;
> and on it have bestowed more contrite tears
> than from it issued forced drops of blood.
> (Act Four, scene 1, ll. 291–3)

We must think, as so often in Shakespeare, of a ritual that restores the order of nature. The climax of the theme is not only in the magnificent and contrasted lists of the French and English dead: it is also in the renewed fertility of France. In Burgundy's speech in praise of peace in act five, scene two, many threatening and warlike speeches throughout the play are gently transmuted. Of course as a single poem the play is a lament of a kind for Henry V and his lost victories, though the note of lament is not dominant. The sense of remoteness and loss just touches the very end of the play. It is a praise poem really, as the lamentation of the dead so often is, and it is also the expression of an ideal England.

I felt that I owed these few opening words to this day, and to Shakespeare, the genius of our poetry, and in this part of England the genius of the place. I was pleased and fascinated to discover that this exalted poetry was so conscious of the lamentation of the dead.

The lamentation that I mean belongs in its pure form to simpler and more coherent societies than ours. It is performed, and in an illiterate world it may perish in the performance, though there are fortunate exceptions. We have lost the habit and the tradition, but not the need, I suppose. The dead are lamented nowadays in impure forms. Lorca at the end of *Bodas de Sangre* has a very pure lyrical lament,[1] almost too pure to ring true, yet it does ring true. But Lorca had put down roots into a powerful popular tradition. Éluard, in his poem for Gabriel Péri, a Communist painter shot by the Germans during the war, a poem that I still find almost unbearably moving, could not resist a line or two about hope and the future. No doubt that is forgivable under the Nazi occupation, and I have been carried away, as in the greater case of Shakespeare, by his rhetoric and sentiment: by the truth of his lamentation.

6

Il y a des mots qui font vivre
et ce sont des mots innocents
le mot chaleur le mot confiance
amour justice et le mot liberté
le mot enfant et le mot gentillesse
et certains noms de fleurs et certains noms de fruits
le mot courage et le mot découvrir
et le mot frère et le mot camarade
et certains noms de pays de villages
et certains noms de femmes et d'amis
ajoutons-y Péri
Péri est mort pour ce qui nous fait vivre.... [2]

Underneath this modern, metaphysical poem, in which every formality and every idea seems to be an invention of the poet, there does of course lie a traditional theme of lamentation, an identity with nature. 'Péri est mort pour ce qui nous fait vivre.' Odd as it is, one ought to remark that the survival of the natural cycle, the fields and countryside and so on, have often been felt at a popular level to be the deepest purpose of the wars of this afflicted century. 'The shepherd will herd his sheep, the valley will bloom again, and Johnny will go to sleep in his own little bed again. There'll be blue skies over the white cliffs of Dover, tomorrow when the world is free.' No doubt patriotism is extremely local, but a sense of place could scarcely generate or justify a war. 'Il y a des mots innocents.' I am inclined to think that the theme of the reintegration of nature after war may have strayed from the lamentation of the dead.

Elegy is a lament that has strayed from its pure origins. Pastoral elegy, which survived at least to touch the work of Tennyson and of Matthew Arnold, begins with Theokritos, with the death of Daphnis: it is already literary, meant to be read and not to be performed. The ritual of Adonis was an influence, but one would greatly like to know what deeper roots if any the deathbed of Daphnis had in folk poetry. The refrain in the first Idyll of Theokritos at least makes it plain that this is meant to be herdsmen's poetry: but in a highly literary version. Daphnis dies of love, and the song is rather about love than about death. But some themes that do occur in genuine lamentation occur here. He says goodbye to the natural world. He will come no longer to the forest and the wood. He summons Pan to lament him. 'And now let violets grow on brambles and the deer chase the dog, and the order of nature be reversed, and mountain owls contend with nightingales', because Daphnis is dying. Popular, proverbial rhetoric underlies the rhetoric of poetry, and in a dead language they are hard to distinguish. When Moschos adapted this poem as a lament for the poet Bion, the pastoral elegy was well on its way to immortality. One of Bion's characters, taken from two stray mentions in Theokritos, was Lycidas. The fact that genuine and very ancient elements of lamentation of the dead survive in Milton and in Matthew Arnold contributes to the profound force of those poets, I suppose.

In the case of Milton it may be worth noticing that these ancient elements are what lie deepest, certainly what came first, in the composition of his *Lycidas*. Having written the first version of his opening lines, he went on at once to write down and then to correct the eight lines beginning 'Bring the rathe primrose that forsaken dies',[3] then on the opposite page of his manuscript he began the whole poem again from the beginning. When he came to the place where the lines about flowers now stand, he did not bother to copy them out again, since they were already perfect and legible, but simply noted that they belonged at line 142. This slight laziness has tempted scholars to the view that the flower passage is an afterthought, inserted on a separate sheet. The Trinity manuscript strongly suggests otherwise. Milton ended *Comus* on one side of a page and began *Lycidas* with its opening lines and the flower passage on the other. The whole of *Lycidas* then follows in order. This pedantic detail has a certain importance because it shows how Milton conceived his poem, and rules out some interpretations of the whole poem and even some that have been advanced about Milton's prosody. And I dislike the idea that this passage was just an extra flourish, an unnecessary ornament. *Lycidas* is one of the finest poems in our language, and these emblematic flowers with their freshness and strangeness lie at the heart of it.

Milton strays a long way in the course of *Lycidas* from lamentation of the dead. To study a genuine lament we should go back to the Bible and the *Iliad*. There is curiously little ritual lamenting in the Bible, and for an interesting reason. Lamenting the dead has usually, perhaps always, been the role of women.[4] The true lament is women's poetry, and the Bible is mostly men's. Even what pretends to be women's poetry in the Bible often has a mannish quality. Men's lamentation for dead heroes contains boasting and praises and usually some talk of vengeance. Lamenting women are more intimate and more lyrical. Still, some elements are in common.

And David lamented with this lamentation over Saul, and over Jonathan his son;

The beauty of Israel is slain upon thy high places; how are the mighty fallen!

Tell it not in Gath, publish it not in the streets of Ashkelon; lest the daughters of the Philistines rejoice, lest the daughters of the uncircumcised triumph.

Ye mountains of Gilboa, let there be no dew, neither let there be rain upon you, nor fields of offerings; for there the shield of the mighty is vilely cast away, the shield of Saul, as though he had not been anointed with oil.

From the blood of the slain, from the fat of the mighty, the bow of Jonathan turned not back, and the sword of Saul returned not empty.

Saul and Jonathan were lovely and pleasant in their lives, and in their death they were not divided: they were swifter than eagles, they were stronger than lions.

Ye daughters of Israel, weep over Saul, who clothed you in scarlet, with other delights; who put on ornaments of gold upon your apparel.

How are the mighty fallen in the midst of the battle! O Jonathan, thou wast slain in thine high places.

I am distressed for thee, my brother Jonathan; very pleasant hast thou been unto me: thy love to me was wonderful, passing the love of women.

How are the mighty fallen, and weapons of war perished![5]

It appears that David may be usurping a woman's role, but this is not the only epic touch in the story of David, and any impurity or intermingling of form may well be due to successive stages of a long transmission. As we now have it at least, this lament is as close to invented poetry as it is to popular ritual. Its heroic quality is common to all the great surviving lamentations of the dead: they are for dead heroes or the dead in battle. They raise the question of an influence of epic poetry, that is heroic narrative poetry, on laments, and of the reverse influence. We have in the *Iliad* a mature heroic narrative that contains lamenting of the dead, as the Second Book of Samuel does, but there also exists on a smaller scale, in Greek and in Irish in the eighteenth century for example, lamentation which includes heroic narrative.

I do not really believe that the poetry of Homer, or Norse epic poetry or prose saga, could in any serious sense arise from laments or praise poetry. Zulu praise poetry, as Maurice Bowra[6] pointed out, is as pure in form as any: it is moving and thrilling, but it never generated an epic. Praise poems are to narrative verse rather as church hymns are to the Christian narratives and the Bible. Epic poetry presupposes a professional tradition. True epic has multiple roots and it transforms everything it touches into itself. The living were praised and the dead lamented in a more formal style, but the lamentation of the dead has a special position in epic poetry as it has in life; lamentation is the closure of the *Iliad*, death ends the First Book of Samuel and lamentation begins the Second. The laments in the *Iliad* are heavily influenced by the fluent and flexible style of Homer, and yet their formality is clear.

In the Second Book of Samuel, women seem to be called on only to weep and to wail. In the *Odyssey*, Thetis mother of Achilles comes ashore with her daughters the Nereids to lament over his dead body. 'They wailed pitifully, and tore their immortal robes. And the nine Muses all replying with beautiful voice lamented him. And all men wept.'[7] The lamentation for Hektor in the last book of the *Iliad* is fuller, but the form is similar. 'They put him on the carved bed, and stood singers beside him [the same word is used for professional poets], leaders of laments, who lamented in grievous song, and the women wailed. And white-armed Andromache began their wailing.'[8] Andromache wails in words, briefly, eloquently and personally: Hecuba follows more briefly, then Helen, that is first the widow, then the mother, then the sister-in-law. Hektor's burial follows at once, and the *Iliad* is over. The lamenting verses are not without formality, particularly Hecuba's, which end with Hector's beauty in death, 'like one that Apollo of the silver bow has killed with gentle weapons'.

But taken together these verses are a deliberate device. They embody and conclude the great themes of the *Iliad*. Homer has utterly altered the narrative of war to a tragic and compassionate poetry on as vast a moral scale as *War and Peace*. That alteration is radical, it is intimately interwoven into line after line, and it certainly does not begin with Book XXIV. No serious scholar can ever feel again after reading Colin MacLeod's recent commentary[9] that the end of the *Iliad* is an afterthought. And yet the final, essential moment, and the climax of this vast transformation of values, of the whole *Iliad*, is the lamentation of the dead Hektor. However Homer may have cooled down the ritual laments of women, which appear in a wilder form a little earlier in the conclusion, it remains true that it was by adapting women's poetry at the climax, and by accepting women's views, that he gave the *Iliad* its extraordinary power. The lamentation of Hektor is not a stray incident, nor a merely formal closure.[10]

Unfortunately, this is really too civilized to bring us close to genuine ritual. What is the function of Homer's male singers? Did they sing antiphonally? In the end it was women who sang, as the Muses sang and the Nereids wailed for Achilles, but the male singers suggest professional dirges. The closest women of the family then took over, as they might in a village, where I suppose no professional singer might exist. In the Mani,[11] in southern Greece, where the art of lamenting the dead in poetry survived until our own generation, every village or group of villages used to have one or two women who were professional lamenters. Everyone can wail in every family, but not everyone can make or sing the dirge. What Homer records at the end of the *Iliad* is not quite a dirge, however close; at this point there is something almost novelistic about him. He records inarticulate crying only in the most general terms. One would greatly like to know in what antiphonal songs the Muses lamented Achilles. Aeschylus has some antiphonal lamentation in the *Oresteia*, but that is little help. Perhaps a dirge was always a passionate conversation of laments with a background of weeping and wailing.

Margaret Alexiou[12] has looked for 'the origin of the lament in the antiphonal singing of two groups of mourners, strangers and kinswomen, each singing a verse in turn and followed by a refrain sung in unison'. One is reluctant to give professional poets so important a role so early in the history of poetry. Poetry is a natural communication, before it becomes a professional activity, and if women could compose laments of great power apparently impromptu in the Mani thirty years ago, and if Homer gives similar powers to his women, we ought to accept that personal and ritual poetry are the common inheritance of traditional societies. That is not to say that every village woman could compose the *Iliad*: mature epic poetry cannot arise without long time and labour over generations, and it cannot arise without what we call genius. Perhaps Homer's male singers of dirges are a piece of grandeur remembered or imagined from a courtly society, but the laments of village women were all he had ever heard.

Heroic narrative hinges on heroic death, and it is not surprising that the greatest epics are continually haunted by undertones of lamentation. The ironies[13] and dark comments that attend the death of the most minor Homeric heroes constitute such an undertone; they are

close to the epigrams carved on gravestones, in some of which the
dead speak their own lament and praise, epigrams in many cases
inscribed by fathers for their dead sons. These early Greek verse
epigrams are heavily overshadowed by the *Iliad*. The father who lives
to lament his own son is a fundamental theme of the *Iliad*, and we
should think of the *Iliad*'s audience as older than the heroes it commemorates. In Irish folksong the old lament the young, and the
conclusion of Atlamál in the Norse poetic *Edda*[14] implies an audience
of the old.

> Happy is any man since
> who can beget such offspring,
> so great in deeds.
> Their defiance
> will live after them,
> in every land
> where there are men to hear.

Undertones and fragments of lamentation are to be found in many
traditions, probably in all mature epic poetry. In the Balkans, both in
Yugoslavia and in Greece, they haunt the ballads and lays (and in
Serbo-Croat the epic fragments) of the Turkish period. In 'The Wed-
ding of Milich the Ensign'[15] a young man laments his dead bride.

> Forest of darkness, do not frighten her,
> dark earth, do not lie heavily on her.
> Slim fir, put out your branches further now,
> drop your cold shadows over my bride's head.
> Cuckoo, do not wake up my bride early,
> let her rest peacefully under the earth.

In this tradition, the cuckoo is a bird of ill omen. The young man
also dies and his mother laments him.

> She called out like a cuckoo in her grief. . . .

In fact she went mad. She watered a vine with her tears and whispered
to the vine. She spoke to the setting sun and the rising sun. She was
alone.

> Only the mother's grief and her lament,
> calling out like a cuckoo in her grief,
> reeling as the swallow does in mid-air,
> and will cry so until her fated day.

In this poetry the identification with nature is not as simple as it looks.[16] The sun is a death-symbol, the cuckoo and the swallow carry complex traditional meanings, both nature and social ritual are ironically reversed. All these messages are compressed into simple-looking poetry of powerful density. In 'The Mother of the Jugovichi'[17] it has an epic swiftness, and sinuousness, and force. It flickers as Homer does between formality and the most daring originality, with no disruption of its lucid, traditional language. The Jugovichi were killed at the lost battle of Kosovo, which in epic tradition was a symbol like the fall of Troy.

> And in the morning, daybreak of morning,
> two black ravens flying,
> with bloody wings to the shoulder-bone,
> with beaks dripping white foam,
> they are carrying a hero's hand
> with a gold ring on his hand,
> they throw the hand down on his mother's lap.
> The mother of the Jugovichi holds it,
> she turns it around and over,
> she cries out to Damjan's bride:
> 'My daughter, Damjan's bride,
> do you know this hand?'
> Damjan's bride speaks:
> 'Mother, Damjan's mother,
> this is our Damjan's hand.
> I know the ring, mother,
> I brought him the ring at my wedding.'
> The mother takes Damjan's hand,
> she turns it around and over,
> she is whispering to the hand:
> 'My hand, O green apple,
> where did you grow from, where were you torn off?
> You grew in my lap,
> you were torn off on flat Kosovo.'

This terrible poem, with its appalling reversals of nature and of ritual, is surely built on the simple ritual lamentation of two women under normal circumstances, with no Twa Corbies, and no dismenbering of the dead. 'The mother takes Damjan's hand,' that is all. The traditional ritual underlies the amazing poem. It was recorded in the nineteenth century from an unknown singer in Croatia; the battle of Kosovo was in the fifteenth.

In Greek of the same period we have the greatest quantity of laments that we have from any language, and the tradition lived long enough to be observed by anthropologists and by travellers. Because this was a living tradition, and perhaps in a few villages it still is, a lot of what survives is simple village poetry. But of course the form as it survived was not untouched by other influences, including narrative poetry, and the liturgical lamentation of the dead Christ. The language is not unpretentious, and some of the laments Passow collected and Teubner published in 1860[18] are impersonal, they are set pieces or special passages that could be reused and adapted on many occasions; that is why they were remembered, to be used in performance. They are in some sense professional. The dramatization is extremely lively and the ironies are dense. Of certain set themes or metaphors, like the 'river of the dead', we have several versions, and here at last we have laments for simple, unrecorded people, sailors and shepherds. Ancient Greek epigrams make it clear enough that the style of country lamentation had always had a simplicity.

> I shall arise at break of dawn, the sun two hours unrisen,
> I will take water, I will wash, water and I will waken,
> and I will take the track, the track, the path so beautiful,
> and come upon the rooted rock, and crouch and sit below,
> to hear the speaking of the hawk, the stone-hawk's whistling,
> to hear the partridge speaking in the voice of nightingale,
> where to the eagle she laments and weeps to the stone-hawk:
> 'My stone-hawk of the stony land, cross-eagle of the field,
> you have eaten my true lover and I am left alone.'[19]

Perhaps that is just village music, a faint echo of lament. The true performance of lament was seldom repeated, at least in the Mani. It was considered terribly bad luck to sing the true lamentation of the dead outside its proper occasion. The real thing is passionate and formal. But people were so fond of this poetry and so impressed by it that they did sing imitations and scraps and variations of it. For instance I heard an old woman on a cross-country bus sing a lamentation for the dead Christ that lasted something like an hour. The true style survives best in couplets and short fragments.

> Wake, though you have not had enough of sleep,
> this sleep is heavy, it will bring you harm,

your youth spoils in your sleep and beauty spoils,
youth runs to earth and beauty runs to grass.[20]

Gentleness that suddenly turns to harshness has been the essential style of lamentation since the time of the *Iliad*, and I do not think a fragment like that is the worse for its gentleness. But from what I have said so far, one great example is missing, a heroic lamentation that includes a narrative. It was composed in Irish at the end of the eighteenth century, and recovered in several different versions from illiterate or scarcely literate countrymen and fishermen in the south of Ireland in the 1890s and later. It is called the 'Keen for Art Leary', the 'Lament for Arthur O'Leary'. The chief purpose of this lecture is simply to read you this poem, and to set it in its true context, among the greatest examples that we have of the lamentation of the dead. One cannot comprehend in a single lecture all the branches of this enormous subject, but the 'Lament for Arthur O'Leary' is both a vital piece of evidence and a very great poem. I think it is the greatest poem written in these islands in the whole eighteenth century. I believe that Goethe, and Thomas Gray, and Wordsworth, and Matthew Arnold, in whose place I am honoured and awed to stand, might all have thought so. Arnold was keen on Celtic poetry, but he failed to discover this, though he travelled where it was known. It is a disgrace to us all that so few of us know Irish.[21] I shall read the English version by Eilís Dillon, which seems to me the best.[22]

The lament was composed by Arthur O'Leary's widow, Black Eileen or Dark Eileen, but in the course of it his sister and his father also speak. The tradition of lamentation of the dead in Irish is strong, and we have some fine earlier examples. Arthur O'Leary died young on 4 May 1773. His widow was born about 1743, her mother was a poet and her family had been patrons of traditional, wandering Irish poets. Hence the mysterious touches of epic convention and of epic power in this lament. Eileen was an elder kinswoman of Daniel O'Connell, the Liberator; she was married at fifteen to an old man who died at once; she lamented him, and the lament was remembered for many years. It is now lost. In 1767 she fell in love with Arthur O'Leary at Macroom. He was twenty-one years old, and a captain in the Austrian army. He wore a sword, an illegal act for a Catholic, and when he had won a race against Abraham Morris, High Sheriff of Cork, he refused to sell his horse for five pounds, once again an illegal act. He became effectively an outlaw; he was betrayed by John Cooney at Millstreet. He was shot on the run by a soldier; Abraham

Morris was tried for murder and acquitted. Morris then left the area, and died soon afterwards. Arthur O'Leary was buried in unconsecrated ground at Killnamartyr, but later his body was moved to his family's burial place in Kilcrea Abbey. Eileen wrote his epitaph in English:

> Lo! Arthur Leary, generous, handsome, brave,
> Slain in his bloom, lies in this humble grave.

The lament was apparently composed before the second burial, and perhaps for a wake that was held the night before that occasion, which the last stanza foresees. This poem contains many traditional and common elements, and it dramatizes several stages of the story; it is a poem with many elements, not an impromptu lamentation. The true wake would be held in the O'Leary house. So we have lamentation at the death, then the quarrel over the wake, then lamentation before burial, and finally two stanzas for the second burial. I do not believe these were all composed separately; what we have here is a single poem of many elements of lamentation.[23] With this poem a world ended; we had not known that it had lived so long.

APPENDIX

The Lament for Arthur O'Leary

From the Irish of Eibhlín Dhubh Ní Chonaill

I

EILEEN SPEAKS:

My love forever!
The day I first saw you
At the end of the market-house,
My eye observed you,
My heart approved you,
I fled from my father with you,
Far from my home with you.

II

I never repented it:
You whitened a parlour for me,
Painted rooms for me,
Reddened ovens for me,
Baked fine bread for me,
Basted meat for me,

Slaughtered beasts for me;
I slept in ducks' feathers
Till midday milking-time,
Or more if it pleased me.

III
My friend forever!
My mind remembers
That fine spring day
How well your hat suited you,
Bright gold banded,
Sword silver-hilted –
Right hand steady –
Threatening aspect –
Trembling terror
On treacherous enemy –
You poised for a canter
On your slender bay horse.
The Saxons bowed to you,
Down to the ground to you,
Not for love of you
But for deadly fear of you,
Though you lost your life to them,
Oh my soul's darling.

IV

Oh white-handed rider!
How fine your brooch was
Fastened in cambric,
And your hat with laces.
When you crossed the sea to us,
They would clear the street for you,
And not for love of you
But for deadly hatred.

V

My friend you were forever!
When they will come home to me,
Gentle little Conor
And Farr O'Leary, the baby,
They will question me so quickly,
Where did I leave their father.
I'll answer in my anguish
That I left him in Killnamartyr.
They will call out to their father;
And he won't be there to answer.

VI

My friend and my love!
Of the blood of Lord Antrim,
And of Barry of Allchoill,
How well your sword suited you,
Hat gold-banded,
Boots of fine leather,
Coat of broadcloth,
Spun overseas for you.

VII

My friend you were forever!
I knew nothing of your murder
Till your horse came to the stable
With the reins beneath her trailing,
And your heart's blood on her shoulders
Staining the tooled saddle
Where you used to sit and stand.
My first leap reached the threshold,
My second reached the gateway,
My third leap reached the saddle.

VIII

I struck my hands together
And I made the bay horse gallop
As fast as I was able,
Till I found you dead before me
Beside a little furze-bush.
Without Pope or bishop,
Without priest or cleric
To read the death-psalms for you,
But a spent old woman only
Who spread her cloak to shroud you –
Your heart's blood was still flowing;
I did not stay to wipe it
But filled my hands and drank it.

IX

My love you'll be forever!
Rise up from where you're lying
And we'll be going homewards.
We'll have a bullock slaughtered,
We'll call our friends together,
We'll get the music going.
I'll make a fine bed ready
With sheets of snow-white linen,
And fine embroidered covers

18

That will bring the sweat out through you
Instead of the cold that's on you!

X

ARTHUR O'LEARY'S
SISTER SPEAKS:

My friend and my treasure!
There's many a handsome woman
From Cork of the sails
To the bridge of Toames
With a great herd of cattle
And gold for her dowry,
That would not have slept soundly
On the night we were waking you.

XI

EILEEN SPEAKS:

My friend and my lamb;
You must never believe it,
Nor the whisper that reached you,
Nor the venomous stories
That said I was sleeping.
It was not sleep was on me,
But your children were weeping,
And they needed me with them
To bring their sleep to them.

XII

Now judge, my people,
What woman in Ireland
That at every nightfall
Lay down beside him,
That bore his three children,
Would not lose her reason
After Art O'Leary
That's here with me vanquished
Since yesterday morning?

XIII

ARTHUR O'LEARY'S
FATHER SPEAKS:

Bad luck to you, Morris! —
May your heart's blood poison you!
With your squint eyes gaping!
And your knock-knees breaking! —
That murdered my darling,
And no man in Ireland
To fill you with bullets.

XIV

My friend and my heart!
Rise up again now, Art,
Leap up on your horse,

19

Make straight for Macroom town,
Then to Inchigeela back,
A bottle for wine in your fist,
The same as you drank with your dad.

XV

EILEEN SPEAKS: My bitter, long torment
That I was not with you
When the bullet came towards you,
My right side would have taken it
Or a fold of my tunic,
And I would have saved you
Oh smooth-handed rider.

XVI

ARTHUR O'LEARY'S My sore sharp sorrow
SISTER SPEAKS: That I was not behind you
When the gun-powder blazed at you,
My right side would have taken it,
Or a fold of my gown,
And you would have gone free then
Oh grey-eyed rider,
Since you were a match for them.

XVII

EILEEN SPEAKS: My friend and my treasure!
It's bad treatment for a hero
To lie hooded in a coffin,
The warm-hearted rider
That fished in bright rivers,
That drank in great houses
With white-breasted women.
My thousand sorrows
That I've lost my companion.

XVIII

Bad luck and misfortune
Come down on you, Morris!
That snatched my protector,
My unborn child's father:
Two of them walking
And the third still within me,
And not likely I'll bear it.

XIX

My friend and my pleasure!
When you went out through the gateway

The Lamentation of the Dead

You turned and came back quickly,
You kissed your two children,
You kissed me on the forehead,
You said: 'Eileen, rise up quickly,
Put your affairs in order
With speed and with decision.
I am leaving home now
And there's no telling if I'll return.'
I mocked this way of talking,
He had said it to me so often.

XX

My friend and my dear!
Oh bright-sworded rider,
Rise up this moment,
Put on your fine suit
Of clean, noble cloth,
Put on your black beaver,
Pull on your gauntlets.
Up with your whip;
Outside your mare is waiting.
Take the narrow road east,
Where the trees thin before you,
Where streams narrow before you,
Where men and women will bow before you,
If they keep their old manners –
But I fear they have lost them.

XXI

My love and my treasure!
Not my dead ancestors,
Nor the deaths of my three children,
Nor Domhnall Mór O'Connell,
Nor Connall that drowned at sea,
Nor the twenty-six years woman
Who went across the water
And held kings in conversation –
It's not on all of them I'm calling
But on Art who was slain last night
At the inch of Carriganima! –
The brown mare's rider
That's here with me only –
With no living soul near him
But the dark little women of the mill,
And my thousand sorrows worsened
That their eyes were dry of tears.

XXII
My friend and my lamb!
Arthur O'Leary,
Of Connor, of Keady,
Of Louis O'Leary,
From west in Geeragh
And from east in Caolchnoc,
Where berries grow freely
And gold nuts on branches
And great floods of apples
All in their seasons.
Would it be a wonder
If Ive Leary were blazing
Besides Ballingeary
And Guagán of the saint
For the firm-handed rider
That hunted the stag down,
All out from Grenagh
When slim hounds fell behind?
And Oh clear-sighted rider,
What happened last night?
For I thought to myself
That nothing could kill you
Though I bought your habit.

XXIII

ARTHUR O'LEARY'S   My friend and my love!
SISTER SPEAKS: Of the country's best blood,
That kept eighteen wet-nurses at work,
And each received her pay —
A heifer and a mare,
A sow and her litter,
A mill at the ford,
Yellow gold and white silver,
Silks and fine velvets,
A holding of land —
To give her milk freely
To the flower of fair manhood.

XXIV
My love and my treasure
And my love, my white dove!
Though I did not come to you,
Nor bring my troops with me,
That was no shame to me
For they were all enclosed

22

In shut-up rooms,
In narrow coffins,
In sleep without waking.

XXV
Were it not for the small-pox
And the black death
And the spotted fever,
That powerful army
Would be shaking their harness
And making a clatter
On their way to your funeral,
Oh white-breasted Art.

XXVI
My love you were and my joy!
Of the blood of those rough horsemen
That hunted in the valley,
Till you turned them homewards
And brought them to your hall,
Where knives were being sharpened,
Pork laid out for carving
And countless ribs of mutton,
The red-brown oats were flowing
To make the horses gallop –
Slender, powerful horses
And stable-boys to care them
Who would not think of sleeping
Nor of deserting their horses
If their owners stayed a week,
Oh brother of many friends.

XXVII
My friend and my lamb!
A cloudy vision
Came last night to me
In Cork at midnight
Alone in my bed:
That our white court fell,
That the Geeragh withered,
That your slim hounds were still
And the birds without sweetness
When you were found vanquished
On the side of the mountain,
Without priest or cleric
But an old shrivelled woman

That spread her cloak over you,
Arthur O'Leary,
While your blood flowed freely
On the breast of your shirt.

XXVIII
My love and my treasure!
And well they suited you,
Five-ply stockings,
Boots to your knees,
A three-cornered Caroline,
A lively whip,
On a frisky horse —
Many a modest, mannerly maiden
Would turn to gaze after you.

EILEEN SPEAKS:

XXIX
My love forever!
And when you went in cities,
Strong and powerful,
The wives of the merchants
All bowed down to you
For they knew in their hearts
What a fine man in bed you were,
And what a fine horseman
And father for children.

XXX
Jesus Christ knows
I'll have no cap on my head,
Nor a shift on my back,
Nor shoes on my feet,
Nor goods in my house,
Nor the brown mare's harness
That I won't spend on lawyers;
That I'll cross the seas
And talk to the king,
And if no one listens
That I'll come back
To the black-blooded clown
That took my treasure from me.

XXXI
My love and my darling!
If my cry were heard westwards
To great Derrynane
And to gold-appled Capling,

24

Many swift, hearty riders
And white-kerchiefed women
Would be coming here quickly
To weep at your waking,
Beloved Art O'Leary.

XXXII
My heart is warming
To the fine women of the mill
For their goodness in lamenting
The brown mare's rider.

XXXIII
May your black heart fail you,
Oh false John Cooney!
If you wanted a bribe,
You should have asked me.
I'd have given you plenty:
A powerful horse
That would carry you safely
Through the mob
When the hunt is out for you,
Or a fine herd of cattle,
Or ewes to bear lambs for you,
Or the suit of a gentleman
With spurs and top-boots –
Though it's sorry I'd be
To see you done up in them,
For I've always heard
You're a piddling lout.

XXXIV
Oh white-handed rider,
Since you are struck down,
Rise and go after Baldwin,[24]
The ugly wretch
With the spindle shanks,
And take your revenge
For the loss of your mare –
May he never enjoy her.
May his six children wither!
But no bad wish to Máire
Though I have no love for her,
But that my own mother
Gave space in her womb to her
For three long seasons.

XXXV
My love and my dear!
Your stooks are standing,
Your yellow cows milking;
On my heart is such sorrow
That all Munster could not cure it,
Nor the wisdom of the sages.
Till Art O'Leary returns
There will be no end to the grief
That presses down on my heart,
Closed up tight and firm
Like a trunk that is locked
And the key is mislaid.

XXXVI
All you women out there weeping,
Wait a little longer;
We'll drink to Art son of Connor
And the souls of all the dead,
Before he enters the school –
Not learning wisdom or music
But weighed down by earth and stones.

Translated by Eilís Dillon

From Aeschylus to James Fenton

I can still remember my youthful excitement thirty or forty years ago at discovering a book by Maurice Bowra called *From Virgil to Milton*: it turned out to be no more than an honourable attempt, excellent on Virgil and fascinating on Milton, and I think on Ariosto, but rather thin in between. So why Aeschylus and why James Fenton? Aeschylus no longer looks like a mighty crag, a lesser Homer or an almost adequate substitute for epic poetry: we see him now as a conscious, very intelligent writer of astounding and unfair greatness, bold in devices, exciting in conceptions, and in the power of his language incomparable. Given a mere anonymous scrap of papyrus, it will not take you long to recognize the implicit signature of Aeschylus in every line. Of all the ancient dramatists he has most to say, and carries the most contradictions in his verse. He is greater than Pindar because dramatic poetry concentrates, it exhausts a subject, it is or seems to us a greater medium than the Olympic ode. Of course there is no universal truth or eternal value to be found in his writings, any more than in James Fenton's. But the same intellectual or spiritual processes that accompanied the emergence of democracy are to be sensed in the dramatic poetry of Aeschylus: and particularly in the *Agamemnon* he has roots in ancient society, and when he offers a powerful variation, it is almost the illusion of a choice.

At the level of verbal texture, the ancient and the modern poet share an interest in riddles. Aeschylus has fewer riddles than Browning's Aeschylus, but they are an irreducible element in his verse: Fenton's 'The Kingfisher's Boxing Gloves' is an old example, 'The Ballad of the Shrieking Man' is a recent one, in his.

Like James Fenton, Aeschylus is a poet of war and of the consequences of war. A number of Fenton's poems are almost purely playful: Aeschylus is not renowned today for his lightness of touch, but in antiquity he was considered the greatest writer of those playful

27

plays that always had a chorus of satyrs: we have only a few miserable fragments, but enough to substantiate that reputation. Aeschylus is more obviously patriotic than Fenton, but in our day there has been no great patriotic war since 1945. Both poets deal with the events of war with a compassion not always easy to detect, not sentimental, but extremely ironic. Between the Athenian poet's observation of Salamis and the detachment of a hard-bitten journalist in South-East Asia, a persona James Fenton adopts, the difference is smaller than you might expect. To write a tragedy you have to conceive of tragic suffering, and those who suffer worst are formally the heroes, Agamemnon or Oedipus. To write a tragedy about the Persian wars of the Greeks and make the Greeks triumph you have to turn the Persians into tragic heroes. When Phynichos presented the fall of Miletos to the Persians[1] with the Milesians as tragic heroes, the play was thought unacceptably sad, and the poet was prosecuted and fined. The whole excitement of Aeschylus is that his dramatic poetry is always so close to the bone, but when he died he was overshadowed at once by Sophocles and by Euripides, neither of them to my mind quite as thrilling: revivals of his work took the form of spectacular 'epic' productions (enter the Greek army with chariots and the spoils of Troy)[2] and he was never really rediscovered as he is, at least until the romantic movement. Romantic theorists were interested in romantic conflict: that is to be found in Aeschylus, but it is not the point. His poetry is rooted in the values that lay under the surface of his world. I find a curiously rooted quality of the same kind underlying the impressive tranquillity of James Fenton.

Perhaps you are already tired of this extravagantly distant comparison. The differences of these poets are obviously greater than their similarities. They both give the impression of having new things to say about poetry, and to do in it, but not the same things. Aeschylus has the advantage of dramatic form, and of its freshness in his time. Fenton has the disadvantage of the tail end of modernism and the ghost of Auden, of a poetry and a language that tend towards decomposition. Of all that stands between them, the two biggest influences are perhaps Shakespeare, who has made so much seem impossible to later generations, and the history of this nation and this language, both exhausted from the great debauch that came to its climax in 1914. If we are to relearn the art of poetry, we must go further back; we must study not only the classics of our own language, the poets by whom or in whom that language itself most lives, poets we should recognize by ear and learn by heart, and not only every hole and corner where the language flourishes, but also we would do well to cross-question Aeschylus. He is easy enough to question; he intended his works to be heard not read, and not all his effects depend on surprise.[3]

> Now to this roof this household and this hearth
> I have come home: first I salute the gods,
> who sent me from it and brought me again.
> May Victory that went with me, settle here.[4]

The content of poetry is seldom good news, the lovers are all untrue, the dead after a battle remain dead.

> Beauty, danger and dismay
> Met me on the public way.
> Whichever I chose, I chose dismay.[5]

The Persians is not the greatest play even among those few by Aeschylus that survive, but its handling of the battle of Salamis is unique: it appears to be an eyewitness account of a naval action, or something close to that. In its syntactic structure and lucid organization it goes beyond what prose historians could do except for the greatest passages in Thucydides, a generation later. Its tragic force depends on a momentum that carries it beyond the Athenian triumph and beyond the climax of horror. If the island of Psyttakia where the Persian army was massacred has been rightly identified, the plan of the action has been formalized, even mythologized. Aeschylus is terribly clear-eyed about men, about war and about the gods: more so I think than Herodotos on the same battle. It is typical of the cadences of Aeschylus that the messenger bringing the news of Salamis to the Persian Queen begins his story with sunset and ends it with the dark.[6] The last details have to be wrung out of him. (See Appendix 1.)

In the context of the play, Xerxes the Queen's son has a crucial importance, but it must surely be conventional that the messenger's speech about the battle begins and ends with him. Rather in the same way, when Thucydides at the end of Book Seven describes the Athenian disaster in Sicily, between the sentences 'Nikias when it was day led on his army' (7, 84, 1) and 'Nikias surrendered himself to Gylippos' (7, 85, 1), the Athenians whose disaster it was died anonymously: they were a crowd that could only say 'Rhubarb', hence the tragic impersonality and inevitability of Thucydides. Aeschylus is freer, yet still more terrible. Oliver Taplin has pointed out that although there was a grammar of dramatic convention, grammar is not quite the right word, because there were always departures from the norm.[7] The point is that Aeschylus was conscious of conventions and patterns in life as on the stage, but he felt free to use them thoroughly, as if they had never been used before. Today a poet chooses his own conventions and does so fastidiously. Consider James Fenton on 'Dead Soldiers'. (See Appendix 2.)

The ancient battle stories are straightforward and deadly, the modern story is sidelong, elegant, almost freakish, but the elegance increases the horror, and the knowingness makes you shiver: this Prince is a more convincing figure than Xerxes, let alone the ghost of Darius. This poem could hardly be more sinister, but Aeschylus is more terrible, because the thunder breaks and the lightning strikes. Today, poetry of every kind is available to us in abundance: we do not need to reject one kind in order to prefer another, and I assume that a modern poet learning his or her trade in English will take lessons from more than one language and more than one generation. I am giving this lecture in order to make the point that there is a lot to be said for James Fenton, but also a great deal to be said for Aeschylus. I would like to add the minor point that under the initial impulse of Auden and perhaps of Brecht, and in the course of the expression of life and reality which is a poet's task, James Fenton has veered in the direction of Aeschylus, his plain and godlike and intensely self-dramatizing speech. This is not a conscious direction or a theory, but the search for plainness and for strength is a strong current under the surface of our poetry in this century. Also, although to my mind he recalls Robert Wood's description of the intellectual world of Homer,[8] where 'there was no school but that of Life, and no philosophy but that of Common Sense', yet he takes a view of ultimate justice of almost Aeschylean gloom. (See Appendix 3.)

Death in Aeschylus is more powerful than Zeus, it is taken even more seriously, and his religion is to that extent humane. He is bold but never crude in conception: here I must take issue with Oliver Taplin's brilliant and reliable book about Aeschylus, where in discussing the difficult matter of whether the *Prometheus* is genuine[9] he writes, 'Primeval grandeur of conception is *per se* no guarantee of the greatness of the author. Any inflated poetaster may have grandiose conceptions: most do. In more recent times there have been only too many allegories of basic forces, a piece of fundamental symbolism, which are disasters as works of art.' The word 'primeval' is romantic and out of place, and the verbal slide from 'grandeur' to 'grandiose' masks a disjointed argument. Simple grandeur is very rare in every period: Aeschylus often achieved it and it is not beyond the grasp of modern poetry. The disastrous pseudo-epics of modern times are not worth mentioning in the same breath. But how are we to tell the difference between the grandiose and the grand, between real Aeschylus and phoney Aeschylus (I admit, for example, after resisting the modern view for ten years, that *Prometheus* is probably not genuine) or the difference between the true and the false, the genuine and the corrupt in modern poetry?

Not by the application of rules, and not by any degree of subtlety attainable by a computer: a computer is not even able to tune a piano. But by experience of poetry and of life, testing one against the other. The genuine rings true in the ear. If this is dismissed as a bizarre criterion, or a recurrence of old-fashioned taste, of the old claret-tasting school of literary criticism, so be it: every generation has its own taste, and in this hunger for the genuine, in the recognition of what is genuine, poets will often be found a little bit in advance of their contemporaries. But we can all agree about certain passages of poetry which are exemplary, which serve as a criterion of what genuineness is. Some of them are single lines: Κατεῖδον ἀνθοῦν πέλαγος Αἰγαῖον νέκροις. 'I saw the corpses blossom on the sea', the bodies of Greeks and the ruins of shipping. But those longer passages are a safer touchstone in which something that can be thought and felt as important is being said.

In the great lyrics of Aeschylus there is an intense consciousness of the gods in their many disguises, and a sense of violence, that is of their violence, but very little theology, very little intellectual joy or dogmatic liberation. For that reason, as one grows older, one may come to prefer Aeschylus to more optimistic writers: one can understand him even with no knowledge of his allusive mythology or the painful succession of supreme gods that ended in Zeus. (See Appendix 4.) In this case more than another it is worth listening to the solemn and dramatic words of the Greek, because the musicality of supreme poetry is so intensely individual to great poets, and yet in another sense the same in all languages. You could never mistake Aeschylean verse for anything but poetry that often touches greatness, even not knowing a word of Greek. He is not a poet who expresses everlasting values, least of all here where he claims to do so. He is more compact or dense or contorted than Marlowe or most of Shakespeare, solemn and strong in a way that one can only call archaic, rather as Langland seems to us, only more concentrated, something like Everyman: 'Where art thou Death thou dreadful messenger?' But he has very clear, simple images: 'printing their proud hooves in the receiving earth' could be by him, and 'blasting their proud whinny through the shrill pipes' is one he really wrote. He might also, except for the names of the small birds, have written those lines of Webster:

> Call for the robin red-breast and the wren,
> which with the fallen leaves do cover
> the friendless bodies of unburied men.[10]

That last line in particular has the exact quality and rhythm of Aeschylus, as Maurice Baring noticed. I do not want to press the analogy with James Fenton until it becomes a game. They are in numerous ways very unlike. But the criterion is the same, always, for all poetry. There is a seriousness that you can hear and to which you are compelled to attend. Not all poets have it, not even all great poets. Villon has it, and at his incomparable best so has Auden. In a few poems so has Fenton. You are always surprised by this degree of seriousness, when you find it in a modern poem. Lucky Greeks, who had a right to expect it whenever they sat down in the theatre, but that is another story. This sense of surprise or shock at great and simple poetry is why we speak proverbially of what oft was thought but ne'er so well expressed. It is almost as if you had written the poem, as if some unconscious power in you had been released. Eliot says somewhere that there are many things to get right in a poem before ever you set pen to paper, above all its tone: and that seems to me true of a poem like 'In a Notebook'.[11] (See Appendix 5.)

Aeschylus is a quite different kind of poet from Shakespeare; if they overlap at all it is only in a few phrases: he is possibly a little closer to Marlowe, but the closeness is unimportant, it is a function of the nature of dramatic poetry. Shakespeare's dramatic poetry depends essentially on the immediacy of his theatre, and on the enormous number of actors available to him in London. No doubt at times it depends on the smaller number of actors available in the provinces, hence no doubt the process of tightening and shedding that took place in revision: a process still largely unexplored by scholars, because it is only now beginning to be admitted.[12] The multiplicity of Shakespeare, and his dramatization of great historical events, even of a world, like Tolstoy's in *War and Peace*, arise from his grasping of the opportunities of the loose unclassical English theatre.

Take the battle in Act One of *Henry VI Part 3*. To an Elizabethan audience, part of the attraction was novelty. They mostly knew much less about the intricacies of fifteenth-century dynastic conflict than the Athens of Aeschylus knew about the Seven against Thebes, so the action dramatized had to be made very clear. The first line of scene 1 opens the plot: the Yorkists break into a building and Warwick says, 'I wonder how the King escaped our hands.' The Duke of York and his sons name the dead in a recent battle: the play is about nemesis, so the dead must sooner or later be avenged. No battle need be final in Shakespeare except in Act Five, but in Aeschylus battle and death are more portentous: the unity of short time and a single intelligible and felt event in general confine him. His efforts to break out are instructive: the need for Delphi and Athens in the *Eumenides* for example, and the geographical outburst of the beacon fires right across Greece in the *Agamemnon*. Shakespeare wanders at ease, except in the confusing travels of *Pericles*, which are based on a romance and rather hard to follow.

King Henry abdicates, but the Queen goes on with the war. Scene 3 is the first battle. Once again clarity is all, and the characters speak only to dramatize their roles, the parts they must inevitably play: none of this goes unexplained. A little boy with a tutor to underline his innocence is caught by a man whose father the boy's father murdered. The institutions of chivalry are founded on the inheritance of one's dead father's shield, or at least the design on it, so the characters are easy to identify (in Aeschylus, all that has to be spelt out slowly so that the inherited curse in the *Agamemnon* remains obscure to this day). (See Appendix 6.) What little Rutland spells out is his own fearful perception of Lord Clifford. Aeschylus might have used the lines about the lion, though a pent-up lion would be unknown to him, but in Aeschylus the poet's sympathy would be with the lion. The sophistry of the last lines is like Euripides, not like Aeschylus. The point of this scene is to paint Clifford black, so that in the dingdong of vengeance he in his turn has to die. He does so at the end of Act Two, and but for this scene he might have seemed a pure and saintlike character, an incarnation of feudal loyalty: but there is room for only one saint in *Henry VI*. I do not think Aeschylus would have so blackened a minor character simply because he had to die. He is uninterested in Aigisthos, but he does blacken Agamemnon with the death of Iphigeneia. Lions, by the way, crop up again in Clifford's speech to the King in Act Two, scene 2. They are quite rhetorical, but Shakespeare remembers Rutland's lines, and taken together these lines suggest a basis in real life.

> To whom do lions cast their gentle looks?
> Not to the beast that would usurp their den.

Whose hand is that the forest bear doth lick?
Not his that spoils her young before her face.

Elizabethan London was more barbarous and more savage than the Athens of Aeschylus; no doubt that is why we have so deep a feeling for it. Aeschylus goes to the deepest point of human anxiety, he plays on anxiety as on an instrument of music, and releases from it a kind of cataclysm of suffering. Shakespeare deals with what is savage, wild and unacknowledged in human nature and reveals himself as a supreme poet; he is Orpheus to the animal nine-tenths of humanity. Yet all these amazing revelations of poetry depend on the stage, on its piling up of context, its human multiplicity and conflict, and its deadly weapon of dramatic concentration. And to these events and these revelations the modern poet is no more than an epilogue.

Modern poetry takes place within comparatively narrow limits, not only because it occurs later in time, and in a period conscious of history, which has easy access to Shakespeare and to Aeschylus,[13] but because the verse theatre is dead, and every attempt to revive it makes it look deader still: the more successful the attempt, the more irrecoverably dead it looks. Auden's theatre was light verse, Eliot's became too solemn, Christopher Fry's was popular but individual, never imitated. Tony Harrison's dramatic verse has been a nine days' wonder. Many more poets than I have named have all burnt their hands in the same embers without relighting the fire: in any culture, the theatre of prose has always followed the theatre of verse quite swiftly, and that process is apparently irreversible. Both Aeschylus and Shakespeare wrote in the first few years of the newly invented theatre in their own languages. Aeschylus was one of the first Greek tragedians and Shakespeare was one of the first English secular theatrical writers: the earlier exceptions hardly count.

But modern poetry has to invent its means. It has no lightness and little delicacy because modern European society has none. Poetry can scarcely be said to follow social changes decade by decade, but it does so generation by generation. Poets have been driven back on formal inventiveness, something that James Fenton has shown to a remarkable degree: that is the source of his light verse, as it was of Auden's. The consciousness of what happened in 1914, and of the consequences of what happened in 1914, and of the consequences of Hitler's policies, and of the war and of the atom bomb, and the stunning consciousness of the extent of Stalin's inhumanity, which is only now spreading, have affected the post-war generation lethally: the reaction has been a serious kind of silence; we have lost the confidence that these sufferings can be comprehended. Hope is the privilege of action; you will find it in the most stricken verses of that old soldier of 1914, David Jones. But we are doomed to know the world as no earlier generation has ever known it, and to be conscious of our own futility, our inaction and our wrong action and their appalling consequences.

I hope these gloomy thoughts may throw some light on the quandary of James Fenton, and on his poems, though I have no idea whether he thinks the same as I do. Because he is a little more serious than his contemporaries, a bit deeper, and also because of his gleeful cleverness, I rank him with the best German poets of the post-war period: with Peter Huchel for instance, born long ago in 1903, but only a left-wing schoolboy and later a quiet, country poet before the war: it was Hitler and what followed Hitler that made him a great and genuine poet.

> The heavens will drift off
> but as a fall of snow
> sinks in the black water
> we will not say Te Deum any more.
>
> A smashed house between heaven and earth.
> Toad in the gateway
> still at this moment
> with the crown of gold on his head.[14]

Even in this simple poem, which is both allusive and powerful, one has the sense of a depth of meaning that struggles to the surface. In those poems where it plainly surfaces, Peter Huchel is a master. In the 1950s it was not Brecht alone, but Brecht and Huchel together who dominated and inspired East German poetry, which yielded a richer harvest than our own. Later Huchel moved to the West. What he has in common, odd as it may be, with Fenton and with Aeschylus, but not in common with Marlowe and Shakespeare, is that the necessary element of freshness and strangeness in his poems is usually the smell of freshly spilt blood. The shadows of fish are knife-sharp and the wings of his swans are daggers that cut; the strangled sunsets end in corpses whose wounds are covered with a humming sheet of flies.

> Once there was fire enough and gold
> under the heavy roots of woods,
> Germany is dark, Germany is cold.
> Where the fire darkened in the ring

the salted tears clung to the jug,
blood seeped painfully through the shroud. . . .

Or consider his 'Warsaw Memorial', which I take it refers to the
rising in the Warsaw ghetto in the 1939 war, and the consequences of
the rising.

(i)

The lightning flash of slaughtered summer
has left ashes in the trees.
The wound-scars of the walls blaze with the dead.
Unshod feet freeze in the dew of roses.

(ii)

O holy blood, it burned
in all the veins of this city.
A heap of wounded flesh the mouth of it.
On the silence behind the teeth, iron broke.[16]

Peter Huchel wrote for his son a calm poem about Theophrastus,
the pupil of Aristotle and the great botanist. It occurs in the same 1963
collection.

At midday when the white fire of poems
dances over the urns, my son, remember.
Remember those that planted conversations
like planting trees. The garden is dead,
my breath comes harsher, preserve the moment,
here walked Theophrastus, feeding the soil
with oak-bark, bandaging the wounded trunk
with fibres. Now an olive-tree has split
the moulded brickwork, there is a stillness
in the heat where the swarm of midges hangs.
Their orders were to take it by the root.
Your light is sinking, leaves without defence.[17]

Maybe the power of this poem arises from the very obscurity of the
allegory, yet in Germany when it was written the allegory was sharp
enough. But the meaning is deeply sunk in the metaphor, and the
metaphor deeply sunk in the cold, physical earth, in natural process
and the invasion of it, in our sense of ruined, heroic antiquity, the
unattainable peace of Theophrastus which by a metaphor we do
attain. What makes the poem tragic and moving is not the garden but
the allegory of those who once planted conversations like planting

trees. Compare with this an admittedly lesser poem by James Fenton: it belongs to a sequence, so it offers no sharp allegorical insight, but it has a narrative momentum; Fenton wrote stronger poems later in life, this one is quite interestingly like and unlike Peter Huchel. It is about a character at least as enchanting as Theophrastus, the Japanese poet Basho. James Fenton wrote it as an undergraduate in his Newdigate Prize Poem, on the opening of Japan, 'Our Western Furniture'.[18] (See Appendix 7.)

Of course this poem bites less sharply than 'The Garden of Theophrastus', because what it lacks is the experience of life. But it remains instructive to observe the work of a very young poet who is going to develop. The picture of Basho is uncompromising and incisive: it abstracts or selects stray revealing phrases from his own work. The Penguin translation appeared in 1966, and, without being unfair, one is free to judge it better than this miniature portrait in a single sonnet: yet now twenty years have gone by, and who is writing this trim, Auden-like form of sonnet today? One poet in twenty years is no doubt more than our ration as a university, but I do not think it is only the sheer ability of young poets that has altered, but the radical stance of a poet. Still, from Aeschylus to James Fenton is a long enough gap to have covered; I shall not pretend to peer into the future of poetry, at least not at the moment. Every modern poet is thrust back on to devices, of which we have a uniquely wide number available from the past and from our contemporaries; even so, it is a matter of pride for poets to add to the stock of devices, and we admire in every modern poem its intelligence as a device.

Many of these devices are humorous or half-humorous: more kinds of humorous or half-humorous poem are available to James Fenton than Aeschylus could have conceived. That is surely because tragedy today is all but universal, our predicament is universal, the tragic stage has widened to include the world. It is a wandering spotlight moving about the world, and, in order to speak at all, the poet is ironic: his lack of belief or his absence of gods are not causes of his irony but symptoms or consequences of his predicament. The difference between tragedy and humour is only the throwing of a switch: ironic laughter is much like the catharsis,[19] the venting of emotions at a tragedy; it is an evasion or a dissolution of complex passions. They both result from the artist's aspiration to be serious. Beyond humour lies bad-taste humour, the kind that plays on our knowledge that our good taste is really false. That subdivision of humour delighted us in a muted form in Housman and in Belloc, it broke loose in Brecht and rioted in Auden. 'Two Cheers for Tramconductors in Partingtime Hall' (1987), poems of mingled authorship by James Fenton and John Fuller, is not a bad example. Its formal disadvantage is that it always has to go further than what we are used to reading. But is there not a similar formal disadvantage in Greek tragedy? Late productions and demanding actors turned a dead man struck by lightning in the *Seven against Thebes* into a blazing comet spinning like a catherine wheel; Oedipus entered singing, wheeling his dead children on a trolley. The bad taste of the Greeks is an interesting and neglected subject. The closest style we have to that of Aeschylus in recent times is to be found in certain works of Robert Lowell, but between his earliest poems and the long series of late sonnets, there is some sense of diminishing returns. However great a poet Lowell always was, Aeschylus was only one of his devices.

Wit, when it exists at all in English poetry, is often obtrusive, insistent and repetitive, even to the point of being a bore. 'Riddle on a Gooseberry', by the largely unpublished minor writer William Skipwith, a contemporary of Shakespeare, was perhaps much relished by his friends in the Inner Temple, but as poetry it hardly exists. In the best witty poems the wit goes up in a sheet of flame, becoming something of another order; this often happens in Aeschylus, and it can happen in James Fenton.

Cambodia

One man shall smile one day and say goodbye.
Two shall be left, two shall be left to die.

One man shall give his best advice.
Three men shall pay the price.

One man shall live, live to regret.
Four men shall meet the debt.

One man shall wake from terror to his bed.
Five men shall be dead.

One man to five. A million men to one.
And still they die. And still the war goes on.

What has happened here is that wit is only part of the structure that furnishes the poem. Effectively the poem is made by its last line, which more than fulfils the expectation of its form. Wit looks like frustration, and when wit dies down the poem lives. When the poem succeeds, there seems to be nothing there but poetry, in Greek as in English.

> The curses of Oedipus have burst open
> and the fantasticness of dreams is true
> which have divided his inheritance.[20]

These lines of Aeschylus are densely written and difficult to translate; I follow only the principal meaning of words which have many levels of meaning: but here again the underlying structure of wit has been consumed into poetry. Oedipus has cursed his sons and here one of them speaks: the curse has fallen on them both and they are going to kill each other. The curses have boiled over or burst out like eczema (the word is the same). Dreams of inheriting his wealth have come true in their equal inheritance of his curses. 'O proud destroying Death-fates and Furies That have consumed the race of Oedipus And swallowed them down whole'.[21] It appears that there is more to the tone of Aeschylus than can easily be accommodated into our verse. If that is true, so much the worse for us.

APPENDIX 1

Aesch. *Pers.* 377–464

MESSENGER: And when the light of the sun had perished
and night came on, the masters of the oar
and men at arms went down into the ships;
then line to line the longships passed the word,
and every one sailed in commanded line.
All that night long the captains of the ships
ordered the sea people at their stations.
The night went by, and still the Greek fleet
gave order for no secret sailing out.
But when the white horses of the daylight
took over the whole earth, clear to be seen,
the first noise was the Greeks shouting with joy,
like singing, like triumph, and then again
echoes rebounded from the island rocks.
The barbarians were afraid, our strategy
was lost, there was no Greek panic in
that solemn battle-song they chanted then,
but battle-hunger, courage of spirit;
the trumpet's note set everything ablaze.
Suddenly by command their foaming oars
beat, beat in the deep of the salt water,
and all at once they were clear to be seen.

First the right wing in perfect order leading,
then the whole fleet followed out after them,
and one great voice was shouting in our ears:
'Sons of the Greeks, go forward, and set free
your fathers' country and set free your sons,
your wives, the holy places of your gods,
the monuments of your own ancestors:
now is the one battle for everything.'
Our Persian voices answered roaring out,
and there was no time left before the clash.
Ships smashed their bronze beaks into ships;
it was a Greek ship in the first assault
that cut away the entire towering stern
from a Phoenician, and another rammed
timber into another. Still, at first
the great flood of the Persian shipping held,
but multitudes of ships crammed up together,
no help could come from one to the other,
they smashed one another with brazen beaks,
and the whole rowing fleet shattered itself.
So then the Greek fleet with a certain skill
ran inwards from a circle around us,
and the bottoms of ships were overturned,
there was no sea-water in eyesight,
only wreckage and bodies of dead men,
and beaches and the rocks all full of dead.
Whatever ships were left out of our fleet
rowed away in no order in panic.
The Greeks with broken oars and bits of wreck
smashed and shattered the men in the water
like tunny, like gaffed fish. One great scream
filled up all the sea's surface with lament,
until the eye of darkness took it all.
I could not tell the whole tale of that harm,
not if I strung words together ten days.
Understand one thing well: that on one day
there never died so many men before.

THE QUEEN: How great a sea of evil has broken
on the Persians and all the Asian race.
MESSENGER: Understand this: the evil is not small,
such a catastrophe of suffering
had come on them it struck another stroke.
THE QUEEN: What fortune could be worse hostile than this?

              Say what disastrous thing you mean that brought
              even a greater evil on our men?
MESSENGER: The most high-natured and high-spirited
              and bravest Persians and most nobly bred,
              in whom their lord had highest trust always,
              died by an infamous, inglorious death.
THE QUEEN: O misery, O evil! O my friends!
              Tell me what the death was by which they died.
MESSENGER: There is an island beside Salamis,
              a small isle, a bad anchorage for ships:
              dancing Pan is the god of the island
              and lives there on the edges of the sea.
              There he set them to kill those agile Greeks
              reaching the island from their ruined ships,
              and save their friends out of the arm of sea,
              ill foreseeing what the future would be.
              When the god gave the Greeks the sea-battle
              that very day they walled their bodies up
              in brazen armament, leapt from their ships,
              and ringed the island in one metal ring,
              so that our men had no way they could turn.
              Then they smashed them with rocks thrown with their hands,
              and deathly arrows flew from the bowstring.
              At last they rushed them in one breaking wave,
              battered and butchered their unhappy limbs,
              until they all wasted away their lives.

APPENDIX 2

Dead Soldiers

When His Excellency Prince Norodom Chantaraingsey
Invited me to lunch on the battlefield
I was glad of my white suit for the first time that day.
They lived well, the mad Norodoms, they had style.
The brandy and the soda arrived in crates.
Bricks of ice, tied around with raffia,
Dripped from the orderlies' handlebars.

And I remember the dazzling tablecloth
As the APCs fanned out along the road,
The dishes piled high with frogs' legs,
Pregnant turtles, their eggs boiled in the carapace,

Marsh irises in fish sauce
And inflorescence of a banana salad.

On every bottle, Napoleon Bonaparte
Pleaded for the authenticity of the spirit.
They called the empties Dead Soldiers
And rejoiced to see them pile up at our feet.

Each diner was attended by one of the other ranks
Whirling a table-napkin to keep off the flies.
It was like eating between rows of morris dancers –
Only they didn't kick.

On my left sat the prince;
On my right, his drunken aide.
The frogs' thighs leapt into the sad purple face
Like fish to the sound of a Chinese flute.
I wanted to talk to the prince. I wish now
I had collared his aide, who was Saloth Sar's brother,
And whom we treated as the club bore. He was always
Boasting of his connections, boasting with a headshake
Or by pronouncing of some doubtful phrase.
And well might be boast. Saloth Sar, for instance,
Was Pol Pot's real name. The APCs
Fired into the sugar palms but met no resistance.

In a diary, I refer to Pol Pot's brother as the Jockey Cap.
A few weeks later, I find him 'in good form
And very sceptical about Chantaraingsey'.
'But one eats well there,' I remark.
'So one should,' says the Jockey Cap:
'The tiger always eats well,
It eats the raw flesh of the deer,
And Chantaraingsey was born in the year of the tiger.
So, did they show you the things they do
With the young refugee girls?'

And he tells me how he will one day give me the gen.
He will tell me how the prince financed the casino
And how the casino brought Lon Nol to power.
He will tell me this.
He will tell me all these things.
All I must do is drink and listen.

In those days, I thought that when the game was up
The prince would be far, far away –
In a limestone faubourg, on the promenade at Nice,
Reduced in circumstances but well enough provided for.

In Paris, he would hardly require his private army.
The Jockey Cap might suffice for café warfare,
And matchboxes for APCs.

But we were always wrong in these predictions.
It was a family war. Whatever happened,
The principals were obliged to attend its issue.
A few were cajoled into leaving, a few were expelled,
And there were villains enough, but none of them
Slipped away with the swag.

For the prince was fighting Sihanouk, his nephew,
And the Jockey Cap was ranged against his brother
Of whom I remember nothing more
Than an obscure reputation for virtue.

I have been told that the prince is still fighting
Somewhere in the Cardamoms or the Elephant Mountains.
But I doubt that the Jockey Cap would have survived his good connections.
I think the lunches would have done for him –
Either the lunches or the dead soldiers.

James Fenton

APPENDIX 3

Supp. 222–31

Worship the common altar of these Lords,
and like a flock of doves in purity
crouch here in fear of hawks that wing together,
that hate your blood's kin and defile your race.
How can a bird that eats a bird be pure?
Mated unwilling with a man unwilling
how is one to be pure? Dead and in hell
one would not fly from it, having done this.
Another Zeus judges all ravellings
down there, and gives last justice to the dead.

APPENDIX 4

Zeus, whoever Zeus may be, if he
is pleased so to be called,
by this I speak to him:
I find no likeness though I weigh
all things in the scales but Zeus,

43

if I must truly throw
useless weight from my mind.

And now not even he who once was great
who with his fighting courage swelled,
he shall not be spoken: he once was:
and he that was born then
was thrown and he has gone.
Who gladly cries Zeus champion
will hit the centre mark of thought:

who has put men on the road to be wise
by the authentic law
to learn by suffering,
and painful memory drips
like sleep into the heart
and those unwilling have learnt to be wise;
maybe the blessing of those gods by force
throned on the dreadful steering-bench.

APPENDIX 5

In a Notebook

There was a river overhung with trees
With wooden houses built along its shallows
From which the morning sun drew up a haze.
And the gyrations of the early swallows
Paid no attention to the gentle breeze
Which spoke discreetly from the weeping willows.
There was a jetty by the forest clearing
Where a small boat was tugging at its mooring.

And night still lingered underneath the eaves.
In the dark houseboats families were stirring
And Chinese soup was cooked on charcoal stoves.
Then one by one there came into the clearing
Mothers and daughters bowed beneath their sheaves.
The silent children gathered round me staring
And the shy soldiers setting out for battle
Asked for a cigarette and laughed a little.

From low canoes old men laid out their nets
While on the bank young boys with lines were fishing.
The wicker traps were drawn up by their floats.
The girls stood waist-deep in the river washing

44

Or tossed the day's rice on enamel plates
And I sat drinking bitter coffee wishing
The tide would turn to bring me to my senses
After the pleasant war and the evasive answers.

There was a river overhung with trees.
The girls stood waist-deep in the river washing,
And night still lingered underneath the eaves
While on the bank young boys with lines were fishing.
Mothers and daughters bowed beneath their sheaves
While I sat drinking bitter coffee wishing –
And the tide turned and brought me to my senses.
The pleasant war brought the unpleasant answers.

The villages are burnt, the cities void;
The morning light has left the river view;
The distant followers have been dismayed;
And I'm afraid, reading this passage now,
That everything I knew has been destroyed
By those whom I admired but never knew;
The laughing soldiers fought to their defeat
And I'm afraid most of my friends are dead.

James Fenton

APPENDIX 6

Henry VI Part 3, Act One, scene 3

RUTLAND: Ah whither shall I fly to scape their hands?
            Ah, tutor, look where bloody Clifford comes!
CLIFFORD: Chaplain, away! thy priesthood saves thy life.
            As for the brat of this accursed duke,
            Whose father slew my father, he shall die.
TUTOR: And I my lord will bear him company.
CLIFFORD: Soldiers, away with him!
TUTOR: Ah Clifford, murder not this innocent child,
            Lest thou be hated both of God and man.
CLIFFORD: How now! is he dead already? Or is it fear
            That makes him close his eyes? I'll open them.
RUTLAND: So looks the pent-up lion o'er the wretch
            That trembles under his devouring paws,
            And so he walks, insulting o'er his prey,
            And so he comes to rend his limbs insunder.
            Ah, gentle Clifford, kill me with thy sword,
            And not with such a cruel threatening look....

APPENDIX 7

from Our Western Furniture

I am Bashō: a dead man travelling
Through flat and withered moorland where the trees
Cruelly sculpted by the winds and skies
Are hung with icicles and know no spring.

I am a man who watched the flowering
Of breathless blossoms in the cherry trees
And knew the swirling currents of the breeze
That spread their scent and petals through the spring.

The wind has made my skeleton its home.
The frost is native to my heart, my skin
Withered and leprous, white with age.
Now all my former fire of life is gone.

I am Bashō, who lived for flowers and moons
And found instead clouds and a carapace.

James Fenton

Horace[1]

Most of my life I made a mistake which I think has been common in England for several hundred years: I thought I understood Horace. I thought I communicated with him quite directly and immediately, and knew him as a poet and as a friend, particularly through the odes. Admittedly poets do have an instinct for other poets. Wystan Auden thought he knew Horace without even knowing much Latin, Milton did know Latin, and his version of an ode of Horace in English is classical, perfect and quite unlike anything else in our language. Hopkins of all people translated two odes of Horace with a certain sensuous inwardness. The only other[2] adequate reflection of Horatian lyric poetry in English, literally the only other, at least until Housman and Basil Bunting and modern times (to which I will return), is Marvell's 'Horatian Ode'. Duncombe put together a four-volume anthology in the eighteenth century of translations of Horace by various hands, some poets and some not. It is a treasure-house of charming, clever, obscure poetry, but not one poem in it adequately conveys Horace, except for the Milton.[3] Milton conveys the obstinacy, almost awkwardness of the Latin, with its melodic momentum and its pervasive sweetness.

Milton and Horace meet in a sense of rhythm derived directly from music, and Marvell belonged to Milton's generation. Under the influence of Italian music in the 1590s, when every London barber's shop kept a lute to play while you were waiting, and with the melting tones and long sighing or dying notes of our native music at that time, from the 1590s until the Civil War, also with a certain primitive consciousness of syllabic length and brevity which crops up in the theoretical work of Thomas Campion for example, English was prolific in the creation of new lyric stanza forms. That ability was necessary for an adequate translation of Horace's odes. It began with Spenser and died with the court of Charles I. The court ode, which survived or was revived, was another matter: its music was more pompous and its lyric more artificial, splendidly pompous in Purcell, beautifully artificial in Pope and Dryden, but the old simple ability was gone in 1660, and it never came back.

It is curious that Shakespeare felt so little influence of Horace's odes. He knew of them, since *Antony and Cleopatra* is Plutarch with a touch or two of Horace's 'Cleopatra' ode, and his heart was in the right place, because the death of Cinna the poet – 'tear him for his bad verses' – is funny as well as terrible, but the odes seem not to have been taught at his school; he knew Seneca and absorbed Ovid. The Elizabethans who praised him as a new Propertius, a new Ovid and a new Catullus never called him a new Horace. His ideas of the lyric ode probably came from Ronsard, or from Italian songs. A verse he is supposed to have taken from Petronius is really closer to the *Carmina Burana*. When the revellers sing in *Antony and Cleopatra*, there is nothing very Horatian about them.

> Come, thou monarch of the vine,
> Plumpy Bacchus with pink eyen,
> In thy vats our cares be drown'd,
> With thy grapes our hairs be crown'd,
> Cup us, till the world go round,
> Cup us, till the world go round!

For two hundred years after Shakespeare's death, every stray squire thought he could do Horace; many of them thought they *were* Horace, but between the age of Augustus and British history there is a great gulf fixed. At the end of the seventeenth century the greatest English scholar, Richard Bentley, tried to explain to the squirearchy what Horace's metres were like; his examples were strict and formal in Latin and in Greek, but on occasion he illustrated them by stress accent from British popular songs.

In fact the only poem of Shakespeare over which Horace does cast an indirect shadow is one of the most famous, a poem central to the Renaissance and to everyone's idea of Horace as a lyric poet, his boast: the epilogue and signature to the third, or rather to the first three books of odes, which he published together, 'Exegi monumentum'. Yet I doubt whether the shadow fell directly: there are similar sentiments linking poetry to immortality in Propertius and in Ovid, and it was Ovid not Horace that Shakespeare quoted like a manifesto, in the epigraph to *Venus and Adonis*. The idea that poetry is immortal and therefore poets and those they celebrate are immortal is close to the core of Renaissance culture: Horace's statement is classic for them, so it is not surprising that Shakespeare's different statement still strikes us as classic. Yet one should remember that in his case this was only one among many boasts, only one variation of an amazing theme. For Horace it stood rather alone, being the fullest version of many hints elsewhere: he was claiming to be a kind of priest, in a way a kind of Greek, but Horace's poem is moving because it is so intensely localized in the far south of Italy, in that undistinguished military colony where his father was an auctioneer, the nest from which he soared.[4]

The letter m and the word monuments connect these poems. But Shakespeare knows ruins, abbey ruins if not the ruins of Rome, 'unswept stones besmear'd with sluttish time'; and he knows how Rome ended: 'When wasteful war shall statues overturn'. His concern is the beloved immortalized, a more gallant and Propertian, but more artificial device than Horace's security of his own fame. Horace identifies himself with Rome, and with his own countryside as part of Rome. I find that braver and more momentous. Indeed, the deepest contradictions in all Horace's poetry arise from his headlong commitment or his by no means headlong commitment, to his friends and to the Roman state. But 'Exegi monumentum' has something unusual in Horace that was a favourite quality of writers like Marlowe and Shakespeare: the unmistakable and amazing sweep and swoop of great verse in the grandest and simplest manner, from the first line to the last, such as a sonnet might have. Two things at least about Horace have been subtly traced by an immensely great scholar, Eduard Fraenkel, his relations with Augustus and his Greek influences: since that book is in print and easy to find I do not intend to trespass on its territory more than I must. Fraenkel said elsewhere that the deeper any Roman was, the deeper was the Greek influence on him, and Horace is the supreme case of that saying. As for Horace's sentiment about the state, I want to leave it aside, saying only that I have a deep, uneasy respect for it, more than I have for Virgil's, and to add the observation that it may have some analogy to Boris Pasternak's Russian patriotism.

So let us turn to Horace's odes.[5] The first thing to say about the odes is that they are not his first or his only poems: they are sandwiched among his satires and epistles from which one learns more about him and with which they share philosophy, social attitudes one might not notice, and the names of people. The second is their abundant and contrived variety, not just their metrical abundance, which let us take for granted, but a variety of that inward core of poetic form which he learnt about as a very young man, probably as a student in Athens. Thirdly he made progress, he became better as a poet: he reworked later in life poems that would have won our applause in their first state. The most obvious example of that is the one Housman translated in its final version. When he had read that translation aloud during his rather dry and knotty Horace lectures, in May 1914, he wept and left the room.[6]

It will easily be seen in what ways this is a typical Housman poem (see Appendix 1), a perfectly poised and composed later-Victorian poem which is a distant cousin of the songs of Heine. Housman casually remarked that Conington's was the best English version of Horace he knew, and one of the best translations in the language. It is indeed one of the rarest flowers of its long-lost culture. In our poem the love of comrades in the final stanza is almost but not quite an intrusion; it is certainly intrusive in tone. the original myth had been that Pirithous sat on a rock in the underworld and the rock and his naked flesh grew into one thing; he was stuck to it by the bottom. There is some consciousness of that myth in fifth-century Greek vase-painting, but one is safe to assume that Horace was unconscious of it: he speaks of chains, that Theseus the famous strong athlete is not strong enough to break. Hippolytus is chaste or pure, but once again 'pure of stain' is intrusive. Earlier in the poem 'audet ducere nuda choros' becomes 'unapparelled in the woodland play', which is a clever enough equivalent, but one that brings the goddess a fatal step closer to the draped or the undraped ladies of Burne-Jones. Still, what Housman captures is the speed and movement of the poem as a whole: he offers at least some remote equivalent of the experience of reading Horace in Latin. It is no mere coincidence that Housman and Milton, the two great translators of Horace into English, were (with Thomas Gray) the greatest English writers of Latin verse.[7] The half-suppressed intensity of sentiment that makes Housman's Horace a little whiskery and Victorian can be felt also in his Latin verses – 'cito casurae tactus virtutis amore'.[8] It was part of his personality, as a certain humorous reticence was part of Horace's.

Kipling was even more crazy on Horace and had a strong feeling of inwardness with his political verse, but here as elsewhere he took the imperial message too seriously.[9] He contributed two poems to that curious enterprise, the fifth book of Horace's odes, by A. D. Godley, 1920, with translations by Kipling and Charles Graves of *Punch*, published by Basil Blackwell. That must be the high-water mark of English Horatiomania: it is moving, I suppose, as well as ridiculous, and the *apparatus criticus* to which I think R. A. Knox contributed, and the Latin preface, which is a spirited parody of Housman *furiosus*, still raise the ghost of a smile. It must be nearly the last of a long series of European volumes that flatter Horace by at least the intention of imitation. It is no fault of Kipling's that he differs utterly from Horace in sound values, and psychologically at least as much as an industrious, middle-class, colonial Englishman of 1900 differs from a Whig aristocrat of the eighteenth century.[10]

Horace's odes are various and his first three books were planned or laid out to demonstrate that. He was reviving and adapting Greek metres that had the glamour of antiquity but were nearly lost. Catullus in the last generation had pointed the way, but Horace's exploitation of the new sounds was thorough and full-blooded, and technically extremely able. The tones were almost more various than the metres, but when his poetry is taken together there is something tragic about it as well as something delicate.[11] Many of those to whom he dedicated poems died by violence or suicide. Life under Augustus was uneasy and he reflects that unease. When he signs off the last poem, number twenty of his first book of epistles, with a self-portrait, he deliberately underlines the year of riots over a disputed consular election, when Augustus was out of the city and Rome had to be put under military law, under a garrison. I was forty-four in that year, he says. He had lived and written through civil war, and every kind of crisis and military occupation.[12]

One of the most appealing things about him is the sadness of his personal philosophy, which is eclectic but partly stoic and partly epicurean ('tristis illa et exilis voluptas'), and the vividness of his consolations is outlined against that darkness. Hence I assume his appeal to the despairing, stubbornly private English squirearchy, and hence the alternative he offers to Christianity. The philosophy of life of English villages has not for centuries been the philosophy preached in the village churches with their translations from Hebrew and Greek and Latin, but rather the philosophy insinuated by the surrounding graveyards, which is closer to Horace than we may like to think. Part of Horace's sadness is his social position as an outsider, the son of an ex-slave, educated and promoted beyond his station, and patronized by great men he was obliged to please: first Brutus took him from a lecture hall in Athens and made him an officer, but he sensibly ran away. Then Virgil introduced him as a poet to the difficult Maecenas, with whom his relationship was not untroubled; then came Augustus. His first Roman promotion was to be head archivist of the central legal and political library: a job that normally went to an *eques Romanus*, that is to a minor peer or a baronet, the backbone of the aristocracy. I hazard the conjecture that from that time onward it was impossible for Horace to marry the women he knew, the daughters of the circles in which he moved. The marriage of a Roman noble to anyone beneath him was automatically invalid, and the alliance of a nobleman to the son of an ex-slave was unthinkable. His verses contain much fooling about with sex and even with love, but the names are not real: he had no wife and the homosexuality in some of his verses is hardly more than a schoolboy's guidebook to the homosexuality of their Greek originals. It is literary love.

All the same it can be convincing, most of all when it is painful. Ligurinus in the first ode of the fourth book, one of his last writings,[13] is surely a contemporary slave, named from his country of origin, not a Greek imitation. The poem is addressed to a rich and promising young man, a favourite at court, who was later disgraced like so many, and permitted to die by suicide. Horace begs Venus, the savage mother of desires, that at fifty she should let him go. 'I am not what I was in Cinara's day,' he says; 'go and torment young Paulus Maximus. He is *nobilis et decens*, and a fine advocate. He will give you a marble statue under the fruit trees[14] by the Alban lake, with incense and the lyre and flute and pipe. There twice a day the boys and the young girls will dance to you. No woman and no boy can tempt me now.' The poem ends with tears and silence and a dream of pursuit that is terribly convincing: probably it was a real dream, but maybe not a real boy. Of all the erotic boys and girls in Horace's odes, I find Ligurinus the most unforgettable. Cinara seems to be a real person, perhaps uniquely in his poetry of this kind, but she remains shadowy, we hardly know her, she belongs to private life and to the past. It is the dream, not Ligurinus, that is so real. If he was a slave his naked exercise on the Campus Martius is highly improbable. Horace's sex life has disappeared into dreams.

What remains overwhelmingly real in the fourth book as it was in the first is his consciousness of death. It is most real when it is most conventional. In the seventh ode he uses a set of words for the ancient dead that occurs on real Roman epitaphs, but the rhythm makes them awe-inspiring.[15]

> damna tamen celeres reparant caelestia lunae:
> nos ubi decidimus
> quo pater Aeneas, quo dives Tullus et Ancus,
> pulvis et umbra sumus.

Part of the force of this great poem lies certainly in the solemn, full beat of its hexameters interspersed with the deadly precision of its half-lines. The whole metre is almost elegiac couplets, but sharper and more penetrating: its reticence and its solemnity are audible. The early poem it improves (1,4) has a less satisfactory rhythm, once again not far from elegiac couplets, but more tripping: 'Pale Death with equal foot beats on the door of poor men's cottages and rich men's castles' is in itself less convincing, less formal, though I like 'Pluto's narrow house', and 'iam te premet nox fabulaeque Manes' ('Night will press on you and the fabled Shades').

The English have traditionally taken a curiously purified view of Horace,[16] rather ignoring the constant use he makes of mythology. Sometimes he invokes it as an example, sometimes to give meaning to the state: 'son of Maia, Caesar's avenger' (1,2, 43–4) or 'Pollux and wandering Hercules in the citadels of fire where Augustus shall lie among them to drink nectar with his shining mouth' (1,3, 9–12). Sometimes it gives body to a poem like 'the hundred-handed Giant' or Gyges (2,17, 14 and 3,4, 69), the names of constellations, the Scorpion and the Scales and 'Capricorn hard master of the western sea'. Sometimes a myth is like some marvellous unexpected ornament, perfectly concrete like Hyacinthus in the poems of Góngora, caught motionless in arrested motion against the light, poised between the poem and eternity. This gets better as he grows older, and it seems to derive from a close study of Pindar, of all unlikely authors. Consider the eagles and the lions that introduce Drusus in Odes 4,4 and the Muse herself in Odes 4,3 who can give the swan's sound to the voiceless fish: 'quod spiro et placeo, si placeo, tuum est'. This mythology has many uses as a common language, for instance to bring alive and make concrete a latent value or belief, but other functions too. They all raise the awkward question of what Horace really believed about the gods.

At times he is only telling a story, however seriously, or retelling an old story, like the story of Regulus tortured to death, which he took from Naevius,[17] a poet of genuinely archaic quality, lost to us but magnificent in his fragments. I assume that Naevius based his story of Regulus going out to die on the *Iliad* and on Hector. The story is of course mythical: such accusations and counter-accusations about torture between Romans and Carthaginians filled the air when Naevius was writing. This[18] is the most memorable of the six patriotic odes that open the third book: yet its theme is personal and philosophic, it is about heroism. All these odes, in spite of their divine fulminations and their Augustan gestures, are essentially the state-

ment of a private philosophy in a public tone we would nowadays
think unbecoming. They are about virtue, and the relevance of the
divine machinery for the refounding of Troy in ode three remains
obscure to this day, as Horace (3,3, 69–72) felt it to be. On the
whole, Horace is far less personal and less revealing of himself in the
odes than he is in the satires and epistles. I well remember as a boy at
school floundering through these so-called state odes, and pouncing
with relief on the lighter subject of adultery in number seven, though
its mythological allusions to Bellerophon and Hippolyte, which attract me today as the scent of fox attracts a pensioned-off fox-hound,
then passed me by. Horace found the Greek names glamorous and
beautiful, as Virgil did, but I found them hard to learn by heart and
inconsequential. I preferred the flute in the streets at night, and the
girl's name Asterie.

> prima nocte domum claude, neque in vias
> sub cantu querulae despice tibiae
> et te saepe vocanti
> duram difficilis mane.

What does he really believe about the gods? Horace attaches the gods
to the state, so that they take on something of the state's meaning-
lessness, the emptiness and formality behind the terror. Virgil attaches
the gods of the *Georgics* to the earth, so that we half believe in them,
but the gods of the *Aeneid* to the past, which makes them merely
fabulous, or in Book Six to the Roman future, which is a baroque
triumph of barbarous unpleasantness. In his poetry meanings and
images swim beneath the glassy surface, and Greek names preen
themselves like exotic fishes. Horace is a more pungent poet, just as
Baudelaire is more pungent than Tennyson. His range, being wider, is
more uneven. He reveals oddly little of his intimate beliefs: when the
gods are visionary, which is rare and mostly about Bacchus and his
gang, then the visions are real, but in 'Parcus deorum cultor et in-
frequens' (Odes 1,34) the lightning and the landslide are real and yet
the god perhaps not. In 'Faune nympharum fugientum amator', the
peasants believe and he identifies with the peasants. At the Bandusian
spring[19] something similar happens, but the poem is an ornamental
exercise as well, a tribute not to a god but to a beautiful place. Horace
prefers the Roman names for rustic gods, even though his peasant
woman has the Greek name Phidyle. He calls Pan Faunus, and the
Muses often enough Camenae, or Greek Camena (2,16, 38). 'To me
truthful Fate gave small fields and the thin breath of the Greek Muse

and to despise the envious crowd.' His hatred and fear of envy and his triumph over it are an Italian villager's feelings. He does refer to Pan, but not by name: he calls him 'that god whom Arcadia's black mountains please'.

That is in 4,12. The winds that are spring's companions waft the boats, the nightingale with the glamour of Greek mythology makes her nest, the shepherds' pipes chant to their fat sheep, 'delectantque deum, cui pecus et nigri colles Arcadiae placent'. Black because the snow has melted. These are thirsty times, a time to open the expensive scent, so if these joys move you, come to my poor house, remember the dark fires, mingle some folly with your wisdom: 'dulce est desipere in loco'. The dark fires are thrilling, are they not, and boldly unexpected after the dark hills? This light-looking poem holds many elements of image and insinuation in balance: you can turn over its elements in your hand. This is a function of the short lines and swaying rhythms and the crispness of lyric stanzas, and of Horace's varying syntax, here at its simplest, so that no two stanzas have the same rhythm; vernacular rhythms colonize them gradually as the poem advances. Several stanzas are memorably beautiful, but he never pauses for long over any one kind of verbal felicity or beauty of language. In this way I believe that to a meditative, lifelong reader Horace more than any other poet except perhaps early Virgil reveals what is essential in the art of Latin poetry.[20] To put it another way, Horace is the most Chinese of Roman poets.

He is not a poet whom it is easy to sum up, for the same reason. I choose to concentrate on the odes, because they are so queer, such a daring mixture of contradictory experiments. Punctuation is an important, often an all-important clue to what he is up to as a poet, in any given ode: in punctuation I include the length of sentences, which is by no means predictable from one poem to the next. This series of seven end-stopped stanzas, all but one of which are four-line sentences, must be nearly unique. The exception indicates a pause, and the turn of the poem into its closer subject. 'Adduxere sitim tempora, Vergili'. 'These are thirsty times, Vergilius. But if you want to drink Calian wine, O associate of young noblemen, some scent will win you some drink.' Spring wind and the nightingales' sad and sexual story and the ready tunes of shepherds to their sweating sheep introduce drink and a scent, the cool storehouse, the bitterness of care and so to the end. The entire poem has a subtly linked undertone of sensuality.

Horace's landscape belongs to him as the farmer and owner of a long, steep-sided valley not far from Rome; the *fons Bandusiae* is close to his estate. An estate of course means an income as well: the wandering herds and the olive trees are his living, and the Sabine farm to judge by its archaeology is a substantial and an enviable house. By virtue of memory the landscape of the far south of Italy with its chestnut woods and its rushing rivers also belongs to him:[21] it was where he grew up among the enormous children of enormous centurions, the veterans of the military colony of Venusia. But the landscape belongs to him specially as a poet. 'Me doctarum hederae praemia frontium / dis miscent superis, me gelidum nemus, / Nympharumque leves cum Satyris chori.' He is a poet of place: 'quo pinus ingens albaque populus umbram hospitalem consociare amant ramis' . . . he likes a long spring, a warm autumn and a fine vintage (2,6, 17). The Muse smiled on him at his birth and he remains grateful. The most remarkable feature of his landscape vignettes in the odes is their smallness of scale, the tiny babble of the Bandusian spring and the single ilex overhanging it. For all his grand utterances he remains essentially a witty and laconic writer. He might waste a stanza or even a poem, but he never wastes words. His simple poems like the one to Faunus, which I take as a single sentence, and the Bandusian spring poem, are often quite perfect, and our grandfathers were right to admire them. He is also capable of wonderfully elaborate and effective structures, particularly in the fourth book. That is hardly surprising in view of his carefully modulated hexameter poems. Of those I want to say only that Alexander Pope comes very close to the spirit and tone and to the material of Horace's epistles. If you add the satires and epistles to the odes, Horace becomes a very great poet indeed. His only major work that disappoints is the *Art of Poetry*, which is pedantic, possibly juvenile, and I think unfinished.

Lawrence Durrell gives a curiously truthful and intuitive account of Horace in his poem 'On First Looking into Loeb's Horace'. (See Appendix 2.) It does not depend on that inwardness of his with Mediterranean life which was expressed in 'Deus Loci', a poem Horatian in another way, written at Forio d'Ischia in 1950 and revised in 1955, but rather on the sense of what it is to be a poet. It was written in the 1940s, and what it presents is a diagnosis of Horace which is accurate enough to be worth consideration.[22] The smallholder's ambitions, though Horace was more than a smallholder, and the sense of seasons must surely be right, and I like the uncomfortable chair. The cypress may be wrong, because cypress wood was used to burn the dead: it was not confined to cemeteries and I doubt whether it marked graves.[23] But the solitary at the upper window revising metaphors for the winter sea is a brilliant insight, and the winter that left his words pure but very few expresses a truth of some kind. The following two stanzas about Horace in the Sabine hills sound to me after many rereadings over thirty years very close to the truth about such a poet. Only the very last couplet of the poem drifts away off target. Most of the great books about Horace were written long ago, but this poem adds to them. Lawrence Durrell speaks as a poet about another poet because he has a right to do so, and he treats Horace as responsibly as he treats Cavafy. I think I like his Horace poem so much because it genuinely reminds me of Horace. Anyway, Durrell like Horace is a poet whom it is pleasant to quote.

It is quite hard for one who knows English as well as Latin to get rid of the lurking notion that Horace is an English minor poet of the eighteenth century or the Regency, the poet perhaps of Branwell Brontë's talented version of Book One of the Odes:[24]

> Here thou mayest, in long-drawn vale,
> Fly the sun and court the gale;
> Here with old Anacreon's string,
> Faith or frailty thou mayest sing:
> Here beneath the shade recline
> Quaffing cups of sober wine;
> Far from scenes when furious Mars
> With the joyful wine gods wars;
> Nor suspicious Cyrus fear
> Lest his boisterous passion tear
> From thy head the festal crown,
> And rend thy unoffending gown.[25]

But Horace is technically more ambitious and physically more sensuous, and intellectually more fresh and strange. The poem is an invitation to Tyndaris, beginning with a charming picture of Faunus piping to the cool goats, and ending (as so often) with a sudden moment of frozen violence like a snapshot. Tyndaris is just anyone, a Greek name because the bad behaviour at the end of the poem cannot be addressed to a Roman nobleman. The same is true of the famous Soracte ode, which follows a Greek original that a fragment about cushions suggests had some degree of impropriety. A full criticism of Branwell Brontë's version would be breaking a gnat on a wheel, but Horace exploits a far more complex verse form, and his verse leads

in more suggestive directions. Much has disappeared in Branwell
Brontë's translation:

> hic in reducta valle cuniculae
> vitabis aestus et fide Teia
> dices laborantis in uno
> Penelopen vitreamque Circen.

That is hardly conveyed by the clever phrase 'faith or frailty', and
'cups of innocent Lesbian in the shade' are more specific than 'cups of
sober wine'. Penelope and Circe, who imply Odysseus of course, make
an important transition in this simple, beautiful poem. However that
may be, it will be well to glance at something technically complex and
daring, and we are lucky to be able to do so with the serious, sober
modern version by James Michie, which contains for our generation a
valuable series of insights into Horace's odes. The fourth ode of Book
Four is mechanically perfect: it is not uncommon nowadays to see his
odes as perfect pieces of antique machinery, wonderful working
models: but they are something more. (See Appendix 3.) Horace is
interested in honesty, and passionate about his poetry. Philip Larkin
expressed the positivist view that 'today a poet cannot be a priest of a
mystery, because a mystery is either hokum or ignorance'. Horace
knew exactly where he stood as the priest of a mystery that was
neither. How much mystery there is in a poem or in poetry itself or in
what stanzas of a poem, all that was under Horace's control.[26] This
fourth ode of Book Four is written to Augustus and his stepsons, the
two Nerones; it is solemn, formal and brilliant. It is what Horace, with
all his devices in old age, can make of a formal compliment. It is not
among my favourite odes because it is too little personal, except in the
thrilling and Pindaric series of its images. I prefer the ritual and the
real language of his late poems to Augustus himself. But ode four
never gets lost, and Hannibal's speech is an extraordinary *tour de
force*.[27]

If war can be glorified, if Rome can be glorified, this is how. The
monstrous tree in the hills is as real as Hercules and Colchi and Thebes
are fabulous. The death of Hasdrubal, which is the occasion of this
dramatic speech,[28] is both fabulous and historical. The Alpine enemy
is virtually mythologized. The aristocratic belief in breeding is a
Pindaric doctrine, and I think from the way he speaks of Sabine
peasants and Marsians and Apulians that Horace wanted to believe in
it. He was a lover of freedom and an admirer of 'the terrible mind of
Cato' in that great man's refusal to be vanquished by Caesar and in his

suicide: his pride in his own father the ex-slave is famous, and he was high-handed on occasion with Maecenas and even Augustus, but he was not an egalitarian socialist. Whatever rings hollow to us in this poem does so because our view of Rome is determined by Roman historians of later generations, including the Greek Plutarch and a malcontent of genius, Tacitus. The hard edges of the poem are rubbed for us like those of some magnificent Roman coin or medal, and softened for us by death. This is not the greatest of Horace's late odes and it hardly fits at all into that moving increase of personality and of reconciliation that Fraenkel has traced in late Horace. I have deliberately (as I said) steered as clear as I could of his book on Horace[29] because I find its influence overwhelming. He did discuss it in moving terms, I think in a class in the 1960s on 'Those poems of Horace on which I have not yet spoken'. It represents a phenomenal technical achievement, and the climax of Horace's long wrestle with Pindar. In a number of details it recalls Virgil. It is a monumental poem, with the hollowness of monumental poems, but in its way perfect. And it is not at all like a minor poem by a squire or a young candidate of poetry. No official poet in French or Italian or Spanish or English has outdone it: not Pope, not Dryden, for its energy and wit, its mastery of its astonishing means, or its bite, its *morbidezza*.

So intense was the English cult of Horace 150 years ago that Augustus Hare says that the local peasants of the Sabine farm in his day thought Horace must have been an Englishman, because so many English came there asking questions about him. In the same way the peasants of Delphi thought the ancient pagans who built it were called Milordi, who came back to worship their old stones. The likely site of Horace's house was bought by a Mr Searle in 1878, whose daughter married a Harrow schoolmaster, Mr G.H. Hallam. The place was excavated in 1914, in the last hours of the old Europe. Nearby one can visit the Bandusian spring, and the woods where Horace met a wolf that ran away from him, luckily for us.[30] What protected him from the wolf was poetry itself, he says, a song about Lalage, and the fact that as an innocent poet he is 'integer vitae, scelerisque purus'. Horace's poems are as charming as his letters, and in liking them one must overcome one's resistance to giving way to charm. Charm that lasts so many hundreds of years is hard to distinguish from his formidable technique, yet his greatness in the odes is very much a technical thing, a musical and flowing line or momentum, beautifully disturbed by controlled cross-currents and constantly enlivened by visual excitements. His naturalism and realism and his personal tone are conditions of his astounding visual quality. You can hear his power as a poet, and you can see it.

Take a brief, unpretentious poem, 3,22.[31] (See Appendix 4.) The goddess is the ancient Mistress of the wild beasts, to whom the mountains and the forests belong: she is 'diva triformis', the Moon, the Virgin huntress and the Queen of hell, Hecate. The pregnant woman and the wild animals come equally under her protection: one believes in her because the girls believe. 'Imminens villae tua pinus esto'; he dedicates the tree. Vivid reality saves this poem from being a neo-classic epigram: the same touch of the genuine that rescues so many Greek epigrams and makes them wonderful. The poem is one sentence, the metre is light-footed, and the wild boar, 'obliquum meditantis ictum', is unforgettable. This is not a new or a different style from the longer odes: the odes are more like each other than their Greek originals were, the eye and the craftsmanship of Horace are almost the same as those of the sculptors of the Ara Pacis Augusti, the same in a bee or an insect crawling on a sway of stone flowers, on the free and beautiful drawing of the goddess Earth or Italia, and on solemn but individual portraits of the imperial family, and on the miniature allusion to the Parthenon procession. It is not just that many of the odes end in frozen violence, or include a scene of dancing, it is Horace's crispness and his perfectly persuasive music. The shepherds are tired out, the sun bites, drink is a dignified remedy for irremediable despair: at the year's end stands death and if necessary suicide. 'Ipse deus simul atque volam me solvet: opinor, hoc sentit moriar, mors ultima linea rerum est'.[32] Meanwhile Horace invites his insomniac patron Maecenas to dinner, in a long poem of bleak consolations.[33] 'Iam pastor umbras cum grege languido rivumque fessus quaerit et horridi dumeta Silvani caretque ripa vagis taciturna ventis'.

APPENDIX 1

Diffugere Nives

Horace, *Odes* 4, 7

The snows are fled away, leaves on the shaws
    And grasses in the mead renew their birth,
The river to the river-bed withdraws,
    And altered is the fashion of the earth.

Horace

The Nymphs and Graces three put off their fear
  And unapparelled in the woodland play.
The swift hour and the brief prime of the year
  Say to the soul, *Thou wast not born for aye.*

Thaw follows frost; hard on the heel of spring
  Treads summer sure to die, for hard on hers
Comes autumn, with his apples scattering;
  Then back to wintertide, when nothing stirs.

But oh, whate'er the sky-led seasons mar,
  Moon upon moon rebuilds it with her beams:
Come *we* where Tullus and where Ancus are,
  And good Aeneas, we are dust and dreams.

Torquatus, if the gods in heaven shall add
  The morrow to the day, what tongue has told?
Feast then thy heart, for what thy heart has had
  The fingers of no heir will ever hold.

When thou descendest once the shades among,
  The stern assize and equal judgement o'er,
Not thy long lineage nor thy golden tongue,
  No, nor thy righteousness, shall friend thee more.

Night holds Hippolytus the pure of stain,
  Diana steads him nothing, he must stay;
And Theseus leaves Pirithoüs in the chain
  The love of comrades cannot take away.
                                                A. E. Housman

APPENDIX 2

On First Looking into Loeb's Horace

I found your Horace with the writing in it;
Out of time and context came upon
This lover of vines and slave to quietness,
Walking like a figure of smoke here, musing
Among his high and lovely Tuscan pines.

All the smallholder's ambitions, the yield
Of wine-bearing grape, pruning and drainage
Laid out by laws, almost like the austere
Shell of his verses – a pattern of Latin thrift;
Waiting so patiently in a library for

Autumn and the drying of the apples;
The betraying hour-glass and its deathward drift.

Surely the hard blue winterset
Must have conveyed a message to him –
The premonitions that the garden heard
Shrunk in its shirt of hair beneath the stars,
How rude and feeble a tenant was the self,
An Empire, the body with its members dying –
And unwhistling now the vanished Roman bird?

The fruit-trees dropping apples; he counted them;
The soft bounding fruit on leafy terraces,
And turned to the consoling winter rooms
Where, facing south, began the great prayer,
With his reed laid upon the margins
Of the dead, his stainless authors,
Upright, severe on an uncomfortable chair.

Here, where your clear hand marked up
'The hated cypress' I added 'Because it grew
On tombs, revealed his fear of autumn and the urns',
Depicting a solitary at an upper window
Revising metaphors for the winter sea: 'O
Dark head of storm-tossed curls'; or silently
Watching the North Star which like a fever burns

Away the envy and neglect of the common,
Shining on this terrace, lifting up in recreation
The sad heart of Horace who must have seen it only
As a metaphor for the self and its perfection –
A burning heart quite constant in its station.

Easy to be patient in the summer,
The light running like fishes among the leaves,
Easy in August with its cones of blue
Sky uninvaded from the north; but winter
With its bareness pared his words to points
Like stars, leaving them pure but very few.

He will not know how we discerned him, disregarding
The pose of sufficiency, the landed man,
Found a suffering limb on the great Latin tree
Whose roots live in the barbarian grammar we
Use, yet based in him, his mason's tongue;
Describing clearly a bachelor, sedentary,
With a fond weakness for bronze-age conversation,
Disguising a sense of failure in a hatred for the young,

Horace

Who built in the Sabine hills this forgery
Of completeness, an orchard with a view of Rome;
Who studiously developed his sense of death
Till it was all around him, walking at the circus,
At the baths, playing dominoes in a shop –
The escape from self-knowledge with its tragic
Imperatives: *Seek, suffer, endure*. The Roman
In him feared the Law and told him where to stop.

So perfect a disguise for one who had
Exhausted death in art – yet who could guess
You would discern the liar by a line,
The suffering hidden under gentleness
And add upon the flyleaf in your tall
Clear hand: 'Fat, human and unloved,
And held from loving by a sort of wall,
Laid down his books and lovers one by one,
Indifference and success had crowned them all.'

1946/1943

On Ithaca Standing
(1937)

Tread softly, for here you stand
On miracle ground, boy.
A breath would cloud this water of glass,
Honey, bush, berry and swallow.
This rock, then, is more pastoral, than
Arcadia is, Illyria was.

Here the cold spring lilts on sand.
The temperature of the toad
Swallowing under a stone whispers: 'Diamonds,
Boy, diamonds, and juice of minerals!'
Be a saint here, dig for foxes, and water,
Mere water springs in the bones of the hands.

Turn from the hearth of the hero. Think:
Other men have their emblems, I this:
The heart's dark anvil and the crucifix
Are one, have hammered and shall hammer
A nail of flesh, me to an island cross,
Where the kestrel's arrow falls only,
The green sea licks.

1943/1943

Lawrence Durrell

Horace, *Odes*, Book Four

Have you seen the feathered servant of the lightning,
Made by the king of gods king of his wandering
   Kind for his trusty part
In kidnapping the blond boy Ganymede?

Young blood and eagle's energy first launch him
Out of the nest to meet a sky of troubles,
   And the spring winds conspire,
Now storms are past, to teach his timid wings

Airy adventures. Soon his great sweep sends him
Plummeting down to terrify the sheepfold,
   Or, rage- and hunger-driven,
He lugs the wrestling serpent in his grip.

Have you seen a roe-deer browsing in contentment,
And then a lion whelp come upon her, freshly
   Weaned from the tawny teat –
Doomed she looks up, food for his unfleshed tooth?

Eagle or lion was Drusus to the warring
Vindelici among the Rhaetian passes,
   Whose right hands have preferred
The Amazon axe from immemorial time

(Custom whose origin we cannot guess here,
Nor should men sound all knowledge). Long unconquered,
   Victors on many fields,
Their armies scattered by a young man's skill

Have learnt what power accrues when mind and heart are
Fed with religion in a reverent household,
   Learnt what paternal love
Can do, when it is Caesar's, for two boys.

Brave noble men father brave noble children.
In bulls and horses likewise the male's stamp shows
   Clearly; we never find
Fear bred from fierceness, eagles hatching doves.

Yet it is training that promotes the inborn
Talent, and morals that shore up the spirit.
   When laws of conduct fail,
Vice mars what nature once formed excellent.

Horace

How deep the debt you owe the clan of Nero,
Rome, the Metaurus witnesses, and routed
   Hasdrubal, and that day
When darkness lifted over Latium

And victory had its first fair Roman dawn since
The terrible African rode through our cities
   Like fire through pine-woods, like
An east wind whipping the Sicilian waves.

From that day Roman manhood plucked momentum
And marched from strength to strength. The shrines that Carthage
   Laid barbarously waste
Refurbished saw their gods stand straight again,

Till the perfidious Hannibal in despair cried,
'We are like deer, predestined prey, who yet would
   Run after ravening wolves.
Triumph for us lies in retreat and stealth.

This race that, risen undaunted from Troy's ashes,
Ferried its gods, old men and children over
   The tossing Tuscan sea
To house them safely in Italian towns,

Is like some tough-grained oak, lopped by the woodman
On Algidus, that dark-boughed, verdurous mountain:
   It bleeds, it feels the shock,
Yet draws in vigour from the very axe,

Flourishing as fiercely as the severed Hydra
Sprouted at chafing Hercules. Old Cadmus'
   Dragon-sown fields at Thebes
Never pushed up a prodigy like this.

Whelm it in water, it will come up brighter.
Throw it, and it will grapple with the winner
   Again and take the applause.
The wars they wage breed tales for wives to tell.

Henceforward I'll no more send home to Carthage
Arrogant messengers to proclaim my triumphs.
   Lost, lost all hope and sunk
Our nation's star now Hasdrubal is dead.'

There's not a feat that cannot be accomplished
By Claudian hands. Jupiter smiles upon their
   Works, and their wise designs
Pilot us through the rapids of our wars.

James Michie

APPENDIX 4

Horace, *Odes*, Book Three

Friend of hills and woody places,
Goddess of three shapes and faces,
Virgin who, when summonéd
Thrice by young wives in childbed,
Givest ear to the hard-pressed
And from death deliverest,
Henceforth I declare this pine
Shadowing my villa, thine.
Blood of a wild boar that's just
Aiming his first sidelong thrust
Shall at each year's turning be
Gladly given to it by me.

James Michie

Dryden's Virgil[*]

John Dryden was nearly thirty when Charles II was crowned, and if ever a poet seemed to have a hard road ahead of him it was Dryden. His parents were a daughter of a rector and the third son of a baronet. The baronet had been imprisoned by Charles I, the poet's father had been a JP and a committee man under Cromwell, and his cousin, for whom he worked as a clerk, was Cromwell's Chamberlain, and one of the judges who condemned Charles I to death, though he luckily contrived to be absent on the day the death warrant was signed. In 1660, John Dryden had nothing but his education, his worldly ambition and his poetry; throughout his life, his poetry served his ambition, he made it work for him. If that is shocking it is also remarkable. He climbed far and high: he was at school at Westminster under Busby, to whom not only his Latin but his poetry[1] owed a great deal. Locke and South were among his fellow pupils. He was also at Trinity College, Cambridge, but without any obvious effect, though he was known there as a poet. In 1664 Samuel Pepys saw 'the poet I knew at Cambridge' sitting in a famous literary coffee-house, 'with all the wits in town'.

He wrote well-conceived public poetry: celebrating Cromwell in 1658 and the King in 1660 in memorable phrases. He is said to have worked as a publisher's hack for nineteen years, between the ages of twenty-nine and forty-eight.[2] His career was largely in the theatre, and in the theatre he gradually moulded his style. In his middle age, in the vital thirteen years between the ages of thirty-seven and fifty, he turned out fourteen plays. Social promotion came more swiftly, but financial security very much more slowly.[3] He was a Fellow of the Royal Society in 1662, he wrote his first plays and married above himself in 1663, in 1668 he was made a Master of Arts of Canterbury, and in

[*] This lecture, unlike the others, has been shortened.

1670, at thirty-nine, he succeeded Davenant as Poet Laureate and Historiographer Royal. Of the two theatres that first opened at the Restoration, Killigrew had the King's and Davenant had the Duke's; Dryden cultivated them both, they were his royal road. In them he worked on equal terms with literary courtiers, and by the late 1660s he had a share in management.[4]

He was ingenious in adaptation, and set his sails to catch the mood of the moment. It is curiously hard to say of Dryden, as it is of Eliot, whose criticism by the way often seems founded on stray remarks of Dryden's, whether they were creatures of their age in literature or whether in some sense they created it. One may say that Dryden was over-bold in adaptation; at times he was ridiculous, but never merely ridiculous. He adapted a translation of Molière by the Duke of Newcastle. He adapted Shakespeare with Davenant. In 1669 he adapted Milton's *Paradise Lost* in rhyming verse as an opera called *The Age of Innocence*. 'Ah,' said Milton, 'you may bag my verses if you will.' Dryden loved Milton, and learnt from him.[5] Some element of Milton's style has seeped into the best lines of Dryden's Virgil. Dryden also loved Shakespeare: though in adapting *The Tempest* Dryden and Davenant made Miranda male and Caliban female. Dryden returned to Shakespeare in 1679 to adapt *Antony and Cleopatra* as *All for Love*, and then *Troilus*. The fashion of rewriting Shakespeare that Dryden and Davenant founded was long lived and catastrophic, but *All for Love* is still a most interesting play, even in its difference from Shakespeare. By 1679 Dryden had learnt a great deal.

He took what is to my mind a strange line about the age of Fletcher and Shakespeare. It was partly nostalgic. As he said in *Astraea Redux* in 1660, 'Youth, that with joys had unacquainted been, Envied grey hairs that once good days had seen.' In the *Essay on Dramatic Poetry* (1668), where he meant to establish the supremacy of Shakespeare, he did so by citing the opinion of John Hales, the venerable and long since dead Fellow of Eton, and that of Sir John Suckling in the court of Charles I 'and with him the greater part of the courtiers'. Yet in Dryden's Epilogue to *The Conquest of Granada*, he refers to that same past age in boastful tones: 'In this one praise he has their fame surpast, To please an age more gallant than the last'; and in his prose defence of this Epilogue, he censures Shakespeare and Fletcher and Jonson, singling out that magnificent play *Bartholomew Fair* for particular contempt, as unfit for a polished audience. 'In those days,' he says, 'authors were not admitted to the best society ... there was less gallantry.' Did Dryden really think the court knew best? Did he

identify courtly polish with metrical smoothness? His personal
annotations to the 1679 edition of Spenser tend to regularize and
smooth down Spenser's metre. In the prefaces to the three volumes of
the appalling *Astrée of Durfé*, the young Dryden, if it really was
Dryden,[6] hazards the view that romances are 'the highest, noblest
productions of man's wit'. Was he just not thinking? Or is the
corruption of literary taste a reflection of some public corruption of
social standards?

This is a question that must I think be opened before we advance on
Dryden's Virgil. His style then was already formed, but formed by
what? Sir Walter Scott, his great biographer[7] and best critic, accepted
Dr Johnson's low view of metaphysical poetry, but he forgave the
remaining traces of it in early Dryden.[8] 'As he wrote from necessity,
Dryden was obliged to pay a certain deference to the public opinion.'
Another interesting critic of Dryden, George Saintsbury,[9] notices that
'Except his great editor [Walter Scott], it is doubtful whether any man
of letters ever knew the public taste better than Dryden.... The work
of the translator is to bridge over the interval between his author and
his public. The question arises who Dryden's public were, beyond the
audiences of London theatres.[10] Surely in the background there was
another, an ideal audience, the perfect audience that every poet
imagines, of which the courtiers of Charles II prided themselves as
members, an everlasting audience like Virgil's.[11] All the same I do not
believe such an imaginary audience, the one for which Dryden
translated Virgil, was more than a background or a vague backcloth to
his ambitions. In the foreground of his mind and of his style other
considerations jostled for his attention.

I greatly sympathize with a remark of Robert Lowell about Dryden
in an essay called 'Epics' on which he was working in 1977, in the last
summer of his life.[12] 'Homer', he says,

> is blinding Greek sunlight; Virgil is dark, narrow, morbid, mys-
> terious, and artistic. He fades in translation, unlike Homer who
> barely survives. By combining the plots of the *Iliad* and *Odyssey*,
> Virgil has seemed a plagiarist, attempting an epic as a task for
> rhetoric. He is as original as Milton. Dryden and the restoration
> critics were wrong in thinking the *Aeneid* something like their
> regilding of Jacobean tragedy . . . giving alloy and polish to old gold.

Of course he is talking about the *Aeneid*, and my contention is that
Dryden's *Eclogues* are a staggering achievement, and his *Georgics* the
best translation of what he himself called the best poem of the best

poet, though in this judgement I believe Dryden underrated Shakespeare, let alone Homer. Saintsbury thought the *Georgics* were Dryden's best effort but the *Eclogues* his worst. He thought the *Aeneid* the most uneven, an easy judgement to make, but at its best he thought it the best of all.[13] It is partly to clear up my own doubts on this matter that I am giving this lecture.

The problem goes back to Virgil himself. The *Aeneid* is an amazing mixture of episodes and fragments, subtly sewn together and intermingled; its unit is not the episode or the fragment or the phrase, though those are easy to recognize, but the book. Book Five is held together by water, Book Four by fire, Book Six by darkness and the flickering of shadows, and so on. Within the book the verse system is cumulative, and almost too smooth to be noticed. But we have little experience today of verse construction on so vast a scale, and modern criticisms of the construction of the whole *Aeneid*, which is precisely what is in question, lack authority. Any attempt to improve the *Aeneid* would make it worse. Its meaning for its first audience depended on a counterpoint of feelings, some more official and others more truthful: today some of these feelings are rotten and hollow, but others much sharper than before. I cannot ask you to enter into Virgil's private feelings – he has mostly made them impenetrable – but only to pick out as far as possible Dryden's from Virgil's. Virgil agreed to give a central force in his *Aeneid* to Rome, Roman values, the role of Augustus and the Roman empire. By doing so he came near to ruining his poem, which was most of his lifework.[14]

Virgil did also import more into his poem than is often realized of Italy and Italian values, but that is another matter. No poet not in two minds ought to undertake an epic poem, because poetry belongs to the defeated and the dead. One can say this at least for Dryden: he translated Virgil in retirement, stripped of his offices by the Glorious Revolution. When his publisher insisted on identifying Aeneas in the plates to Dryden's Virgil with the hooked nose of William III, Dryden was very angry indeed.

Dryden's best work was always done in retirement from London, as I think Shakespeare's was. In 1665–6 London was afflicted with plague and then fire. Dryden withdrew to Charlton in Wiltshire; he produced *Annus Mirabilis* and his *Essay on Dramatic Poesy*. By 1675, in which year *Aureng-Zebe*, his last rhymed tragedy, was revised by Charles II to give better lines to Nell Gwynn, Dryden's thoughts were already turning towards epic, and he considered the Black Prince or King Arthur. Luckily those were busy years and these awful epics remained unwritten.[15] In 1681–2 an attack on his political loyalty stung him to *Absalom and Achitophel* and to *The Medal*. When James II became king Dryden was seen by Evelyn on 19 January 1686, going to Mass with his sons and Nell Gwynn. He wrote *The Hind and the Panther* in Northamptonshire. In 1688 at the Revolution he was fifty-seven, and Shadwell was preferred to him as Laureate. He retired to the country, published his brilliant *Miscellanies*, which show him in supreme command of the English language, as of Latin literature, and translated Virgil.[16]

It would be thrilling to trace in detail the whole course of Dryden's progression as a poet, but that would have to be a long critical book.[17] Some of his finest verses are in his theatrical prologues, particularly the Oxford ones, in which he consciously encountered an audience more rewarding to him than the court. He was always talented, but often too explosively witty, and his robustness had a coarse, rough edge which today we might be in danger of overvaluing. I find it fascinating that the prologues, which were sold on stray sheets at the theatre door, and which are therefore bibliographical rarities, were more obscene than the official versions printed later. He was not far at times from being what W. B. Yeats called 'a coarse-witted pamphleteer'. But he could transmute into admirable and even mellow poetry, quite unexpectedly on any occasion: sometimes he was rather too automatic in plucking these golden strings, as in his verses to Sir Robert Howard in 1660; 'In those wild notes which with a merry heart The birds in unfrequented shades express.'

There are constant touches of Virgil throughout his career. At first he seemed to feel his poetry was a kind of mausoleum for the music of the past. That music was rather Ovidian than Virgilian.

> Musique herself is lost, in vain she brings
> Her choicest notes to praise the best of Kings:
> Her melting strains in you a tomb have found.[18]

Elsewhere:

> O'er whom Time gently shakes her wings of Down
> Till with his silent sickle they are mown.

And:

> Of some black star infecting all the skies.

It seems strange at first sight that he invokes Virgil in one of the most baroque of all his poems, the *Annus Mirabilis*. 'Virgil has been my Master in this Poem: I have followed him everywhere.... my images are many of them copied from him, and the rest are imitations of him.' When one looks into the poem in detail, one sees what he means, and it suddenly appears in what way Virgil really is a baroque poet.

> So hear the skaly Herd when *Proteus* blows,
> And so to pasture follow through the the sea....
> So glides some trodden Serpent on the grass,
> And long behind his wounded volume trails.

Here it is again in verses to the Lord Chancellor.[19]

> And as the *Indies* were not found before
> Those rich perfumes, which from the happy shore
> The winds upon their balmy wings convey'd,
> Whose guilty sweetness first their World betray'd....
> Thus once when *Troy* was wrapt in fire and smoak
> The helpless Gods their burning shrines forsook....

It appears that Dryden had discovered not only the mellifluous sweetness easily attributed to Virgil but even more easily derived from Ovid; he had a sense of the sting in Virgil's lines and of his remarkable unevenness of tone, which is one of the most exciting things about him.

Virgil is already a great poet in the *Eclogues*, but their composition is extremely peculiar, intellectually sharp and sensually wild. Their intimacy and the self-echoing music of single lines, the perfect footfall of his phrasing and its abundant variety, are based of course on Greek idylls and Greek epigrams, particularly on Theocritus. Dryden's case is quite otherwise. Dryden thought himself the most perfect versifier, at least in couplets; he felt he had smoothed and refined English metrical practice. Contemporaries and later critics took him at his word, and the fashion remains to this day of tracing a progressive evolution of this metre. Within Dryden's own work, there was indeed such a progression, and by the 1680s his verses were certainly supple, versatile and under exquisite control. But the evolutionary theory of the couplet towards smoothness is wrong, I think. (See Appendix.) Dryden's principal contribution was that his verses were bolder and more spirited than the others. They show the influence of the theatre and of wit.

It is worth pausing for a moment on the idea of refinement, which I assume is first Latin and then Italian and French. Eliot defines it well in a poem written to Walter de la Mare (1958) as:

those deceptive cadences
Wherewith the common measure is refined.
By conscious art practiced with natural ease....

The succession in English rhyming couplets is supposed to be from
Fairfax, Waller and Denham, Dryden perhaps invented it under the
influence of Boileau's *The Art of Poetry*. Dryden even uttered his
amazing view of Milton that 'rhyme was not his talent . . . he lacked
the ease and grace of it even in his youth'. Milton in his turn thought
Dryden 'no poet but a good rhymist'. There is indeed a strain of prose
eloquence and prosaic strength in Dryden's verse which today we may
choose to think admirable,[20] but he is surely a powerful poet on more
levels than one, and in more ways. I am not sure whether the idea of
the refinement of verse goes back to the history of Latin verse, with the
insistence on correctness, on a smooth, liquid sound pattern, and on
wit. John Aubrey had got hold of the word, possibly from Dryden, and
used it in his life of Edmund Waller: 'One of the first refiners of our
English language and poetry. When he was a brisk young spark, and
first studied poetry, "Methought," said he, "I never saw a good copy
of English verses; they want smoothness: that I began to essay."' The
word 'copy' surely refers to school exercises. Waller was at Eton; he
was no good at Latin verse and had his verses written for him there by
another boy, but a lesson seems to have sunk in, for better and worse.

Dryden was born in 1631; he had fond memories of Sir John
Ogilby's translation of Virgil, which was a big, beautiful, illustrated
book he knew in youth. Its annotations and choice of words heavily
influenced his own version. Ogilby's Virgil appeared in 1653, when
Dryden was twenty-two. It was in couplets, awkward and amateurish
at times, but readable as a book. Six years later, James Harington
produced another version, much more spirited and vigorous, in
couplets that recall Cowley except for their unevenness, but Dryden
seems to have ignored him. Denham and Waller had both published
versions of odd books of Virgil in couplets, Denham in 1656 though
he wrote in 1636, and Waller in 1658, finishing a pre-war book.
Dryden ignored them both.[21] Denham's couplets collapse into bathos
like very small waves on a beach, yet they do echo some whisper of the
Muse. He was a faint, expiring kind of poet. Waller's couplets had
Sydney Godolphin for co-author, though Godolphin died in 1643;
Waller finished his work on Dido and Aeneas, and printed it in 1658.
The verse is as fine as Dryden's here and there, but less robust. The
lusty Trojans sweep Neptune's smooth face, and cleave the yielding
deep. These poets are all roughly the same generation. They are not

precisely a school or group. Everyone in their generation with any pretension to poetry could write smooth, dull, accomplished rhyming couplets; much of this verse remains unpublished, and almost all of it unread. It had no influence on Dryden. Dryden, like Virgil, went backwards in time for what he thought to be the best models. In the defence of his verse practices in his Dedication, we hear of Spenser, of Chapman's Homer, of Sidney and of Cowley. In his Postscript to the reader, he growls against Chaucer, compliments Addison, Cowley and Lord Roscommon, and highly praises the anonymous translator of *The Power of Love*, a version of the third *Georgic* I have not been able to trace. One assumes he was unable to scan Chaucer, and one sadly notes that the text of Shakespeare he used will have been full of irregularities; he never read Marlowe's Ovid. But he does situate himself. He likes vigorous and lucid modern English, he toys with vernacular phrases, and with archaisms:

> Then on the broiling Entrails Oyl he pours;
> Which, ointed thus, the raging Flame devours.[22]

His verse is accomplished and his ear excellent. He is, however, recorded as having admitted to Richardson that, if he had Virgil to do again, he would not have used couplets at all, and he writes in the Postscript that he found each book more difficult than the last. He found it hard to think of fresh rhymes.

In the *Eclogues*, Dryden's obvious master was Spenser, whom he thought to be a match for Theocritus and for Virgil, and uniquely great in modern times.[23] Both as a critic and as a stylist, Dryden passes over *Lycidas* as if it had never been written.

> Now the green Lizard in the Grove is laid,
> The Sheep enjoy the coolness of the Shade;
> And Thestilis wild thime and Garlike beats
> For Harvest Hinds, o'respent with Toyle and Heats:
> While in the scorching Sun I trace in vain
> Thy flying footsteps o're the burning Plain,
> The creeking Locusts with my voice conspire,
> They fry'd with Heat, and I with fierce Desire.[24]

This poetry lives by contrast of heat and cold, greenness and burnt grass, quiet and motion. It constantly stings you with the unexpected sharpness of a sensory expression, and yet it appears restrained, almost understated. Line after line is paradoxically melodious, more so in Latin of course, but Dryden begged his readers to put aside the original before they read his translation.

> *Pan* taught to joyn with Wax unequal Reeds,
> *Pan* loves the Shepherds, and their Flocks he feeds:
> Nor scorn the Pipe: *Amyntas* to be taught,
> With all his Kisses would my Skill have bought.
> Of seven smooth joints a mellow Pipe I have,
> Which with his dying breath *Damaetas* gave:
> And said, This, *Corydon* I leave to thee:
> For only thou deservst it after me.

Virgil is syntactically energetic, and so is Dryden: both their sentences have the perfection of epigrams, and draw on epigrams for that perfection. But the poetry generates a half-conscious erotic force; it deals cumulatively with reeds, pipe-music, smoothness, kisses and dying breath. Virgil manipulates these images and symbols quite deliberately. Every small touch is restrained, but the power of the whole poem is complex. Roman critics praised Virgil for his exact and telling use of quite simple words; he achieved it by the study of late Greek poetry and how that worked. Dryden can follow him; he knows how this kind of poetry works.

There is a special scholarship that arises from the needs of poets. They need to have texts, often of obscure, unfashionable writers, and they need to make up their own minds about the history of their own literature. One can see that necessity and some elements of that understanding in Dryden, though he lacked a proper library. A poet is compelled to study the art of poetry. I take it that the Oxford English School embodies some faint reflection of that need. Scholarship and criticism are secondary pursuits that arise from the real needs of living poets, but scholarship and criticism seem to come too late to meet the fresh needs of each successive generation. It was not from critics or scholars that Dryden took his inwardness with Virgil's style.

> Come to my longing Arms, my lovely care,
> And take the Presents which the Nymphs prepare.
> White Lillies in full Canisters they bring,
> With all the Glories of the purple Spring:
> The Daughters of the Flood have search'd the Mead
> For Violets pale, and cropt the Poppy's Head:
> The Short *Narcissus* and fair Daffodil,
> Pancies to please the Sight, and Cassia sweet to smell:

And set soft Hyacinths with Iris blue,
To shade marsh Marigolds of shining Hue.
Some bound in Order, others loosely strow'd,
To dress thy Bow'r, and trim thy new Abode.
My self will search our planted Grounds at home,
For downy Peaches and the glossie Plum:
And thrash the Chestnuts in the neighb'ring Grove,
Such as my *Amaryllis* used to love.

This is not a mere list, though I share Auden's respect for lists in poetry. But these verses drag their reader into a kind of sensuous intimacy. He feels the texture of the plum and the peach as if he handled them, the flowers have a strangeness which makes them fresh and ghostly at the same time, and the sudden realism of 'cropt the Poppy's Head' and 'thrash the Chestnuts in the neighb'ring Grove' is thrilling. If these are small delights, this is a poetry that depends on them, though its ultimate power is far greater than its ingredients. In reading one of the shorter eclogues complete, one must remember that the ten eclogues are intended to be read as a book, as one complete work.

Here as elsewhere in his works, Virgil foresees the widening of his own range as a poet. It is not so much that he had a programme, but the form of the eclogue in his hands is already bursting its bounds. Theocritus wrote quite different kinds of poetry which are bundled together as idylls, which means vignettes. The bucolic ones are different mixtures of not always the same elements. They are essentially variations, and so are Virgil's. Among other things, they are a catalogue of unhappy lovers, an idea that recurs as the *Ecatommiti* of Cintio, which includes the germ of Shakespeare's *Othello*. One can see in these poems that Virgil was already interested in extended narrative, and in Italy, in the earth and its values. In the *Georgics* he adapted Hesiod, but also drew on a tradition of Greek natural history that goes back to Theophrastus. These poems alternate vast perspectives with intimate details. The reader is drawn into the poem not only by physical sensation, but because the *Georgics* are full of instruction, and activities rather than landscapes. Their landscapes are consequences. This poetry is almost as much a mixture of elements as the *Eclogues* were, but on a bigger scale. Each of the four books shows a different application of Virgil's constructive sense, and I do not think that the early books of the *Aeneid* are any better constructed. Virgil had clearly studied the construction of long poems, 566 lines or so for a georgic and 860 or so for a book of the *Aeneid*; his unit from now on is the poem of that length. Within it, his sub-unit is the verse paragraph, which may be as long as he chooses.

An entire georgic is too long to be considered here, but throughout all Virgil's works, the *Aeneid* not least, one's eye constantly lingers on a paragraph.

> For sundry Foes the Rural Realm surround:
> The Field Mouse builds her Garner under Ground;
> For gather'd Grain the blind laborious Mole,
> In winding Mazes works her hidden Hole.
> In hollow Caverns Vermine make abode,
> The hissing Serpent, and the swelling Toad:
> The Corn devouring Weevel here abides,
> And the wise Ant her wintry Store provides.

At times Dryden's language seems to go dead for a few words, but I am not certain whether that may not be a useful strategy in so long a poem. In a long poem of rhyming couplets it seems inevitable: Virgil also used mouldering antique language as an element in his verse texture. This passage about the enemies underground is full of contrasts and ironies: it works well in English, though it is of course closer to a bestiary than to any modern book about the same creatures. It conveys a childhood sense of an entire world underground. Virgil's paragraphs always have a satisfying closure, but not always such a quiet one. These are just the introductory lines to the storm in the first *Georgic*.

> For e're the rising Winds begin to roar,
> The working Seas advance to wash the Shoar:
> Soft whispers run along the leavy Woods,
> And Mountains whistle to the murm'ring Floods:
> Ev'n then the doubtful Billows scarce abstain
> From the toss'd Vessel on the troubled Main:
> When crying Cormorants forsake the Sea,
> And stretching to the Covert wing their way:
> When sportful Coots run skimming o're the Strand;
> When watchful Herons leave their watry Stand,
> And mounting upward, with erected flight,
> Gain on the Skyes, and soar above the sight.
> And oft before tempestuous Winds arise,
> The seeming Stars fall headlong from the Skies;

And, shooting through the darkness, gild the Night
With sweeping Glories, and long trails of Light:
And Chaff with eddy Winds is whirl'd around,
And dancing Leaves are lifted from the Ground;
And floating Feathers on the Waters play.

Dryden is often more baroque than Virgil, but Virgil gives him plenty of excuse, particularly in the introduction to each georgic, in the praises of rustic solitude at the end of the second, the classic description of Virgil's innermost soul and ambitions I suppose, and in the famous setpieces of the fourth. Dryden does exaggerate though, and that entails missing the point of perfectly simple-looking lines: 'et viridi in campo templum de marmore ponam', a white temple in a green field,[25] becomes 'of *Parian* stone a temple will I raise', but the field is lost. The invitation to Bacchus to join the grape-treading:

huc, pater O Lenaee, veni, nudataque musto
tingue novo mecum dereptis crura cothurnis,[26]

which means tear off your boots and colour your legs like mine with the fresh vintage (a scene of which Dryden can have had no experience), becomes:

Come strip with me, my God, come drench all o're
Thy Limbs in Must of Wine, and drink at ev'ry Pore.

At heart Dryden is an admirably unclassical poet: however deeply he entered into Virgil, it was only to transform him, to make him write like an English theatrical poet of the 1690s. In so far as Dryden has a classical side at all, that is Boileau, it is not Virgil. Dryden's Virgilianism is baroque and sensuous. It makes Dryden for us an important gateway to Virgil: he helps us to understand what Virgil was like when he was alive, before he was called classical. He was a far wilder, livelier and sharper poet than Eliot thought he was. Even his humanism is more human than it looks. The *Georgics* are full of pains and pestilence and dire events. Virgil's only mention of gardens and his symbol of the good gardener is a retired Levantine pirate, settled in the far south of Italy.

Lord of few Acres, and those barren too;
Unfit for Sheep or Vines, and more unfit to sow:
Yet lab'ring well his little Spot of Ground,
Some scatt'ring Potherbs here and there he found:
Which cultivated with his daily Care,

And bruis'd with Vervain, were his daily Fare.
Sometimes white Lillies did their Leaves afford,
With wholsom Poppy-flow'rs, to mend his homely Board.[27]

We are not allowed to enjoy even the pleasures of successful small-holding without a strong sensation of frugality, and of the labours of cultivation.[28]

Even in the *Aeneid*, Dryden never quite founders. His poem has passages of floating darkness and light, and many mysterious refreshments.[29] Dryden had little critical understanding at all of the *Aeneid* or even the *Iliad*, as complete poems. He thought Virgil was writing about the acceptance of victorious monarchy after civil war and still showed the traces of an old republican; he thought the *Iliad* was about the need for unity between allies and for discipline in war. These are superficial views.[30] Dryden was accurate enough as translators go, but his pretensions to personal scholarship are impertinent by modern standards. How could such a man translate the *Aeneid*? I think the answer is that he had or developed an extreme inwardness[31] with Virgil as a stylist.[32] It was Virgil as a stylist that he tracked through book after book of the *Aeneid*. And it may be that is all Virgil ever was, and all Dryden ever was. Poetry after all is made of words, and lines, and paragraphs. Wherever a continuous thrust or impetus is to be found in the *Aeneid*, Dryden mirrors it. The *Aeneid* is a dense, laborious construction, and Virgil's intelligence, fine as it is, fails in the end to penetrate Homer: there is something wrong with Aeneas because there is something wrong with Rome. The *Aeneid* contains some shocking aesthetic misjudgements: the boy who exchanges with Cupid for example, the disgusting boxing match, the frigid parody of the shield of Achilles, the imperial prophecy in the underworld, the endless delayed climax of the war books, and the violently nasty conclusion. And yet it remains the shadow of a great poem. It shows Virgil often at his best, and Dryden sometimes at his best. Dryden's *Aeneid* is not an everyday poem, it is a confused, wonderful, baroque monument to Virgil, a sustained series of interlocking masques. It is a remarkably sustained performance.

APPENDIX

Dryden contributed the English names substituted for Boileau's French ones to his version of *L'Art Poétique*. For Boileau, the evolution of French verse was from Villon through Marot to Ronsard, but the first perfect metrist was his hero Malherbe:

> Enfin Malherbe vint, et, le premier en France,
> Fit sentir dans les vers une juste cadence,
> D'un mot mis en sa place enseigne le pouvoir,
> Et reduisit la muse aux règles du devoir.
> Par ce sage écrivain la langue réparée. . . .

There was one Malherbe, and Boileau was his successor. In English verse Dryden gave himself the same climactic position. It is true that Waller's Virgil, which supplements Godolphin's, has merits but it lacks momentum. The Sandys translation of Ovid is in capable couplets. Jonson's 'Penshurst' is in admirable couplets. Jonson, unlike his successors, will have read Marlowe's couplets. Atterbury, in the second, 1690 edition of Waller, takes the view that Dryden made the couplet supple, and that in Donne's hands the couplet was obscure, a view that Dryden himself had suggested, and from that time on-wards some such view of the refinement of the couplet prevailed. It is hard to see why Dryden in substituting English for French names in the version of Boileau's *Art of Poetry*, to which he contributed, made so much of Fairfax, whose translation of Tasso is dull, sub-Shakespearean stanzas. Waller was born in 1606, Denham in 1615; neither of them knew Ben Jonson personally, but Lord Falkland, a close friend of Waller, certainly knew him and wrote similar smooth couplets before the Civil War, as they all did. Godolphin belonged to the same circle.

Visionary Poets

Very few visionary poets can be called classical. This is because visions and revelations occur mostly on the outer limits of a given culture, they belong to the deprived and the unrecognized and to those who cultivate secret wisdom, whose ambitions may be on the march towards the centre. Our own culture rests on reason and on science, our morality is practical and our philosophy is distrustful of visions. If we are still hungry for visions then we seek them in the realm of poetry. There, on the outer limits of our culture, we allow them to exist.

But if we assume that visions are not genuine, or at least not what the visionaries claim them to be, what is the validity or authenticity of visionary poetry? Can one imagine a valid and authentic poem based on an unreal vision, a fiction or a lie, or must one treat visions as a special language, only the meaning or translation of which one might dispute? Some people think that is the status of all or nearly all poetry whatsoever (wrongly in my view), or of all the prophetic and religious poetry in the Bible, but that needs some sorting out. The question remains, in a visionary poem which we call genuine, like Blake's 'Jerusalem', is the genuineness in the poet's mind? Does the vision, and does the poem, exist like music in the ear and on the page, or only in the reader's mind, or on the poet's lips, in the poet's mind? This is an important question about all poetry. It was with such questions in mind that I wanted to explore visionary poetry.

Philip Larkin wrote in 1955, 'I write poems to preserve things I have seen, thought, felt (if I may so indicate a composite and complex experience) both for myself and for others, though I feel that my prime responsibility is to the experience itself, which I am trying to keep from oblivion for its own sake.'[1] In 1964 he wrote, 'Some years ago I came to the conclusion that to write a poem was to construct a verbal device that would preserve an experience indefinitely by reproducing it in whoever read the poem.'[2] I do not think he would ever have claimed universal validity for these definitions. They were working principles that enabled him to write certain poems that only he could write. He admitted to mystery about the selection of experiences, the subject matter of poetry, and the personal urge to write one poem and not another.[3] But his definitions are admirably crisp and lucid. My own immediate feeling was that I disagreed entirely.

I thought poetry was more like making something out of a given material. It was a profoundly musical exercise in a given language, in what had been said and what could be said in that language, and therefore in the name of all the anonymous creators of the language. I thought the essential experience was the poem itself, not something remembered, not even anything known by the poet except in the closing stages of writing, though it might well be sensed at the beginning. I thought revision was somehow to strengthen but not necessarily to clarify an original idea or an old experience. In fact I thought of poetry as like writing a long novel, not as making a record. You may suspect that my reactions were as much designed to protect my habitual disorganized way of working as Philip Larkin's definitions were to protect his, only that I had not attained the dignity of rational definition. I still do feel some of the reservations I have expressed, and yet I share the prejudice I am sure Philip Larkin would feel, that only a genuine visionary ought to write visionary poems. Truthfulness to one's own experience is a moral imperative, and that is what made Philip Larkin, and might make anyone, an important writer. The fact that he was also a great poet only intensifies his truthfulness. And yet there are a few Larkin poems, particularly in *High Windows*, that have something very close to a visionary quality. Perhaps this is an illusion arising from his brilliance at recapturing and his purity of tone.

God in the Bible, whenever he appears to be choosing his own words, has a particular purity of tone. Biblical scholars have not all agreed about what bits of the Bible are poetry and what bits are not.[4] There is very little narrative poetry in it, not because of any lack of talent for verse, but because Hebrew written prose developed earlier than Greek, and the Hebrews had written prose when the Greeks had nothing but orally transmitted poetry. But it is interesting from the point of view of visionary poetry that God himself in the Bible generally speaks prose and yet God's speech mediated through or reported by a prophet will be poetry. Poetry is a performance, it speaks to the people as Solon spoke. Public poetry is something we have lost, and the more it gets revived the more it looks dead, but there can be no doubt that the first visionary records were in verse, or that the earliest visionary poetry was public poetry. In the Bible the Book of Job is a special case, since I take it to be a work of fiction, a morality. There God convinces Job by his powers of poetry, poet against poet.[5] God's visionary poem works like a vision on Job.[6] It overwhelms him by convincing him that his mind cannot comprehend such a poem, or such a world of monstrous creatures as the poem encompasses. The lasting resonance of the Hebrew prophets is not really the product of their visions, nor is it a projection of the earnest beliefs of later generations. It is the property of the poetry in which they spoke. Christ is as much the fulfilment of their poetry as of their prophecy; it was only in poetry that the morning stars sang together and all the sons of God shouted for joy.

Ancient Hebrew poetry often took an apocalyptic tone. It scarcely touches the fringes of classical literature. Homer appealed to the Muses only to supplement his memory as a historian. Hesiod claimed a visionary vocation, but his vision of the Muses was only a pastoral incident. They gave him a magic stick 'and breathed into me divine utterance, to cry aloud what shall be and what was. And they commanded me to sing the birth of the blessed ones who for ever are, and to sing first of them and ever last of them.' One is inclined to think that English visionary poetry has more of a Christian and Platonic than a classical basis. But the Greeks did have their visions, as one can see from the *Bacchae* of Euripides, and apocalyptic Hebrew poetry did leave some traces in Greek.[7] The so-called Sibylline Oracles are written in Greek hexameters and seem to have a Jewish origin, though the immense power of the Revelation of John is all the greater through being written prose. One can sense the Hebrew poetry under its surface with no distractions from educated rhetoric.

Virgil's visions are mostly rhetoric and so are Horace's. Eduard Fraenkel's treatment of Horace's Ode 3,25 caused a lasting scandal among scholars. He took the rather invulnerable and sympathetic view that the poet ought to be taken at his word, that he means what he says and that if he claims a vision then we should accept that he had one.[8] Maurice Bowra took a similar line about a vision that Pindar had. The difference is instructive. I do think it likely that if Pindar says he had a vision, then he probably thought he had one: that would not be abnormal in his day, inside or outside poetry. But the question about Horace and the age of Horace is whether by publishing a poem about a vision he intended his readers to think he seriously claimed to have had one, or whether he offered them a literary exercise, to be enjoyed as such and assessed as such, as if it were written by an eighteenth-century clergyman in a wig. A similar question arises with the visionary poems of William Blake, and some people really are prepared to take all his claims to visions seriously. They think he was preserving an experience. That would certainly make interpretation easier than I feel it is. Yet I find myself unscandalized by Fraenkel on Horace. Maybe Horace's poem was about an experience of some kind, something passionately thought and felt before the poem was written. In what sense it was really a vision we have no way of knowing. The point is that thinking one has a vision is not different from having one, from the poet's point of view. When T. S. Eliot was asked by an Oxford undergraduate what he meant by the line, 'Three white leopards sat under a juniper tree', he replied, 'Three white leopards sat under a juniper tree.' Horace might have given a similar answer.

Visionary poetry is as ancient as it is widespread. I would like to distinguish it from mystical poetry. As J. M. Cohen puts it in the Preface to his fine *Rider Book of Mystical Verse* (1983), mystical means 'poetry of spiritual apprehension'. 'Ways of expression are many. But the fundamental truths are one.' Visionary poetry is more personal. If it is true that most of modern art conveys whatever can be conveyed of intense and separate personal visions, that is because of an emptiness at the centre of our culture, a breakdown of society expressed as an absence of shared belief. In the modern arts, the edges and extremes are on the march towards the centre: that is the hypothesis I entertain.[9] And yet in the past there were visionary poems that were central to their cultures. They were composed at times when the visionary had a more central place in society. The Babylonian hymn of the fifty names of Marduk is visionary; it is a revelation meant to be recited by heart from generation to generation, not only by the wise but by herdsmen and shepherds. Inanna's Journey to Hell in the same collection is certainly visionary and so is the Epic of Gilgamesh,[10] though these are visionary fictions. As intense personal visions I doubt whether they have ever been bettered. The Canaanite myths and legends, which no one reads now but specialists, have something of the same hypnotic quality.

> And Baal will give abundantly:
> abundant rain and moisture and snow,
> he will utter his voice in the clouds,

and his flashings and his lightnings on the earth.
Let his temple be built up with cedar wood,
let his house be made solid with hardened brick.
Say to Baal the victorious,
summon a caravan into thy dwelling-place,
and a multitude within thy palaces,
the rock shall yield much silver unto thee
and the mountains the most choice gold,
with the most noble gems,
a mansion of bright stones, even the sky-stone.[11]

The extraordinary religious poetry of the Byzantine Greeks is rather mystical than visionary; it derives as much from Platonism as it does from the details of Christianity. Something similar could probably be said about the thrilling poetry of the Sufis, who often disguise their true meaning so that it is difficult for an outsider to distinguish the disguise from the mystical vision. The great example of a visionary poet central to European and Christian culture is Dante, but here again much of his poetry is allegory and fiction. He does not really intend us to believe he descended into hell or to take his description of hell literally. Hell is a grotesque entertainment. Most of his *Inferno* and *Purgatorio* are crammed with contemporary life and interest, and particularly in the *Paradiso* he has a lot to say about Italian politics. In his secular love poetry, allegory and fiction and something like vision mingle or overlap in a similar way. We value Dante as a poet for earthly, technical qualities. And yet no poet has so fully and clearly expressed Christian belief in a visionary poetry. It may be worth observing that I find rather little of the famous influence of Thomas Aquinas in the *Divina Commedia*.

To enquire where genuinely visionary poetry begins and the allegory and fiction fall away in Dante's great poem is probably useless. There was a young girl in need of a poetic counsellor who chose George Seferis for that difficult role. In the end she turned on him, as young people will, and accused him of loving her for her body and not her soul. He answered, 'Je ne suis pas alchémiste, moi; qui sait où le corps finit, et où l'âme commence?' That has an application to Dante's poetry, I think. In the structure of the *Divina Commedia*, a big change comes at the twenty-seventh canto of *Purgatorio*.[12] From that point until he enters heaven, Dante is being purified, and he is learning what he had not known; it is suddenly as if he himself were passing through his own purgatory, he is no longer a spectator. He has just left the Provençal poet Arnaut Daniel, for whom of all these shades he shows the most love.

> Ara vos prec per aquella valor
> Que vos guida al som de l'escalina
> Sovenha vos a temps de ma dolor.

Dante clearly intends to go beyond the tradition of love poetry, and the idea of love, in which he grew up and of which Arnaut was the great example. He intends to write a new kind of poetry. In fact he has invented and explored this poetry in the long course of writing the *Divina Commedia*, and he must have foreseen the change of style, so far as there is one, to suit his heavenly subject matter, from the very beginning. All the same, the twenty-seventh canto opens memorably.

> As the sun's first rays shiver in his hand
> where the sun's Maker scattered his own blood
> and Ebro sprawls under the toppling Scales
> and Ganges water burns again for noon
> so stood the sun, day drew to its ending,
> that hour God's glad angel revealed himself
> standing outside the flame above the cliff
> and chanted: Blessed are the pure in heart.[13]

> Si come quando i primi raggi vibra
> Là dove il suo Fattore il sangue sparse,
> Cadendo Ibero sotto l'alta Libra,
> E l'onde in Gange da nona riarse,
> Sì stava il sole; onde il giorno sen giva,
> Quando l'Angel di Dio lieto ci apparse.
> Fuor della fiamma stava in sulla riva,
> E cantava: Beati mundo corde.

In this canto Dante passes through the wall of fire, Virgil speaks of Beatrice and a voice sings 'Come ye blessed of my father.' The sun sets, and they sleep. At the hour when Venus rises in the east as morning star, Dante dreams a strange beautiful dream, and Virgil leaves him alone in the earthly paradise.

> Those sweet apples so sought with mortal cares
> on all the branches of the fruitless world
> will bring your hungers to their peace today.[14]

Quel dolce pome che per tanti rami
Urcando va la cura dei mortali,
oggi porrà in pace le tui fami.

In the next canto Dante goes forward to explore the dense, living woods; 'la divine foresta spessa e viva', the gentle breeze, the sweet smell, the singing birds whose refrain the leaves in the wind sang; and then we come suddenly back to earth, in one of those moments that always give such pleasure in the *Divina Commedia*. He says it was just like the pine forest at Chiassi, when Aeolus has let Sirocco loose.

tal qual di ramo in ramo si raccoglie
per la pineta in sul lito di Chiassi,
quand' Eolo scirocco fuor discioglie....[15]

Visionary poetry always has its roots in personal earthly experience. Even the sky-stone, the heavenly blue of the Canaanites, is really lapis lazuli, an important luxury. That is another difference between visionary poetry and mysticism. As the *Divina Commedia* approaches and enters heaven, its visionary quality intensifies until it almost freezes with light. The visions that make the best poetry are very often tranquil and serene, like the contemplation of the stars, from which in part they may arise. But in whatever visionary state Dante may have conceived or even composed his final cantos, poetry is a mortal terrestrial thing, and all our languages are earthly and mortal.

Even a genuine mystic like John of the Cross, the unique case of a great saint and a great poet, composed his mystical songs in earthly language. Their mysterious fire and lightness arise from centuries of meditation on the Song of Songs, and the tradition of adapting the Song of Songs both for earthly and for heavenly love-songs, throughout the middle ages. That fire and that lightness also owe something to Renaissance metrical technique and Renaissance pastoral poetry,[16] which were new in Spanish when John of the Cross was a young man. The rigorous scholastic pedantry of his prose commentaries[17] on his own poems, wonderful as those commentaries may be, and of far more practical use than the poems to genuine mystics, makes an extraordinary contrast to his obvious freedom of spirit as a poet. I suppose what we would nowadays call his sexuality has free and innocent play, at least in a sublimated way, in his poetry, but the monastic prose tradition of his time rigorously excludes it. These two separate sides of him meet in his drawings. He offers a plan of the way to mystical union with God, which in one way is like one of those Victorian Biblical games of snakes and ladders constructed for children by Bible societies, but in another way has an extraordinary innocence and beauty. This drawing originated, as much of his lyrical verse did, as a communication with nuns.

It seems to be Teresa of Avila, who wrote at least one poem of her own, who first spurred him into verse, but his great productive period as a poet was in prison at Toledo in 1578, when Shakespeare was a schoolboy. He heard a love-song sung in the street outside the prison walls. 'Of love I die, dear love what shall I do? Die, alas, die.'

> Muérome de amores
> Carillo. ¿Qué haré?
> Que tu mueras alahé.

This song inspired him, and his mystical poetry does show other traces of anonymous, popular songs. It also contains a lot of allegory and encoded doctrine, a code being highly advisable in his times, with mysticism in Spain rather a Jewish monopoly, suspected by the Inquisition. By blood John of the Cross was probably Jewish, as Teresa of Avila certainly was. The allegory in his verse was undoubtedly secondary to the poetry, as one can observe in the failure and jejuneness of his own allegoric commentary on the 'Spiritual Canticle', which exists in two versions.[18] The first version is a magnificent poem full of light and freedom. The second one has been rearranged and dislocated, for the sake of the commentary. Allegory is an important element in most visionary poetry, but it trails away into vision as vision trails away into allegory. Is there an allegorical meaning to Blake's Tiger? I expect that there is, but the poem is surely visionary. With allegory goes a certain degree of surrealism, particularly noticeable in John of the Cross.

> Our bed with flowers scented
> And by the lions in their lairs surrounded,
> in royal purple tented,
> on peace builded and founded,
> a thousand shields of graven gold have crowned it.[19]

> Nuestro lecho florido
> de cuevas de leones enlazado,
> en púrpura tendido,
> de paz edificado,
> de mil escudos de oro coronado.

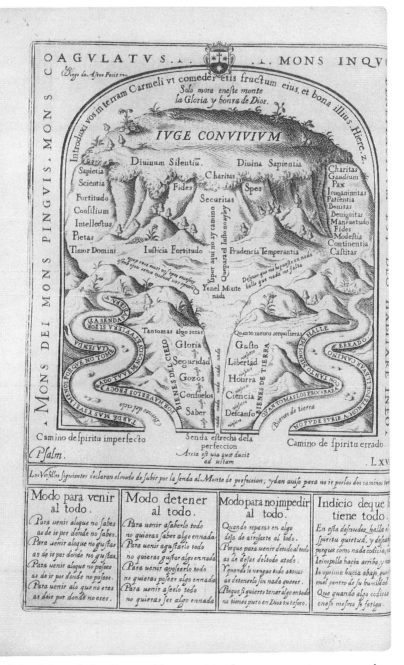

1. Saint John of the Cross, *Obras espirituales que encaminana vna alma perfecta vnion con Dios...*(Barcelona, 1619). Photo British Library.

2. Drawing of Shakespeare by William Blake (1757–1827), *c.* 1800. By kind permission of Manchester City Art Galleries.

This is neither one of the greatest stanzas nor by any means the oddest. The surrealism in this case is Biblical. The stanza form is the *lyra* invented in Italian by B. Tasso as an equivalent to Horace and inherited by John of the Cross from Garcilaso de la Vega. Spenser learnt similar devices from Ronsard; but I think John of the Cross is even swifter, smoother and more brilliant than Spenser. He is also in his best stanzas quite untranslatable into English verse.

> My beloved, the mountains,
> The woods in the solitary valleys,
> The foreign islands,
> The echoing rivers,
> The whisper of the amorous airs....
>
> Mi Amado, las montañas,
> los valles solitarios nemorosos,
> los ínsulas extrañas,
> los ríos sonorosos,
> el silbo de los aires amorosos....[20]

John of the Cross has a very precise sense of the placing of words, within a rhyme scheme, and also a very exact sense of meaning. He is a poet of fire and swiftness and darkness. It may be that his experience goes too deep in him to be called vision.

Vision and allegory and mere poetry are often hard to distinguish, and nowhere more so than in the Hebrew poetry of antiquity and of the middle ages. I doubt whether John of the Cross was conscious of any Jewish inheritance. He had never heard of 'Night like a Negress in embroidery of gold, or the moon like a letter Yod written in golden ink on the robes of Night'.[21] But the air that he breathed in sixteenth-century Spain was an intoxicating mixture of elements. He wrote of the night tranquillized, kindness before dawn, silent music, sounding solitude, the supper of refreshment and *eros*.

> La noche sosegada
> en par de los levantes de la aurora,
> la música callada,
> la soledad sonora,
> la cena que recrea y enamora.

In English, the vision and the dream have been a convention of our poetry since pre-Christian times. Some of the more detailed Christian visions of the middle ages are gruesome, but the *Dream of the Rood* is one of the necessary poems of our language, and so is the *Vision of Piers Plowman*. But when the wind of the Reformation blew, which in England happened before the Renaissance had very much effect, the wilder visions of the outer limits, among which I think we must class *Piers Plowman*, suffered a frost, and the individual apprehension of God became central to the national religion. Yet the tradition that descends from the Lollards to the Civil War, to poets like Bunyan and George Fox, is fascinating in many ways, though not central to English poetry in the way that Milton is central, and not quite as central to English life as one is often tempted to believe. The Elizabethans were fond of ghosts and spirits; the Cambridge Platonists and even John Aubrey investigated them with earnest care, and the power of second sight was still a real issue when Dr Johnson explored the western islands of Scotland. But England achieved a remarkable degree of literacy very early, and English written poetry is a function of grammar school culture. And yet what language is richer in visionary poetry? Blake's drawing of Shakespeare in the Manchester City Art Gallery is the portrait of a supreme visionary, wreathed in dark leaves and ghostly scenes.

Inga-Stina Ewbank pointed out in an interesting essay on Shakespeare as a poet that 'Part of Shakespeare's poetic belief is that what is cannot always be said.' She instances the wordless reunion of Leontes and Hermione in *The Winter's Tale*, and of course 'The Phoenix and the Turtle',[22] 'his furthest reaching out in words towards what cannot be articulated'. One might add the almost wordless words of Lear. This belief was certainly shared by John of the Cross, who believed that not only his subject matter but even somehow his own poems were beyond his comprehension.

> Y déjame muriendo
> Un no sé qui que quedan balbuciendo.

I have always thought of 'The Phoenix and the Turtle' as a visionary poem, though like the poetry of John of the Cross it doubtless has an element of allegory. Inga-Stina Ewbank observes, 'It is an incantatory celebration of a love so great and pure and mysterious as to be able to transcend nature and reason, and it is in that sense an extension, in one particular direction, of the sonnets, as well as an anticipation of central themes in the Romances. But in its structure and handling of language it strangely anticipates the dramatic rhythm of the closing scenes of *King Lear*.' 'The Phoenix and the Turtle' was printed in 1601. Part of its mystery can be penetrated by comparing it with a rambling poem by Robert Chester, to which it was an answer by Shakespeare, and with which it was printed. Marston, Chapman and Ben Jonson contributed answers of their own in the same volume. Their subject was the nature of human love.

The Phoenix and the Turtle

Let the bird of loudest lay,
On the sole Arabian tree,
Herald sad and trumpet be,
To whose sound chaste wings obey.

But thou shrieking harbinger,
Foul precurrer of the fiend,
Augur of the Fever's end,
To this troop come thou not near!

From this session interdict
Every fowl of tyrant wing,
Save the Eagle, feathered king:
Keep the obsequy so strict.

Let the priest in surplice white,
That defunctive music can,
Be the death-divining swan,
Lest the requiem lack his right.

And thou treble-dated Crow,
That thy sable gender mak'st
With the breath thou giv'st and tak'st,
'Mongst our mourners shalt thou go.

Here the anthem doth commence:
Love and constancy is dead;
Phoenix and the Turtle fled
In a mutual flame from hence.

So they loved, as love in twain
Had the essence but in one;
Two distincts, division none:
Number there in love was slain.

Hearts remote, yet not asunder;
Distance, and no space was seen

'Twixt this Turtle and his queen:
But in them it were a wonder.

So between them love did shine,
That the Turtle saw his right
Flaming in the Phoenix's sight:
Either was the other's mine.

Property was thus appallèd,
That the self was not the same;
Single nature's double name
Neither two nor one was callèd.

Reason, in itself confounded,
Saw division grow together,
To themselves yet either neither,
Simple were so well compounded;

That it cried, 'How true a twain
Seemeth this concordant one!
Love hath reason, reason none,
If what parts can so remain.'

Whereupon it made this threne
To the Phoenix and the Dove,
Co-supremes and start of love,
As chorus to their tragic scene.

THRENOS

Beauty, Truth, and rarity,
Grace in all simplicity,
Here enclosed in cinders lie.

Death is now the Phoenix' nest;
And the Turtle's loyal breast
To eternity doth rest.

Leaving no posterity:
'Twas not their infirmity,
It was married chastity.

Truth may seem, but cannot be;
Beauty brag, but 'tis not she;
Truth and Beauty buried be.

> To this urn let those repair
> That are either true or fair;
> For these dead birds sigh a prayer.

The intense images, the daring devices and the sheer freshness of those poets Dr Johnson called 'metaphysical', and their amazing intermingling of science and mystery, natural philosophy and divinity, makes it tempting to call them all visionaries of some kind. But their playfulness is too conscious, their consciousness of ornament and device and pretension is too easy to see, for that to be true. None the less there are visionary passages in the poetry of John Donne, just as there are visionary sentences in his sermons. I hope I have made it clear in what sense I called Shakespeare a visionary poet. The vision is not an experience outside the poem, though it refers to something real and independent of the poet. The vision is not a precise experience he went through before he wrote, or even as he wrote, and sought to preserve by writing 'The Phoenix and Turtle'. He expresses a mystical extreme of earthly love, just as John of the Cross does of unearthly love.[23] Shakespeare's poem rests as our understanding of it must rest, on the experience of life. The vision in fact is ours: the poem communicates it, and it has no other existence. Shakespeare can experience it only by the intensity and purity of his own poem, first by writing it then by reading it. That is why it is an incantation. T. S. Eliot has something of the same hypnotic effect. So in some poems has John Donne; some of them are about secular love, some about divine love. I do not see how one kind is less visionary than the other.

And yet Donne never maintains visionary intensity throughout an entire secular poem. That is partly because his art is more self-conscious, he is more consciously dandyish than Shakespeare; also he is not quite so good a poet. His 'Nocturnal upon Saint Lucy's Day' is thrilling and faultless, but one is made aware that the metaphors are only metaphors, because he several times changes them. Donne's 'Nocturnal' is a series of breathtaking insights and devices, much like one of his sermons, and it surely has moments of great intensity. 'The Ecstasy' is a fine poem too, but a little too long, a little over-clever. Neither of them taken as a whole can be called visionary. The solution to this paradox may be that Donne is only truly visionary when he is most physical, both in his sermons and in earthly love-poems. Still, he is certainly capable of unearthly visions:[24]

> At the round earth's imagined corners, blow
> Your trumpets, angels, and arise, arise

From death, you numberless infinities
Of souls, and to your scattered bodies go,
All whom the flood did, and fire shall o'erthrow,
All whom war, death, age, agues, tyrannies,
Despair, law, chance, hath slain, and you whose eyes
Shall behold God, and never taste death's woe.
But let them sleep, Lord, and me mourn a space....[25]

His constant urge is to outsoar his own mind's boundaries, to race towards a receding horizon,[26] to come close to saying what cannot be said. But he was too passionate for innocent visions, and too thoughtful for simple ones; his greatness lies elsewhere. This sonnet droops away into religious melancholy about sin, as so many of Donne's religious poems do, and so many of Henry Vaughan's. I think it is this miserable obsession with sin and bloodshed that breaks down Vaughan's startling and wonderful poems after their first flights, rather than what David Cecil calls wooden and formless in him. As he said, 'Vaughan is a mystic of nature. Hills and streams, a primrose lurking in the cranny of a river bank, the majestic tranquillity of night, each of those conveys to him some aspect of the Divine spirit. At its best his vision has an extraordinary still intensity; awestruck we seem to watch the very face of God unveiled before us.'[27]

Yet to call him a 'mystic of nature' is imprecise. Visionary poetry cannot but be a vision of nature, however transmuted, purified or glorified, but Vaughan is not a nature poet in the same sense as the Georgian poets or as Wordsworth. He is not pondering on nature for the vestiges of God or the expressions of the soul. His experience is religious and peculiar: even if it is habitual it is his own alone, and he wants not exactly to share it, but to induce it in us. He is like that brilliant eccentric Henry More;[28] he prepares himself with meditation:

Collect thy soul into one sphere
Of light, and 'bove the earth it rear:
Those wild scatter'd thoughts that erst
Lay loosely in the world dispersed
Call in: thy spirit thus knit in one
Fair lucid orb; those fears be gone
Like vain impostures of the night
That fly before the morning bright.
Then with pure eyes thou shalt behold
How the first Goodness doth infold
All things....[29]

Henry Vaughan is a far greater poet than this. In him perhaps the visionary and the romantic first meet. He loves childhood and innocence, though his thoughts on the subject are rather sad than visionary. I assume that Wordsworth knew and loved the poetry of Henry Vaughan, but where Wordsworth is a great intellectual, Vaughan has a directness like Blake's, which belongs only to authentic visionaries. Henry Vaughan speaks to Night:

> God's silent, searching flight:
> When my Lord's head is fill'd with dew, and all
> His locks are wet with the clear drops of night;
> His still, soft call;
> His knocking time; the soul's dumb watch,
> When Spirits their fair kindred catch.
>
> Were my loud, evil days
> Calm and unhaunted as is thy dark tent,
> Whose peace but by some Angel's wing or voice
> Is seldom rent;
> Then I in heaven all the long year
> Would keep, and never wander here.
>
> But living where the sun
> Doth all things wake, and where all mix and tire
> Themselves and others, I consent and run
> To ev'ry mire,
> And by this world's ill guiding light,
> Err more than I can do by night.
>
> There is in God (some say)
> A deep, but dazzling darkness; as men here
> Say it is late and dusky, because they
> See not all clear;
> O for that night! where I in him
> Might live invisible and dim.

The darkness, the swiftness, the lyric metre and the strong Biblical overtones of the images recall John of the Cross, so far as anything in English can do so. Henry Vaughan soars in and out of allegory and literary devices, but when he claims to have seen something, one believes him, and for a moment one sees it too.

> I saw Eternity the other night,
> Like a great ring of pure and endless light,

All calm, as it was bright;
And round beneath it, Time, in hours, days, years,
   Driven by the spheres,
Like a vast shadow moved; in which the world
   And all her train were hurl'd.

The doting Lover in his quaintest strain
   Did there complain;
Near him, his lute, his fancy, and his slights,
   Wit's sour delights;
With gloves and knots, the silly snares of pleasure;
   Yet his dear treasure
All scatter'd lay, while he his eyes did pour
   Upon a flower.[30]

George Herbert was an incomparable religious poet, but seldom a visionary. Herbert is Vaughan's master, but Vaughan's visions are his own: 'A way where you might tread the Sun, and be More bright than he!' Henry Vaughan was most at home in poems of dawn and early morning. He spoke more than once of the earthly paradise restored:

   those groves,
And leaves thy spirit doth still fan,
I see in each shade that there grows
An angel talking with a man.

Under a juniper, some house,
Or the cool myrtle's canopy,
Others beneath an oak's green boughs,
Or at some fountain's bubbling eye....[31]

Even his poem about death is a poem about the light: 'They are all gone into the world of light'.

This visionary language became in the seventeenth century an ordinary way for poets to express themselves. Some of Marvell's poems have the hallucinating clarity of visions. Milton in his blindness was a profoundly religious, profoundly sensuous and genuinely visionary poet. The change that comes over him is more than technical. Too much technique can drive away visions just as it can drive out love, and in that century it sometimes did so. I will not linger among doubtful or disputed examples. No one can doubt the visionary quality of Thomas Traherne, if only because the material he transmutes is so ordinary, being simply nature, without the mystical component, the pure contemplation of God alone, that one finds in Henry Vaughan.[32] In fact what Traherne seeks to communicate both in poetry and in his rhythmic, incantatory prose is not an experience but his whole mind, his condensed theology (of a kind never known before or since except perhaps in Malebranche), and his way of looking at things. Readers are attracted by his enthusiastic optimism; his poems are a do-it-yourself kit for intending visionaries.

> For Nature teacheth Nothing but the Truth,
> I'm Sure mine did in my Virgin Youth.
> The very Day my Spirit did inspire,
> The Worlds fair Beauty did my Soul inspire.[33]

He was fascinated by Dreams, by Angels and by his own Childhood, and not incapable of philosophy and paradox; his poems have moments of passing grace and sensual pleasures, but he was less than a great poet, and his visions were a rather simple mating of the world with divinity.

> Thus Hony flows from Rocks of Stone;
> Thus Oil from Wood; thus Cider, Milk, and Wine,
> From Trees and Flesh; thus Corn from Earth; to one
>   That's hev'nly and divine.
> But he that cannot like an Angel see,
> In Heven its self shall dwell in Misery.[34]

In prose he says that 'To sit in the Throne of GOD is the most Supreme Estate that can befall a Creature. It is Promised in the Revelations. But few understand what is promised there, and but few believe it.[35] Death meant to him a restoration of the angelic vision and felicity of his life on earth. He was not a very usual man. Even his vision of nature is less pure and less convincing than the visionary poetry of an early Irish hermit that Seamus Heaney discusses.[36] The intellectual construction that underlies Traherne is not as powerful as that primitive sense of the world which was once present in the Irish language, and which is lost now, so that we must seek to recover it in poetry, as Traherne did in imaginary innocence, and in theology.

The nonconformist hymn-writers are too stern and deliberate to be called visionary poets, though one might make a case for Bunyan. For more than a hundred years after Traherne the visionaries in English poetry were disorientated and slightly mad, or at least just mad enough to liberate their mighty genius. It really was mighty. Christopher Smart's mad poetry, *Jubilate Agno*, goes far beyond even his magnificent *Ode to David*, a perfectly sane and classic poem that plays with full eighteenth-century brilliance on every one of his wild organ-notes, and yet beside *Jubilate Agno* it looks at first like a formal exercise. *Jubilate Agno* was written while his mind degenerated, a line a day ending on his last day in the madhouse. Yet it marked and embodied his transition from a minor talent to a great poet. The *Ode to David* was written soon afterwards: its sanity and its greatness are undoubted. If we wish in our personal research as poets to prune the bush back to the sound wood and the living sap, I believe we must go back to the *Ode to David*, to *Jubilate Agno*, and to William Blake. Or we must go back as David Gascoyne did to Hölderlin. Not for their visions but for their poetry, their purity and power as poets, which may perhaps be inseparable from visionary poetry. I believe this quality is what the public still demand of poetry and demand in vain. Christopher Smart by being visionary makes things more real, as the Irish hermit does.

Consider Smart on his cat Jeoffry, who leaps up to catch the musk. In these famous lines the visionary is the cat and the poet is a scientific observer. The poetry is as pure and clear as a documentary film. Its form has a scriptural resonance,[37] but its language has no scriptural obscurities. The musk is real, I suppose; it used to be grown in every cottage for the sake of its smell, but for some reason musk lost its smell early in this century. I sometimes think visionary poetry is almost the only kind that never loses its freshness and immediacy. It is constantly refreshed by subterranean rivers in the mind of every generation of its readers.

The great example is Blake (1757–1827). He was three years younger than Crabbe and thirteen years older than Wordsworth, but closer to us in a way than any poet since Shakespeare. Yet one must ask whether Smart's visions were distant from his madness, and whether Blake simply adopted the pose of a prophet. In the case of Smart the construction of *Jubilate Agno* is mad, and its details have a mad ingenuity; as his mind begins to fail he loses sight of his own mad plan, but his eye is not mad and his voice is mad only in the sense of being obsessive. Blake was certainly playful about visions, but they were real to him, and he makes them real to us. The more we discover about his ideas, about Thomas Taylor the neo-Platonist for example, and about William Stukeley the archaeologist, who interested Blake in Druids and brought divinity down to the suburbs of eighteenth-century London, the less mad Blake seems.[38] Stukeley's seriously held opinion that the Druids were pure descendants of the religion of the patriarchs lies behind Blake's 'Jerusalem, builded here Among these dark Satanic mills'.[39] And yet Blake's visions and his apocalyptic boldness lie somewhere beyond these explanations. The sum of everything knowable about Blake would not explain him. He is more like a heretic than like a prophet, and his vision in the long poem 'Jerusalem'[40] was wonderfully wild. Blake was jealously proud of the privacy of his visions, and at the same time he treated them as a revelation to mankind. The authority of his poetry and the brilliance of his paintings and drawings make him look in retrospect like a much more central figure than he must have seemed at the time.[41]

> The Vision of Christ that thou dost see
> Is my Vision's Greatest Enemy:
> Thine has a great hook nose like thine,
> Mine has a snub nose like to mine:
> Thine is the friend of All Mankind,
> Mine speaks in parables to the Blind:
> Thine loves the same world that mine hates,
> Thy heaven doors are my Hell Gates.[42]

Blake believed in what he called Poetic Genius as Traherne believed in nature and childish vision. In the first book of Blake's *Milton*,

> The Bard replied: 'I am Inspired! I know it is Truth! for I Sing
> According to the inspiration of the Poet Genius
> Who is the eternal all-protecting Divine Humanity,
> To whom be Glory and Power and Dominion Evermore. Amen.'...
>
> The Seven Angels of the Presence wept over Milton's Shadow.

In solemn utterances like these Blake challenges us to believe him, yet we cannot quite do so. We cannot treat his prophetic books as scripture. His visions convince us most in his simplest personal lyrics.

> Away to sweet Felpham, for Heaven is there;
> The Ladder of Angels descends thro' the air;
> On the Turret its spiral does softly descend,
> Thro' the village then winds, at My Cot it does end.

That is part of a letter to Mrs Flaxman from Mrs Blake, from Hercules Buildings, Lambeth. Everyone referred to in this letter seems to be enveloped in a weird, mystical light, and Mrs Blake's prose is very beautiful.

The Bread of sweet Thought and the Wine of Delight
Feeds the Village of Felpham by day and by night;
And at his own door the bless'd Hermit does stand,
Dispensing, unceasing, to all the whole Land.

In this case the visionary is Hayley, the Hermit of Eartham, and it was on Hayley's Turret that the Angels descended. In fact everyone in the poem and everyone in the letter is a visionary. The vision is shared between friends. The Blakes were longing for Felpham, they were longing to get out of London.[43] But the affectation of an earlier generation that they were all Arcadians, or of Stukeley and his friends that they were all Druids, are dust and ashes in comparison to this. A week later Blake wrote to John Flaxman from Felpham, 'And Now Begins a New life, because another covering of earth is shaken off.... In my Brain are studies and Chambers fill'd with books and pictures of old, which I wrote and painted in ages of Eternity before my mortal life; and those works are the delight and Study of Archangels.' What can one do but believe him? To judge from his youthful *Poetical Sketches*, he began as a great poet, and became a great visionary poet.

But with Blake we have come to the beginning of modern times. There is something wilful about his eccentricity, and something deliberate about Hölderlin's madness. From this time onwards vision is swallowed up in romanticism, which has reached a fever pitch, and authenticity is to be found only among passionate individuals, whom the world neglects as Blake was more or less neglected for forty years, John Clare utterly for longer, and Gerard Hopkins for nearly as long. The intensity of these poets is no doubt magnified by their loneliness, although loneliness is not a guarantee of greatness. 'The City of Dreadful Night' is a fascinating and a formidable poem, it is authentic enough, but not without weakness; one remembers only the rhythm, the realism and the refrain. John Clare has no pretension to be a visionary, though in our eyes he may be one, because his consciousness is so much purer than ours. Generations that lose religious intensity of vision have turned to Hopkins, and losing deep relationship with green nature they turn to John Clare. No one can move history backwards; every age is soon irrecoverable, and we do well to pay close attention to the poetry of the past. Generations pass so swiftly that I include the recent past. The great visionary poets in English in this century have been T. S. Eliot and David Jones, in stray passages throughout their works, but particularly in *Four Quartets* and *The Anathemata*. These poems are too great and too mysterious to be sensibly treated at the end of a lecture. In a sense I think that even *In Parenthesis* is a visionary poem, an utter transformation of experience that draws on the deepest roots of poetry and remains real. Its innocence makes it the more powerful.

David Gascoyne translated or adapted Hölderlin with an essay and four linking poems of his own.[44] It is very rare for a visionary poem to be equally convincing in another language, though I suppose that one might say the Song of Songs becomes visionary only in translation.[45] Hölderlin like his predecessors transfigures nature, and so does David Gascoyne. This lyric is not as frail as it looks.

> Adorned with yellow pears
> And with wild roses filled,
> The earth hangs in the lake.
> And wondrous love-intoxicated swans
> In peaceful holy waters dip their heads.
>
> My woe! When winter comes
> Where shall I find the rose?
> Where shall I find the sunshine and
> The shadows of the earth?
> The cold unspeaking walls rise up,
> The flags flap in the wind.

The walls are mountains and the final image is memorable by any standard. It makes one feel that all poetry aspires to be visionary, yet that is not true. The truth is just that visionary poets if they are authentic often have qualities to which other poets do aspire. This lyric is called 'Hälfte des Lebens', Halfway through Life. Here is Michael Hamburger's more literal translation.[46]

> With yellow pears the land
> And full of wild roses
> Hangs down into the lake,
> You lovely swans,
> And drunk with kisses
> You dip your heads
> Into the hallowed, the sober water.
>
> But oh, where shall I find
> When winter comes, the flowers, and where
> The sunshine
> And shade of the earth?
> The walls loom

Speechless and cold, in the wind
Weathercocks clatter.

The swans now seem to be so drunk with love they have to cool
their heads. *O sobria ebrietas, O ebria sobrietas.* Hamburger is more
clipped and somehow more secular than Gascoyne, though the poem
is not lost. Only now it might be a song by Heine. The reason is, or so I
believe, that David Gascoyne always was, as he still is, an authentic
visionary poet. (See Appendix 2.) As for the experience, for Hölderlin
it lay outside the poem, and he preserved it for us; for David
Gascoyne, it was surely the experience of someone else's poem
powerfully intermingled with his own experience, and liberated by his
innocence of the fine points of German. Some of Hölderlin's
conceptions are inseparable from the particular poem itself. 'Nah ist
und schwer zu fassen der Gott'.

The God is near, and
difficult to grasp.
But danger fortifies the rescuing power.
In sombre places dwell the eagles; the Alps' sons
Go fearless forth upon the roads of the abyss
Across lightly constructed bridges. And since all round there press

The peaks of time, and those so close
In love, are worn out on the separate heights,
Then give us the innocent waters,
O give us wings, that with the truest thought
We may fly yonder and return to this same place.

I spoke thus. And then rose
A guardian spirit, carried me away
More swiftly and still further than I dreamed,
Far from my house and home.
And as I passed, the light of dawn
Glowed on the shady woods and longed-for streams. . . .

Hölderlin's atmosphere of wingbeats goes back to Pindar, and his
visionary journey, to which this is only the introduction, goes back to
Gilgamesh. And he serves to make the point that not all visionaries are
optimistic, or necessarily Christians; least of all are they orthodox. It is
hard to discuss the quality of visionary poems without discussing the
quality of visions. Hölderlin seems to have moved in his lifetime from
an ordinary pure-minded romanticism to a country of intensifying

visions that his psychological make-up was unable to bear. His visions were like a drug habit: except that drugs give one the illusion of wonderful communications while in fact one babbles banalities and physically abuses one's braincells. Drugs furnish no close analogy to visionary poetry. As for quality of vision, even of earthly vision, we can sense that only in some quality of the poem: not precisely in its merit, but in some quality of it. Traherne's vision of the world is as clear to us as Henry Vaughan's. Shakespeare's vision of love is here and there revealed in his comedies and pondered in his sonnets, but never I think beyond argument: he normally requires an active, discursive understanding like his own. Yet in 'The Phoenix and the Turtle' we have a sudden, immediate sense of the depth of that vision. It is an effect of poetry, not of mysticism. It may well be among the most ancient uses, the most ancient social functions of poetry, and it has outlived many of the others.

A poet may move in and out of this visionary mode at different times of life. Hölderlin fulfilled in his life an early epigram that he wrote when he still had his sanity.

> In younger times I joyed in the sun's ray
> and wept at nightfall, now in my sunset
> daylight begins in doubtfulness, and yet
> holy and tranquil is the end of day.[47]

Eliot was not always visionary. Whatever was visionary in him was lost in the end: I think in his struggle to be central to the culture of his time. *The Waste Land* and the *Four Quartets* arose from low points in his life. It is always true for artists that failure makes one freer to experiment. The most isolated artist is the most free. Of all modern poets, of all intense visions, that seems to me truest of David Jones. And the loneliest poems of Philip Larkin are visionary poems.

APPENDIX 1

See Fraenkel on 'Quo me Bacche rapis', and its translation by Novalis.[48] Fraenkel's view of this poem (3,25) is really an extension of his view of 2,19. He says, 'I think Horace means what he says. He did see Dionysus.... He had only to close his eyes to see the god before him.' The lines in question are as follows:

> I have seen Bacchus in the remote rocks
> chanting his songs, believe me world to come,

the nymphs attending and the pointed ears
of the goat-footed satyrs attending.
Ehuoe: my mind shivers with the fresh fear
and my chest heaves breathing in Bacchus and
rejoicing. Ehuoe: have mercy Liber
dreadful and heavy-rodded, have mercy.[49]

William Stukeley published a pamphlet in 1736 to show that what Horace really saw was Jehovah teaching songs to the women of Israel. (*Palaeographia Sacra* No. 1.) 'I saw the LORD (let future times believe) Teaching to Israel's godlike race, a song of triumph: from mount Sinai's rocky cliff, Echoed by Miriam and her female throng ...

'As *Bacchus* represents our Saviour, so *Ariadne* is his spouse the church....'

APPENDIX 2

Marsh Acres
Saxmundham

Christmas Day, 1986

Dear Peter Levi,

This is the wrong day on which to write about literary things, my letter will not move, and I don't even have your address; but I have just read the *Agenda* issue devoted to you, at one sitting, and shall be trying to write something on Philip Larkin after Christmas – a difficult account of difficult relations. (I was most interested in your Larkin quotation and comments on it, because they touch on what I have to say; but it is your remarks on Hölderlin that urged me to write to you now, while I can.)

I do not think that there was anything 'deliberate about Hölderlin's madness', as you write (p. 46). For one thing, his madness itself is highly questionable – at least in the period in which he wrote his visionary poems. Recent research has shown that he was working on these much later than previously believed, and that the collapse of his former identity and concerns did not occur until he had been *treated* as a madman, dragged against his will into an institution whose methods of 'treatment' (torture) have now been studied and exposed. That institution killed quite a number of its patients. What was done to Hölderlin there was enough to have changed the character of a man far less sensitive, and one who had not already suffered the loss of the woman he loved and the frustration of all his other needs and ambitions. The only 'madness' that Hölderlin could have willed was the 'holy drunkenness' he attributed to the ancient Greeks, as opposed to the 'sobriety' of the moderns; and that, of course, has a bearing on his being a visionary poet; but he had renounced that 'holy drunkenness' in his grappling with those same differences between the ancients and moderns and in his later concern with European, Christian history (as in fragments of poems to be devoted to the Vatican, to the Virgin Mary and to Luther, as well as Columbus and other modern figures). Deliberateness strikes me as an attribute as inappropriate to Hölderlin as Auden's 'dotty'. (I remember protesting to Auden about his use of that word in writing about Hölderlin.) There may have been something deliberate about H.'s refusal to be the person he had been, after the treatment and after the writing of his visionary poems, when he called himself 'Scardanelli' or other names and would not speak of his past; but that cannot be what you meant.

William Cowper, too, was regarded as mad by his contemporaries, at times, and even by himself; but I have not found a trace of madness in any of his poems, including those written in such phases. In fact I should say that Cowper is one of the sanest of all English poets, despite his religious obsession with personal damnation and the depressions it induced.

About the two versions of 'Hälfte des Lebens': I am glad that you quote David Gascoyne's version – he is a dear friend, and has been for some forty-five years – but it was made from the French of Pierre Jean Jouve, with hardly any knowledge of German. A French rendering could not convey the noise made by the original. The very first word, 'adorned', is quite out of place, since it belongs to the eighteenth-century aesthetic that H. demolished with his immediacy. David's 'peaceful holy waters' also miss the clash of opposites (see above) in the contraction 'heilignüchtern'. (I did not have the courage to make one word out of the two in English, but 'nüchtern' (sober), to H., was the opposite of that ancient 'holy drunkenness'.) My version was a mimetic one, getting as close as possible to rendering even the wholly unorthodox syntax of the original. The last line is a conundrum, and will remain one, because H's 'Fahnen' could be flags or weather-vanes. In either case they do not 'flap' but 'clatter' or 'tinkle'. (Tinkle is closer to the German sound, but there would have been something a bit funny or grotesque about it in the context.) I chose weathercocks rather than vanes only because of the 'k'-sound, the harshness of it, because it is the sounds that create a stark contrast between the two stanzas – liquid and mellifluent in the first, dark and harsh in the second. 'Clatter' must have been chosen for related reasons – though 'reasons' is the wrong word, when all one's choices in translation are hardly conscious or deliberate.

With all good wishes for the coming year,

Michael Hamburger

Anon.

Who was it remarked, having read an anthology of the whole of English poetry, that the best poet was Anon.? There is something to be said for this extreme view, but the virtue of anonymous poetry has a special obscurity however sharply we may feel it, because the anonymous ballads have often been reworked by several singers and several generations, so that the original version is lost, and no one version of those that survive is necessarily supreme over the others. Nor would the original be supreme even if it did survive, because each version is only the working material for another, and every version is essentially the material of a performance. It is also true that the fact of anonymity gives poems an unpersonal authority. If the style itself of a poem is anonymous, even the original or the first recognizable form of the poem may be derivative from other poems; the power of a tradition, in the hands of one great poet, is more formidable than a purely personal style, as it is in the case of the *Iliad* and the *Odyssey*, and in the case of the Oxford manuscript of the *Song of Roland*. With the coming of writing and of personal signatures, the power of anonymous tradition is doomed to die out. It was never absolute. The individual singers were famous in their own day and their names were once known. Even now scholarship can diminish their anonymity, place them by region and by dialect, fit them into a social history defined partly by archaeology, as in the case of *Beowulf*, date them more or less by historical events, and map their popularity and influence by physical monuments and by the imitations and transmutations that their poetry underwent after their time.

Sometimes a poem is anonymous only because the poet's name chances to be lost, in an age of poetry where other names survive: in the manuscript anthologies of sixteenth- and seventeenth-century

106

poetry for example. But there the slapdash attributions in manuscripts convey the important lesson that one might expect to know the author by personal style. Everyone is certain by now that the song 'Shall I die?' is not by Shakespeare. I believe Robert Graves was right to attribute the best version of Tom of Bedlam's song, which was neither the first nor the last, to Shakespeare at the time of *King Lear*. We have the criterion of excellence, and another of personal style, including little tricks and faults of style, even when we are dealing with poems that the manuscripts leave unattributed. In these cases the criteria are multiple. They call for exhaustive scholarship and tact, and they admit of little in the way of certainty: but when we know a poet, any new addition to his poems has a special fascination, because then we are not studying poems but poets.

Take the poem which occurs without attribution in an unpublished Bodleian manuscript (Sancroft 53, p. 45), 'On a beautifull Virgin'. (See Appendix 1.) The style is highly conventional and yet highly personal. It falls somewhere between Shakespeare and Herrick. The metre is that of 'The Phoenix and the Turtle', the poem is easy to place, easy to date, but I find it impossible to attribute. We can see it was written by a wonderful poet, in a generation of wonderful poets, that is all. The conventions and conceits of this poetry are not the same as the traditional manner or mannerisms of orally transmitted poetry, which is anonymous in another sense, being heavily influenced by performance, by the conditions of performance and the received values of popular audiences. It is on that second and deeper anonymity that I wish to concentrate. If the lines 'On a beautifull Virgin' were signed, they would probably fall into place at once in the lifework of a poet who is already famous. Its lyrical freshness is in common with anonymous songs, but the poet is deliberately clever and fashionable and even his freshness is deliberate. He chose to be fresh and his sadness was a musical fashion. He does sound like Herrick. Radically anonymous poetry is another matter.

The study of a named poet and his lifework and the study of anonymous poetry call for different skills. One of the purposes of this lecture is to subdivide the kinds of poem we call anonymous, and to point out that all of them, even the most extreme cases, have a lot in common with personal poetry. Many of the skills of personal poetry, is fact, are impersonal: they are intuitively learnt from a tradition and might as well be anonymous. Many or all truly anonymous poems are better studied in the assurance that a personal poet wrote every one of them. The people is not a poet, the folk is not a composer of songs; the shape

of a scythe-handle was invented and adapted by a long series of individual craftsmen, it was not created by the people under the pressure
of social history: the same rule holds for ballad poetry, even though
we lack the names of poets.

Poem XXVII of the *Unpublished Poems* of Sir Thomas Wyatt and
his circle, published from Sir George Blage's manuscript in Trinity
College, Dublin by Kenneth Muir in 1961 (see Appendix 2), looks
like an anonymous poem, but Muir saw that its place in the manuscripts, Blage being a friend of Wyatt and the manuscript containing
plenty of Wyatt's work, points to his authorship: it fits his viewpoint,
his treatment of a similar theme in poem XLIII 'Circo regna tonat',
and it fits the same occasion, the execution of Anne Boleyn's lovers
in 1536, which we know Wyatt saw from a window in the Tower.
But, above all, this very moving poem is good enough and certainly
personal enough to be by Wyatt. If not it was by another unrecorded
court poet of the same power as Wyatt's. In form it belongs to a
popular tradition of which the greatest example is Villon's *Ballade*
while he was waiting to be hanged. Wyatt is likely to have known
Villon's work through Marot, but there were poets nearer home who
wrote in expectation of their executions, including ten years later his
own friend Sir George Blage, who was condemned for heresy in 1546
and saved only by the King from burning alive.

> And I O Lord into thy hands do yield
> My faithful soul appointed now of thee
> This life to leave through fire at Smithfield.

Blage was not as good a poet as Wyatt, but his verses have the force
of reality. Wyatt's verses have that and more. They are a fine example
of what happens to traditional form and language when they are shot
through with the personality and the suppleness, the unwoodenness
of a great poet. Something of the same effect can be sensed in Homer's
short epitaphs or lamenting obituaries for the obscure dead in the
Iliad. Milton's *Lycidas* may be in some other sense a greater poem,
but the personal crisis underlying it is less and it moves us less immediately. Wyatt's poem winds its way inward, from wooden, formal
phrases to personal power of utterance. It was Mark, the young
Italian musician, who betrayed the others from jealousy and who died
anyway, who was the last straw in the breakdown of the poem. He
and Lord Rockford, the first named, are known to have been close
to Wyatt.

Anon.

> The Axe is home, your heads be in the street;
> The trickling tears doth fall so from my eyes,
> I scarce may write, my paper is so wet.

Wyatt is not incapable elsewhere of wooden or derivative lines, and
they occur here, mostly early in the poem; in other cases they sometimes derive from a faulty or maybe from an unrevised text (the same
kind of thing seems to happen in the text of Shakespeare), but in this
poem I doubt it. One can watch from stanza to stanza the process by
which Wyatt takes over the wooden popular form and personalizes
it. That is not to say that the greatness of poetry is always in the personal quality of poems. There is another process by which the greatest
of personal poets may gain by achieving a certain impersonality:
Shakespeare in 'The Phoenix and the Turtle' for example, and in 'Fear
no more the heat o'the sun'. The most personal poetry is only an
adaptation of the impersonal, both within and well beyond the sixteenth century.

A form handled personally by named, self-naming artists for generations will become exhausted, like the shapes of Greek painted
pottery. But a form handled anonymously for generations because of
its usefulness and because of the rhythms of life that belong to it
becomes subtle beyond the scope of one artist, and peculiarly beautiful, like the wooden handle of a scythe. The sonnet in its long career
has fallen on bad days more than once, because its devices have been
deliberately exhausted by personal poets, each of whom competes to
write the sonnet to end all sonnets. Yet the genuine worksong has an
irresistible attraction, and the best children's rhymes are excellent
examples of the power of anonymous verse to flourish through centuries of rehandling. Admittedly, the older versions, when they exist,
are sometimes better poetry, better anonymous music, than what was
printed more recently. 'There were two blackbirds sat upon a hill, The
one was nam'd Jack, The other nam'd Gill; Fly away Jack, Fly away
Gill, Come again Jack, Come again Gill.' That is about 1765: it has
more melody than 'Come back Peter, Come back Paul.' On the other
hand, 'Jack boy, ho boy, news, the cat is in the well, let us ring now
for her knell, ding dong, ding dong bell' (recorded by an organist of
Winchester Cathedral in 1580 and alluded to in three plays by Shakespeare) is less perfectly mellifluous, less Tennysonian than 'Ding dong
dell, Pussy's in the well.' The reformers of nursery rhymes particularly
hate this one, as they say it teaches children to throw cats into ponds.

In the judgement of these durable, fragile-looking children's songs, their rhythm is primary. Some are based on such things as trumpet calls. 'Go to bed Tom' consists of words used in the Warwickshire Regiment for tattoo,[1] chanted on one note with drumming of the fists. A musical offering called 'The Battle of Prague', about 1800, ends with 'Go to bed home.' A version in about 1780 has 'Then to bed Tom, Then to bed Tom, Drunk or sober go to bed Tom'. Soldiers the world over must have put words to rhythms in this way; as late as the 1914 war Edward Thomas wrote poems with the same inspiration. But soldiers around 1800 were simpler, and their rhymes closer to children's rhymes. Beethoven noted down the similar words that Austrian soldiers used to sing to the Lights Out trumpet-call, and they gave him the motif of the Waldstein sonata. Eduard Fraenkel used to sing Beethoven's soldiers' words from a lost notebook that was in Berlin before the war. The English nursery rhyme does away with drunkenness, 'Tired or not Tom, Go to bed Tom.' Some old soldier must have chanted it in that form to a child, and so it became immortal.

A number of the most memorable nursery rhymes have no explanation at all. This commends them to children, and suggests an element in all poetry. They are concrete, strange and resonant, they suggest a whole new world which is left to the listener's imagination, yet they are constructed of familiar things. 'Little Tommy Tittlemouse Lived in a little house; He caught fishes in other men's ditches.' That seems to be first recorded by Halliday the great Shakespeare scholar in 1844. I dimly recall the variant, 'he put fishes in other folks' breeches'. Children's rhymes are specially strong in nonsense words,[2] which I take to be partly mimicry of sound, partly forgotten languages like very ancient counting rhymes and the shepherd's counting rhymes, 'Yan, tan, tethera'. Similar rhymes exist in German and doubtless in other languages. The only point I want to make about them here is their amazing musicality and rhythm: they constitute a basic element, probably *the* basic element, in the art of poetry. They make perfect sense in the ear, but none of any other kind. They are the groundswell of poetry, being uncluttered by syntax or logic or rhetoric. The prose sense of children's rhymes is secondary to the rhythm, and something similar is often true of traditional, illiterate poetry, in its adaptation and in its transmission. Those children's rhymes that are anonymous by chance, and began as political verses, like 'Dr Foster went to Gloucester' and 'Little Jack Horner sat in a corner', survive only because of their riddling quality, their inviting strangeness, like 'Little Tommy Tittlemouse', which may in fact belong among them.

The characters are memorable in the same way as Edward Lear's characters in his limericks. The intense personal sadness and the fragile humour of Edward Lear's poems are unlike anything else, but he drew on anonymous children's rhymes. In turn he contributed to anonymous tradition not his unique personality, but only the metrical form of the anonymous limerick. His longer poems have the same essential tone and music and characterization as his limericks. In the same way one of the longest and the most mysterious of traditional children's rhymes is the same in nature as the shorter ones: 'Who Killed Cock Robin?'[3]

> Who killed Cock Robin?
> I, said the Sparrow,
> With my bow and arrow,
> I killed Cock Robin.
>
> Who saw him die?
> I, said the Fly,
> With my little eye,
> I saw him die.
>
> Who caught his blood?
> I, said the Fish,
> With my little dish,
> I caught his blood.
>
> Who'll make the shroud?
> I, said the Beetle,
> With my thread and needle,
> I'll make the shroud.
>
> Who'll dig his grave?
> I, said the Owl,
> With my pick and shovel,
> I'll dig his grave.
>
> Who'll be the parson?
> I, said the Rook,
> With my little book,
> I'll be the parson.
>
> Who'll be the clerk?
> I, said the Lark,
> If it's not in the dark,
> I'll be the clerk.

Who'll carry the link?
I, said the Linnet,
I'll fetch it in a minute,
I'll carry the link.

Who'll be chief mourner?
I, said the Dove,
I mourn for my love,
I'll be chief mourner.

Who'll carry the coffin?
I, said the Kite,
If it's not through the night,
I'll carry the coffin,

Who'll bear the pall?
We, said the Wren,
Both the cock and the hen,
We'll bear the pall.

Who'll sing a psalm?
I, said the Thrush,
As she sat on a bush,
I'll sing a psalm.

Who'll toll the bell?
I, said the Bull,
Because I can pull,
I'll toll the bell.

All the birds of the air
Fell a-sighing and a-sobbing,
When they heard the bell toll
For poor Cock Robin.

The fact that this extraordinary poem was recorded in 1744, and referred to the fall of Walpole, is a matter of historical chance: the tradition of such a poem is much earlier, and has an influence on Skelton's 'Philip Sparrow', which is based on Catullus, and on Shakespeare's 'Phoenix and the Turtle', which draws on Ovid and on all these. The tradition of this poem exists in Germany also, and it occurs in a fifteenth-century stained-glass window at Buckland Rectory (Gloucester). 'Kukuk is de kulengräver, Adebor is de klokkentreder, Kiwitt is de schäuler Mit all sin schwester un bräuder.' The tradition was lively enough to provoke Byron in 1821:

Anon.

Who kill'd John Keats?
I says the Quarterly
So savage and Tartarly;
'Twas one of my feats.

The German version helps with the English. The robin is forgotten in the German: it just says 'Who's dead? Lackbread' ('Wer is dod? Sporbrod'), but the point remains the bird's funeral. The names have a lot to do with verbal music, but the typical cuckoo grieves and mourns in German, as it does in Slav folklore, and the stork nests in towers, the peewit chants like a boy and comes in flocks. In English the names are often used for the sake of rhymes, what German calls *wohlklang*, but the English poem does embody a folklore not all of which I understand. Is the Fish connected with the Fisher King, with Balder or with Christ? Did the Owl once have a trowel? I accept that the Bull is a bullfinch, but the combination of a pun and rhyme (Bull, because I can pull) must have been irresistible. One day, among the immense treasury of unpublished, unread poetry, I hope someone may find a version of 'Cock Robin' earlier than Walpole, and perhaps better, because more traditional, more closely moulded by the ear of children than the one we have. The simple-minded question, What are the birds saying or thinking?, is closely related to What are the bells saying?

Oranges and lemons,
Say the bells of St Clement's.

You owe me five farthings,
Say the bells of St Martin's.

When will you pay me?
Say the bells of Old Bailey.

When I grow rich,
Say the bells of Shoreditch.

When will that be?
Say the bells of Stepney.

I'm sure I don't know,
Says the great bell at Bow.

Here comes a candle to light you to bed,
Here comes a chopper to chop off your head.

Chop Chop Chop Chop Chop.

The wonderful and terrible words at the end of the poem are not what the bells say. They belong to a game, which if it is not about public execution is about the plague.[4] Dekker records that, of all those Londoners who fled downriver from the plague of 1603 to Gravesend, not one ever returned; they were all murdered for fear they were plague-bearers. The bell verses make a serious attempt to imitate the individual music of the bells. Once again the form is common; bells had verse inscriptions in which the bell itself speaks, and verses like 'Oranges and Lemons' exist for Derbyshire, Shropshire, Northamptonshire and the city of Northampton. John Holloway collected them in his *Oxford Book of Local Verse* (1987); he calls them bell-jingles.

> 'Pancakes and fritters,'
>   says the bells of Saint Peter's.
> 'Where must we fry 'em?'
>   says the bells of Cold Higham.
> 'In yonder land-thurrow,'
>   says the bells of Wellingborough.
> 'You owe me a shilling,'
>   says the bells of Great Billing.
> 'When will you pay me?'
>   says the bells at Middleton Cheney.
> 'When I am able,'
>   says the bells at Dunstable.
> 'That will never be,'
>   says the bells at Coventry.
> 'Oh, yes it will,'
>   says Northampton Great Bell.
> 'White bread and sop,'
>   says the bells at Kingsthrop.
> 'Trundle a lantern,'
>   says the bells at Northampton.
>
> 'Roast-beef and marsh-mallows,'
>   says the bells at All Hallows.
> 'Pancake and fritters,'
>   says the bells of Saint Peter's.
> 'Roast beef and boil'd,'
>   says the bells of Saint Giles.
> 'Poker and tongs,'
>   says the bells of Saint John's.

Anon.

'Shovel, tongs, and poker,'
     says the bells of Saint Pulchre's.

I doubt whether bell-jingles were written by or for children:
'Oranges and Lemons' appears to me to be written by a skilful musician and poet of the circle and generation of Orlando Gibbons.
That would make it earlier than the others. Church bells imitate
abbey bells; the English art of change-ringing began with hand-bells
at the end of the middle ages. Country churches began to get bells at
the dissolution of the monasteries. Even in 1600 it was very unlikely
for any English town to have so many bells as London. In southern
Greece there is still a proverb about a wind strong enough to ring all
the bells of Areoupolis. The sharpest image in the Greek lament for
the fall of Constantinople to the Turks is the number of its tolling
bells. The earliest-recorded version of the London bell-jingles is about
1744, and if I may argue against my own conjecture it remains quite
uncertain whether the classic version is the original, extended in
1744, or a slowly polished, anonymously perfected work of art. I
suspect it was cut or adapted from a wilder series of rhymes to give it
a coherent plot, which in the 1744 version is overgrown. Northampton borrows the London plot, but the Shropshire jingles have
only the faintest, feeble attempt at coherent narrative. That, I take it,
gives them a special authenticity: they belong more to tradition less
to poetry; no real poet has laid a finger on them. It is possible to like
them all the better for that fact.
    The moment at which individual genius most typically intervenes
in the creation of traditional poetry is simple and unexpected: it
consists of the reversal of meaning of an inherited phrase or image:
the moment in the *Iliad* when the Greek King's words are suddenly
given to Hector: 'the day is coming when holy Troy shall perish.' The
meaning of a phrase or of an image is very often reversed in what we
call folksong, but often also in common speech. The same device lies
at the heart of the poetry of Aeschylus, and of Serbian folksong, and
of ballads in English.

> It shall come to pass on a summer's day
> When the sun shines bright on every stane
> I shall come and take my little young son
> And teach him how to swim the faem.
> And ye shall marry a gunner good,
> And a very good gunner I'm sure he'll be,

115

And the very first shot that ever he'll shoot
Shall kill both my young son and me.[5]

To define the inherited skill of poets must reveal the technical nature of poetry, but one of the fascinating things about this skill is that it remains intuitive, never wholly articulate. This is because the way a poem hangs together is primitive, it exists in the language of children, and operates with the same strength and subtlety in the verse of illiterate poets in illiterate societies as it does in the works of Milton and T. S. Eliot. It is learnt by ear, by imitation and permitted variation, as all the tricks of language and unwritten rhetoric are learnt by children. If it seems that tricks of alliteration, of singsong or repeated rhythm, and of punning and rhyming would appeal mostly to children, that may be because children use language for many more purposes than most adults, they are exploring and discovering the many uses and qualities of sound, and in this as in other matters genius may well consist in the survival of childish powers with adult intelligence and experience of life.

It is important not to be mystical about this. The devices of poetry can be objectively studied after all, and some of them must always have been articulately learnt, even by illiterate poets, just as some of the devices of singing must have been deliberately taught and learnt. David Fowler[6] has pointed out the usefulness to a ballad-singer of a certain kind of formula in the second line which adds nothing much to the narrative but gives the singer time to think or remember and offers him a rhyme for line four, the climax of the stanza.

They filled in wine and made them glad
    Under the leaves small,
And set pasties of venison
    That good was with ale.

The second line is like the refrain line of a song like 'King Orfeo', which I shall discuss, and like the early English carols. In the case of the stanza from 'Robin Hood and the Monk' I have just quoted, the narrative is brisk and hearty, and only the traditional formula, with its change of tone and rhythm, convinces us that this is truly a poem. I think Fowler is mistaken in calling it a filler, a weak line, 'which because of its perfunctory or formulaic character gives the improvising minstrel a chance to plan his rhyme scheme'. Formulaic poetry is not perfunctory; the second-line formula is all that holds this stanza together. It does more than fill a space.

The elements of detail that make a poem work do so by making the lines memorable, attractive to the ear, and so by creating that expectation of important meaning which it is the easy task of traditional poetry and the despairing task of overcivilized poetry to fulfil. But from language to language and from century to century the elements of detail alter because the language has altered on the tongue and in the ear. The Germanic alliterative chanted verse of *Beowulf* suffered a mutation into stress metre in which regular beats were embellished with regular rhymes. Sometimes a refrain in one language is preserved with a ballad in another, one kind of sound is set against another. The same kind of effect can occur within one language.

> Lully lulley, lully lulley,
> The faucon hath borne my make away.
> He bare him up, he bare him down,
> He bare him into an orchard brown.
> In that orchard there was an hall
> Which was hanged with purple and pall.
> And in that hall there was a bed,
> It was hanged with gold so red.
> And in that bed there lies a knight,
> His woundes bleeding day and night.
> By that bed side kneeleth a may,
> And she weepeth both night and day.
> And by that bed there standeth a stone
> With *Corpus Christi* writ theron.

The poem has many origins: the mysterious lullaby and the lover's lament among others, yet the focus is very clear, the momentum is unflagging, and the climax utterly unexpected. It is a simple reversal, an intervention of genius. As Lorca says in his essay on *Duende* (a quality which this poem abundantly has), the form has been used to the marrow of its bone. Yet in all its individual details it depends on a tradition. 'Lully lulley, lully lulley, the faucon hath borne my make away. He bare him up, he bare him down, he bare him into an orchard brown.' Technically, this is not so very far from children's rhymes, and that is its strength, but in climax and in contrast it has a resonance in our experience of life, and that is its sharpness.

The extraordinary lyric intensity of ballad poetry is often inherited, concentrated and distilled through generations of singers of songs until it reaches the pure and intense form we find so surprising and think of as so rare. The very old Orkney ballad of 'King Orfeo' for example[7] has two lines of refrain in a mangled or half-remembered form of Danish. They must have been understood once, and survived I assume because of their music.

> Der lived a king ina da aste,
>   Scowan ürla grün,
> Der lived a lady in da wast,
>   Whar giorten han grün oarlac.

The refrain is quite irrelevant, but works wonderfully. Its meaning is 'The woods are green early, and where the deer run yearly.' Of course ballads can be dramatic as well as lyrical, and the situation of their narratives gets worn down to the bare bones, which increases their force. Antiquity and dialect add to the mystery, at least for us. The Danish refrain of 'King Orfeo' suggests a very ancient source for the kind of phrase we think of as late medieval or Tudor, and essentially English: a source much earlier than the fifteenth century, when the earliest versions of ballads to survive in writing began to appear in French.[8]

Today we suppose that every poet, in order to be recognizable as a poet, has to have an individual style and tone and personality in verse. He is a poet when he can write as no one else can write. This is peculiar, because in the past you were recognized as a poet only when you could write just the same as everyone else, with no lapses from the common standard. My own feeling is that even in epics and in ballads individuals were always recognizable to the connoisseur, but the combination of inherited elements and the flattening force of oral transmissions confuses individuality of style.[9] Sveto Koljevic has shown the very strong personal influence of nineteenth-century Serbian singers on the inherited heroic songs that each of them sang. In modern poetry individuality may be a matter of form – no one else can write an Elizabeth Bishop poem or a late Auden poem or a David Jones poem – or of tone of voice, which in the mature work of any poet at ease in their language becomes as personal as a signature, more so in verse than when poets write in prose.

This particularly modern phenomenon of personal tone has arisen because poetry, at least from Tennyson onwards, has become more intimate. It is personal speech conveying a full personality in all its ramifications, including even the brain and the view of the world. Those young poets who have yet to develop individual views or personalities stand small chance of detaining our attention. But when we catch the personal tone of just one line of Eliot or Seferis, we are captivated. In fact in Eliot's case it takes two lines, the second swerving inwards from the first.

> Let us go then, you and I,
> When the evening is spread out against the sky. . . .

> Here I am, an old man in a dry month,
> Being read to by a boy, waiting for rain. . . .

With Seferis one recognizes the voice at once, though the tone may vary. 'The garden with the fountains in the rain ... On the track, on the track again, on the track, what Circles and what bloody laps, what black Benches, people watching me ...'.

There is an element in this modern cultivation of personal style which I think is a result of the modern movement. I take it that the modern movement arose from the recent decay of heavy stresses in European languages as they were spoken, noticed first in French, then through Pound's review of a book by Duhamel and Vildrac and through the influence of Laforgue on Eliot, in English. Modern poets were tempted, by the way their language sounded in their ears, to abandon regular stress metres and abandon the rhyme schemes that were a feature of those metres, and to pay new attention to 'quantity', to the length of syllables. This is a subtle, not a simple matter, as the best practitioners of free verse have always pointed out. When free verse reaches its third or fourth generation and appears to come naturally, it pays diminishing returns. Once the old stress system with its innumerable tricks of detail has gone, the technique of poetry has to be thought through or worked through from the beginning, by every serious writer individually. In every case the relation of a formal style to the poet's own individual inward vernacular, and to the poet's observation of a common vernacular, is a crucial element at the heart of style. Small wonder therefore that modern styles are personal.

A close inspection of the great modernists will reveal that the small, instinctive techniques that have always been used to hold a verse of poetry together, even in traditional, anonymous poems, have now become all the more important because the obvious conscious rules have dissolved. The modern poets have sharpened exactly that musical and rhythmic sense, and exactly those instinctive ways of handling language, that they have in common with the ancient makers of traditional, anonymous poetry. I mean things like paradox, riddle, alliteration, refrain, self-echo and half-rhyme and the balancing of spaces of time, the leaning of lines against a silence. I have suffered some perplexity over choosing a passage of modern poetry strong enough to carry this argument. You would have to hear the technical side of the poem, and the poem would have to be powerfully successful at the same time, because in the technique of poetry only what has worked is worth describing: technique is only an explanation, indeed only a part of the explanation, how a poem has worked. No amount of explaining the technique can make a poem work. You heard it or you failed to hear it. If a critic and a reader disagree, the only appeal is to the judgement of generations, which in the case of the most modern, the most living poetry is not yet available. For example, all I have just said about the coherence of modern verse, about the nature of which I have no doubts, arose from a rereading of Ezra Pound, but to find a single, overwhelming example in his work is another matter.

At least there need be no doubt at all that Pound had studied the rhythms and the physical sound of traditional music. On this subject as on others he was opinionated, but the effect on his poetry was invigorating.

> Once only in Burgos, once in Cortona
>   was the song firm and well given
> old buffers keeping the stiffness,
>   Gregory damned, always was damned, obscurantist.
> Know then:
>   Toward summer when the sun is in Hyades
> Sovran is Lord of the Fire
>   to this month are birds.
> with bitter smell and with the odour of burning
> To the hearth god, lungs of the victim
>   The green frog lifts up his voice
>   and the white latex is in flower.[10]

In discussing later poetry, which has strayed far from the declining art of modern music, though Pound did something to bring it back into contact with ancient music, which is more alive, it is important to remember that the physical sound of traditional poetry was a sub-branch of popular music. Music as an instinctive traditional art was freer: the cattle-calls, the street cries of the past, and the jubilus or grace-notes of the church, were free of formal discipline and based on folk tradition – 'iubilare est rustice inclamare', says Festus – and the techniques of traditional poetry had the same origin; they must at one time have been as widespread.

120

In the monethe of Maye when mirthes bene fele,
And the sesone of somere when softe bene the wedres,
Als I went to the wodde my werdes to dreghe,
Into the shawes myselfe a shotte me to gete
At ane hert or ane hinde, happen as it mighte:
And as Drighten the day drove from the heven....[11]

This is certainly traditional poetry, from the same late-medieval re-vival or survival of early-English verse technique that produced *Gawain and the Green Knight*. It is held together by repeated rhythms and by alliterations and echoes of other kinds. It is neither incom-petent nor undramatic, and it has a certain Homeric zest and vivid-ness in the death of the stag ('Dede als a dore-naile doun was he fallen'), but one catches little feeling of a personal poet. This poet is excellent and vivid, alive, but not unique. Yet some of the same elements recur in the work of a greater, far more personal poet of the same date. The difference lies in the personal interventions and sudden surprises, even in the opening lines of William Langland.

In a somer seson whan soft was the sunne
I shope me in shroudes as I a sheepe were,
In habite as a heremite unholy of workes
Went wide in this world wondres to here.
Ac on a May morninge on Malverne hilles
Me befel a ferly, of fairy me thoughte.
I was very forwandred and went me to reste
Under a brode banke bi a burnes side,
And as I lay and lened and loked in the wateres,
I slombered in a sleping....

Langland is a personal poet in style or tone, but also in intellect; he plans a great work, just as Dante does before him and Gower after him. But the texture of the verse itself, although as usual it is more or less in common between close contemporaries to a later, untrained ear, is not automatic: I mean that it is never quite automatic. Even the adoption of some received formula is never quite automatic for Langland or for Homer or for a ballad singer. Poetry has no auto-pilot; it can be analysed in mechanical terms only fruitlessly because it is not mechanical.[12] What I have called the intervention of personal genius in traditional poetry is commoner than we think. It may occur at any stage in transmission of a ballad, for example. When many versions of the same ballad have been collected, we may pick out the oldest from antiquarian curiosity, but to select the best, the classic version, is a matter for the ear, and a matter of the instinctive recognition of a form, just as it was for every singer of that ballad. Traditional, anonymous poetry shows us that genius is commoner than we imagine, and great poetry is as common as blackberries; it is not always personal poetry; its anonymity may even be essential to the impression it makes.

> I must be going, no longer staying,
> The burning Thames I have to cross;
> Oh I must be guided without a stumble
> Into the arms of my dear lass.
>
> When he came to his true love's window
> He knelt down gently on a stone
> And it's through a pane he whispered slowly,
> My dear girl, are you alone?
>
> She rose her head from her down-soft pillow,
> And snowy were her milk-white breast,
> Who's there, who's there at my bedroom window
> Disturbing me from my long night's rest?
>
> Oh I'm your lover, don't discover,
> I pray you rise love, and let me in,
> For I am fatigued of my long night's journey,
> And I am wet unto the skin.
>
> Now the young girl rose, and put on her clothing,
> Till she quickly let her true love in,
> Oh they kissed, shook hands, and embraced each other,
> Till that long night was near at an end....[13]

This song has a pathos that arises partly from its apparent artlessness, and an ominous resonance that arises from its form. It has a tense ambivalence which arises from the fact that it mingles three or four quite different ballads into one.[14] Confusion in fact, and the poet's way of dealing with confusion and exploiting it, resolving or refusing to resolve it, are features both of modern and of ancient poetry. The poet is an angler in the lake of darkness. The conscious coverage of those poets of the age of reason who defied the darkness was their tribute to its existence. But as for those more recent, necromantic writers who accept and embrace what they take to be the dark side of poetry, I think they simply fell into the lake.

Anon.

Behind this strangely personal and disturbing Birmingham song lies not only the ghostly lover in the much earlier song called 'Clerk Saunders', with its sequel about the grave and the ghost which F. J. Child cut off from 'Clerk Saunders', as a separate song, but also another closely related ballad, possibly the greatest of all English folksongs, 'The Unquiet Grave'.

> The wind doth blow today, my love,
>   And a few small drops of rain.
> I never had but one true-love,
>   In cold grave she was lain.
>
> I'll do as much for my true-love
>   As any young man may,
> I'll sit and mourn all at her grave
>   For a twelvemonth and a day.
>
> The twelvemonth and a day being up,
>   The dead began to speak:
> Oh who sits weeping on my grave,
>   And will not let me sleep?
>
> 'Tis I, my love, sits on your grave,
>   And will not let you sleep,
> For I crave one kiss of your clay-cold lips,
>   And that is all I seek.
>
> You crave one kiss of my clay-cold lips,
>   But my breath smells earthy strong.
> If you have one kiss of my clay-cold lips,
>   Your time will not be long.
>
> 'Tis down in yonder garden green,
>   Love, where we used to walk,
> The finest flower that ere was seen
>   Is withered to a stalk.
>
> The stalk is withered dry, my love,
>   So will our hearts decay.
> So make yourself content, my love,
>   Till God calls you away.

'The Unquiet Grave' has a classic finality. It took the shape it has in the hands of some very great unknown poet. From the point of view of craft and technique it seems to me faultless, a rare, nearly unknown phenomenon in ballads in any language. Yet its virtues are impersonal, only the decay of love in the last stanza, the faintest touch of a different theme, hints at the personality of the singer. Was that singer or poet of individual genius a woman? The surrounding darkness adds something to the stature of the poem. We are not at the moment scholars attempting to appraise and understand a known writer or singer in his or her entire lifework, in its historical or its critical context. This poem stands alone, anonymous and perfect, as the classic statement of what we most deeply feel: it is quite unpersonal and yet intensely personal. It is like the voice of the most passionate and skilled singer heard once only.

Finally, let me set you a puzzle, since time allows. Epitaphs are usually anonymous, but some have been written by great and famous poets. Verse epitaphs at a popular level sometimes imitate or vary the words already inscribed on other tombs.[15] I am puzzled by the fine anonymous epitaph on the Tanfield monument in Burford Church (1628). The tomb was not built by Lucius Carey, Lord Falkland, who was only eighteen, but by his mother, who was a Tanfield daughter.

> Here Shadowe lie,
> Whilst life is sadd,
> still hopes to die,
> to him she hadd.
>
> In bliss is hee
> whom I lov'd best,
> thrise happie shee,
> with him to rest.
>
> So shall I be
> with him I loved,
> and he with mee,
> and both us blessed.
>
> Love made me poet,
> and this I write,
> my harte did do it,
> and not my witt.

The verses are apparently naively written, in the name of Lady Tanfield, but are they naive, or is her simplicity deliberate? Is the grammatical incoherence in the first stanza a sign of amateur poetry, or the fault of a copyist ('hope' for 'hopes' would correct that)? And then

'My heart did do it and not my wit'? But someone's wit did it really. So who wrote it? Not Lord Falkland: he wrote couplets. Can it be his mother, writing in the name of her mother? The verses are too loving, and Elizabeth Carey's husband, Falkland's father, was still alive. Old Lady Tanfield was a brutal old woman and a confirmed oppressor of the poor; can she have been a poet as well? (See Appendix 3.) The metre is old, easy and popular. But Lord Falkland was a patron of Ben Jonson: if these verses were commissioned, Ben Jonson might have written them.

APPENDIX 1

On a beautifull Virgin

Under this marble buried lies
Beauty may enrich the skies,
And add light to phoebus' eyes.

Sweeter than Aurora's Aire
When she paints the lillies fair,
And gilds Cowslips with her hair.

Chaster than ye Virgin-spring
Ere, her blossoms she doth bring,
Or cause philomel to sing.

If such Goodness lives mongst Men,
Bring it me: For I know then,
She is come from Heaven agen.

But if not, ye Standers-by,
Comfort me; saying that I
Am ye next design'd to dy.

APPENDIX 2

XXVII

In morning wyse syns daylye I increas,
   Thus shuld I cloke the cause of all my greffe;
   So pensyve mynd with tong to hold his pease,
   My reasone sayethe ther can be no relyeffe:
   Wherffor geve ere, I vmble you requyre,   [5
   The affectes to know that thus dothe mak me mone.

The cause ys great of all my dolffull chere,
Ffor those that were, and now be dead and gonne.

What thoughe to Dethe Desert be now ther call,
As by ther ffautis yt dothe apere ryght playne, [10
Of fforce I must lament that suche a ffall
Shuld lyght on those so welthy dyd Raygne;
Thoughe some perchaunce wyll saye of crewell hart,
A trators dethe why shuld we thus be mone?
But I, Alas, set this offence apart, [15
Must nedis bewayle the dethe of some begonn.

As ffor them all I do not thus lament,
But as of Ryght my Reason dothe me bynd;
But as the most doth all ther dethes repent,
Evyn so do I by fforce of mornyng mynd. [20
Some say: 'Rochefford, hadyst thou benne not so prowde,
For thy gryt wytte eche man wold the be mone;
Syns as yt ys so, many crye alowde:
Yt ys great losse that thow art dead and gonne.'

A! Norrys, Norres, my tearys begyne to Rune [25
To thynk what hap dyd the so led or gyd,
Wherby thou hast bothe the and thyn vndone.
That ys bewaylyd in court of euery syde;
In place also wher thou hast neuer bene
Both man and chyld doth petusly the mone. [30
They say: 'Alas, thou art ffar ouer seene
By there offences to be thus ded and gonne.'

A! Weston, Weston, that pleasant was and yonge;
In actyve thynges who myght with the compayre?
All wordis exsept that thou dydyst speake with tonge; [35
So well estemyd with eche wher thou dydyst fare.
And we that now in court dothe led our lyffe
Most part in mynd doth the lament and mone;
But that thy ffaultis we daylye here so Ryffe,
All we shuld weppe that thou art dead and gone. [40

Brewton, ffarwell, as one that lest I knewe.
Great was thy love with dyuers as I here;
But common voyce dothe not so sore the Rewe,
As other twayne that dothe beffore appere.
But yet no dobt but thy ffrendes lament yee, [45
And other her ther petus crye and mone.
So dothe eche hart ffor the lykwyse Relent,
That thou gevyst cause thus to be ded and gonne.

A! Mark, what mone shuld I ffor the mak more
  Syns that thy dethe thou hast deseruyd best,   [50
  Save only that my ny ys fforsyd sore
  With petus playnt to mone the with the Rest?
  A tym thou haddyst aboue thy poore degre,
  The ffall wherof thy frendis may well bemone.
  A Rottyn twygge apon so hyghe a tree   [55
  Hathe slepyd thy hold and thou art dead and goonn.

And thus ffarwell eche one in hartye wyse!
  The Axe ys home, your hedys be in the stret;
  The trykklyngge tearys dothe ffall so from my yes,
  I skarse may wryt, my paper ys so wet.   [60
  But what can hepe when dethe hath playd his part,
  Thoughe naturs cours wyll thus lament and mone?
  Leve sobes therffor, and euery crestyn hart
  Pray ffor the sowlis of thos be dead and gone.

2 Thus]this MS.	5 vmble]humbly.	6 thus]this MS.
12 those]those who	17 thus]this MS.	32 thus]this MS.
35 exsept]accept.	46 her]hear.	51 my ny] mine eye.
61 hepe]help	63 crestyn]Christian.	

APPENDIX 3

Edward FitzGerald comments (12 May 1883) on Mrs Oliphant's *History of Eighteenth-Century Literature*:[16]

By the way there was one good observation. I think, in Mrs Oliphant's superficial or hasty History of English 18th century Literature, viz., that when the Beatties, Blacks, and other recognized Poets of the Day were all writing in a 'classical' way, and tried to persuade Burns to do the like, it was certain Old Ladies who wrote so many of the Ballads, which, many of them, have passed as ancient. Sir Patrick Spens for one, I think.

Shakespeare's Sonnets

Sometimes Shakespeare's sonnets seem to be windows of clear glass that open into his soul, but if so they raise the question where is the soul, what is the soul, can the self or any situation of the self be translated into words, how can what is most personal and intimate seem to be the most universal poetry? Those who seek for traces of Shakespeare's personal life in the sonnets, for the silver trail of a snail on a blackcurrant leaf, find them in abundance. Those who treat the sonnet as a poetic exercise, cat's cradle played with traditional forms and with images meant to be deciphered, discover only what they are fitted to discover. The Latin poet Horace has had both kinds of critic, the wet and the dry, and as with Shakespeare the pendulum of criticism is now swinging too far in the dry direction; the problems are similar. I find it curious that scholars think they know more about Horace's personality than they do about Shakespeare's: it may be because Shakespeare was a dramatist and Horace a lyric poet, but those categories do not exhaust the truth either about Horace or about Shakespeare.

The sonnets do not announce themselves as fictions, yet if we read the sonnets as dramatic speeches in which Shakespeare himself is the character who speaks, they remain enigmatic, because he changes tone so often, so subtly and so utterly. Katherine Duncan-Jones,[1] in a very far-reaching study that sets a new standard and creates a new basis for Elizabethan sonnet scholarship, has shown that the range of tones is deliberate, and not only planned but adapted from the existing plan of Daniel's sonnets. He followed Daniel's themes in some detail; Dr Johnson's friend Malone, the first serious Shakespeare scholar, observed that much in the eighteenth century, but Katherine Duncan-Jones goes much further. In several ways her study comes as a relief. It should put an end to the wholesale rearrangements of the order of the sonnets as they were printed in the first quarto, though

I would reserve the right to consider shifting just one or two towards the end of the series. It explains the presence of the 'Lover's Complaint', the long, very funny poem that concludes the collection, and the rag-bag of the last four sonnets, one of cheerful and robust obscenity, one that I feel might be out of order, and two adaptations of a minor epigram about Cupid or Eros from the Greek Anthology.

The fact that Shakespeare wrote two versions of the same conventional original throws some light on the Venus and Adonis sonnets in *The Passionate Pilgrim*, at least one of which he may well have written. If that is so, they probably date from 1592. The only earlier sonnets by Shakespeare might be the sonnet signed Phaethon, printed as a compliment to Florio in *Second Fruits* (1591),[2] if he wrote that, as I feel sure he did, and possibly sonnet 145, that seems to name Anne Hathaway (if, that is, you accept the pun on the name Hathaway). These are the early fringes of Shakespeare's work in this form. The form of the sonnet continued to influence his dramatic poetry, but within the main series of the sonnets individual poems are usually hard to date. We know only that they were arranged as a collection before 1609. They were a book, a sequence, not a miscellany of verses. Shakespeare had written more than he included. He did include the 'Lover's Complaint', which much as I enjoy it I feel to be very early work, and the Hathaway couplets, which are jejune and have nothing to do with the Dark Lady, but he left out the sonnet for Florio, the Venus and Adonis sonnets, and very likely others that have perished. I want to accept that the main series were not only arranged, but conceived from an early stage and written as a collection. At the rate of only one a week, it would take three years to write Shakespeare's sonnets; I doubt whether he took more than that time in a series of swiftly written groups composed at intervals. They show an absolute mastery of poetry, but he shows the same mastery in *Love's Labour's Lost* at about the same date. The argument that he wrote the sonnets over a period of more than ten years, like fragments of a diary, seems to rest on the belief that the sonnet 'Not mine own fears nor the prophetic soul', is about the Earl of Southampton's release from the Tower at the death of Queen Elizabeth in 1603.

Before we wind our way into the core of Shakespeare's sonnets I would like to deal with the poems I have mentioned, first the Phaethon sonnet.

> Sweet friend whose name agrees with thy increase,
> How fit a rival art thou of the Spring?

For when each branch hath left his flourishing,
And green-lockt Summer's shady pleasures cease:
She makes the Winter's storms repose in peace,
And spends her franchise on each living thing:
The daisies sprout, the little birds do sing,
Herbs, gums, and plants do vaunt of their release.
So – when that all our English wits lay dead,
(Except the Laurel that is ever green),
Thou with thy fruits our barrenness o'er-spread,
And yet thy flowery pleasance to be seen.
Such fruits, such flowerets of morality,
Were ne'er before brought out of Italy.

This sonnet sounds to me like Shakespeare's because of a certain quality in its seasonal imagery, and because no one else I can discover was writing as well in that vein in 1592. The only exception is Spenser, but Spenser would have signed it. Shakespeare was nobody. But Florio was a member of Lord Southampton's household. Scholars trace him as an influence on *Love's Labour's Lost*, and on Shakespeare's knowledge of Italy and Italian. They will have met through Southampton if in no other way, at the time of *Venus and Adonis* and *The Rape of Lucrece*. The story of Phaethon occurs early in the *Metamorphoses* of Ovid, which Shakespeare knew, and the use of this name as a signature expressed the same soaring ambition as the bit of Ovid that Shakespeare put on the title page of his first book, *Venus and Adonis*:

Envy, why carp'st thou my time is spent ill,
And term'st my works fruits of an idle quill?
Or that unlike the line from whence I sprung,
War's dusty honours are refused, being young?
Nor that I study not the brawling laws,
Nor set my voice to sail in every cause?
Thy scope is mortal, mine eternal fame,
That all the world may ever chant my name.
Homer shall live while Tenedos stands and Ide,
Or into sea swift Simois doth slide.
Ascraeus lives while grapes with new wine swell,
Or men with crooked sickles corn down fell.
The world shall of Callimachus ever speak;
His art excelled, although his wit was weak.
For ever lasts high Sophocles' proud vein,

With sun and moon Aratus shall remain.
While bondmen cheat, fathers be hard, bawds whorish,
And strumpets flatter, shall Menander flourish.
Rude Ennius, and Plautus full of wit,
Are both in fame's eternal legend writ.
What age of Varro's name shall not be told,
And Jason's Argos and the fleece of gold?
Lofty Lucretius shall outlive that hour
That nature shall dissolve this earthly bower.
Aeneas' war, and Tityrus shall be read,
While Rome of all the conquered world is head.
Till Cupid's bow and fiery shafts be broken,
Thy verses, sweet Tibullus, shall be spoken.
And Gallus shall be known from east to west;
So shall Lycoris whom he lovèd best.
Therefore when flint and iron wear away,
Verse is immortal, and shall ne'er decay.
To verse let kings give place, and kingly shows,
And banks o'er which gold-bearing Tagus flows.
Let base-conceited wits admire vile things,
Fair Phoebus lead me to the Muses' springs.
And my head be with quivering myrtle wound,
And in sad lovers' heads let me be found.
The living, not the dead, can envy bite,
For after death all men receive their right.
Then though death rakes my bones in funeral fire,
I'll live, and as he pulls me down mount higher.

The couplet in its context expresses just the same ambition and dedication of himself as a poet. Shakespeare had not been to a university,
but he was hungry for knowledge and for fame; he aspired to be a
learned and a sophisticated poet, and he staked his claim. He was
already a successful theatrical writer. It follows from his sonnet to
Florio that it was probably Florio who introduced him to Southampton. We shall return to that story.

The Hathaway sonnet, 'Those lips that love's own hand did make',
is in tetrameters, which make it unusual. If it really is about Mrs
Shakespeare it casts an interesting and amusing light on their relationship, but in terms of biography and occasion it might mean anything or nothing. This poem (145) is such a trifle, and its metre is so
out of step with the other sonnets, that one is free to regard it as a

scrap of Shakespeare's apprentice poetry that survived by chance, an occasional poem, a piece of playfulness.

The sonnet 'Not mine own fears' (107) is more powerful, but the attempts of some scholars to tie it to the defeat of the Armada, making it early, and of others to 1603, making it late, are without foundation. I take its common-sense meaning to be this: Neither my own fear nor the cosmic prophecies of nature can set a limit to my love. Eclipses pass, auguries are false, the uncertain thing happens, the threat of war disappears. Now in this time of healing my love looks fresh and overcomes death, because I live in these verses and so shall you. 'Tyrants' crests and tombs of brass' cannot possibly refer to Queen Elizabeth; balm means healing as it does in Gilead, the plague seems to be over. 'My love looks fresh' cannot refer to Lord Southampton's complexion after three years in the Tower of London under sentence of death, locked up in a dark room with a cat.

The question of Southampton comes before the question of the dedication of the sonnets, which I take to be deliberately enigmatic. We were meant to be kept guessing about that, as we have been. But the person to whom the first sonnets in the collection were written certainly knew who he was, and so it appears did his family and friends. He was a young man of noble lineage who had to be persuaded to marry. The striking coincidence of phrases between sonnet 26 and the dedication to *The Rape of Lucrece* makes it virtually certain that he was Southampton, who fits in every way, as no other person does.[3] The crisis about his refusal to marry began when he was seventeen. His father was dead and he was a ward of Lord Burghley, who wanted him to marry Lord Burghley's grand-daughter. Southampton was extremely rich and eligible. His mother favoured this marriage but he refused it. At the age of twenty-one he came into his money, though he had to pay vast fines and penalties. At that time he built his father's and his grandfather's monument in Titchfield Church, on which he had himself represented with his family arms impaling the arms of a bride, but the bride's side of the shield is blank, unpainted stone. There could be no clearer way of declaring that the crisis over his marriage was still going on. When it began he was sent a nasty Latin poem about Narcissus by Lord Burghley's secretary. The sonnets were an alternative and more comforting approach, Shakespeare being a kinder man. They mention a period of three years of friendship, which the Titchfield monument confirms.

It appears from this small group of the sonnets that having begun by writing a number, Shakespeare then let time pass so that he had to excuse himself for idleness and then write more. Is this fantasy or biography? Are the quarrels and reconciliations real? The sonnets are about love, but a love with more than one aspect. Love is slightly contaminated by literature, but a literature which admittedly comments with some daring on life. 'Such force and virtue hath an amorous look.... Who ever loved that loved not at first sight?' (Marlowe, *Hero and Leander*). Are the poems about neo-Platonic, sublimated love, the kind of *eros* that Socrates discusses in Plato's Symposium?[4] They are not inhuman: love is a ladder that can be climbed upwards or downwards, but the word immortality hints at a secular version of religion, a God that is not in the hands of the Church, beyond the doctrine set out by Sir Thomas Browne in *Hydriotaphia*, or more extreme, an unorthodox, private, poet's and lover's religion, drawing on the unorthodoxies of the Italian Renaissance and of Sir Walter Raleigh. 'There is nothing strictly immortal,' says Sir T. Browne,

> but immortality; whatever hath no beginning may be confident of no end.... But the sufficiency of Christian Immortality frustrates all earthly glory, and the quality of either state after death, makes a folly of posthumous memory. God who can only destroy our souls, and hath assured our resurrection, either of our bodies or names hath directly promised no duration. Wherein there is so much of chance that the boldest expectations have found unhappy frustration; and to hold long subsistence, seems but a scape in oblivion. But man is a noble animal, splendid in ashes, and pompous in the grave.... Life is a pure flame, and we live by an invisible sun within us.

The only one of the sonnets that comes close to this kind of Christian humanism is 146, 'Poor soul the centre of my sinful earth'.[5]

This is not set in a position of climax. It comes after the 'hate away she threw' poem, at a point where the Dark Lady sonnets have degenerated into a miscellany. It is like a versified sermon. After it come sonnets about love as a fever and passion as a blindness. It looks as if Shakespeare has deliberately assembled many kinds of love and many reactions to it, including repentance and the longing for death, but immortality in love is the deep theme of the sonnets: an earthly immortality through the power of verse to transmit beauty, a refusal to die, a defiance of death and age.[6] At the centre of every sonnet lies a paradox; sonnets are versified paradoxes, they contradict common sense and refuse worldly values. We are moved by them today as the old are moved by the young, but they were first addressed to a very young man. I take even the Dark Lady sonnets to be intended not for her eyes but for his.

The first sonnet of Shakespeare's book is a realistic statement of the theme, its paradoxes are about wasting by hoarding, and eating what is due to the world by being eaten by the grave.

> From fairest creatures we desire increase,
> That thereby beauty's rose might never die,
> But as the riper should by time decrease
> His tender heir might bear his memory.

The second sonnet is clearer still; in the third he remembers Southampton's mother: 'Thou art thy mother's glass, and she in thee Calls back the lovely April of her prime.' Since Southampton's mother and father were married in 1565 when Shakespeare was an infant in arms, he can hardly have remembered the lovely April of her prime, but he may have heard of it, and she may have been paying for this early series of poems, though she will not have liked what followed. The first strange note is in the tenth poem, 'Make thee another self for love of me.' In the thirteenth, Southampton is 'Love' and 'Dear my love'. Shakespeare has stepped into his role. The poems may still be formal variations, however wonderfully executed, but his role is to write as an intimate friend and lover. He speaks of his 'barren rhyme' and his 'pupil pen', thinks of his 'papers yellow'd with their age', and begs Southampton to outdo him and to redeem his verses by getting children. Then, in the first of the great and best-known sonnets (18), the power and the dignity of poetry take over, and Southampton must be content to live by that.

The handful of poems that follows are all astonishing: they celebrate but they incarnate the pride of poetry and the confidence of its worth, which I take to be Shakespeare's most important quality as a young man. There is no other example in Elizabethan society of a poet placing himself on equal terms in love with an earl. Nashe is knowing, Jonson is insinuating, but nothing comes anywhere near this. I think Shakespeare's ideas of poetry and love go back through Chaucer and Gower to medieval courtly convention; he has no roots in ordinary social practice. He was drunk with poetry and the poetic idea of love. In his own century, he could have found examples in French, but not in English. (See Appendix 2.) He was also the only Elizabethan poet of his generation and kind who rose above a bohemian way of life: his dream came true because the Earl of Southampton made it come true. The Elizabethan aristocracy were brought up to love and to respect poetry, and many of them wrote it: like Wyatt and Surrey in an earlier generation, Raleigh and Greville are important English poets; John Donne, George Herbert and Robert Southwell were gentlemen by birth as well as priests and poets by profession. All the same, Shakespeare in his relation with Southampton is conscious of standing on a dizzy pinnacle. His excitement is real, you cannot mistake it; this is not a literary game or a courtly persuasion. He often suggests in his plays, and the writer of *Edward III* says of him, quoting one of the sonnets to Southampton, that sonnet writers are false: one person may write a sonnet for another to use. That is not true of Shakespeare's greatest sonnets. In them reality has taken over. Our problem is that we cannot tell where the reality starts or finishes, and the same may be said of the soul, and of the self, or wherever else we discover the roots of our language.

For me it was an act of great daring to lecture on these poems. They are not meant for lecturing or for learned commentaries. They are so simple, so beautiful; there is so little to add to what is obvious about them, and the unknown factors are rather unknowable. Was this great love sequence partly a fiction, partly a private game? It is far easier not to answer, but if one must answer, then: yes. The poem about the gift of a notebook is quite conventional, like a rhyme on a Christmas card if one wrote it oneself, observing the conventions. Were Horace's poems about women and boys with Greek names real? Some of them ring true. They all have elements of the experience of life, but the least real and most conventional are the contemptuous and terrible poems about women who had hurt him. I think the same may be said of Shakespeare's nastiest sonnets to the Dark Lady, but of course without knowing his life independently of his poetry, we can never absolutely determine where reality begins and ends in the sonnets. It is not possible to disentangle the experience from the poetry, and all the more impossible because we recognize as experience of life little more than we experience ourselves, though I hope that art extends our experience in some way.

Let us dispose of one problem at least: that of 'Mr. W. H. the only begetter of these ensuing sonnets'. Southampton's mother married William Harvey as her third husband. When she died he married again, and that is when the sonnets were printed. It looks highly likely that the publisher, Thomas Thorpe, thought they were addressed to Harvey. But it remains possible, though rather an outside possibility, that 'begetter' might mean the person who got hold of the manuscript, the getter. Dekker uses the word begetter in that sense, of a friend at court begetting the reversion of the office of Master of the Revels. Sir Sidney Lee, in his *Life of Shakespeare*, favoured an obscure theological publisher called William Hall as the getter of the manuscript in that sense. But Thomas Thorpe himself was far closer to the circle of Shakespeare's friends than William Hall, so that horse is a non-starter.

If begetter means getter, I would like to propose William Hole, the first English engraver of music. He engraved maps for Camden in 1607 and portraits of half a dozen friends of Shakespeare at just the right period, including Drayton, a close friend. Shakespeare is supposed to have died the morning after getting drunk with Drayton; his son-in-law was Drayton's doctor. William Hole acted from 1618 on as chief engraver of the mint 'in the Tower of London and elsewhere', the Cuneator, engraver of the King's coinage, his ensigns and arms and seals. Hugh Holland wrote a complimentary poem in *Parthenia* (1611), works for the virginals by William Byrd, John Bull and Orlando Gibbons, an extremely rare book of which Bodley has a copy; the poem is dedicated to 'his worthy friend W. H. and his triumviri of music'. Hugh Holland knew Shakespeare, and contributed another complimentary poem to the first folio. My only reason for not making more of William Hole is that I believe the enigmatic and lamentable dedication imposed on Shakespeare's sonnets when they were first printed in 1609 is intended to refer in a riddling manner to Harvey. The dedication is a piece of homosexual knowingness, a piece of voyeurism about the secret subculture, and, like most gossip of that kind, wrong.

There is something physical, as impossible to fake as seasickness, about Shakespeare's sonnets of disgust and self-disgust. There is something just as physically genuine about his gaiety and high spirits. But, in spite of the many hints he drops, he is not giving a fully continuous account of a relationship, a complete story, whether autobiography or fiction. And if not, then deliberately not. The series of 125 sonnets and an envoi is meant to show many aspects of a relationship but not to tell a story. Realistic fiction and realistic autobiography had not yet been invented, though Horace in Latin and much personal poetry is Italian and French were available influences.[7] Shakespeare had read Latin and loved Latin poetry, because he quotes it; Marlowe translated it in sufficiently clear terms for his version of Ovid's *Amores*, when it reaches print long after his death, to be burnt by order of the Bishop of London. But no accumulation of literary sources can explain away the breath of life that blows here and there through Shakespeare's sonnets.

He inherited the lesson that Giordano Bruno taught to Philip Sidney when he visited England in 1583–5, that a sonnet can be a kind of code, a secret but full expression of one's inmost feelings. For Bruno, the feelings likeliest to be dangerous are unorthodox and mystical views about God. If Shakespeare adapted that kind of hermetic poetry to love, a long tradition of Renaissance poetry in more than one language might have suggested the adaptation. But Shakespeare was particularly delicate. To see this one has only to compare his sonnet to the young man with the knowing obscenity of Thomas Nashe, in poems dedicated to the same Earl of Southampton, possibly in the same year.[8] I do not deny that on other subjects in *Summer's Last Will and Testament* (1593) Nashe is one of the greatest poets of the greatest age of poetry in English. In his 'Choice of Valentines', the poet tells of a visit to the brothel in search of his lost love. The verse is a spirited parody of Chaucer. Elizabethan imitations of Chaucer are often hard to spot (Spenser's for example) because the poets were not clear how Chaucer's verses scan. In the sonnet (20) about Southampton as a boy–girl or a girl–boy, Shakespeare makes it clear what kind of love he is talking about, but clearer still that this is sublimated, unconsummated love.

He wants to write about love itself, he is in love with love, but his belief and his instinct are that love with women must (except under conditions of restrictive chivalry, such as prevail in The Two Gentlemen of Verona) be consummated; love of another young man or boy can and indeed must be sublimated. It is therefore love in a purer form. Socrates would have understood this Renaissance point of view. The sonnets are not about *la vice anglaise*. The sonnets of disgust and self-disgust are addressed to the Dark Lady, so is the sonnet of comic obscenity, because without consummated love there would be no room for them, and they are part of the spectrum of love, or the ladder of *eros*, which Shakespeare desires to reveal. Shakespeare may never have had a mistress for all we know, but Southampton was interested in everything. If the Dark Lady refers to anyone real, then I am sure that A. L. Rowse has found the right person, but I find myself reluctant to take her literally; I remain agnostic.

To Shakespeare the sonnet is a jack-in-the-box of paradox and passion, but what we call sexuality, for which I think he had no word but gender, was to him an infinite nest of Chinese boxes: one inside the next. It is not uncommon in his plays for a boy actor playing a girl character to play her at some point disguised as a boy pretending to be a girl. I think he thought the mystery of gender was fathomless and extremely amusing. But his sonnets are an exercise of wit, and their subject is seldom gender, rather love. In the Dark Lady sonnets the wit cooled the passion in the course of writing. His moral sonnet against lust is oddly impersonal compared to the impassioned sonnets of social regret that he addressed directly to Lord Southampton: consider 129 for example, 'The expense of spirit in a waste of shame'.

It was not only male chauvinism in the regulation of Elizabethan society that excluded women from serious consideration in Shakespeare's sonnets. Nor was it that atmosphere of tense falsity generated by Queen Elizabeth, all of whose favourite young noblemen were supposed to be in love with the Queen alone, with the result that they were constantly going to prison for getting the ladies in waiting pregnant: Southampton did, so did Raleigh, so did Pembroke. It was the idealization of the intensity of love itself, love that transcended even mutual lovers. I discussed 'The Phoenix and the Turtle' in an earlier lecture. This ideal of love as a thing in itself, love independent of a shared life, is an astonishing human phenomenon. It derives from a strange and heady compound of ancient philosophy, Christian religion, medieval rules of behaviour, and art as the supreme or the only comfort in life. Did Shakespeare (let alone Mrs Shakespeare) believe in all that? I greatly doubt it, on the common-sense evidence of the first ten sonnets, and of the undoubted fact that in his plays he became the greatest poet of women's love the world had ever known. But in the sonnets, the ideal of love in itself has intertwined with the ideal power of poetry to live for ever, as it did in the sonnets of Ronsard.[9]

Ronsard is an interesting case, because his ideal loves were women. But Ronsard was not only Catholic; I think he was inhibited from marriage by being legally speaking a clergyman. A normal poet who writes love poetry of the most intense power, subtle, sensuous and memorable poetry, confined within itself as the sonnet is confined and yet pungently memorable, is either suggesting a seduction or making a proposal of marriage. Otherwise he makes himself ridiculous. Yet after Drayton had written 'Since there's no help, come let us kiss and part' to his *Idea*, with many more amorous sonnets, he used to stay with her and her husband every summer as an unamorous guest at Clifford Chambers. In the dedication of his sonnets he denies that they are passionate writings:

> My verse is the true image of my mind,
> Ever in motion, still desiring change.

To be perfect, I fear that sonnets have to be self-confined, their reality has to be rendered unfulfillable by some external circumstance which all likely readers know. This of course means that they have to be unreal. But one notices that the circulation of most of Shakespeare's was restricted. Francis Meres in 1598[10] refers to 'Mr. Shakespeare's sugared sonnets circulated among his private friends', and yet only twelve Shakespeare sonnets have been recorded in any private manuscript or miscellany that survives, and nearly all of those were copied from the book published in 1609. The second edition of that had to wait until 1640, an incomplete and bowdlerized version, based perhaps on an incomplete and bowdlerized manuscript. (Nashe's obscene verses to Southampton were not printed at all until the nineteenth century; they survive in only two manuscripts.) Louise Labé was a near-contemporary woman writer of sonnets; she can write with the freedom of Catullus, whom she adapts, but I take it the fact of her being a woman made that a literary exercise, rather than a declaration of intention.[11] If a sonnet is set to music, as Daniel's were by his brother and some of Shakespeare's were, that is another implicit barrier against real life. Campion's magnificent song, 'My sweetest Lesbia let us live and love',[12] was doubly defended by reference to the classics and by the privileged status of songs.

Exceptions exist, but Shakespeare favours the form of sonnet with three four-line stanzas, rhyming abab, cdcd, efef, concluding in a couplet.[13] It is usually in the couplet that the bird flies free, more excitingly than it would with an octet followed by a sextet.[14] Even in the two forms of the limerick, with and without the first line repeated as the last, the form does a lot to determine the kind of message by pre-opting its rhythmic and musical nature. Shakespeare varies the use he makes of his chosen form in several ways. It is instructive to watch where he puts his full stops; there are single-sentence sonnets, five-sentence sonnets, and sonnets with a full stop in mid-line. It is even more instructive to observe the variety of his syntax, each syntactic form a rhythm of its own, and yet all controlled within the unbroken rhythmic form of the fourteen lines. For practical purposes its possible permutations in a given language are infinite. But it is meaning, modulating the rhythms of syntax, that gives the great sonnets their force, and it is by the force of meaning, dammed up into the closure of the final couplet, that the bird flies free, as in sonnet 94 (cf. 87).

The last five or six syllables of the final couplet are quite often separated with a comma or a semi-colon, throwing a slow, heavy emphasis on the closure. In some ways this is like the classical elegiac couplet as that is used in epigrams and epitaphs: but in Shakespeare's usage the mid-line stop is not part of the metrical system, it is in descant with it. The descant of syntax with the metronome of metre is part of the fundamental nature of poetry, and the best poets most exploit it. Even the Greek elegiac couplet has minor syntactic stops where the metre would not expect them: the famous epitaph for the dead at Thermopylae for example owes its noble closure to this device. Some of the greatest poetry gives the impression of being verse only by the skin of its teeth, yet it is perfect verse: the impression arises from the overriding, genuine rhythm of syntax, the force of meaning. In other words, in order to be a poet, to be named in a list with Shakespeare at its head, you have to have something to say, and something that demands a classic statement. Sonnet 81 has subsidiary syntactic stops in both lines of the final couplet. This has another rhythmic life, a very much sadder cadence. Technically speaking, these differences are what the sonnets were written to embody.

Sonnet 73 is a classical use of the form. It consists of a single sentence, with almost a stop at the end of each stanza,[15] but then the sentence revives and fades again each time in a similar way, the rhymes in the third stanza (fire, lie, expire, by) being particularly close, and the first line of the final couplet having a comma in mid-line and another at the end, flinging the final line into relief, like a long, expiring stroke of the strings of a violin. The entire sonnet shows the effect: 'That time of year thou mayst in me behold'.

The poems of Sidney, Spenser and Shakespeare mark the triumph of what C. S. Lewis calls the golden line in English, a line with an origin in the sound of foreign and above all in Latin poetry. One would not know from Shakespeare's sonnets that it was not a native English invention. Shakespeare's fondness for Chaucer is at least equally important from this point of view, with his country background and provincial education. The imagery of his early poetry has an extreme vividness that matches the energy of his syntax, an energy attained only in the sonnets, but the particular Englishness of his images is only intermittent. 'That time of year', the yellow leaves, the sunset and the dying fire, might be anywhere in Europe, unless the 'Bare ruin'd choirs' convey the subliminal message of English monastic ruins. That is an important point, because the sonnets work not exactly by what they say, but by their quasi-musical phrasing, and by those thoughts and feelings and experiences of life that we are subliminally invited to bring to them.[16] This is a case of poetry that arises in the mind of the reader, in the solitary repetition of the verses.

They are chamber music, the opposite of dramatic poetry. They are not intended for a single, continuous, unlingering performance. The idea of such a poetry may well arise from the slow and necessary pondering of foreign or of Latin poetry as one translates it.

Shakespeare's two Cupid and Venus sonnets based on the Palatine Anthology have a crisp charm,[17] but they tell us little of Shakespeare as a translator; they are adaptations, not immediate versions of the Greek. In fact they depart so far from it that no one now really knows what text Shakespeare had to work on, or in what language; it has probably perished. He was certainly interested in foreign and in ancient styles. His parody of the style and characteristic metre of Gower in *Pericles* is a polished performance, both comic and affectionate. His summary of the plot of *The Rape of Lucrece* is a brilliant pastiche of the prose style of Livy, but not a translation of Livy. The epitaph on the grave of Timon of Athens is a pastiche of the style of such epitaphs in North's *Plutarch* and elsewhere. He imitates the style of Warwick's tomb inscription at Rouen in *Henry VI*. The song 'Take O take those lips away' is said to be adapted from a Renaissance Latin poem, though the adaptation is not at all close, and I doubt it. Jan Kott pointed out a constant referring to Virgil's *Aeneid* in *The Tempest*. The question Shakespeare asks himself throughout his sonnets – what is to be said by the lover in this or that situation of love, what can wit and paradox make of it? – seems to me to arise from Ovid's *Heroides*, the love letters of legendary women, which he certainly knew. But I assume it was little more than the idea, the conception of amatory variation in poetry, that came from Ovid. The immortality of poetry, of the poet and therefore of his subject surely comes from Latin poetry, from Ovid and from Horace. Many things about Shakespeare, and about the 350 years of poetry between his death in 1616 and 1966, can be understood through the grammar school curriculum and the ambitions it generated.

Shakespeare seems to grow old in his sonnets, but if he was a bookish twenty-seven to thirty years old, addressing a boy or a very young man, the feeling is not implausible. He makes it plain to Southampton that he thinks forty years old means being extremely old and ugly and at sixty one would be dead. He himself died in his very early fifties. Although at one point he seems so confident in love, and so excited by its permanence, he does reveal elsewhere that he knows this affair cannot last. It is impossible after all that he could believe in the permanent attachment of Lord Southampton exclusively to one poet, let alone one admiring, elder male lover who was not even a member of his household. Here again we are thrust back on to the unknowable frontier between playacting and genuine passion, between playacting that becomes passionate and a passionate truth expressed in gentle playacting.

In the sonnets, Shakespeare already has the crispness of impression and something of the interplay of formal clang and informal speech that mark his great setpieces in the theatre. He conveys the process of thought, the time it takes to think and to speak. But every sonnet, even when he links them, is itself alone, a single device from beginning to end, one idea. The sonnet as a form is essentially self-echoing and self-contained. The themes are capable of expansion as well as variation: therefore the first statement of an important theme in the plays is sometimes in a sonnet. 'Tired with all these for restful death I cry' recurs not only in *Hamlet*, but in a whole series of satiric characters and setpieces of satiric poetry, from the melancholy Jacques in *As You Like It* to *Timon of Athens*, Shakespeare's full and final statement as a satirist. One might have thought that in those plays Shakespeare was influenced by a younger generation of satiric poets such as Marston and Ben Jonson, but his reproaches against the world he knew are quite fully listed in the sonnets at what I take to be a much earlier period of his career as a writer. His ability to make classic, impersonal statements, which are still felt as well as thought to be universal, and personal to ourselves, into the mere warmth of his breath and voice dates from the sonnets. The ghost of the sonnet persisted in his plays to the end. The speech of about fourteen lines that echoes itself and ends formally is one of his favourite and most useful instruments. His sense of time and of the tragedy and vanity of time, imitated in the steady fall of his verses, and even in the overall rhythm of individual plays like *Richard II* and *Macbeth*, is first established in his sonnets.

> Like as the waves make toward the pebbled shore,
> So do our minutes hasten to their end;
> Each changing place with that which goes before
> In sequent toil all forwards do contend.
> Nativity, once in the main of light,
> Crawls to maturity, wherewith being crown'd,
> Crooked eclipses gainst his glory fight,
> And time that gave doth now his gift confound. . . .

This sonnet is a case in which the momentum of the early stanzas is so powerful that the final couplet is overshadowed, one can hardly believe what it says. There are other sonnets in which it hardly needs saying, because the momentum is single from the first line to the last, overriding all changes of rhyme and all full stops until the last. The most obvious example is one that recalls and adapts the last poem of the third book of Horace's odes, the climax that is the signature of those three books: 'Exegi monumentum aere perennius' (Sonnet 55).[18] Shakespeare has cut out the signature and the personal part of the boast. Horace names himself and his birthplace, which in a signature he was bound to do, but in Shakespeare's poem the position of honour goes to Southampton, though he is not of course named. He is never named. He is so idealized that a personal name would be inappropriate.

Katherine Duncan-Jones has put a strong case for the proposition that Shakespeare had some hand in the publication of his own sonnets in 1609. I have some reservations about the possibility she undoubtedly opens of thinking so, but no substantial argument against it. Whatever happened in 1609, the prophecy of immortality has come true, and Shakespeare knew it would come true when he wrote it. That was early in the series; even if the series went on longer than I believe, this sonnet recalls the mood of the young Shakespeare at the time when Richard Field, his old friend from Stratford, first printed *Venus and Adonis*. His confidence in the staying power of his verse was astounding, and justified. Whether his confidence in love was justified, readers must judge for themselves according to their experience of life. Daniel in a sonnet to Delia makes the boastful assertion,

> Though th'error of my youth they shall discover,
> Suffice they shew I liv'd and was thy lover.

The claim was untrue and the implied boast of the future was unjustified.

What happened to all these people? Shakespeare was out of London when the sonnets were published in 1609. An edition of 'The Amours of J. D. and sonnets of W. S.' had been projected nearly ten years before, but it never appeared. Does that mean Donne and Shakespeare, and was the publication suppressed? After 1609 no harm came to Shakespeare. He was then writing his last comedies; then he retired to Stratford, and there he died. Thomas Thorpe, the publisher of the sonnets, was a renegade Catholic and a government spy against his fellow Catholics. He died in the royal almshouses at Ewelme, and was forgotten. Lord Southampton went to prison for his stupid part in Essex's rebellion, but he came out of the Tower when the Queen died in 1603, settled down, became respectable, gave a cartload of theological books to his old Cambridge college, St John's, and begot legitimate children. His portrait was painted more often than that of any other contemporary nobleman; his looks were remarkable. The Princess of Wales is his direct lineal descendant. Samuel Daniel mouldered into the condition of a neglected poet. He ran the same races with Shakespeare for esteem for fifteen years; in 1599 he is supposed to have been Poet Laureate, but in the next reign he was only a gentleman usher of the Queen's privy chamber, complaining of the neglect of his poetry that has increased ever since. He took to court masques, and then to prose, and that was the end of him. And yet a thorough, complete study of Daniel's losing races with Shakespeare might throw light on many things.

APPENDIX 1

from The Romanesque Renaissance

It is in the conception of love that this rejection of force reaches its fulfilment. In Languedoc, chivalrous love was the same thing as Greek love, although this identity is masked by the very different rôle played by woman. But it was not contempt for woman that led the Greeks to honour love between men, which to-day is something base and vile. They equally honoured love between women, as is seen in Plato's *Banquet* and in the example of Sappho. What they were thus honouring was nothing other than impossible love. Consequently, it was nothing other than chastity. Owing to the too great licence of manners, there was practically no obstacle to sexual indulgence between men and women, whereas every well-ordered soul was inhibited by shame from contemplating an indulgence which the Greeks themselves qualified as un-natural. When Christianity and the high purity of manners introduced by the Germanic peoples had placed between man and woman that barrier which was lacking in Greece, they became for one another objects of Platonic love. The sacred tie of marriage was an obstacle equivalent to that provided by identity of sex. The authentic troubadours had no more taste for adultery than Sappho and Socrates for vice; what they aspired to was impossible love. To-day, we can only think of Platonic love in the form of chivalrous love; but indeed it is the same love.

The essence of this love is expressed in some marvellous lines of *The Banquet*:

> The most important point is that in his dealing with gods and men Love never inflicts any injustice nor suffers one. For whatever he may suffer, it is not because he is forced, since force never touches Love. And when he is active he never employs it; for everyone willingly obeys Love in everything.

144

According to the laws of the royal city, when consent is freely granted by both parties it is just.

Everything that is subjected to the contact of force is defiled, whatever the contact. To strike or to be struck is one and the same defilement. The chill of steel is equally mortal at the hilt and at the point. Whatever is exposed to the contact of force is liable to degradation. Everything in the world is exposed to the contact of force, with only one single exception, which is love. Not natural love, like that of Phaedra or Arnolphe, which is slavery and tends to constrain; but supernatural love, which in its truth goes directly to God and descends again directly, united with the love God bears towards his creation; which always goes directly or indirectly to the divine.

In chivalrous love, the object was a human being; but it is not covetousness. It is simply a patient attention towards the loved person and an appeal for that person's consent. The word *merci* by which the troubadours designated this consent is very close to the notion of grace. Such a love, in its plenitude, is the love of God through the person loved. In this land, as in Greece, human love was one of the bridges between man and God.

In Romanesque art there shines the same inspiration. The architecture, although it borrowed a form from Rome, has no regard for power and force, but solely for balance; whereas there is a certain taint of power and pride in the thrust of Gothic spires and lofty pointed arches. The Romanesque church is suspended like a balance around its point of equilibrium, a point which is real although there is nothing to show where it is. This is what is needed to enclose that cross which was a balance on which Christ's body counter-balanced the universe. The sculptured figures are never people; they never play a rôle; they are not aware they are being looked at. Their pose is dictated solely by feeling and architectural proportion. Their awkwardness is a naked-ness. Gregorian chant slowly rises until, at the moment when it seems to be gaining assurance, the ascending movement is broken off and goes down; the ascending movement is always conditioned by the descending. The source of all this art is grace.

Simone Weil

APPENDIX 2

I Love the Laurel Green
(after Étienne Jodelle)

I love the laurel green, whose verdant flame
Burns its bright victory on the winter day,
Calls to eternity its happy name
And neither death nor time shall wear away.

I love the holly tree with branches keen,
Each leaflet fringed with daggers sharp and small.

I love the ivy, too, winding its green,
Its ardent stem about the oak, the wall.

I love these three, whose living green and true
Is as unfailing as my love for you
Always by night and day whom I adore.

Yet the green wound that stays within me more
Is ever greener than these three shall be:
Laurel and ivy and the holly tree.

Charles Causley[19]

APPENDIX 3

Edward FitzGerald in a letter to W. A. Wright on 16 May 1870[20] discusses a sonnet by Tusser as the origin of Shakespeare's Sonnet 104. (Tusser is supposed to have died about 1580.)

Sev'n times hath Janus tane New Year by hand;
  Sev'n times hath blust'ring March blown forth his power
To drive out April Buds by Sea and Land,
  For minion May to deck most trim with flower.
Sev'n times hath temperate Ver like pageant played,
  And pleasant Aestas eke his flowers told;
Sev'n times Autumnus heat hath been delay'd
  With Hyems' boisterous blasts and bitter cold.
Sev'n times the thirteen Moons have changed hue;
  Sev'n times that Sun his course has gone about;
Sev'n times each bird her Nest hath built anew;
  Since first time you to serve I choosed out.
Still yours I am though thus the time hath past,
  And trust to be so long as time shall last.

Milton's Early Verse

This lecture is about Milton as a self-made poet, who slowly at first but with energy and gathering speed finds his own way, always increasing his distance from other poets. Milton wrote his first thrilling lines at the age of fifteen, in verse adaptations of the Psalms. The lines were religious, but almost too playful to be called pious, and they were derivative, from the Bible and from Sylvester's version of Du Bartas, yet with touches of sparkling originality.[1]

> They saw the troubled sea, that shivering fled,
> And sought to hide his froth-becurled head
> Low in the earth....[2]

Or again:

> And caused the golden-tressed sun,
> All the day long his course to run,...
>
> The horned moon to shine by night.
> Amongst her spangled sisters bright.[3]

It sounds as if Milton has been reading Shakespeare, and Milton was born in 1608, and these verses date from 1624; he was too young for the theatre in Shakespeare's lifetime, and the first folio of Shakespeare's plays came out in 1623. To the generation that was young then, Shakespeare's works were fresh and fascinating; any study of English poetry in the early seventeenth century must take Shakespeare's liberating influence into account.[4] That influence seems to have increased for a time after his death, but there were others, and in the mind of any writer the swirls and eddies of memory and imagination are hard to analyse. Still, it is interesting to see the young Milton, in poems that are hardly more than school exercises, however brilliant, taking part in that free movement of transfiguring the Bible

147

in English of which the Authorized Version of 1611 is only the sober spearhead.

My thesis is that poetry is always in some sense a learned art. It cannot be taught, but it has to be learnt. Milton like all poets was self-taught, in spite of St Paul's School and the University of Cambridge. Because we have so many of his juvenilia, we can trace the process. It has its mere exercises but it has its seriousness. It is a parable of how a young poet should behave today. Milton is sportive, but with a graceful awkwardness, an exquisite heaviness, like a baroque dolphin. He puts more of himself into it than other young poets. The same liberated glee, the same sunlight of Shakespeare, shows in his early Latin verses, which were certainly school exercises, as in his English verses. It may well be that Ovid transformed Christopher Marlowe in his translation of the *Amores*, and so liberated Shakespeare's English poetry: what liberated Milton in Latin as in English is as much Shakespearean as Ovidian, to our ears.

> Rise up, arise, shake away your light sleeps,
> the light is eastern, spring from your hot beds,
> the cock crows wake, that winged herald is
> to the new sun and shall our task appoint.

> Surge, age surge, leves, iam convenit, excute somnos,
>   Lux oritur, tepidi fulcra relinque tori
> Iam canit excubitor gallus praenuntius ales
>   Solis et invigilans ad sua quemque vocat.[5]

Milton was still about fifteen. His Latin verses were as remarkable at that age as his English verses were, and in much the same way. I am unable to distinguish the same personal tone in his Greek verse exercises, but then very little classical Greek verse of genuine merit has been written in modern times. Good, or at least interesting Latin verse by English poets is commoner than one would expect. George Herbert is as individual in Latin verse as Milton is. A substantial part of Milton's early self-expression as a poet was in Latin. He did not stop at school exercises. I believe he found his voice as an English poet partly through his Latin verse. The only phrase Tennyson remembered from school was *desilientis aquae*, and its music haunted his poetry.[6] Milton was haunted by the sound of his own poetry in Latin. In his mature style, F. T. Prince has demonstrated beyond doubt that Italian poetry was a crucial influence, but in the earlier, purer style I believe Latin was a vital element. I think the attentive and faultless play of sound and image in 'Soft silken primrose fading timelessly' and in 'Down he descended from his snow-soft chair'[7] owe as much to analysis of the sound-combinations of Ovid as they do to the practice of Spenser and of Shakespeare. Even if that is not so, his best Latin poems are worth attention for their own sake.

To take the trivial beginnings of an important matter, Milton's mythology, which meant so much to him and still communicates an excitement by its very strangeness, has roots in his education. It is typical of Milton that in schoolboy elegiacs he refers to Venus as Zephyritis: 'Ecce novo campos Zephyritis gramine vestit' ('Now Venus dresses meadows with new grass'). The word Zephyritis is not just an affected piece of obscurity. Milton is what Walter de la Mare called a lively reader, he imagines very fully, he goes beyond his author. He must have found Zephyritis in a dictionary, where it was a piece of freakish learning, or else he read it in Catullus. The title Zephyritis comes from the temple of Queen Arsinoe on the promontory of Zephyritis. Kallimachos wrote about her and Catullus translated Kallimachos: in that poem the west wind Zephyrus, the one who blows in Botticelli's *Primavera*, attends on the deified Queen. I tell this story as a curiosity, but observe how Milton transforms the word. Out of a jejune royal compliment he takes a simple element in his early summer morning. The west wind dresses meadows in new grass. His Latin is more innocent and more robust than its models.

The besetting sin of classical mythology in later poetry is that it becomes a mere ornament frivolously applied, without depth or meaning. But by his seventeenth year Milton was a serious poet in English: his imagery is entertaining, surprising, even delicious, but the intention of the poem he wrote his mother, 'On the Death of a Fair Infant Dying of a Cough', was deadly serious. It was to console her for a child that died before Milton was born, and was buried unbaptized. Milton maintains in the climax of his poem, against the orthodox belief of Christians in his day, that the dead child went to heaven.[8] In the last line he promises immortal fame to the name of Milton. He had found a voice and knew he had found it. One might expect that from that time on he would devote himself to English poetry, being conscious of his own seriousness, and conscious of having written a great poem. On the contrary, it was now that he settled to serious attempts at original poetry in Latin.

Artifice can be serious. Devices may be seriously intended whether the artist has made them his second nature or controls them with a cooler intelligence. And most of the devices of language are inherited:

they are social gestures learnt in childhood and somewhat intuitively used. A poet in the course of self-education seeks a wider range and a sureness of tone: both a consistency and a variation of texture. Milton in his first Latin elegy to his schoolfriend Charles Diodati touches for the first time on themes we know better in English in 'L'Allegro' and 'Il Penseroso', where he mingles them with deliberate imitations of Shakespeare and of Virgil's *Eclogues*. It was apparently spring of 1626, about the end of Milton's first year at Cambridge, and he addressed his poem to Chester, where his friend was spending the Oxford Easter vacation. He speaks of London and the theatre, and of country pleasures including girls. He shows off in an intimate way, as young people do. Some of his shorter, minor verses are awkward enough, but the first elegy to Diodati is a smoothly executed, a brilliantly full expression of adolescence. The 'shady roof of branching elm star-proof' in the 'Arcades'[9] and the 'Dancing in the chequered shade' in 'L'Allegro'[10] have their origin in the elm groves of the Thames valley.

> Nos quoque lucus habet vicina consitus ulmo
> atque suburbani nobilis umbra loci. . . .
> I dwell within a close elm-planted grove
> of noble shadows in suburban fields.
> Often the stars breathe down their gentle fire,
> and I see virgin dances that go by.
> Oh, I see miracles of loveliness
> that could refresh old Jove's antiquity. . . .[11]

This is a pleasing poem, not a great one. Milton at seventeen was still learning the range of his instrument, and of every instrument he could master. He was still feeding back every attempt into a later attempt. There are no final statements in his years at Cambridge. The seventh elegy, written at nineteen, was no better and no worse than the first. He wrote a number of formal poems, which were exercises of a kind, on the academic dead: one in lyric verses on the Bishop of Ely, in which he complains to Death and gets consoled by a visitation from the Bishop's ghost, another in lyrics on the Vice-Chancellor, an elegy on the University Beadle, and another on Lancelot Andrewes, Bishop of Winchester, who appears to Milton in a vision dressed as a druid and applauded by angels who clap their butterfly wings.

> Beside me suddenly stood Winchester
> star-glitter glowing in his splendid face,

snow-white his clothing flowed to gilded boots
his holy head was banded with milk-white.
So dressed he came, so old, so venerable
The flowered ground shook at the happy noise.
The regiments of heaven, spotty-winged,
Blasted the heights with trumpets of triumph.
Each hails him with embraces and with song....[12]

The odd thing about these Latin exercises, which were such as all young scholars were expected to produce, is that Milton's were so extremely capable, with flashes of almost Shakespearean strangeness and freshness, and on a fuller scale than most verses of the kind. They were genuinely ambitious, and maybe what they chiefly express is the literary ambition which was their principal motive. That is another sense in which Milton was serious, and far more so than his contemporaries. These exercises could only have been written by a real poet. Milton knew it, I suppose, and they were published in later life by Milton himself. The ambition to be glorious, the ambition to be a famous poet, is closely related to the ambition to be taken seriously, which with any luck begets the personal resolution actually to be serious intellectually and morally. How is that possible within the limits of these artificial, formal exercises? The answer is probably to be found in the circumstances of *Lycidas*.

Milton was at his worst where he was most like the others. His Latin epigrams on Guy Faux and his long hexameter poem on the fifth of November are impersonal and more or less indefensible, though the fifth of November poem does contain a first sketch of hell as an infested ruin, and a buzzing of flies like the bee-buzzing of the devils in *Paradise Lost*. Cambridge in some ways was a backward period for Milton, an artificial frost; he learnt a lot, and maybe that exhausted him. Still, under the frozen ground he developed as a poet: as a man, therefore as a poet. This shows wherever he commits himself as a poet and therefore commits himself as a man. The same is true in English as in Latin. His 'Vacation Exercise' written in 1628, about the same time as the seventh elegy, which is in its way capable, is partly in Latin and partly in English. Its scheme is obscene in Latin, and pedantic and foolish in English, and Milton must have hated writing it. The English part is as bad as anything he wrote in Latin. It is like Miltonic verse churned out by a computer. He disliked the official studies at Cambridge and he hated the pedantry and coarseness of Cambridge jollifications. That fastidiousness shows in the 'Vacation Exercise'. He published the English part of it with other early work in 1673, and the Latin with a bundle of other Latin, in 1674, the year of his death.

Another sign of Milton's fastidiousness is the poems that he refused to write. He was still pouring his imagination into Latin poetry, and no Latin versifier in Cambridge could begin to compete with him. His spring elegy with the perfumed Zephyrus 'who lightly claps his wing of cinnamon' – 'Cinnamea Zephyrus leve plaudit odorifer ala'[13] – has not fluttered over anyone else. This is a Renaissance theme, it is almost a classical poem, it is not a Cambridge exercise. 'And the gods choose the forest not the sky, all groves are haunted and by private gods.'[14] But Milton was either not asked or he refused to contribute to any official collection of Latin verses for a royal occasion. These curious publications appeared in numbers both at Oxford and at Cambridge. By Milton's time they were a traditional display and highly competitive between the two universities and within each one. They were clearly intended to attract court patronage. (Cf. Appendix.)

In 1631, when Milton was twenty-two and still at Cambridge, the University Press published *Anthologia in Regis Exanthemata*, On the King's Pimples, to congratulate Charles I on a recovery from small-pox. It had a Latin verse dedication by the Vice-Chancellor, and it appears to have been organized by Ralph Winterton, a medical Fellow of King's, whose poem comes last. There were nearly eighty versifiers, including real poets like Henry More and Richard Crashaw, and a few young noblemen evidently writing under instruction on a suitably political aspect, but members of King's predominated. One of the contributors was Edward King of Christ's College, who was drowned in 1637 and became Lycidas. His contribution was severely sober and glum, and rather long. He clearly took himself seriously as a Calvinistic clergyman, and (in his way) as a poet. He was four years younger than Milton, fourteen when he entered the college in 1626, eighteen when he was made Fellow by royal mandate, the year before The King's Pimples. He was dead at twenty-five. It has been suggested that Milton wanted the fellowship that Edward King got. He can hardly have expected it, since King's father Sir John King was an official of the Crown in Northern Ireland, and Milton was middle class; he had still to find his patron. And I cannot believe that Milton would have accepted to follow George Herbert (1626) and John Donne (1615) into office in the Anglican Church.

It is worth glancing at the favoured styles of the poems on the royal pustules. They are full of terrible jokes; not even a dead language can disguise their creaking levity. For instance: 'Why palest thou, Pest, and

Pustule, why swellest thou? . . . Grows Death fastidious of plebeian gut? And seeks she now a rarer meat to cut? Gustavit Carolum, sed non deglutiit. Euge, Morbe, quid impalles? pustula, quidve tumes?'[15] Crashaw, who was about seventeen and in his first year at Pembroke, is worse in a way.

> Return O Muse our father has returned,
> With his true voice Apollo has returned:
> And his true face for there his purple lives
> and runs as lover in commingling snows. . . .[16]

As a description of the ravages of smallpox on a face, this is remarkable. Dryden wrote his contribution to the *Lachrymae Musarum* for the death of Lord Hastings (ed. R. B. 1649) when he was eighteen, at Westminster under Busby. The more startling lines of his poem had precise origins in *Exanthemata Regis*.[17] Several contributors have lines like 'O insolentes pustulae . . . Audaces papulaeque pustulaeque'. As Mr Booth of Corpus Christi put it, 'The Muse erupted where the doctor's been, In clouds of pimples on the august skin, And every pustule has a poet now. . . .'[18] Henry More wrote elegantly in Greek, a rare accomplishment, but his heart was not in it. A number of contributors seem to imitate English rather than Latin poetry: Donne maybe, and Sydney. Mostly the verses exist in a world of their own, on a neglected margin of poetry and social history. One can see why Milton despised it and why Edward King looked out of place in it. The Vice-Chancellor set the tone: 'Thy sickness is our foe: away it turns, And for thy pustules banished, incense burns.'[19]

In the same year, 1632, Milton's sixteen-line epitaph on Shakespeare was printed in the second folio edition of Shakespeare's works. He was writing sonnets, in English and in Italian, and learning from the texture of the Italian language how by analogy to produce the crispness and complexity of Latin poetry in English. He had already translated Horace in a version that reads like a sonnet too crisply compressed. He had already written the ode 'On the Morning of Christ's Nativity'. He was a great poet entering maturity. His good genius was Shakespeare and he knew it. He was like the sparrow that climbed on the eagle's back; he attained his tranquil assurance of tone by the time he was twenty-four.

> O nightingale, that on yon blooming spray
> Warblest at eve, when all the woods are still . . .
> Thy liquid notes that close the eye of day,

First heard before the shallow cuckoo's bill
portend success in love....

It is on the period of these poems of early maturity that I wish to
concentrate attention. The great London poet of the day was Ben
Jonson in the final, Shakespearean phase of his life. He died in August
1637, within four days of the drowning of Edward King. It is some-
times said to have been the news of the coming Oxford[20] publications
of *Jonsonus Virbius* in Ben Jonson's honour that provided *Justa
Eduardo King naufrago*, and its supplement called *Obsequies for
Edward King*, including *Lycidas*, as a rival effort at memorial verse
from Cambridge. But there are two poems in the *Lycidas* volume by
Henry King; one is in Latin by Edward King's brother. The other is in
English, and I suspect or believe it to be by Henry King, Canon of
Christ Church and after Milton and Shakespeare the greatest of all
English elegists, the intimate friend of John Donne; if I am right he
seems to have contributed to both books.[21] In that case one may
discount the rivalry. Donne had died in 1631 and George Herbert in
1632. The poets of Cambridge in the 1630s who furnish a context for
the early mature work of Milton are one twenty years older and the
other ten years younger than he was: Giles Fletcher and Abraham
Cowley. One should perhaps add Herrick (born 1591, entered St
John's 1613, ordained 1629, died 1674).

Giles Fletcher wrote his brilliant poem 'Christ's Victory' as a
student at Trinity at the age of twenty-two in 1610, when Milton was
two years old. He died young in 1623, but in 1632 his work was
reissued in Cambridge. It was luxuriant, sensuous, spirited, brisk and
lucid. Its influence on Milton and Cowley was vital to them both,
because he opened the possibility of treating Christ and Christianity in
an Ovidian spirit, with great freedom. He paid homage to the
drowsy Greek poet Nonnus, to Sannazaro's Christmas poem, to
Spenser and Du Bartas, but he went far beyond them by sheer force of
youthfulness and high spirits. His Christian poetry is constantly
enjoyable; it is new wine in old bottles.

> the Heav'ns to spread
> Their wings to save him? Heav'n itself shall slide,
> And rowle away like melting starres, that glide
> Along their oylie threads....
>
> (Stanza 38)
>
> 'Bring, bring, ye Graces, all your silver flaskets,
> Painted with every choicest flower that growes,

That I may soone unflower your fragrant baskets,
To strowe the field with odours whear He goes,
Let whatsoe'er he treads on be a rose.'
So downe she ,let her eyelids fall, to shine
Upon the rivers of bright Palestine,
Whose woods drop honie, and her rivers skip with wine.

(Stanza 85)

That is the fitting conclusion of 'Christ's Victory in Heaven'. 'Christ's Victory on Earth', the second part of his cheerful enterprise, contains a comic hermit in the manner of Spenser, a monstrous serpent, some ghosts and an exciting garden.

The garden like a ladie faire was cut,
That lay as if she slumbered in delight,
And to the open skies her eyes did shut.
Over the hedge depends the graping elme,
Whose greener head empurpuled in wine,
Seemed to wonder at his bloodie helme,
And halfe suspect the bunches of the vine;
Least they perhaps, his wit should undermine.
For well he knew such fruit he never bore:
But her weake arms embraced him the more,
And with her ruby grapes laughed at her paramour.

(Stanza 45)

As for the person of Christ, Giles Fletcher becomes even wilder and more wanton, taking his licence here from the classics and here from the Songs of Songs. The verses are as fresh as *Venus and Adonis*.

Upon a grassie hillock He was laid,
With woodie primroses befreckeled;
Over His head the wanton shadowes plaid
Of a wild olive, that her bowghs so spread,
As with her leavs she seem'd to crowne His head,
And her green armes to embrace the Prince of Peace;
The sunne so neere, needs must the Winter cease,
The sunne so neere, another Spring seem'd to increase.

. . . Under His lovely locks, her head to shroude,
Did make Humilitie her selfe grow proude: –
Hither, to light their lamps, did all the Graces croude.

His cheeks as snowie apples, sop't in wine,
Had their red roses quencht with lilies white,
And like to garden strawberries did shine,
Wash't in a bowle of milk, or rose-buds bright
Unbosoming their breasts against the light.
Here love-sick soules did eat, thear drank, and made
Sweete-smelling posies, that could never fade, –
But worldly eyes Him thought more like some living shade.

This is not the atmosphere of the Cambridge that we know, nor of Milton's Cambridge. He remembered Giles Fletcher's amazing verses and learnt deeply from them. But the melting Spenserian tones were not strong enough for a poet under the influence of Shakespeare. Milton loved the density and the intricacy of Fletcher, but Fletcher wrote with a certain naivety and gusto, and by 1632 Milton had acquired a simplicity of tone which could be the base line of a more complex music. The trouble with Giles Fletcher's stanza form is that weary concluding line, which seems a sort of boast: Look, I've done it again. And his profusion is old-fashioned, like Ben Jonson's comic profusion. Elizabethan abundance did need to be pruned; even the language needed to be less riotous. In 1632 the age of prose was still a distant but already a legitimate aspiration.

Cowley only got to Cambridge at nineteen in 1637. He had been publishing poetry since he was fifteen, and precocious facility may have done harm to his schoolwork. He is said to have failed the Trinity election of 1636. He wrote in Latin verse as seriously as ever he wrote in English, and he was an able prose writer. The late-seventeenth-century English verse translations of Cowley's Latin didactic poem on herbs, flowers and trees make the same point about his Latin verse that I tried to make about Milton's: it was genuinely poetry. Cowley is a lighter, giddier Milton, more diverse and less great. Milton in old age thought Dryden, who was his fan, a mere versifier, 'a good rhymist' (Dryden was very young then); the only younger poet he admired was Cowley. Maybe Cowley was the last poet in the tradition as Milton understood it: his favourite English poets were Shakespeare, Spenser and Cowley. Had he forgotten Donne? Had he not read Herbert? Did he never guess that Marvell wrote lyric poetry? What was it about Cowley that attracted him? I can only think it was a certain closeness to himself, and a virtuoso quality and perhaps the sheer ambition of the 'Pindarique Odes'. It is after all notorious that the cult and imitation of Milton as a great poet were slow to begin.

They started years after his death as affectionate parody. Cowley died before Milton, in 1667, and his reputation began to sink at once.

The poem by Cowley that shows the jolly influence of Giles Fletcher is his 'Davideis, A Sacred Poem of the Troubles of David', which he published in 1656. He finished only four books where he intended twelve; 1656 was a low point of his life, and he had no appetite to complete what must once have been intended for his masterpiece. But Thomas Sprat, Cowley's biographer and the historian of the Royal Society, called Pindaric Sprat because of an ode on *The Plague of Athens* in Cowley's style, says the 'Davideis' was written much earlier. He addresses the *Life of Cowley* to Matthew Clifford, a conservative, rationalist wit who later became Master of Charterhouse. Sprat became a bishop. Dryden calls them Malicious Matt Clifford and Spiritual Sprat. All the same Sprat's *Life of Cowley* is excellent, like all his prose.

He says: 'His Davideis was wholly written in so young an Age; that if we shall reflect on the vastness of the Argument, and his manner of handling it, he may seem like one of the Miracles, that he there adorns, like a Boy attempting *Goliah*. I have often heard you declare, that he had finish'd the greatest Part of it, while he was yet a young Student at *Cambridge*. This may perhaps be the Reason, that in some few Places, there is more Youthfulness, and redundance of Fancy, than his riper Judgement would have allow'd.' Sprat then takes on a defensive tone. He likes the 'Davideis' because 'The Contrivance is perfectly Ancient.... The Digressions beautiful and proportionable: The Design to submit mortal Wit to heavenly Truths: In all there is an admirable mixture of Human Virtues and Passions, with religious Raptures.'

It is worth the time it takes to glance at one of those passages Sprat thought frivolously youthful and high-spirited. They are splendid, but the Civil War was a cultural chasm, and the high-spirited seriousness of Cambridge poetry at the time of Milton's early maturity, I was tempted to say of the arts under the early Stuarts, had become irrecoverable and incomprehensible. Cowley's descriptions in David's vision, first of Christ and then of the Angel Gabriel dressing for an earthly mission, must have looked very eccentric in the late 1660s and 1670s. He has a shimmering surface quality that recalls Ovid, and in a different way perhaps Tiepolo.

In her chaste Arms th' *Eternal Infant* lyes,
Th' *Almighty Voice* chang'd into feeble Cries.

Heav'n contained *Virgins* oft, and will do more;
Never did *Virgin contain Heav'n* before.
Angels peep round to view this mystick thing,
And *Halleluiah* round, all *Halleluiah* sing.
No longer could old *David* quiet bear
Th' *Unwieldy Pleasure*, which o'erflow'd him here . . . .
. . . When *Gabriel* (no blest *Spirit* more kind or fair)
Bodies and Cloaths himself with thicken'd Air,
All like a comely *Youth* in Life's fresh Bloom;
Rare Workmanship, and wrought by heav'nly Loom!
He took for Skin a Cloud most soft and bright,
That e'er the mid-day Sun pierc'd through with Light,
Upon his Cheeks a lively Blush he spread,
Wash'd from the Morning Beauties deepest Red.
An harmless flaming *Meteor* shone for Hair,
And fell adown his Shoulders with loose Care.
He cuts out a silk *Mantle* from the Skies,
Where the most sprightly Azure pleas'd the Eyes.
This he with starry Vapours spangles all,
Took in their Prime e'er they grow *ripe*, and *fall*.
Of a new *Rainbow* e'er it *fret* or *fade*
The choicest piece took out, a Scarf is made.
Small streaming Clouds he does for Wings display,
Not virtuous Lovers Sighs more soft than they.
These he gilds o'er with the Suns richest Rays,
Caught gliding o'er pure Streams on which he plays. . . .

One ought to register that Cowley has been out of fashion for a long time, and yet we have come round to a time when these verses appear as clever, as funny and as delightful to us (or at least to me) as they would have done when Milton was in his twenties. What they are not is great poetry; I am afraid that the couplet which he uses with such dash confines his effects in a way that will just not do in literary epic. Pope used it intensely seriously, but it prevented his *Iliad*, with all its great moments, from being the powerful poem that Homer's *Iliad* is, even if nothing else had prevented that. Yet Cowley has a narrative grace, and the tone of these verses is sensitive to the swiftest and the subtlest alterations. He lacked Milton's Shakespearean lustre and his gravity: he was not so great a poet, that is all.

> O nightingale, that on yon bloomy spray
> Warblest at eve, when all the woods are still. . . .

One is impressed by the simple texture of these words, and their musicality, which appears simple in the same way as birdsong appears to be, and their gravity, all of which the young Milton had learnt, on his own, from Latin and in this case Italian poetry, transferring sound-patterns from one language into another.[22] But in terms of sound these are simple effects compared to the opening few lines of *Lycidas*, and even to the restrained, swelling stanza of the 'Hymn on the Morning of Christ's Nativity', which he began to write before dawn on Christmas Day 1629, when he was twenty-one. Sannazaro, as Giles Fletcher tells us,[23] 'Sanazar, the late-living image, and happy imitator of Virgil, bestowing ten years upon a song, only to celebrate that one day when Christ was borne . . . ', had been the source of a tradition of Renaissance Nativity poems. Milton adapted Tasso, Prudentius and other writers, including Plutarch, because this was intended to be, was conceived as, a learned poem, and as a great poem. The attempt at greatness undertaken too early is silly and embarrassing, and for most of us it will always be too early. But when a poet has found his or her voice, different from every other poet's voice as one signature differs from another and consistent from poem to poem, then I am inclined to believe that they should set out to master their language and to master those techniques that seem impossible, that separate the individual poet, or even their own period or generation of poets, from greatness. As for the attempt at a great poem, there have been authentic, admirable and most moving poets to whom it never occurred: Edward Lear for instance, and possibly Philip Larkin. That is not to say they lack greatness. But by a great poem I mean a major statement and an ambitious construction, a monumental poem, that adds something to the language.

Some poets are multiple, others are or seek to be monumental. The greatness of a multiple poet is a coherence of variety, a continuity of luminous transfigurations. Ovid is such a poet, and so is Tennyson, though they both nourished ambitions to be monumental. Milton is a monumental poet; so is Virgil. Their greatness is inseparable from the audacity of their constructions, it is inseparable from their ambition as poets. They felt their own powers, and they sought deliberately for a great poem which would exhaust every resource and display every power in a single performance. Very few English poets give evidence of such a wish, but it distinguishes Milton's work from an early age. Poetry is artifice, and its discipline extends into personal sincerity only because it extends into seriousness, the serious wish to be taken seriously. The same can be said of all rhetoric and all formal language.

Milton mastered his language and created his range of tones in playfulness and artifice, but what distinguishes him from most of his contemporaries, what underlies his search for a voice, is the force of his sincerity, the force of his seriousness.

His Nativity hymn is an amazing compound of seriousness and playful artifice: the seriousness being expressed largely in its momentum and its slow crescendo. It is an extremely learned and still a highly original poem. One is not supposed to be familiar with all the exotic demons; their strangeness is their charm. One can see from Milton's Latin verses 'De Idea Platonica', which he wrote for a fellow of his college to use in some pedantic joking ceremony, and refers to as a frivolous trifle, that he thought the impressive and obscure names were a bit of a joke. Idle Eternity lolls in his vast cave, keeper of muniments and God's decrees. The thunder was mock thunder. The grandeur of sound was mock grandeur and the obscurity was a humorous device.

> Non hunc sacerdos novit Assyricus, licet
> Longos vetusti commemoret atavos Nini,
> Priscumque Belon, inclytumque Osiridem.
> Non ille trino gloriosus nomine
> Ter magnus Hermes (ut sit arcani sciens)
> Talem reliquit Isidis cultoribus.

The effect of the 'Hymn', as opposed to the Latin verses a year and a half earlier, is fresh and not at all pedantic. The stanza form is original and thrilling. The ability to create complex lyric stanza forms of any merit belongs as much to a particular age in music as it does to an age in poetry. In French it began earlier, with Ronsard; it was part of the classical revival. In English it begins with Spenser, and with Marvell, Milton and Cowley it ends. The court odes of the eighteenth century trundle along in a leaden manner. Of all the lyric poets who followed Spenser and learnt from him, Milton (as usual after Shakespeare) was the freshest and the best, and in Milton Italian influence, musical influence and the sound of Shakespeare, and of Spenser's *Epithalamion*, came together. He makes one think of a line of Oliver Bernard: 'A nightingale the other night taught me a complex stanza form.' It is the naturalness as well as the music of Milton's hymn stanza that gives it zest. And the joyfulness is genuine, I think. Milton loves the old popular festivals. He was continually celebrating Mayday, and dancing round trees; he was as nostalgic for rustic rejoicings as Shakespeare was. I have often thought that the paradise of *Paradise Lost* is the paradise of Shakespearean comedy: particularly the gardening scene and that sleeping scene like a more erotic version of *The Babes in the Wood*. On the other hand, the deliberate quaintness and the stately closure of the stanza of the Christmas hymn do recall Spenser.

When Milton had written this hymn, he had not by any means quitted the world of artifice. The most personal statements he ever makes are in his sonnets, but even they are not ashamed to be ornamental. A few days after finishing the 'Hymn', Milton replied in cool and witty Latin verse to a letter from his friend Diodati which he seems to have received just before starting it.

> Paciferum canimus caelesti semine regem,
>   Faustaque sacratis saecula pacta libris,
> Vagitumque Dei, et stabulantem paupere tecto
>   Qui suprema suo cum patre regna colit,
> Stelliparumque polum, modulantesque aethere turmas,
>   Et subito elisos ad sua fana deos.

> I sing the seed of heaven, peaceful king,
> the happy age promised in holy books,
> cry of an infant God so poorly roofed
> who with his father reigns in highest heaven,
> the dance of stars, squadrons singing in air,
> and the gods in their shrines suddenly dust.[24]

One can see very clearly in the Latin the dramatic impulse of the English poem. One can almost see it growing out of a series of epigrams and paradoxes. Its inner machinery is quite secular I think. Its freshness and its sparkle depend on some chilly imagery and starlight. The pagan gods are rather like a Christmas ghost story, they are its learned equivalent. 'There was a man dwelt by a churchyard: I will tell it softly, yon cricket shall not hear me. . . .' Milton's later poem on the Passion of Christ is less successful, more artificial and as cold as stone. It is written in the grandiose stanza form of the introductory stanzas to the 'Hymn', and it lacks the extraordinary breath of naturalness that breathes through the 'Hymn' even at its most exotic. Its interest is that it reads like a parody of *Paradise Lost*: the first feeble touching of those strings.

> See, see the chariot and those rushing wheels
> That whirled the prophet up at Chebar flood,
> My spirit some transporting cherub feels. . . .

Other minor poems written about the same time are mere fireworks of wit, a poet's wit admittedly, since the substance of poetry was impregnating his witticisms. His epitaph on the University Carrier is charming, even touching: it would be more so if there were not two of them, if death were not made to seem the excuse for cleverness. The epitaph for Lady Winchester is almost equally insubstantial, though it has some wonderful classical lines and a touch of Shakespeare.

> Gentle lady may thy grave
> peace and quiet ever have....[25]

The exciting thing about this epitaph is that here suddenly is the characteristic rhythm and almost the metre of 'L'Allegro', which was probably written later in the same summer of 1631. Its starting point, the idea of its framework, was perhaps a song by a minor poet heard in the theatre.[26] It opens with a frigidly baroque prelude or introduction like a flourish of music, as the Nativity hymn does. Music was a rising star at this time of Milton's life, and there is something masque-like about the verse of 'L'Allegro' and 'Il Penseroso'. I wish I knew if Milton had ever seen a court masque; he had at least probably seen the masque of Hymen in *Midsummer Night's Dream*: and he knew Ben Jonson's masques from the folio of 1616 or the second folio that came out precisely in 1631. His own masque 'Arcades' is difficult to date. We are told only that it was 'Part of an entertainment presented to the Countess Dowager of Darby at Harefield, by some Noble persons of her Family, who appear on the scene in pastoral habit ... '. It consists of three songs and of one speech by the Genius of the Wood. 'Arcades' appears to be a trial run which won Milton the commission for *Comus*, the masque presented at Ludlow Castle by some of the same family, in September 1634.

The one impossible or scarcely possible date for 'Arcades' is 1631, because of Lady Derby's son-in-law Lord Castlehaven's execution for sodomy on 14 May that year.[27] Henry Lawes says in the dedication of the *Ludlow Mask*, which incidentally has the name of Lawes but not the name of Milton on its title page, that he introduced Milton to Lady Derby's family. That is highly likely, since Lawes was a music master to the children; he was also a famous composer of court masques, and of music to words by Andrew Marvell, George Herbert, Herrick, Shirley, Davenant, Donne and others. The poetry of that age owes a great deal to his music. But to return to 'Arcades' and the date of Milton's first interest in the pastoral masque, a date before 1631 seems unpopular with scholars, though 1629 has been suggested. Otherwise

'Arcades' can hardly have been acted very long before *Comus*. In the Trinity manuscript of Milton's poems 'Arcades' is the first poem, before the sonnet on his three and twentieth year, which he describes as 'my nightward thoughts some while since'. Milton was twenty-three on 9 December 1631. So perhaps the scarcely possible date of summer 1631 is the right one for 'Arcades' after all. Perhaps Lady Derby and her family put a brave face on things. I am inclined to believe that.

Scholars have maintained that nothing Milton wrote was precisely a legitimate masque, in spite of Henry Lawes and Milton himself using that title for *Comus*. Milton takes from the pastoral theatre, and he likes the learning, the sweet old-fashioned pedantry he found in the court masque. If you knew the name of one of the three Graces was Euphrosyne, and that they were children:

> Whom lovely Venus at one birth
> With two sister Graces more
> To ivy-crowned Bacchus bore,

information that comes from Servius' commentary on the *Aeneid*, you could more easily use it in a masque than in most poems. Of course, 'In heaven yclept Euphrosyne' suggests Spenser, and Spenserian allegory, from the beginning, because of the word 'yclept'. Milton found a charm, and a fresh strangeness, in Spenser's archaisms and in his classical images, so close to Shakespearean fairy scenes.

> Or whether (as some sager sing)
> The frolic wind that breathes the spring,
> Zephyr with Aurora playing,
> As he met her once a-Maying,
> There on beds of violets blue,
> And fresh-blown roses washed in dew....

This is very much the same world as 'Arcades':

> And ye the breathing roses of the wood,
> Fair silver-buskined nymphs....

There is a lot of dawn poetry in early Milton: his English like his Latin verse constantly summons up the coldness and crispness of dawn:

> To hear the lark begin his flight,
> And singing startle the dull night.

> From his watch-tower in the skies,
> Till the dappled dawn doth rise....

The realism of 'dappled' and of similar words is what makes Milton such an improvement on Du Bartas. Du Bartas prettifies, classicizes and generalizes. In English, in Sylvester's version, I find him unreadable, and in French like a schoolboy's parody of Ronsard.

> Ains d'un doux ventelet l'haleine musquetée
> Coulant dans la forêt de l'Eternel plantée....

This is his Earthly Paradise:

> Car pour lors les corbeaux, horiots et hiboux
> avaient des rossignols le chant doctement doux,
> et les doux rossignols avaient la voix divine
> d'Orphée et d'Amphion, d'Arion et de Line,
> Echo, voix forestière, Echo fille de l'air....

It is a fainter poetry than Milton's, more refined, over-refined, so that the necessary tension between a real voice and a classic tone is lost. The cockcrow, the huntsman's horn and the hedgerow elms,

> Right against the eastern gate,
> Where the great sun begins his state,
> Robed in flames, and amber light ...

belong to Milton's schoolboy Latin verses and his childhood memories. They are an essential element of the subject matter of all his early poetry, because they are his most thrilling experience of life. That is why his poetry seems to us to have such purity and force, where the verses of the Seigneur du Bartas are no more than a charming classic exercise. Milton's mixture of names out of Virgil's *Eclogues* with Faery Mab and the friar's lantern, the tournament and the theatre is as oddly convincing as it is, only because the same or a similar mixture had already been composed by Spenser and Shakespeare.

Observe how Hymen:

> In saffron robe, with taper clear,
> And pomp, and feast, and revelry,
> With mask, and antique pageantry,
> Such sights as youthful poets dream
> On summer eves, by haunted stream ...

leads naturally to the names of Jonson and Shakespeare. Milton at twenty-three had become a second Shakespeare within the narrow limits of pastoral verse. The style of 'Il Penseroso' is more whimsical, and in spite of lines of perfect beauty and many exotic thrills, I find it too full of solemn jokes. I believe that Milton's heart was more in 'L'Allegro'. He had discovered that Cambridge was not his place for learning: his learning was poetry: it was like alchemy, like a mystery. He knew with the force of the new science that the universe was not what it looked like, its natural events were like physical miracles to many in his generation. But the heart of his poetry was terribly old-fashioned, and 'L'Allegro' expresses that: it was Shakespearean.

His Latin hexameter epistle to his father ends by promising the same immortality for the name of Milton he had already promised his mother. The date is uncertain, but the ideas of poetry and science seem to belong quite close to 'Il Penseroso'. Why did Milton, who knew the Copernican system was true, use the old earth-centred Ptolemaic system in poetry? Milton was not a great poet in the manner of Lucretius. Like many later poets, he was thrilled by the idea of science and the image of the scientist, by the breaking down of taboos and the expansion of knowledge, and by every imaginative breakthrough, but to him it was all a *materia poetica*. He used what paradoxes he pleased. Satan could perch on the outer skin of the universe like a bat on a dome, Spenserian artillery roared and smoked in heaven in the wars of the angels. He loved science and he loved reality but his poetry was full of gods and allegories sharply and even seriously imagined. It was no place for scientific truth, or indeed for theological truth either. For Milton, theology and science alike were a masque, a transfiguration scene, a revelation of the physical wonders that his poetry presented.

The best Latin poems he ever wrote were written after *Comus* and after *Lycidas*. They were 'Mansus', addressed to a marquess who was once Tasso's patron and who entertained Milton at Naples, and *Epitaphium Damonis*, the pastoral elegy on the death of his school-friend, Charles Diodati, in some ways a purer and more intimate poem than *Lycidas*. These two poems are the last he published in his 1645 collection, rather near the beginning of his long silence as a poet. They represent, together with *Lycidas*, the final mood of his early poetry. In these two Latin poems, Milton became the supreme poet of the Thames valley.

He writes to Mansi that barbarous England has her poetry. It appears to be an important motive of Milton's Latin verse that it could be read all over Europe, and make him great and famous on an international scale.

> For on our floods the swan is heard to sing,
> heard in the darkest shadow of the night,
> where Thames pours down his water from pure urns,
> drenching old ocean's grey hair in his streams....[28]

Does he mean the cries and the wing-beat of wild geese heard at Gravesend? The *Epitaphium Damonis* has less grandeur and more of familiar memory, very closely interwined with fantasy.

> Who shall go by my side as you would go
> in the hard cold over hoar-frosted ground
> or when the swift[29] sun blights the droughted grass,
> to see the distant lion rear his head
> or fright the wolves away from folded sheep,
> then talk and sing and send the day to sleep?
> Who now shall have my heart, who teach to soothe
> my biting cares, cheat long nights with sweet words,
> and while the soft pear whispers in the flame
> and the black chestnut crackles on the hearth,
> and the storm wind thunders into the elm?[30]

Epitaphium Damonis throws more light than I have time to point out on *Lycidas*. *Lycidas*, being printed in 1638 with twenty-three pieces of Latin and Greek memorial verse entitled *Justa Eduardo King*, in a separate collection of thirteen English poems, suggests that Milton still disapproved of the classical exercises that Cambridge was so ready to produce, and the fact that *Lycidas* comes last in the *Obsequies to the Memory of Mr. Edward King*, the English supplement, suggests, by analogy with *Exanthemata Regis*, that Milton may easily have been the organizer of the poets who wrote in English; some of them on other occasions contributed Latin verses to Cambridge collections. I conjecture that the first poem is by Henry King of Christ Church,[31] whom Milton probably knew and presumably invited, in default of any Cambridge dignitary able to write in English, though the other English poets were not much better than Latin ones.

> So should he, so have cut the Irish strand
> And like a lusty bridegroom leapt to land;
> Or else (like Peter) trod the waves; but he
> Then stood most upright, when he bent his knee....

166

That is Isaac Olivier. Cleiveland is a similarly frigid firework display of paradoxes. This is his first published English poem.

> When we have filled the rundlets of our eyes,
> We'll issue't forth, and vent such elegies,
> As that our tears shall seem the Irish seas,
> We floating Islands, living Hesperides....

To the hectic tone of these poets, Milton is an exception.

> Yet once more, O ye laurels, and once more
> Ye myrtles brown, with ivy never sere,
> I come to pluck your berries harsh and crude,
> And with forced fingers rude,
> Shatter your leaves before the mellowing year.
> Bitter constraint, and sad occasion dear,
> Compels me to disturb your season due:
> For Lycidas is dead, dead ere his prime,
> Young Lycidas, and hath not left his peer....

There are few examples in seventeenth-century English poetry, and none in the Oxford and Cambridge collections of Latin verse, of Milton's tranquil authority of tone. The vision of 'the pilot of the Galilean lake', which scholars have thought a bizarre disturbance of the unity and the texture of *Lycidas*, corresponds to the visions in almost every one of Milton's early elegies. It was appropriate to poor Edward King, with whose religious views, as with Milton's, our own times are out of sympathy. *Lycidas* is nearly 200 lines, the *Epitaphium Damonis* is 210 lines long. Milton was the master of poems of that length. He was never to write except in dramatic verse on any greater scale until the enormous, defiant undertaking of *Paradise Lost*, with its infinity of pendent rhythms and pendent clauses, and its long, wandering harmonies: blind man's poetry.

APPENDIX

The earliest collection of Latin verses for a royal occasion known to me is *Academiae Cantabrigensis lacrymae, tumulo D. Philippi Sidneii sacratae* (1587). They multiplied under James I after the death of the Prince of Wales in 1612. Various collections on funerals, returns home, weddings and so on appeared in 1613, 1617, 1619, 1623, 1624 and 1625 (two). A number of collections of Latin verse by the same versifiers survive unpublished in the

Bodleian Library (Rawlinson mss) and probably elsewhere. Patronage was to the University, not only to individuals, hence the scale of the competition. In 1592 a Cambridge critic attacks Oxford plays put on for the Queen. Sir I. Wake of Merton thanks James I at Christ Church for first visiting the older University. R. Corbet of Christ Church circulated a song satirizing a royal visit to Cambridge.[32]

Edward Lear

Edward Lear is not what we normally call a great poet: and yet his verse is certainly popular and memorable, and the special atmosphere of his poetry is as unmistakable as that of Alexander Pope's mature poetry or Alfred Tennyson's. But Lear was not just a poet and not principally a poet, although at the end of his life he was more proud of his poems than he was of his paintings, perhaps because of their overwhelming success. He is one of those highly individual artists of the period, like Gerard Manley Hopkins and William Morris and William Blake, whose value increases when you take every aspect of their work, and their personality and their life story, together. It may be Lear's enchanting personality, or it may be his tragic life story that prevents his poetry from being taken as seriously as it deserves. It may be that the immediate attraction of his watercolour drawings makes his children's verse seem secondary. But all his best work as an artist, let alone as a comic artist, as a poet, as a letter writer and a travel writer, has the same modest, secondary quality. Very few of his attempts at monumental greatness as a painter accomplish as much as they intend. We call him less than great as a poet only because we commonly deny greatness to everything Auden grouped together as light verse. Wrongly I am sure.

My opinion is that the physical nature and the origins of poetry, the substance of what it is to be a poet, and the basic techniques are best studied in children's verse, and anonymous verse. The deliberately comic and highly personal verses of Lewis Carroll and Edward Lear are another matter: they add a new dimension to the art of poetry. We can get round the question of greatness by speaking of favourite and necessary poets. Lear is almost my favourite nineteenth-century poet. I bask with pleasure in his cadences; and I am always finding something fresh in his technique, I recall stray lines of his continually and with delight. He is one of the most necessary poets because one could not do without him or understand poetry so well without him, or enter into his age of the world half so well without him. William Empson as a young man wrote that poetry is not made of words, it is made of the kind of jokes there are in hymns. In this sense Edward Lear is a very pure and powerful poet.

'How pleasant to know Mr Lear!'
    Who has written such volumes of stuff!
Some think him ill-tempered and queer,
    But a few think him pleasant enough.

His mind is concrete and fastidious,
    His nose is remarkably big;
His visage is more or less hideous,
    His beard it resembles a wig.

He has ears, and two eyes, and ten fingers,
    Leastways if you reckon two thumbs;
Long ago he was one of the singers,
    But now he is one of the dumbs.

He sits in a beautiful parlour,
    With hundreds of books on the wall;
He drinks a great deal of Marsala,
    But never gets tipsy at all.

He has many friends, laymen and clerical,
    Old Foss is the name of his cat;
His body is perfectly spherical,
    He weareth a runcible hat.

When he walks in a waterproof white,
    The children run after him so!
Calling out, 'He's come out in his night-
    gown, that crazy old Englishman, oh!'

He weeps by the side of the ocean,
    He weeps on the top of the hill;
He purchases pancakes and lotion,
    And chocolate shrimps from the mill.

He reads but he cannot speak Spanish,
    He cannot abide ginger-beer:
Ere the days of his pilgrimage vanish,
    How pleasant to know Mr Lear!

As a self-portrait this is remarkable: as a poem beautiful. 'His mind is concrete and fastidious. . . . He weeps by the side of the ocean. . . . He sits in a beautiful parlour, With hundreds of book on the wall.' He wrote this poem with a friend, a young lady called Miss Bevan whom he knew late in life in his retirement at San Remo: but apart from the first line, which someone had actually said, and which tickled his fancy, it has the air of being all his own work. The whole of his biography, and the judgements of his close friends, confirm this insight: he was as funny as he was sad. Henry Strachey wrote of him: 'Mr Lear was by temperament melancholy; it was not the grave air assumed by a humourist to give his jokes more point, but a gentle sadness through which his humour shone. . . . This melancholy never soured his mind nor stopped his matchless flow of humour and bad puns; but it coloured them all.'[1]

The reasons for the melancholy are easy to understand. He was the youngest of twenty-one children brought up by sisters. His father went to prison as a bankrupt. Young Lear suffered from catarrh, bronchitis and minor epileptic seizures. He never went to school, and acquired only the polite women's accomplishments of singing, composing light verse and painting in watercolours. Hence his extraordinary mixture of originality and lack of confidence as a painter, and his pathological dependence and deep loneliness. He was the best and the most loved friend and the most brilliant company anyone knew. Socially he was a success with the upper class: he was Queen Victoria's drawing master, the Prince of Wales never forgot him, he lived with the earls of Derby on and off for years; four earls of Derby were his patrons and nearly as many of the Barings and Stracheys. But he had no money. As a painter of souvenir drawings he was driven out of business by the invention of the picture postcard. The only secure-looking job he was ever offered was £100 a year to be full-time professor of art in the University of the Ionian Islands. At least twice he considered marriage, but like the poet Horace he lacked the means to marry into the social class in which he lived, and his illness was another inhibiting factor. He was a melancholy, but a very loving man.

A rough statistical analysis of his limericks (though he never called them that, the word came into general use later) yields some interesting results all the same. Two of the persons in these verses are thankful to escape, from Lucca and from Basingstoke, but seven or eight are driven out for nonconformity; there are eight cases of unexplained misfortune, two of unexplained grief, fourteen of furious rage and violence, six of crazy attempts to teach things to animals, but nearly thirty cases of happy eccentrics who get away with their eccentricities.

> There was an old person of Tring,
> Who embellished his nose with a ring;
>> He gazed at the moon
>> Every evening in June,
> That ecstatic Old Person of Tring.

Can this be a member of the Rothschild family? A number of Lear's best friends and patrons were Jews, but the limericks contain fifteen or sixteen cases where the nose or sometimes the hair is much too long. The limericks are not a psychopathological casebook, indeed there are eight cases of unhappy persons who get happily cured of their condition, but one can detect something ominous, a lurking nightmare, in some of the most pleasing.

> There was an Old Man of Blackheath,
> Whose head was adorned by a Wreath,
>> Of lobsters and spice,
>> Pickled onions and mice,
> That uncommon Old Man of Blackheath.

A certain element of cruelty is of course traditional in children's humour: they like it and it does them good, reality and nightmare can be coped with in play: 'we all fall down', 'she cut off their tails with a carving knife', 'I killed Cock Robin'. But one unnoticed influence lurks in Edward Lear's poetry that explains a good deal. He and his friend Lord Carlingford[2] were very fond of Butler's *Hudibras* and knew chunks of it by heart. Something of its coarse and heartless humour was already present in Lear's idea of comic verse before he started writing. We know of this only because one evening they forgot a line from what Carlingford calls 'a famous description' (as if a lot of Victorians knew *Hudibras* by heart), and Lear supplied it the next morning with a comic drawing. Significantly, it was about a nose.

> So learned Taliacotius from
> The brawny part of Porter's Bum,
> Cut supplemental Noses, which
> Would last as long as Parent breech:
> But when the Date of *Nock* was out,
> Off dropt the Sympathetick Snout.[3]

This gruesome passage is about a sixteenth-century professor at Bologna called Tagliacozzo who practised plastic surgery, using working-class bums to repair defective syphilitic noses. When the Date of *Nock*, that is the porter's behind, was out, that is he died, off dropt the Sympathetick Snout. Samuel Butler's satiric poem is good in parts like the curate's egg. Few people read it today, and as an influence on nineteenth-century comic verse it is to me a new thought. Samuel Butler has a bluff, damn-your-eyes quality that might appeal to bachelors, but he can often be witty and sometimes funny. Edward Lear may not have quite understood the lines about Taliacotius. He may just have thought all poems about noses were funny; he was certainly over-conscious of his own nose. As for his knowledge of English classics all but unheard of in our generation, it is suggestive that the notebook he used for Uncle Arley and for an unfinished fragment of a sequel to 'The Owl and the Pussycat' was a cheap travelling edition of Addison.

But the process by which he arrived at the full self-expression of his longer lyric poems was slow. He began with parody and small-scale adaptation.[4] He was invited to Knowsley by Lord Edward Stanley, to paint birds and animals, and was soon accepted as a guest there because the children found him so intoxicatingly funny. It was the same Edward Stanley who showed him his first limerick and suggested he could write one of his own. The book was *The Anecdotes and Adventures of Fifteen Gentlemen*, illustrated by Robert Cruikshank and published about 1820, possibly written by R. S. Sharpe: this book, with *Adventures of Fifteen Young Ladies and those of Sixteen Wonderful Old Women ... their principal Eccentricities and Amusements*, first launched the limerick as a comic verse form. Lear appears to have known all these early limerick books. His comic drawing owes something at times to Cruikshank. His illustrated alphabets and alphabet verses were done in an existing nursery tradition. He illustrated common nursery rhymes, as other people did, before he began on his own. For him, comic illustration and parody went together from the beginning. His music was just as original, and yet just as derivative, as his humour. He parodied Thomas Moore's Irish Melodies: 'The Dong with the Luminous Nose' is based on Moore's 'Lake of the Dismal Swamp'. His best comic lyrics, the ones that are so sad, are the essence of Tennyson rewritten in other terms.

He parodied even his favourite poems of Tennyson. When he sang his settings of Tennyson poems, people wept: not only his friends wept but diplomats and grandees in great reception rooms. In 1851 on hearing 'Home they brought her warrior dead', Dean Tait of Carlisle, later Archbishop of Canterbury, told him he ought to have half the laureateship. And yet one night, when he broke down in sobs singing

'Tears Idle Tears', produced a note the next morning with these lines:

> Nhw, fluv bluv, ffluv biours,
> Faith nunfaith kneer beekwl powers
> Unfaith naught zwant a faith in all.

He wept and made others weep, that is, particularly at poems that mentioned tears.

He knew and profoundly admired Alfred Tennyson, though not without a tiff or two, and he reserved his absolute of worship for Lady Tennyson, who understood him better than any of his friends. Tennyson was a vain and difficult man; he was capable even at the height of his powers of sending a poem to the papers under a pseudonym, and then writing again under another pseudonym to say what a good poem it was. Lear in his music and in certain landscapes and above all in his own most moving lyrics sucked out the honey from the core of Tennyson: but that did not inhibit him from parody, which is after all a form of worship, though the poet parodied may resent its intimacy.

Lear sent Tennyson his volume of Greek landscapes. He received in return a poem by Tennyson of a remarkable dexterity. After any great work that requires intense concentration by a poet, a few poems are often written that are in some way fall-out from the great work. Tennyson had just written *In Memoriam*, and the stanza and the landscape theme haunted him. A little later he modulated the metre into something closer to Horace – he used to say he could never appreciate Horace until he was forty, that is 1849 – in his invitation to F. D. Maurice to come to the Isle of Wight. The theme of Mediterranean landscape which he started in his poem to Lear got a fuller statement soon afterwards in 'The Daisy'. The last great failed enterprise of Lear's life was the attempt to illustrate Tennyson's poems[5] with his own landscape drawings. The memorial album of these that was issued after Lear's death, in 100 copies signed by Tennyson, contains only 'To Edward Lear', 'The Palace of Art' and 'The Daisy'. Their mutual friend Franklin Lushington remarks in the introduction that Lear 'was always so to speak finding his subjects in Tennyson. . . . they ware Lear's sermons on texts taken from Tennyson'. It is quite certain that Lear venerated Tennyson's poetry: yet he gleefully and gratuitously parodied the sound.

In September 1873 at the age of sixty-one he writes from San Remo to his old friend Chichester Fortescue about:

some parodies I have been obliged to make, whereby to recall the Tennyson lines of my illustrations: beginning with these serious and beautiful verses:

1. Like the Wag who jumps at evening
   All along the sanded floor.
2. To watch the tipsy cripples on the beach,
   With topsy turvy signs of screamy play.
3. *Tom-Moory* Pathos: all things bare, –
   With such a turkey! such a hen!
   And scrambling forms of distant men,
   O! – ain't you glad you were not there!
4. Delirious Bulldogs; – echoing, calls
   My daughter, – green as summer grass;
   The long supine Plebeian ass,
   The nasty crockery boring falls; –
5. Spoonmeat at Bill Porter's in the Hall,
   With green pomegranates and no end of Bass.

The first couplet is surely 'And the crag that fronts the even', which Lear painted in all seriousness in 1877, that is four years later. The second defeats me, so does the fifth, but the two stanzas beginning 'Tom-Moory' Pathos' come from Tennyson's 'Poem to E. L.', which Lear both illustrated and greatly loved. If this were simply the story of a joke in questionable taste it would be too long in the telling, but these curious, rather secret and innocent parodies of Lear's show an acutely good ear for the texture of Tennyson's verse, which comes into its own long afterwards in the story of aged Uncle Arly, a variation on 'The Lady of Shalott', and indeed in the last verses in his diary, shortly before his death. 'He only said I'm very weary. The rheumatiz he said. He said, it's awful dull and dreary. I think I'll go to bed.' There is something physical about poetry and the talent for poetry. The same fineness of ear underlies all these examples. Victorian soulfulness is a physical tone.

It may be that Tennyson with all his intimacy cowering under the obligation to grandeur was more able than other examples to liberate a poet of intimate sensations, almost a poet of the silence of unexpressed feelings, like Edward Lear. Two critics of Tennyson cast a little more light on this tenuous subject. Professor Walter Raleigh, in a slapdash but fascinating study of Milton published in 1905, discusses the texture of verse: he distinguishes Milton, whose every word is unpredictable and his musical quality infinitely variable, from the diffuse Spenser, over whose verses one may glide without loss. He accuses Tennyson of 'a kind of fluent singsong'.

> So all the ways were safe from shore to shore,
> But in the heart of Arthur pain was lord.

'The elements of musical delight', he remarks, 'here are almost barbarous in their simplicity. There is a surfeit of assonance – The alliteration is without complexity, – a dreary procession of sibilants. Worst of all are the monotonous incidence of stress, and the unrelieved, undistinguished, crowded poverty of Saxon monosyllables. No two such consecutive lines were ever written by Milton.' The technical words in this criticism are unhelpful; they merely skirt the problems of rhythm and texture to be found in the lines. Their slowness is deliberate, archaic, solemn. They are not such bad lines really, in spite of their unlikeness to Milton. But in 1905 English ears were jaded with the sound of Tennyson, which to me is one of the marvels of our literature. Anyway it was not the iron bleakness of these lines that Edward Lear looked for in Tennyson, but something far more delicate, lyrical and sad, which is also to be found there. Both men were sad for the same reason, among others, because they were aesthetes: they were sad simply because the sun had gone down on the past, and their own sun would go down.

That envious popinjay Bulwer-Lytton attacked Tennyson in harsher terms.[6] 'Let schoolmiss Alfred vent her chaste delight' on 'darling rooms so warm and bright! Chaunt I'm aweary! with infectious strain, And catch her blue fly singing i'the pane.' These nasty lines were written when Tennyson got his pension in 1845, before his marriage, before *In Memoriam*, and before the laureateship. They hurt him badly, as they were intended to do. He did have a feminine streak, he did delight in tiny details of life and in visions of domestic happiness: whether these were weaknesses or, as I believe, a basic component of his strength and his hold on reality,[7] he had them in common with Edward Lear. Lear's genius did not lie in the parody of noises, the abstraction of noises from their meaning, but in transmuting intimate emotions and half-revealed meanings; he did not transmute them into the soft language of domestic intimacy, but into the tougher language and sad morality of the nursery.

The relationship between Edward Lear and Lewis Carroll is evidently close, though it remains obscure. They were both friends of the Tennyson family, they might well have met, but neither of them is recorded ever to have mentioned the other. Lear was first in the field of nonsense, and did a good deal to make that field respectable; indeed his first pseudonymous books of lyrics, which were signed Merry Down Derry, were commonly attributed to the Earl of Derby, with at least more show of reason than the attribution of Shakespeare's works to the Earl of Oxford. But between Carroll and Lear the influences were mutual. The railway ticket in Uncle Arly's hat recalls the image of the Mad Hatter, for example. Dodgson was more terribly contorted and frustrated than Lear, and so his prose was in tighter intellectual control. Lear seems to write as naturally as breathing: he is a pleasing prose writer in many styles, but a wonderful and unique poet. Lewis Carroll's poetry has a prickly humour and a profound wit, but the noise it makes is no better than that of Thackeray's comic verse, or that of F. W. N. Bayley, which was reissued in 1850 in the paperback Shilling Books for Railway Travellers.[8] The only occasion on which Lewis Carroll did produce at least one stanza of great verbal beauty, a stanza once learnt never forgotten, was very close to the style of Lear, and to that musical authority which descended from embarrassing Keats to domestic Tennyson. The first stanza of 'Jabberwocky' is a high point of Victorian poetry.

> 'Twas brillig, and the slithy toves
>   Did gyre and gimble in the wabe:
> All mimsy were the borogoves,
>   And the mome raths outgrabe.

What to make of Tennyson, how to digest him, was a central problem of English poetry for more than fifty years, just as what to make of Baudelaire was a central problem in French. If I may be forgiven a moment of autobiography, it was the astounding power of Baudelaire and (as I felt) the comparative weakness of Tennyson that drove me back many years ago now to re-explore Tennyson's poems and so to value them for their unique qualities. The transfiguration of Tennysonian music is not confined to nonsense writers: it can be strongly felt in the Dorset dialect poetry of William Barnes, another personal friend, another great and neglected English poet. When Barnes translated his own poems into standard English, he disimproved them by making them more conventional. But in dialect they have the same streak of unconventionality that Tennyson himself had. Barnes, like Lear, was a self-educated man and a man of many talents. His drawing style was stiffer than Lear's and his lyrical manner limited in a different way; he was a headmaster and a clergyman, but his voice is authentic and stands in an equally interesting relation to the poetry of their mutual friend Tennyson. Thomas Hardy recognized his genuineness.

'Barnes', wrote Hardy, 'really belonged to the literary school of such poets as Tennyson, Gray and Collins, rather than to that of the old unpremeditating singers in dialect. Primarily spontaneous, he was academic closely after; and we find him warbling his native wood-notes with a watchful eye on the predetermined score....'[9] The advantages of dialect to William Barnes are that it was salty where middle-class English lacked salt, musically alive, deeply rooted and tending to truthfulness: all strong cards in the hand of any poet.

I entertain the supposition that English poetry, like a very old garden plant, had begun to go dead in the centre while it flourished at the edges, in Whitman and Hopkins and Edward Lear and William Barnes. Tennyson like a gardener of genius made the centre flourish again, Matthew Arnold hardly had the powers to do so, or only very briefly, Bridges failed altogether, and Eliot's gestures towards the traditional centre were gestures towards something that had long been dead. Poetry is nourished from unexpected edges and margins, by whatever is genuine. It is here that Edward Lear's place is so honour-able, and his originality so valuable. Neither of Tennyson nor of Hopkins, far greater and more ambitious poets, can it be said as it can of Lear, that one never wants to tell him to come off it. His handful of longer nonsense lyrics came late in his life; they are the fullest expression of his experience.

The first of these longer poems was written for Janet, the small daughter of John Addington Symonds, in 1867 when Lear was fifty-five. It was 'The Owl and the Pussycat', which had gentle, lyrical illustrations, and which Lear used to sing to a strange, haunting tune, now forgotten. He was wedded to diminuendo: even in the limerick he chose the diminuendo though he knew the crescendo form with the climax of a new rhyme in the last line. Maurice Baring points out in an important though brief essay on Edward Lear,[10] that 'Poems like "The Owl and the Pussycat" have an organic rhythm. It is quite different from the neat clashing rhymes of most writers of humorous poetry. The whole poem (and not merely the separate lines and stanzas) forms a piece of architectonic music.' Lear's biographer Angus Davidson makes the justified comment that the same is true of the best of Lear's watercolours. 'Behind this sense of rhythm,' he says, 'there lies the emotional force that is an essential quality of all true poetry, a force that is derived from life itself.' Much as I dislike these large terms about what lies behind poetry, I am forced to admit that what Mr Davidson says is substantially true.

'The Owl and the Pussycat' belongs to comparatively early days. The owl that went to sea goes back to a limerick published when Edward Lear was about eight years old.[11] The magical ending of the poem was cannibalized and even improved in 'The Quangle Wangle's Hat'.

> And at night by the light of the Mulberry moon
> They danced to the flute of the Blue Baboon,
> On the broad green leaves of the Crumpetty Tree,
>   And all were as happy as happy could be
>   With the Quangle Wangle Quee.

Lear's limericks overlap with the lyrics and the lyrics with one another because his method was essentially that of variation on a given theme. But the variation could be quite spontaneous, in a letter for example, in a few satiric verses against Gladstone, in a sudden parody of Clough's 'Amours de Voyage' (they were together in Rome) or in the merest twiddles or doodles in verse: 'Thoughts into my head do come, Thick as flies upon a plum',[12] or on payments of a debt, 'Of Carlingford all nature knows – He paid his debts – he blew his nose.' He was capable of impromptu verse. In pitch darkness, after a fifteen hours' journey in Greece, he went to sit on a rock but sat on a cow. He remarked cheerfully, 'There was an old man who said Now I'll sit down on the horns of that cow....'

When his friend Fortescue married, he wrote, 'But never more, O never we Shall meet to eggs and toast and tea.' Deep-seated ideas surfaced casually: the pathetic lover, for example, or the nostalgia for travel.

> Said the Kangaroo, I'm ready
> All in the moonlight pale;
> But to balance me well dear Duck, sit steady
> And quite at the end of my tail!
> So away they went with a hop and a bound,
> And they hopped the whole world three times round,
>   And who so happy, – O who,
>   As the Duck and Kangaroo.

What surfaced in his mind might be a tune or the rhythm of a poem: 'The Yonghy-Bonghy-Bò' echoes Tennyson's 'Row us out from Desenzano'; 'Calico Pie' echoes 'Sweet and Low'; 'How pleasant to know Mr Lear' is meant for the tune of 'How cheerful along the mead'. But both the pseudonym of his first book of limericks, Derry Down Derry, and 'The Yonghy-Bonghy-Bò', which in his diary for 11 December 1871 he calls 'a foolsong', reveal a fascinating taproot into the old English Mummers' plays, where they belong to a fool who goes back to Shakespeare and earlier. His name is Fiddler Wit. This speech was recorded in 1923,[13] but it looks earlier than Lear's lifetime.

> Father died the other night
> And left me all his riches,
> A wooden leg, a feather bed,
> And a pair of leather breeches,
> A coffee pot without a spout,
> A jug without a handle,
> A guinea pig without a wig,
> And half a farthing candle.

The Mummers' plays were mostly not published in Lear's time, and the fact that they were orally transmitted for years at a time has had a very strange effect on any text that has survived. Lear transforms the cheerful rhymes, but he precisely captures the character of the fool, the rejected rustic lover, the pathetic village natural. 'The Yonghy-Bonghy-Bò' commemorates his failure to summon up the courage to propose marriage to Gussie Bethell, a peer's daughter in her twenties he fell in love with in his fifties. In the end she married Paul Nash's uncle Thomas, and died in 1931 aged ninety-three. The poem was written about 1870.

The old age of a bachelor, which Edward Lear feared and which he suffered, finds several expressions in his poems, though more in his letters, some of which are heartrending. In 'The Two Old Bachelors', the two anti-heroes are roughly handled by the sage. In 'The Eclogue', which is a conversation about grumbling between Edward Lear and the Symonds family, severe judgement is passed on the bachelor poet. At the end of 'Calico Pie',

> Calico Drum,
>   The Grasshoppers come,
> The Butterfly, Beetle and Bee,
>   Over the Ground
>   Around and round,

> With a hop and a bound, –
> But they never came back!
> They never came back!
> They never came back!
> They never came back to me!

'The Dong with a Luminous Nose' is an elderly, lonely, abandoned lover. 'Long years ago, The Dong was happy and gay Till he fell in love with a Jumbly Girl. . . .' He goes on singing the Jumbly song: 'Far and few, far and few Are the lands where the Jumblies live; Their heads are green, and their hands are blue, And they went to sea in a Sieve.' So now the Dong is abandoned like some mythical creature in the *Odyssey*. He spends the rest of his quite long poem looking in vain for the girl. But the most striking part of this poem, better as poetry than the bit children like, about how he made himself a nose with a lamp inside it, is simply a parody. By playing with his idiotic original, Edward Lear produces something much more rich and strange. What was his relation to Moore? He has a finer, less orotund version of Moore's musicality, and if one were told that Lear wrote 'The last rose of summer', one might almost believe it. But he mocked Moore worse than Tennyson, and admired him less. In Moore's poem:

> He saw the Lake, and a meteor bright
> Quick over its surface play'd –
> Welcome, he said, my dear one's light!
> And the dim shore echoed, for many a night,
> The name of the death-cold maid! . . . .
>
> But oft, from the Indian hunter's camp,
> This lover and maid so true
> Are seen, at the hour of midnight damp,
> To cross the lake by a fire-fly lamp
> And paddle their white canoe!

The death-cold maid gave Lear his Jumbly girl, the firefly lamp which is a meteor bright; the midnight and the shore give him enough stimulus for a comic poem, not his deepest or best, but a funny one written for Christmas.

> When awful darkness and silence reign
>   Over the great Gromboolian plain,
>   Through the long, long wintry nights; –
> When the angry breakers roar

As they beat on the rocky shore; –
  When Storm-clouds brood on the towering heights
Of the Hills of the Chankly Bore: –

Then, through the vast and gloomy dark,
There moves what seems a fiery spark,
  A lonely spark with silvery rays
  Piercing the coal-black night, –
Hither and thither the vision strays,
  A single lurid light.

Slowly it wanders, – pauses, – creeps, –
Anon it sparkles, – flashes and leaps;
And ever as onward it gleaming goes
A light on the Bong-tree stems it throws.
And those who watch at that midnight hour
From Hall or Terrace, or lofty Tower,
Cry, as the wild light passes along, –
    'The Dong! – the Dong!
  'The wandering Dong through the forest goes!
    'The Dong! The Dong!
  'The Dong with a luminous Nose!'

    Long years ago
  The Dong was happy and gay,
Till he fell in love with a Jumbly Girl
  Who came to those shores one day....

For an artist so penetrated with melancholy, Lear kept up his spirits
and the high quality of his work remarkably well. His only failures
were oil paintings on a monumental scale, and the only thing wrong
with them is pre-Raphaelite theories. *The Cedars of Lebanon* had to
be done from life in a hotel garden in Walton on Thames: it was
wicked to use sketches. *The Temple of Bassae*, where he eviscerated
the architecture, has a foreground of trees and rocks painted in
Leicestershire. At the end of his life his eyes began to fail. But he had
plenty of earthly pleasures, and he was not racked by religious guilt or
so far as I can see by sexual confusion. A man less unfulfilled than Lear
in some ways could not have been so deeply fulfilled in others.

    There was an Old Person of Pett,
    Who was partly consumed by regret,

          He sat in a cart,
          And ate cold Apple Tart,
      Which relieved that Old Person of Pett.

'The Dong' is a sort of sequel to 'The Jumblies', who set out to sea
in a sieve.[14] It is interesting that Lear was so strong in basic comic
images like that, because so was Aristophanes, and Greek comedy in
his time was just as parasitic on tragedy as Edward Lear was on
Tennyson; what is more, Aristophanes shares with Edward Lear an
extraordinary exactness and liveliness of rhythm. There the resem-
blance ends, because their audiences were so different, and Aristophanes was intellectually so vigorous. But the comparison was worth
making, because Aristophanes is a very great poet, and one is free to
prefer Greek comedy to Greek tragedy. The ancient Greeks might
have thought more of Lear than they would have done of Tennyson.
Plato might have preferred Lewis Carroll, William Barnes would
certainly have been popular, but I believe the Greeks would have
named Edward Lear almost in the same sentence as Aristophanes.
Would he have been happier in their society than he was in ours? Very
likely. But only after the European soul had been ploughed and
manured for two thousand years after Christ could he paint his
watercolours. He advised young painters first to study the works of
God and then the works of Turner. His watercolours are his truest
single claim to greatness. Once as a lad he heard Turner sing a comic
song; he remembered the refrain and the tune for the rest of his life: I
wish he knew more about that. His own favourite comic song was
called 'The Cork Leg'.

His songs, his comic lyrics, were parodies of the deepest emotions
they expressed, but they were at least as sad as they were funny, and
when they were in perfect balance, the emotion overcame the parody.
They were not meant to be sung in public houses. It is not our own
special fineness of ear or of temperament that makes us feel so for the
people in his lyrics or even in his limericks: we were meant to do so.
The story of the 'old man of Thermopylae who could never do
anything properly' is one of the saddest poems of its century. It is a
comic or a mild, surreal statement of Lear's deepest fears. 'So they said
if you choose to boil eggs in your shoes, You must go right away from
Thermopylae.' The world of his lyrics and limericks is somehow a
single world. The old man who 'danced with his cat and made tea in
his hat' might easily be an inhabitant of the great Gromboolian plain.

If many of the creatures of his poetry seem to live alone, outlined against the merest sketches of a landscape, that is because the poems are essentially about loneliness.

Wystan Auden in his introduction to the *Oxford Book of Light Verse*[15] maintained that the breakdown of traditional communities left the family as the only surviving social unit 'and the parent–child relationship as the only real social bond', within which nineteenth-century nonsense poetry 'was an attempt to find a world where the divisions of class, sex, occupation did not operate'. But children have surely always had a world of their own and poetry of their own.[16] Ancient Greek children's verse is attractive and yet mysterious in exactly the same way as English nursery rhymes. Edward Lear's poetry entered an ancient tradition so swiftly that poems by him were recorded as anonymous, orally transmitted children's rhymes while he was still alive. Divisions of class and sex and occupation do exist in his poetry, dimly apprehended or distorted by dreams, as in all children's poetry. The adventure of 'The Nutcrackers and Sugar-tongs' is about an escape from servant's hall of kitchen dreariness, an escape from the class system. It sounds almost like a revolution.

> The Frying-pan said, It's an awful delusion!
> The Tea-kettle hissed and grew black in the face,
> And they all rushed downstairs in the wildest confusion....
>
> And still you might hear, as they rode out of hearing,
> The Sugar-tongs snap, and the Crackers say Crack!
> Till far in the distance, their forms disappearing,
> They faded away. – And they never came back!

But this is not just a world of refuge, a fantasy of happy endings. In 'The Broom, the Shovel, the Poker and the Tongs', social order is restored after a furious quarrel: 'they put on the kettle, and little by little, they all became happy again'. All the same the skeleton will not fit back into the cupboard; something too alarming has been revealed. At the end of 'The Eclogue' Edward Lear is condemned to lead his normal life, to make large drawings nobody will buy, to paint oil pictures that will never dry, and so on, until spring returns and 'time restores a world of happier hours'; one believes in his routine sufferings, not in any difference that spring can make. The Pobble loses his toes in verses of seductive charm, his Aunt Jobiska gives him lavender water tinged with pink, and a feast of eggs and buttercups, but one is not meant to believe that Pobbles are happier without their toes.[17]

The poem about 'The Daddy Long-Legs and the Fly' may be less powerful, and to most people less memorable, than the one about the Pobble, but it is probably Lear's most perfect statement of a relationship. It takes place where many of Lear's scenes are set, on the beach: a setting of which Lewis Carroll was for some reason equally fond. Were these sad seashores Tennysonian ('thy cold grey rocks O sea'), or Darwinian ('this London once was middle sea'),[18] or to do with children's seaside holidays, just beginning in those years? The king and queen in red and green seem to belong to a fairy-tale, and the boat with pink and grey sails is equally unreal, unless it means the dawn or sunset. 'The Daddy Long-Legs and the Fly' is full of sadness and longing; it is some people's favourite Lear poem. But maybe the most touching and the final statement of his experience of life and of his own nature is 'Incidents in the Life of My Uncle Arly'.

I

O MY AGED UNCLE ARLY!
 Sitting on a heap of Barley
 Thro' the silent hours of night, –
Close beside a leafy thicket: –
On his nose there was a Cricket, –
In his hat a Railway-Ticket; –
 (But his shoes were far too tight).

II

Long ago, in youth, he squander'd
All his goods away, and wander'd
 To the Tiniskoop-hills afar.
There on golden sunsets blazing,
Every evening found him gazing, –
Singing, – 'Orb! you're quite amazing!
 'How I wonder what you are!'

III

Like the ancient Medes and Persians,
Always by his own exertions
 He subsided on those hills; –
Whiles, – by teaching children spelling, –
Or at times by merely yelling, –
Or at intervals by selling
 'Propter's Nicodemus Pills'.

185

IV

Later, in his morning rambles
He perceived the moving brambles
   Something square and white disclose; –
'Twas a First-class Railway-Ticket;
But, on stooping down to pick it
Off the ground, – a pea-green Cricket
   Settled on my uncle's Nose.

V

Never – never more, – oh! never,
Did that Cricket leave him ever, –
   Dawn or evening, day or night; –
Clinging as a constant treasure, –
Chirping with a cheerious measure, –
Wholly to my uncle's pleasure, –
   (Though his shoes were far too tight).

VI

So for three-and-forty winters,
Till his shoes were worn to splinters,
   All those hills he wander'd o'er, –
Sometimes silent; – sometimes yelling; –
Till he came to Borley-Melling,
Near his old ancestral dwelling; –
   (But his shoes were far too tight).

VII

On a little heap of Barley
Died my agèd uncle Arly,
   And they buried him one night; –
Close beside the leafy thicket; –
There, – his hat and Railway-Ticket; –
There, – his ever-faithful Cricket; –
   (But his shoes were far too tight).

The essence of what Victorian poetry has to offer is present in this poem, in its courageous sadness, in its musical tones, and in its detail. Life is transformed into art without any loss of realistic sharpness. The characterization is Dickensian, and the shoes that are too tight are an ingredient as essential to poetry as Tennyson's bluefly buzzing on the windowpane. It has the poetic substance of a novel in verse. 'Incidents in the Life of My Uncle Arly' is a masterpiece.

Boris Pasternak*

The older I get, the more interest and use I discover in mere biographical criticism, the relation of a poet through his personal history to the history of his times. The old-fashioned Life and Times makes modern academic criticism look thin indeed, and we feel cheated if a modern poet leaves no letters and no journal. But although historical biography is a laborious, demanding pursuit, so that we have few successful examples, I have just embarked on a biography of Boris Pasternak,[1] who was (as I conjecture) the greatest poet of my lifetime and of this century, in this or any language. Before I start to write his life it will give me pleasure to clarify how a foreigner and an amateur can hope to recognize a great poet. Boris Pasternak is a life-giving force, strong enough as it were to make one believe in the resurrection of the dead.

That can be said of few modern poets, not even of Blok or of Yeats, who were powerfully resonant but inwardly somewhat liturgical poets of chanting tones. Those tones were shared by symbolist poets in every European language, and very queer they sound today. Pasternak was as energetic, as dramatic, but more open to life. T. S. Eliot in my own pantheon comes higher than Yeats or Blok, if only because of their admittedly almost negligible admixture of falsity or folly, but Eliot demands to be considered as an intellectual, and there he fails for all his seriousness; his resurrection is the ghost of a rose in air that is full of ashes. He is always trying to rescue something lost to us, and he is more refined than we are and more in anguish about his refinement than most of us.

I do not want to be misunderstood: Eliot's memory is sacred to me, and I have spent a lifetime often rereading his poetry and sometimes

* When this lecture was given, the poet's sister Lydia Pasternak Slater read his poems in Russian.

187

his prose. Even at the height of his fame, his greatness was as great as people said it was, and somehow more real. But when you read Eliot you feel everything is over and the last possible kind of poetry in English has been perfected. If you are a poet you despair in the presence of his mastery. When you read Pasternak you are delighted and you want to write: not to rival his astonishing greatness, which anyway is like a force of nature, both naturally and historically incomparable, but he makes you want to get on with your own work. He communicates energy, and he opens windows. If this description is naive, that will make it true to my experience. As La Rochefoucauld says, 'At every age of life one arrives as a novice.' After nearly forty years, I still read Pasternak with amazement as one reads Shakespeare or Horace or maybe Baudelaire. In the past I have seldom read him in Russian, and then mostly the few poems in the *Penguin Book of Russian Verse*. He is hard to translate and few translators communicate the original shock. That is partly because from the beginning he was a post-symbolist poet, and they are always untranslatable because their poetry depends on the precise penumbra of particular words in a certain language. It is also partly because his Russian was a more strongly stressed language than our English; it is the only European language in which Kipling's 'Boots, boots, boots, boots, moving over Africa' and Wilde's 'Ballad of Reading Gaol' sound like great poetry. Russian in 1910 was still a crisp and fresh language, unexhausted by literature, and in Pushkin's time, just a hundred years before Pasternak's, it was untrodden snow. Boris Pasternak still seems to me, after a lifetime of assessing and exploring the modernist movement, the most exciting modernist poet in any European language, combining the seriousness of Eliot and the freshness of Gatsos or of Mayakovsky: and this without losing the old-fashioned sweetness of Tyutchev, the intensity of Fet or the resonance of Blok. But he is also after 1945 the greatest and the most moving post-modernist and anti-modernist poet. Let me give my first example from a yellow newspaper clipping thirty years old.[2] Eugene Kayden is not a great and famous poet, and he is distinctly unmodern, but what he loses in one way he gains in another.

I Would Go Home Again

I would go home again – to rooms
With sadness large at eventide,
Go in, take off my overcoat,
And in the light of streets outside

Take cheer. I'll pass the thin partitions
Right through; yes, like a beam I'll pass,
As image blends into an image,
As one mass splits another mass.

Let all abiding mooted problems
Deep rooted in our fortunes seem
To some a sedentary habit;
Still even so I brood and dream.

Again the trees and houses breathe
Their old refrain and fragrant air.
Again to right and left old winter
Sets up her household everywhere.

Again by dinner time the dark
Comes suddenly – to blind, to scare,
To teach the narrow lanes and alleys
She'll fool them if they don't take care.

Again the skies seize unawares
The earth; again the whirlwinds blow
And wrap the last few dozen aspens,
Deep in a cloak of drifting snow.

Again, though weak my heart, O Moscow,
I listen, and in words compose
The way you smoke, the way you rise,
The way your great construction goes.

And so I take you as my harness
For the sake of raging days to be,
That you may learn my verse by rote
And for my truth remember me.

In 1958 and 1959,[3] the translations by Pasternak's sister Lydia, which had been appearing here and there since 1945, were collected in a brief but important book. Lydia is an interesting poet in her own right, and as one might expect she conveys qualities of the original not to be found in other versions. Hugh MacDiarmid, introducing her in 1958, pinpointed one of her brother's central attractions: Pasternak wrote that 'There are in the experience of all great poets features of such naturalness that having tasted of them ... it is impossible not to fall ultimately as into heresy, into unheard of simplicity.'

Without intruding too much on biography, which reveals Boris Pasternak like many artists as a complex human being who sets out perhaps unconsciously to cheat the reader of those intimate glimpses for which readers hunger, it is fair to lay down what is known to everybody. He was born in 1890, and his serious awakening took place in his boyhood, in the revolution of 1905; the first great crisis of his life was the Russian revolution in 1917. Symbolist poetry, Blok's in particular, continually demanded an artist saviour, and expected an apocalyptic event: but the only symbolist poetry in which anything actually happened is that of the Russian revolution, just as the only Elizabethan or Stuart court masque in which anything really happened was the beheading of the King at Whitehall. Today in this country it is hard (at least for anyone under fifty) to enter into the fervours of those years: English views of heroic war have always had an element of Dad's Army, ever since Shakespeare. Pasternak's eyes were innocent in another way.

His father was a great painter, and Tolstoy's friend; he was summoned to the railway station at Astapovo to paint Tolstoy's deathbed portrait: his eldest son went with him, Boris Pasternak: the greatest Russian poet since Pushkin at the deathbed of the greatest Russian narrative writer since Pushkin. What is in common between the three of them defies crude definitions, but it exists, and it is particularly Russian. Pasternak was in some ways old-fashioned in his generation: he wrote as a young man in social revolutionary, not in Communist journals, and his heroic record in verse was about 1905,[4] not 1917, though it was published in the mid-1920s. The only poet of ours with whom I can compare Pasternak's revolutionary style is the early Auden, who I imagine had not read him, and who had no idea what to do with such a style, because to Auden revolution was a fantasy from which he developed in quite other directions. All the same I cannot avoid saying that a lot of the most exciting Auden is like a pastiche of Pasternak: I have never been clear whether that excitement is meretricious.

Pasternak turned in later life against his own earlier poetry. Most poets do so to a greater or lesser extent, if they live long enough. Unfortunately the definition of what he rejected is blurred. He spoke of everything before 1940, but he told Isaiah Berlin (1944) that what he really despised and rejected was *Early Trains*. Both stylistically and politically his expressions of self-disgust make nonsense of one another, so we must ignore them; we are thrown back on our own critical resources. There is no doubt that he lived his life and achieved his lifework under terrible pressure: those who suffer such a pressure and such a censorship say whatever they do say with great and disturbing force. That is as true of Shakespeare as of Pasternak, and Pasternak understood the analogy. He knew what they had in common, and in what way Shakespeare was free. Shakespeare, and *Hamlet* in particular, were his examples all his life. From being the inherited lumber of symbolism these texts became terribly real to him; even after he had written his great *Hamlet* poem, the reality increased as if the poem had been a prophecy. A very wild translation of Pasternak, taking more liberties even than Pasternak allowed himself as a translator, though not more I think than he claimed for translators, reveals his extraordinary power, because a great poet in our language wrote it, Robert Lowell, almost all of whose own poetry this translation dwarfs.[5] (See Appendix.)

The quality that Lowell uniquely recaptures is a momentum of meaning and of rhythm, a momentum of excitement, not uncontrolled like Mayakovsky or the upward beat of the beat poets, which thrilled Robert Lowell when he came across it later in life, but a profound vigour, a wind of life. The poems sound like water breaking through rock, which has been under pressure in the rock and become very pure. In Pasternak's case as in Shakespeare's, so much was censored or impossible to say that whatever did get said was very purely itself, and surfaced under pressure: it was a liberation for which we were thirsty. But the disadvantage of this amazing breakthrough style of Robert Lowell in *Imitations* was that all poems sound the same in it, whereas Boris Pasternak's style altered in many ways, developing in a spiral, and reaching his best I believe under the influence of Shakespeare, of that concision and dramatic power which he conveyed in translating Shakespeare, and of that mysterious freedom of which he spoke in his conversations with Gladkov.[6]

Pasternak's translations of Shakespeare have been criticized. They tend to crop and prune Shakespeare's luxuriance, to clarify and compress his meaning, to sharpen and to concentrate. That is a good fault in a verse translation, but it is also the way in which Shakespeare in the theatre as a mature writer revised his own *King Lear*. As a young man he revises by expanding, on the subject of love in *Love's Labour's Lost* and poetry in *Midsummer Night's Dream*; he floats away into an empyrean of poetry like the lark ascending. As he matures he strengthens, he sharpens characterization and he cuts. Pasternak's English was imperfect: at least in one of those long letters of his, to the English publisher of *Dr Zhivago*, it was very stiff. I am not certain that he was the best judge of English translations of his own poetry. But in Russian he was a supreme and a divine poet. I have heard only his powerful *Hamlet*, but that makes one ready to agree with Maurice Bowra's better-informed opinion in his review of Pasternak's *Antony and Cleopatra* in *Horizon* for August 1945: 'He is surely one of the greatest translators who have ever lived, even in Russia.... What matters is the poetry, and in Pasternak's Russian this flows in a full, Shakespearean flood. The magnificence, the variety, the inexhaustible vitality, the "high Roman fashion" are all here.'

It is worth noticing that Bowra's observant review of Pasternak's *Terrestrial Space*, and of his *Antony and Cleopatra*,[7] together with his own pleasing verse translations of Pasternak, which appeared in the next number of *Horizon* in September, were printed before the very influential essay in *The Creative Experiment* (1949). That book was a sequel to the *Heritage of Symbolism* (1943). It was finished in 1948 and the Pasternak essay was based on a lecture given as Professor of Poetry at Oxford. When it was published Maurice got a letter from the poet saying he had dreamed of being discussed by Maurice above all critics, and now that this hope was fulfilled the result exceeded all his expectations. Maurice does indeed make a strong case for his poet, and a prophetic case, that all but foresees *Dr Zhivago*: but he deliberately limits it to 1917–23. That is partly to slot Pasternak into place in a European movement, for the sake of the scheme of his book, partly no doubt for lack of texts, but I think at least partly because of Pasternak's disconcerting changes of style. 'Admirers of Pasternak's early work, so brilliant and provocative, may be surprised and disappointed by his latest manner. Pasternak is now fifty-five, and he has lost some of the exuberance and fire of youth. His poetry is easier to understand than of old.... the emphasis now is less on a mysterious sense of impending doom than on purely human emotions.'

Maurice did not underestimate this post-modernist phase or this emergence of old reservations about modernism, so soon to be validated by the appearance of *Dr Zhivago* and its poems, but he was a romantic at heart and he loved high spirits; I think he liked *The Waste Land* for its high spirits not for its melancholy; he certainly delighted in an Aristophanic play by Mayakovsky in which the hero meets Lloyd George at the North Pole and mistakes him for a sea-lion. In Bowra's mood in the late 1940s, something about Pasternak disconcerted him. And yet he saw in him 'a powerful poet of the Russian world who has done more than anyone to interpret the deep trust in life and nature and humanity which inspires its prodigious achievements'. Perhaps Maurice suspected that the same implacable political forces which had cut down Mayakovsky to size and simplified his style and abolished his wildness had crushed Boris Pasternak, though he would never have published a view so insulting about a living poet he so admired, and by the time I knew Maurice well in the 1960s he had no reservation left about Pasternak's greatness.

I should add that I feel that the downward curve in the graph of Pasternak's work, coinciding with Stalin and lasting to the end of the war, has been much exaggerated. I am unable to condemn or utterly to deplore the years of his silence because out of the pressure of that silence came his greatest work. He disliked his own early writings, but what poet does not? At the end of the war what he deplored (as I have said) was the 1940 collection *Early Trains*. When he had broken through into the full power of his late manner, he wrote: 'I dislike my style up to 1940, just as I quarrel with half Mayakovsky's writings and with some of Yesenin's. I dislike the disintegrating forms, the impoverished thought and the littered and uneven language of those days.... I would not lift a finger to rescue more than a quarter of my writings from oblivion.'

But this is the aged eagle spreading his wings, it is an eagle flying up from the shoulders of an eagle; we can permit ourselves to admire the first eagle as well as the second. With *Zhivago* ready, he criticized his own early prose, perhaps more justifiably for 'its affected manner, the besetting sin of those days'. He was free of this chrysalis, and sure of having said what he had it in him to say, in *Zhivago*. 'The poems scattered over the past years of my life ... are steps preparatory to the novel.'[8] But to a poet everything is preparatory to a great and exhausting work; the work itself as it recedes in time becomes a base for new steps preparatory. Boris Pasternak did not stop working after *Zhivago*. We have great poems of 1956, 1957, 1958 and 1959. *Zhivago* is just an element in their authority.

When It Clears Up

The lake is like a giant saucer;
Beyond – a gathering of clouds;
Like stern and dazzling mountain-ranges
Their massif the horizon crowds.

And with the light that swiftly changes,
The landscape never stays the same.

One moment clad in sooty shadows,
The next – the woods are all aflame.

When, after days of rainy weather,
The heavy curtain is withdrawn,
How festive is the sky, burst open!
How full of triumph is the lawn!

The wind dies down, the distance lightens,
And sunshine spreads upon the grass;
The steaming foliage is translucent
Like figures in stained-window glass.

Thus from the church's narrow windows
In glimmering crowns, on spreading wings
Gaze into time in sleepless vigil
Saints, hermits, prophets, angels, kings.

The whole wide world is a cathedral;
I stand inside, the air is calm,
And from afar at times there reaches
My ear the echo of a psalm.

World, Nature, Universe's Essence,
With a secret trembling, to the end,
I will thy long and moving service
In tears of happiness attend.[9]

It is hardly surprising if Boris Pasternak had not only hidden thoughts but mixed thoughts about many things: about the city of Moscow, for example. In 'Spring 1944' it is:

Moscow I love with all my power.
Here is the source of all the wonderful
With which the centuries will flower.

But in 1956 he is writing about 'the whole town, the whole world under snow'. In the last years of his life he undoubtedly wrote with greater personal freedom and more immediate self-expression than before. It is not surprising that some themes recur with new meanings, some with slighter variations. From early days his thoughts and feelings have been entangled in nature, but nature is seasonal and recurrent, and his thoughts and feelings about nature can no longer be disentangled from that recurrence. His sharpest personal statements therefore, like the *Hamlet* poem, most avoid talking about nature, but his sense of depth and inspiration still inevitably have a great deal to do with natural process. Sometimes this entanglement in nature is so detailed as to be shocking and disoriented, both in prose and in verse: never in any short-story writer was the weather so active. The city rushes forward to meet the train or the train runs towards Moscow laden with an immense crimson sun, newly risen above the swelling land. The touch of dynamic surrealism arises from a certain hunger of modernism to incorporate cities and railways and modern life, a hunger that found little expression in England until Auden and Spender, in whom it was superficial, though if you look for it you will find it in every generation since Tennyson. But the special wildness and strange exactness of Pasternak are based on synaesthesia, that is on a theory of intermingled perceptions based on the intense inter-mingled perceptions of childhood. They can be thrilling.

> The clustered, wax-bespattered flowers
> On massive trees, sedate and old,
> Lit up by raindrops, burn and sparkle
> Above the mansion they enfold.

He expresses a fundamental and intense faith in reality, in the processes of nature and the natural processes of mankind, even in *Zhivago*, to the point of resurrection and an appeal to a kind of Christianity, which for him I think is just an essential part of a Russian acceptance of nature, including the soul and his own nature. Once again, his point of view does not seem to differ much from the late Shakespeare's: it is not dogmatic because they were both among the least dogmatic of men. But the wish to cram the most intense feelings and perceptions into his verse do lead to peculiar effects. He is a perfect example of the general truth that genius is the survival of the powers of childhood, unalloyed and undiminished, among adult intellectual powers.

Maurice Bowra singles out the two phrases, 'that a frosty night is "like a blind puppy lapping its milk" or that the dew "runs shivering like a hedgehog"'. His explanation is that 'a frosty night has really something primitively greedy about it and the shivering of the dew is like the shivering of a hedgehog'. There is surely more to it. Pasternak wants to fills us with a revival of surprise, a reverence of a childlike wonder. That is surely one of the legitimate purposes and procedures of all poetry, but of his more than most.[10] The blind puppy feels in the dark the attractions of the milk it laps: the earth is white under frozen snow, not just an English hoar-frost, and the night is black. The night is like a puppy sniffing the special smell of the frozen earth, and lapping it. The point is not the exactness of the words, but their shock quality, and their complexity of suggestion. I have never seen a hedgehog shivering, nor for that matter dew shivering except in a very early half-light on shivering grass, the time for seeing hedgehogs. Anyone might shiver before the sun is up. The coldness is also an eagerness, just as the puppy expresses an eagerness. The same kind of complexity, the same ramification of the senses, one into another, lies behind both phrases.

God forbid that we should read poetry only in this way, but we must use what intelligence we have, and whatever doglike powers of snuffling we may have, to discover how poetry works on us as it does: and in the case of poetry so essentially original in its procedures as this is, to enter into its new world, to become familiar with all its behaviour, and of course to remove obstacles, including those set up by translation. One can see from the translations of Pasternak's early prose, which often sound very queer indeed, what difficulties of delicately poised perception the translators of his poetry had to face.

'At the final moment absolutely empty, there was the solid stone platform, there the solid stone sonority, the solid stone cry of the conductor: *Pronti! – All away!* And he raced past the window, chasing his own voice. With dignity station columns swept by. Like knitting needles lights twinkled out and intercrossed. Bright station lights flashed in at the train windows, the draught caught swiftly at them and swept them through the compartment and out on the other side, and there the iron railings caught at them and stretched them out.'[11] This is dazzling and exact, but a bit puzzling and unexpected. The power of poetry to integrate meaning and image transforms this kind of language.

> After this the halt and summer
> Parted company, and taking
> Off his cap at night the thunder
> Took a hundred blinding stills.
>
> Lilac clusters faded; plucking
> Off an armful of new lightnings,
> From the field he tried to throw them
> At the mansion in the hills.
>
> And when waves of evil laughter
> Rolled along the iron roofing

And, like charcoal on a drawing,
Showers thundered on the fence,

Then the crumbling mind began to
Blink; it seemed it would be floodlit
Even in those distant corners
Where the light is now intense.[12]

'Thunderstorm, Instantaneous Forever' was written during the
hectic excitement of 1917, when he was twenty-seven, and it was
published in 1922 as a part of the sequence *My Sister, Life*, probably
his most famous single book, the one by which he was generally
recognized as a great poet. He wrote later, 'When *My Sister, Life*
appeared, expressing completely uncontemporary sides of poetry
revealed to me in the revolutionary summer, I did not care at all what
the power was called to which I owed this book, because it was
immeasurably greater than me and the poetic theories surrounding
me.'[13] In early 1922, Boris Pasternak married his first wife. *My Sister,
Life* is about a love affair, among other things. He was a hermetic
poet, in the sense that he constantly alluded to a private life which he
never directly expressed, but the presence and smell and warmth of
which made his poetry resonant. One catches his meaning directly
enough, by an intuitive sympathy, as one was meant to catch it. I think
it was this aspect of Pasternak that I first found spellbinding. There is
more to human communication than mere words, love among other
things breeds heightened awareness, and poetry which touches love
conveys more than it seems to convey. Nothing is so prone as love to
alter the weather: it even alters the definitions of poetry and of the
soul, and of philosophy itself, as Plato would have agreed that it did.

The Definition of Soul

It falls like a ripe pear into the storm
with a single clinging leaf.
How faithful – it quits its branch –
reckless – it chokes in the heat.

It falls like a pear, more askew
than the wind. How faithful –
Look back: it thundered beautifully,
bloomed, scattered – into ashes.

The storm burned our country.
Fledgling, will you know your nest?

O my quivering goldfinch, my leaf,
why do you flutter against my shy silk?

Do not fear, my single clinging song.
What should we strive for?
O indivisible trembling – you don't get
that deadly phrase 'stay put'.[14]

The history of the publication of *Dr Zhivago* and its poems is too complicated, and essentially too well known for me to repeat it. The Nobel prize was a factor, and so was Pasternak's powerful protest against the Russian invasion of Hungary in 1956. He had already refused to condone the execution of Marshal Tukhachevsky and his colleagues in 1937. He gave money to those who were persecuted, he corresponded with people in the camps of the Gulag, he welcomed returned prisoners with open arms in public places. He was sensitive to every event of his lifetime. That part of his life was all but silent in most of his poetry, and yet it pervades his poetry as love pervades *My Sister, Life*. It is true that the *Zhivago* poems gain immeasurably because we are told whose poems they are, but it is also true that Pasternak called them the final chapter and the climax of his novel. Queer as it may seem to us, it was those simple and harmless-looking Christian poems among *Zhivago*'s handful of verses that stuck worst in the throats of the Russian bureaucracy. They are so beautiful and innocent: if they were in English they might almost have been written by the nineteenth-century Dean of a quiet cathedral town: but because they are in Russian, and modern, they have a further quality. They are offensive to the Soviet State because they are part of Pasternak's definition of what it is to be Russian, of what has survived and cannot be changed. But they are not at all like Pushkin's famous 'Prophet', the most famous Russian religious poem, nor do they recall the marmoreal and abstract devotion of Derzhavin ('Vosstal Vsie-vishnii Bog, na sudit . . . '), but the hymns of Charles Wesley, or German Lutheran hymns.

But what can sin now mean to me,
And death, and hell, and sulphur burning,
When, like a graft on to a tree,
I have – for everyone to see –
Grown into being part of thee
In my immeasurable yearning?[15]

The accumulation of our history does not cease to give new meanings to our religion, and the freshness of that reality is raw, and painful, and offensive to many. For him, it was an essential strand in his lifeline, in his identity:

> the gathering of the poor in a hovel,
> the descent into the cellar with a candle,
> the candle snuffing out in fright
> when the resurrected man stood up.[16]

Late in his life, he returned as many poets do to his original themes, but with a new spareness and directness it had taken him a lifetime to achieve. He wrote four poems then about Blok, who had once been the overshadowing master of Russian poetry when Pasternak was in his twenties: much as Eliot or perhaps Auden was in English in my own generation. The generations differ of course; Blok was more like a Russian equivalent of the later Yeats, a poet who exhausted his resources and on whom nobody can improve, any more than they can on Eliot or on Auden. Yeats, like Pasternak, was a poet who learnt much from the theatre, and, like Blok, a poet who remade himself out of the sense of a crisis that he never quite understood. Pasternak's late view of Blok tells us something of his late view of the October revolution. Pasternak's first great breakthrough was between the socialist revolution of February 1917, a more successful version of 1905 (hence his choice of 1905 as a subject for heroic poetry), and the Bolshevik revolution of October 1917, which very soon began to terrify him, though he remained a loyal Russian citizen, loyal above all to Russian poetry, to humanity and to the duty of poets to humanity. It is not nothing to have despised power, to have refused flattery, and to have gone on working as if he had eternity to squander. His last public, official commission that I can trace was to make the Russian translation of Brecht's speech of thanks for the Lenin Prize, about a month before his own final disgrace. One would like to know what they had to say to one another. In 1956 he wanted to teach:

> The essence of past days
> And where they start,
> Foundations, roots,
> The very heart....
>
> So Chopin once enclosed
> The plenitude
> Of farmsteads, parks, groves, graves
> In his *Études*.

> The torment and delight
> Of triumph so
> Achieved tightens the bowstring
> Bending the bow.[17]

The first poem about Blok in the same year was a savage and contemptuous attack on the Soviet authorities who decided what poetry is 'to be stuffed down our throats by fools'. The second celebrates the wild freedom and revolutionary purity of Blok and his grandfather, 'a Jacobite and crystal-souled'. Pasternak had a lifelong interest in the French revolution, and wrote several fragments of a verse play about it. His views of revolution in those fragments are severe, and the verse is as if Racine had lived a hundred years later. 'On staniet mrakom, on soïdiet s uma. On etot dien, i bog, i sbiet, i razum': 'Gloom and obscurity, insanity Engulf our day and God and light and reason.' 'V Parishie ruklopleshut lipi gromu': 'Lime trees applaud the thunder-claps.' These fragments about Paris, Saint-Just and Robespierre were written in 1917, and published in a revolutionary socialist magazine in May of that year. The third of Pasternak's Blok poems, nearly forty years after the unfinished verse play, sets Blok in a landscape and in his childhood.

> Childhood! Boredom of blackboard and chalk!
> Songs of farm-girl and servant!
> As far as the eye can see
> River and meadow stretch away.

The final poem winds into the centre of the subject: it follows by intimate connections of imagery and plot on the third, showing that these four poems are a sequence, they are really one poem. The fourth deals with sunset, bruising of twilight, bloody gashes in the sky, omens of storm and disaster: forked lightning, 'the state is about to be shaken, A hurricane shadows the land'.

> Blok saw the writing in the sky,
> the heavens told him what it meant,
> dirty weather and thunderstorm,
> and the cyclone imminent.
>
> Blok awaited the conclusion,
> heights and deeps engraved in flames,
> desiring and dreading the outcome,
> in his life, in his poems.[18]

He is still, in 1956, very excited by Blok's poems. I do not suppose he thinks that any poet can be redeemed except by his life and his poems, which are somehow one thing, to be assessed together, as we do in fact assess the poets of Pasternak's generation, often enough wrongly it may be. In his own case the life and the poems appear to be simply coherent. I think this simplicity conceals much complexity, but our final judgement of Pasternak's greatness will extend into his life and poems more deeply than it does today, and into the relationship between them, and will lead us to marvel at him more than we do. The virtue of Blok is one he made his own: truthfulness – he was weather-wise. 'Snow is falling, snow is falling ... And perhaps year follows year, as snow falls and as these words fall.' He was a deep and a simple poet, when all is said and done.

With the simplest and deepest poets in every language it is always the same: one can easily abstract the content of their poems, though symbolist poems present more obstacles than others, and at least one can observe their syntax and their form, but the perfect texture of their verses remains mysterious. It is important to remember that detailed study of the texture of poetry was further advanced in Russia than it was elsewhere, when Pasternak was a young poet: as a verse stylist he is not knowing, but he knew a lot about style. Some of it he learnt from Annensky, who oddly turns out to be the Russian translator of Euripides. Much of his knowledge was intuitive, and more or less impenetrable, particularly to foreigners. It can be learnt only by ear, and learning it improves the ear. Greatness is not a general impression, it is a mass of interweaving detail intuitively apprehended, and it is alive. But even simple words can work on us and satisfy us in a way that criticism cannot exactly follow. Consider by analogy to Pasternak the physical sound, the verbal texture, of an awkward-looking stanza by Thomas Hardy. Hardy like Pasternak was trained in early life to be a musician.

> Silently I footed by an uphill road
> That led from my abode to a spot yew-boughed;
> Yellowly the sun sloped low down to westward,
> And dark was the east with cloud.
>
> Then amid the shadow of that livid sad east,
> Where the light was least, and a gate stood wide,
> Something flashed the fire of the sun that was facing it,
> Like a brief blaze on that side.[19]

Hardy is much gloomier than Pasternak, Hardy was a self-educated countryman without social hope, while Pasternak was a progressive, liberal, middle-class boy from the Jewish intelligentsia. But they share a density of nature, an inwardness that animates the landscape. If you translated these verses of Hardy, they would melt away in your hand. You could easily abstract their content, you could observe some of their devices, but the open secret of their perfect verbal texture remains mysterious. We have no exhaustive notation in which to record all the procedures of language. Pasternak and Hardy have this in common. Someone said of Liszt's piano music that to play it well 'calls for a little more technique than he demands': in the same way to enter deeply into Pasternak's poetry calls for a little more technical awareness than he seems to demand. Fortunately for us foreigners, the techniques of poetry are more or less the same in all languages. The big difference between poetic and piano technique is that Liszt took the piano from the salon into the concert hall, but Pasternak, at a time when poetry in Russia was public art, withdrew it from the concert hall, and made it personal, and unforgettably memorable.

> It is a whistle filled to bursting,
> it is the crack and knock of ice,
> it is the night that frosts the leaves,
> it is a duel of two nightingales.
> It is the soundlessness of the sweetpeas,
> the universe weeping in a green pod.... [20]

That was in the summer of 1917. By the 1950s, after the calculated silences and interventions, and after the great public statement of *Zhivago*, poetry was to Pasternak an identity and a conscience, an inward consciousness, with a magnetic north of its own. He had never been unambitious as an artist: his Robespierre fragments can be matched at the very end of his life with a historical play set in 1860 and onwards, *The Blind Beauty*, the first draft of which was about half finished when he died. He wrote in an English letter that he wanted in *The Blind Beauty* as in *Dr Zhivago* 'to give ... a conception of life in general, of life as such, of historical being or existence'. The play was meant to have a vast sweep of characters like the novel, and a sense of destiny, and of the future. Pasternak had already written futuristic heroic verse in his *1905*, a verse novel in his *Spektorsky*, many different kinds of metaphysical lyric, sub-symbolist, modernist and post-modernist, he had translated from German, from English and from Georgian, immensely improving his work as translator in the course of his life, and in *Dr Zhivago* he had written not exactly a novel but something more powerful, just as *The Blind Beauty* is not exactly a play but something more powerful, just as Tolstoy's *War and Peace* evaporates at its climax for philosophical reasons, dying in the attempt to transfigure itself, remaining a novel nd not a novel. But I believe that what is essential in this hyperactivity and hyperambition of the writer is to be found in Boris Pasternak's innocent-looking lyrics.

Finally we must face the question whether our admiration for Pasternak is like the French passion for Heine, the continental passion for Byron, the northern passion for Kazantzakis: is there something false about it? Is it determined by the row about *Zhivago* and the Nobel prize? Does he satisfy our need for a Russian martyr of intellectual freedom, an anti-Communist with battle-scars who can speak for the past and for Russian nature and some kind of everlasting Russia? Certainly not, because Prince Mirsky, a Russian critic who became a Marxist convert, returned to Russia and died there, already knew Pasternak's importance in the 1920s; so did Rilke, so did Valéry. In *How Are Verses Made?* in 1926 Mayakovsky[21] is very respectful indeed to Pasternak. Even those savagely ironic ladies Akhmatova and Madame Mandelshtam allow his pre-eminence. Admittedly Brodsky thinks Pasternak's fame is exaggerated, but Brodsky is opinionated: I have heard him refer to Tolstoy as the Barbara Cartland of Russian literature. As a young man I conceived Pasternak to be a great poet before I had ever heard of *Zhivago*, and no change of opinion of mine about the history of our times has shaken that conception in the least. Maurice Bowra would have admired Pasternak equally if he had died in 1923. Communist anthologies of 1932 allow his overwhelming importance. Forget *Dr Zhivago* for a moment if you can: Boris Pasternak remains the greatest Russian poet of modern times. One of the most impressive things about him, if you want an almost objective test, is the way that he can stand up to Shakespeare. How many other foreign poets in this or the last century could have done so? Even George Seferis never attempted it.

Consider the opinion of younger Russian poets who are not in exile. Twenty-five years ago I had a private conversation with Yevgeni Yevtushenko about the position of Pasternak in Russian literature. When he first arrived in Europe, that was the subject I was most passionately keen to discuss with him, and later I took notes of his reply. He thought Pushkin was the peak of poetry, and therefore not to be counted. Pushkin apart, the very greatest of Russian poets were

Blok, Mayakovsky and Pasternak, and later in the conversation he promoted Yesenin to the same category. The second rank consisted of Nekrasov, Tyutchev and Lermontov, the third rank was 'Mandelshtam and all the others'. This conversation was casual and his opinion may have altered, of course. He spoke of 'the soaring inspiration of Blok, the earthiness of Yesenin, the political seriousness of Mayakovsky, and the power over images of Pasternak'. He explained his admiration for 'those who soar, but also those who have earth on their boots'. If I am not mistaken he remarked on what I certainly noticed, how Pasternak combines all the virtues of the others. In younger poets like Yevtushenko, like Leonid Aranzon (1939–70) and Ilya Bokstein (b.1937), we can trace lessons learnt from him.[22]

> Here apart from the silence there is no poet.
> The surprise of sodden leaves.
> The rain streams down so quietly as though it were light,
> as though it were the secret of its freedom.

If we are to ask in what way is *Dr Zhivago*, in what way is Boris Pasternak's lyric poetry liberating, the answer must be universal, it may be specially Russian but not exclusively so: nothing liberates anyone from Stalin or his successors, or from history, except in some strange and spiritual sense in which this poetry liberates. The acceptance and the love of life itself in Pasternak's poetry is in a way terrifying. Something of the same quality is diffusely present in the paintings of his father, the synagogue cantor's son Leonid Pasternak, but there it looks like a social atmosphere, almost a quality of the lamplight. In Boris Pasternak's poetry it is terribly concentrated, and for him the easy old questions of art in the 1900s have become more serious. He gave up music because of its technical demands: he lacked perfect pitch; he gave up philosophy because of a girl: he was distracted into poetry, but art itself was in his blood and in his bones.

He has a dignity, and he gives it us, just as a human being, as someone who treads on this earth; he assumes it in his poetry, and, by identifying with that poetry, we assume it. He studied philosophy one summer at Marburg: by a freak of chance and a year or two he just missed coinciding there with another young philosopher, and another apprentice poet, T. S. Eliot, who was two years older than Boris Pasternak. Pasternak called *Zhivago* 'my chief and most important work, the only one I am not ashamed of', and wrote that 'all the rest of my writings are devoid of all sense and importance. The most part of my mature years I gave to Goethe, Shakespeare and other translations.' Eliot in 1954 at the end of the *Four Quartets* expressed grave misgivings about the value of his poetry, which he often felt to be futile.[23] Those are the scrupulous feelings and the deadly seriousness of middle age, when a writer begins to know that whatever is to be said must be said now, because years of enchanting development do not lie ahead of one. Boris Pasternak passed the awful test of middle age and its worries as he passed the test of purity and fruitfulness in youth, and the test of courage and snow-haired integrity as he began to grow old.

His father Leonid drew a sketch of Lenin in action, drawn from the life. Boris did the same in verse, in his 'Sublime Malady'.[24] Later he wrote that 'This unique world, the like of which has never been known before, has receded now into the far distance of memory; it hangs suspended on the horizon like mountains seen from the plain or like a great city in the distance seen against the smoky background of a red sunset.' A good critic of his whole work, Helen Muchnic, has written that in this he is right. '*Dr Zhivago* is not about the Revolution; it is about how and why poetry is written.'[25] I am inclined to agree that it is not about the role of the revolutionary, but the role of the poet, his own role. That is why it is so compelling. He was obsessed with modern history, how could he not be? But above all he was a poet. As his sister Lydia once said of him, he liked the modesty of the particular. One of the principal facts about him, which gives the edge and nervous strength to his whole lifework, is his determination to remain an artist, as Shakespeare did. He has not only given us great poetry, he has shown us what poetry is made of and what that stillness is which underlies it: that is something Shakespeare never did. It is the unique contribution of Pasternak's generation of poets to the study of all poetry. It is a large part of his own unique contribution. His political martyrdom was the crown of such a life.

APPENDIX

The Seasons

I

Now the small buds are pronged
to the boughs like candle-butts.
Steaming April! The adolescent park
simmers.

Like a lassoed buffalo, the forest
is noosed in the ropes of shrill feathered throats –
a wrestler, all gratuitous muscle,
caught in the pipes of the grand organ.

The shadows of the young leaves are gummy.
A wet bench streams in the garden.
Poetry is like a pump
with a suction-pad that drinks and drains up

the clouds. They ruffle in hoop-skirts,
talk to the valleys –
all night I squeeze out verses,
my page is hollow and white with thirst.

II

The garden's frightful – all drip and listening.
The rain is loneliness.
A branch splashes white lace on the window.
Is there a witness?

The earth is swollen and smelly,
the pasture is a sponge;
as if it were August, the far off night ripens
and rots in the elm-dissected field.

No sound. No trespasser watches the night.
The rain is alone in the garden –
it starts up again, it drips
off roof and gutter.

I will drink the rain,
I, loneliness . . .
the rain weeps in the darkness.
Is there a witness?

But silence! Not even a wrinkling leaf.
No sign in the darkness,
only a swallowing of sobs and the swish of slippers . . .
in the interval, earth choking its tears . . .

III

Summer says goodbye to the station.
Running in its photographer's black hood,
and blinding us with flash-bulbs, the thunder
takes a hundred souvenir snap-shots.

The lilac bush is a black scarecrow.
From hill and sky armfuls of lightning

crash on the station-agent's cottage
to smash it with light.

Waves of malevolence
lift the coal-dust from the roof;
the rain, coming down in buckets,
is like charcoal that smudges a drawing.

Something in my mind's
most inaccessible corners
registers the thunder's illumination,
stands up, and steadily blinks.

IV

A driving rain whips the air.
The ice is scabby grey. You wait
for the sky to wake up.
Snow drones on the wind.

With unbuckled galoshes, with a muffler
flapping from his unbuttoned coat,
March bulls ahead, and makes rushes
at the frivolous, frenzied birds.

The season cannot miss you. It tries
to scrape up the candle-drippings in a snotty handkerchief –
it is safe now
to snatch off the night-caps of the tulips . . .

He is out of his senses, he musses his mop of hair.
He is buried in his mind's mush,
and stammers scurrilities
against me – my resurrection in the spring.

V

Pinecones pop in the military gloom of our bedroom.
A grey smog boils in the overtime lightbulb.
The blue window simmers
over the snow-desert.
Our lips puff and stick.

Spring! I leave the street of astonished pines,
alarmed distances,
the awkward classical wooden house, apprehending its downfall –
the air blue as piles of faded sky-blue denim
lugged by the prisoners from their wards!

The age is breaking – pagan Rome,
thumbs down on clowns,

the wrestler's vain swansong to the grandstand –
on the true!
The overpaid gladiator must die in earnest.

Robert Lowell

George Seferis

'All the earth, all the air, of love and pleasure speaks: teach thine arms then to embrace.' If you are reading Elizabethan lyric poems you may admire a poem without remembering quite who wrote it: almost anyone might have written it. But we have the opportunity today with our leisure, our languages and our libraries to know the entire works of modern poets: one may trace their progression, engage in what engaged them, distinguish what is personal, what is temporary, what is a stubborn, perhaps unconscious tendency in their work. Our interest begins at the point where one poet differs from another, and one poem from another. The study that satisfies this curiosity is fascinating, and has the slowness of life, and it is deeply technical. A poet often moves in circles, stalking his essential poem for a lifetime. The greatest poets choose themes of central importance and confront them in the end directly. I think of Pasternak doing that, at a bare table in a patch of sunlight in an empty room. The critic must follow the poet, but he has to approach the greatest themes, and the quality of greatness itself, much more indirectly. His nourishment is a few details and particular observations.

> The minefold Bugbears of the Caspian lake
> Sat whistling ebon hornpipes to their ducks; . . . .
>
> Meantime great Sultan Soliman was born,
> And Atlas blew his rustic rumbling horn.[1]

It is in this spirit that I would like to take a new look at George Seferis. His case is classical: no one with any right to an opinion doubts that he was among the greatest European poets in this century, and in his own language a powerful and life-giving force, as Pasternak was in Russian. One may observe without pressing the point that these two masters had a somewhat similar relationship to Orthodox Christianity. In other ways their backgrounds are different. One of Pasternak's earliest memories was hearing music from another room where Tolstoy was listening to a Tchaikovsky trio. George Seferis as a little boy wandered about the seashore among fishermen and their boats. Pasternak as a young man went to Marburg to study German philosophy. Seferis as a young man went to France to perfect his French for the Greek foreign service; one had to know the words for soup-ladle and for back-scratcher, it was that sort of exam. He was not only a brilliant but a profound linguist, with a very exact sense of the right word and the resonance of a phrase, in French, in English and in Greek. I mean exact in a poet's not a diplomat's sense, as Virgil was praised for *proprietas verborum*, the milk-white tooth of a dead lion, the colours sprinkled on a bird's wings. He was like a shepherd to whom his flock of words were familiar friends, and all their behaviour and individuality known to him. He was formidable in language, and viewed translations with a severe eye. He communicated with the marrow of a language, Laforgue in French and Eliot in English and Makriyannis in Greek. He observed with relish every nuance of peasant expression, and when he walked in the street he always came home with those strange floating phrases that one overhears in a crowd. He was intensely humorous and intensely serious. The humour appeared to the public only after his death, when his light and private verse and his diaries and letters began to be published, but in fact it was always a strand in his poems. They are serious, but they are not always as solemn as they seem. Yet a poem with the lightest of incisions may become terrible. It is not just that the surface texture suddenly alters, but the same poem or the same few lines of a poem, even the same image engage us in many ways.[2]

There are a few simple things to be said about his method. He conveys powerful emotion, though one scarcely sees why, as if life were encoded in the poem. The enigmatic, unexplained nature of the images can be terrifying, because it communicates immediately. One reason for this is that George Seferis is a much more political poet than foreigners realize;[3] his poems are rooted in their time. When they were first published they did not need to decoded. In 1937, Greece was suffering under all its usual sufferings, but also under a stupefying fascist dictatorship. The meaning of the poem was an open secret. But the word political is too shallow: I mean only that his poems are engaged in reality, not in timeless myth. Mythology is not timeless; one must pay attention to where and when every poem was written. George wrote somewhere that he had committed himself utterly to public causes only twice in his life, to the war against Hitler and to the struggle for Cyprus.[4] To those two commitments one may add his stand against the Colonels from 1967 onwards, which made him a national hero whether he liked it or not, just as Pasternak became one. In addition to this he was a public servant most of his life with very high standards of decency. He was a critic and lover of Greece and the Greeks, personally not just from principle, and I believe it was the depth of his love for his country that killed him.

That being said, it would be hard to overstress the degree to which he was essentially a poet. His decision to retire from the foreign service as soon as he could do so took shape when a bomb fell not far away from him in Syntagma Square, and he thought what a disgrace that Seferis the poet should be killed by a stray bomb as he crossed Syntagma on the way to the office. When he first came to England, with very little English,[5] he brought along a little edition of *Hamlet* with a facing French translation. He was fond of quoting a line from Yeats, 'In dreams begin responsibilities.' He was a spirited parodist, and an admirer and translator of Edward Lear.[6] He went so far as to achieve the impossible by writing a series of extremely funny and Lear-like limericks in Greek, intended for one of his grandchildren. (See Appendix.) His poetry was in a way his self-identity, which of course was multiple, but he saw the individual poem as a special gift, sent as it were by God. He once said to me with a kind of awed perplexity, 'My poetry has been slow dying.'

In the magazine *Personal Landscape*, which was a quarterly sold around the cafés in Alexandria and Cairo, founded in late summer of 1941, with a core of contributors who had known one another in Greece before the war, George Seferis published a note about poetry, in a series of similar notes where the other contributors were more pretentious, much less amusing and less deep.

All poems written or unwritten exist. I don't mean a platonic but a biological existence.... The special ability of the poet is to see them.... Mere talent without the poetical gift (i.e. the gift of the seer) is inconceivable. Poems do not live alone. Cases of solitary poems are extremely rare. Usually and normally poems form large crowds subject to special 'sociological laws' and suffering all sorts of social diseases, plagues and starvation, revolutions and dissolutions, wars and golden ages, unemployment and kirtle control, etc.... Poems of the same kind meet usually in special places; they have their clubs.... heroic poems meet in ships on calm sea; poems

about slumber in battlefields; poems about rapes in waterless
islands; poems about death in green meadows at noon; poems
about happiness on peaks of mountains; poems about self-indul-
gence on staircases (think of *Ash Wednesday*) and limericks in the
bathroom.

This fantasy is like the best Greek café conversation. Of course he is
fooling about but of course he is perfectly serious. It would be hard to
unpick the seriousness from the humour, but one remembers what he
said, in my case for thirty years, and one knows what he means. In the
same way there are touches of surrealism in many of his poems; he
uses devices of surprising yet very accurate imagery, which inevitably
expresses a kind of alienation, just as they would in our own so-called
Martian school of poetry, which I admire. But Seferis is less a man
from Mars, he is solidly himself, with his inescapable warmth and
humanity.

Neither the druggist who peers between a red orb and a green orb
like a ship petrified....

While the face of Poland altered like ink soaking into
blotting-paper....

If I begin singing I shall shout
and if I shout –
the agapanthuses command silence
lifting the hand of a blue Arab boy
or the footprints of a goose left on the air....[7]

The first of these poems was written on consular service in Albania;
he was in love and not able to marry. The second was written in that
gloomy and confused period before Greece entered the war, the third
in South Africa, in despair of the Greek politicians in exile and in
sadness at the tragic fate of Greece. The context of the whole poems
imposes a meaning on their details, which one senses without disen-
tangling it. The *Three Secret Poems*, which came late in his career,
being mostly written I think when he was Ambassador in London
during the Cyprus crisis that led to the independence of Cyprus, are
like three sequences of shortish poems where a multitude of details
and resonances combine to one powerful effect.

His most famous poem, and the first in which he showed that kind
of mastery, was *Mythistorima*, but I reserve that for later. My chief
aim in this lecture is to explore ways in which Seferis is different

from all other poets. To do that I must set aside *Mythistorima* just because of its perfection. Perfection is mysterious and hard to deal with, in modern poetry as it is in the sonnets of Shakespeare. The sonnets have something in common with a technique of Seferis in that they are personal, more intimate than a diary, and yet they offer only fragments of a plot, they are not a novel and not quite a record. 'Mythistorima' means 'Novel', but the plot has been left out. It also means or implies a myth and a history; that is how Seferis annotated his title, and the same title might be extended to cover much of his work. Similar modern poetry has been written in French, in Spanish, in English, even in German, but the self in Laforgue is more elusive and fugitive, the self in Lorca dissolves in the poetry as moonlight does into crispness and darkness, the self in Ezra Pound is often socially unbearable and in Eliot's poetry the self is enigmatic. In Rilke it is intellectually constipated. In Seferis the self of the poet is solid, and warm, and in a way simple, and as we knew him. The reason may lie in the nature of relationships, in traditional Greek society, expressed in the language which it might almost be said he was the first to write down. I would like to make Seferis easy for you, but I seem already to have reached the alarming conclusion that you would need to know Greek and the Greeks with some degree of inwardness, and something about European poetry in this century. And yet he communicates immediately, as Eliot does in a poem like 'Marina',[8] the one that first drew him to Eliot, and of all foreign poems the one most like his own.

> I want nothing else but to speak simply, that this grace may be
> given me.
> Because we have loaded even our songs with so much music that
> little by little they are sinking
> decorated our art so much that the gold has eaten away its face
> and it is time for us to utter our few words because our soul sets
> sail tomorrow.[9]

He admits us into his meditations without any preliminaries, as Eliot does. One has to listen to him and to take him seriously because one knows at once he is absolutely serious. The necessity to listen to Seferis is something spiritual. It is as if our souls were famished and there had never for us been any other poet. And he refreshes our senses. He is as vivid as Cavafy about particular places and times of day, the images he prints on the mind are unpretentious and yet unforgettable, the indefinite swaying of a tall palm tree, or in another poem unknown languages like dead cigarette ends sticking to ruined lips,[10] or again in a late poem, the 'Letter to Rex Warner':[11]

> the luminous skyscrapers
> show their windows gleaming
> like the skin of a huge sea monster
> as it breaks clear of the waves.

Having summoned up a context he made sense of it. The context included tragedy, the furies, real blood and a great sorrow. It also included gardens, often small, enclosed gardens, the voices of birds and big trees. The morality of his poems is stern. Here is one that ends with words from Marcus Aurelius: part seven of 'Midsummer, or Summer Solstice', the third of the *Three Secret Poems*, or three private poems.

> The poplar in the little garden
> measures your hours with her breath
> all day, all night,
> waterclock the sky fills up.
> When the moon is strong her leaves
> trail black footprints across the white wall.
> The pines not many at the border
> then marbles, gleams of light
> and men as men are constituted.
> But the blackbird whistles
> when he comes to drink
> at times you hear the voice of the ringdove.
>
> In the little garden a few square feet
> you can see the light of the sun falling
> on two red carnations
> one olive tree a bit of honeysuckle.
> Accept yourself.
> Do not drown
> the poem in the depths of the plane trees
> nourish it with your own soil, your own rock.
> For what remains
> dig to find it, dig in this same place.[12]

The harshest advice that George Seferis had to offer was to poets, and to himself. If I repeat it I do so as if I were talking to an audience of poets. It comes from an interview he gave to Edmund Keeley, his friend and translator, in 1986, nearly at the end of his life.

E.K. Since you don't have any grand advice for the younger generations, I've nothing more to ask you.

G.S. I *have* advice.

E.K. Oh, you *do*? Good.

G.S. I have the following advice to give to the younger Greek generation: try to exercise themselves as much as they can in the modern Greek language. And not to write it upside down. I have to tell them that in order to write, one must believe in what one does, not seeming to believe that one is believing something. They must remember that the only job in which one cannot lie is poetry. You can't lie in poetry. If you are a liar you'll always be discovered. Perhaps now, perhaps in five years, in ten years, but you are going to be discovered eventually if you are lying.

E.K. When you speak of lying, you're speaking first of all of lying against your emotional. . . .

G.S. I don't know what I mean. Perhaps it is an emotional thing. In the reality of one's thoughts. I don't know. I mean there is a special sound about the solid, the sound thing. You knock against it, and it renders a sort of sound which proves that it is genuine.

E.K. Do you think every writer always knows himself whether the sound he hears is genuine or not?

G.S. No. It is difficult to say. But he must somehow have an instinct – a guiding instinct – which says to him: 'My dear boy, my dear chap, be careful; you are going to fall. You are exaggerating at this moment.' And then, when he hears that, he should not take a drug in order to say to himself: 'Why, you are all right, my dear.' You are not all right, my dear, at all.[13]

He was a highly original man, his poetry really was a new created world. I suppose Greece was fuller of original, unexpected characters, particularly in his generation, than most countries. It had no Victorian age to speak of because it then had almost no middle class, and it had no Renaissance and no Reformation. The impact of the modern world on Greek intellectuals in the 1920s and 1930s was stunning. The best description, because the freshest, is by Henry Miller in *The Colossus of Maroussi*. Within that generation, George Seferis was still more remarkable. He was born in 1900, he fled from Smyrna in his teens, he was not rich, or in any ordinary sense international in background, but by the age of twenty-two or so he was a jazz addict. He wrote a remarkable and very uninhibited novel. He started out with a powerful and innocent hunger of life, but much of his experience was bitter. He became a sophisticated European and a very successful diplomat, without ever losing his roots, which were expressed in language. His stance and tone in prose essays and in all his public statements are those of a master.

> And now that I have passed an entire lifetime ravaged by military revolutions, dictatorships, political upheavals, uprisings, calamities and despair, after I have lived through all that, I can speak from close to the bone when I say, as a public servant, that I find it a heavy and sorrowful thing as the years go by that I must end in the conclusion that we have not made one inch of progress in these matters.[14]

However warm or humorous or subtle he chooses to be, there is an element of granite in him. It exists even in his diaries, six or more volumes of which are already in print. Among his masterpieces there are modern Greek translations of the Song of Songs and the Book of Revelation. I have no doubt that the element of granite is inseparable from the way George Seferis worked out his language: he had thoroughly steeped himself in medieval Greek and in the Cretan poem *Erotokritos*.[15]

He often comes close to Eliot, not so much by imitation or unconscious reminiscence as by studying the same originals, even Dante in the same edition,[16] and also by the avoidance of false rhetoric, by what he found it possible to leave out of poetry, leaving the poem stronger and more honest. It was George Seferis who told me that Eliot had quoted to him a saying of Sherlock Holmes, 'Cut out the poetry Watson.' 'I have been trying all my life', said Eliot, 'to cut out the poetry.' George approved of that, he saw the point of it, but he also thought it was extremely funny. He was for example delighted to discover that Giacometti had written in a letter, 'The sky is really red, we call it blue only by convention.' In his own poetry there is a certain blackness behind the sky, but that is a real phenomenon of the Greek sky at midday in August. Between Greece and England no difference is greater than that of nature, in which I include all those relationships and that history which nature determines. When Seferis translates Eliot or Yeats, a vast transformation takes place. It makes one agree with a paradox recently formulated by that excellent poet Patrick Kavanagh: poetry is exactly what does survive in translation. It is all that survives.[17]

Yeats' 'Journey to Byzantium' was an obvious subject for Seferis, but his version has more sadness, in a way more seriousness; it is less intoxicating, less taut, and yet it is equally resonant.[18] I think I could argue in detail that his version, being unrhymed and therefore needing to be held together by a subtle, underflowing rhythmic progression, is in a way a better poem. I am sure that his 'Second Coming' is a more decent version of Yeats, because he seems innocently unaware of the excitement, the secret appetite, with which Yeats welcomes violence. Seferis implicitly deplores by the rhythms of his voice the fact that things fall apart, the centre cannot hold. His poem is even more ominous, more tragic than its original. Even his lords and ladies of Byzantium are more innocent, less hieratic; they come from a medieval ballad line that survived in Crete until yesterday as an opening for narrative poems sung to villagers: ἄρχοντες κι ἀρχόντισσες ἀκονᾶτε τραγουδήσω. Hear me ladies and lords and I shall sing. These Yeats versions are translation of very high quality: a poet who merited and obtained the Nobel prize translating another of whom the same may be said. And yet Seferis begins his Introduction by saying, 'The translation of poetry is of all kinds of writing the least satisfying. However well one works, however lucky one is, there will always be something objective – the original – that survives to show that one still falls short, and what is more, the higher one climbs the more one falls short: woe to the poet who tries to improve on the poem he translates.' In spite of this, the gains in these transmutations of language, these transfigurations of poems, more than outweigh the losses in many cases. If they do nothing else, they give us the opportunity for a fresh look at the poets he translates.[19]

Like every other poet whose hair is grey, I have been sometimes translated; I found the experience amusing and informative (I greatly resent the fact that I sound better in German). But the translator is the one who learns most; I have found it a wonderful feeling when it works well, to have a new kind of poem dripping off the end of one's pen as if one had written it oneself. George Seferis shows in his translations a deep sense of the different qualities of his originals. Yet his own poems, which a number of English writers have attempted, have never been successful in English. They go a little better in French. The rhythms and the undertones of the rhythms are the essential material of his poetry. Not only his own language, but once one has heard it his own voice seems to belong to this essential material. The translations he made into Greek, from D. H. Lawrence, Ezra Pound, Marianne Moore, Éluard, Auden and others, were as he says just a part of a wider enterprise, to see what the Greek language was capable of absorbing in his lifetime. The official version of Seferis in English, by Keeley and Sherrard, has a brilliance of accuracy and many neat bits of poetry, but I fear it proves that the English language in our lifetime was incapable of absorbing the living tissue of his poems. Eliot might have managed it, Durrell comes nearest. Could Auden have done it? He lacked the severe tragic sense of Seferis. Seferis trans- figured Auden's 'China' in the same way as he did Yeats; Auden's later censorship of the end of that poem disturbed Seferis; he thought it irresponsible and inadmissible.[20] For him the writing of a poem was such a serious matter that once it was published it must remain.

There is something particularly genuine about him. He follows the natural grain of the wood, in language and in the experiences of life. This is quite easy to see in the *Second Exercise Book*, which was posthumously published,[21] though be began to plan its publication at least ten years before his death; the events of those ten years post- poned it. It contains some minor poems of victoriously laconic power: verses for a sundial at Kardamyli (1968):

> While the light dances
> my voice is true

and this fragment:

> As time proceeds
> and winter takes its course
> and the throat of the redbreast darkens
> like the cyclamens —

and the couplets he wrote for the blades of six knives: Shakespeare speaks of couplets on knife-blades, though I know of no surviving Elizabethan example. In the Greek islands the custom still exists, and Seferis wrote his for a knife-maker in Amorgos. I suppose the style of the English ones must have been that of ballads, or that of the verses on Shakespeare's tombstone. The couplets Seferis wrote are in just such a style. They are like Cretan *Mantinades*, the impromptu traditional couplets sung over drinks, and Spanish *Coplas*, which equally go back to the sixteenth century or earlier. The verses on the knives are epigrams of the same kind: When the blade flashes the blood splashes, or the bayleaf glitters like a thorn on fire, or the new moon stains to crimson. This language has a traditional formality which is still alive, like the language of Lorca. These are small achieve- ments, hardly more than playful poems, but I mention them because of their marvellous certainty of touch, and to indicate something of the range of George Seferis, and the many elements which might come together in any one great poem. The collection includes a very funny pastiche of Eliot, written about 1948 maybe, called 'What the Camel Said',[22] and a mock 'Sapphic Ode' to the poet Papatzonis, but also two very beautiful love epigrams in classical shape written in 1945 and 1946, that Robert Graves would have envied.

It can be said of Seferis, as the more enthusiastic critics have said of Picasso's sketchbooks, that by constant labour at the boundaries of his art, he deserved the appearance of freedom and spontaneity that his great works have. Another analogy with Picasso's sketchbooks is more important. He kept a mass of notes and diaries, able to inter-mingle the intimate and the personal with great themes and public events. The English poets of the 1930s tend to deduce politics, some-times unconvincingly, from personal experience and states of mind in their poems. I do not think George Seferis ever did that. He gives public events a more powerful and more personal resonance in his poems, so that what convinces is the poem and the person whose objective soul the poem is. The poem has snail antennae as a person has. In a letter of 1931 he wrote to the young novelist Theotokas, 'I would like to say a lot more to you about a man in front of white paper and about words ("the probabilities of human utterance"). I am afraid of boring you.'[23] He then quotes two famous lines of Mallarmé, 'Sur le vide papier que la blancheur défend', and 'Donner un sens plus pur aux mots de la tribu'.[24] These themes, modified in various ways, lasted his life; he ended this letter with his usual advice from Marcus Aurelius: Dig within thyself.

Here is a poem written just after the fall of Greece, called 'The Days of June 1941'. It is dated Crete, Alexandria, South Africa, May–September 1941.

> The new moon came out at Alexandria
> holding the old moon in its arms,
> we walked towards the Gate of the Sun
> in the darkness of the heart, three friends.
>
> Who wants now to bathe in the waters of Proteus?
> In youth we looked for metamorphosis,
> desires playing like the great fishes
> in seas that suddenly grew small;
> we believed in the omnipotence of the body.
> And now the new moon has come out embracing
> the old; and the beautiful island is bleeding,
> wounded; tranquil island, powerful, innocent.

Bodies like broken branches
and like uprooted roots.

Our thirst a horseman on guard petrified
at the dark Gate of the Sun
knowing nothing to seek for: stands on guard
in exile hereabouts
close to the tomb of the Great Alexander.[25]

The topography is not necessary to us really, but this is the Rosetta
Gate of the Arabs; the two great gates of ancient Alexandria were the
Gate of the Sun and the Gate of the Moon. Proteus was famous for
changing his shape, and the myth was localized on the Alexandria
coast. Alexander's tomb at Alexandria has never been found, and I
think that here he is as much a figure of folklore as a reference to the
ancient world. He is not only a national but a magically powerful
symbol. The ironic fulcrum of the poem is of course the fall of Greece
and exile in the ruins of the greatest of Greek cities. Its centre is the
terrible experiences of the fall of Crete. George Seferis remembered
the burial of Venizelos in Crete, the vast fleet of small ships at dawn
like a Venetian argosy, and the blossoms of entire orchards of lemon
trees that people had torn off, and the soldiers lining the steps of the
cathedral at Chania presenting arms with the tears streaming down
their faces. It was a powerful and an innocent island. Something
important has to happen to you before you can write a poem like this.
It stands comparison with Aragon's 'Fugue for a Barrel Organ', about
the fall of France, but with Seferis one has more sense of the water
bursting out of the rock. His poems imply the experience of life, they
have a great deal in reserve. The reader like the poet has to dig within
himself. This is not exactly hermetic poetry, because the experience
unstated but implied is in this case a public event. Great poets who
lack any great event to write about write about history. The power of
the event is part of the power of the poem. Shakespeare for example,
for whom honest discussion of religion and politics was forbidden,
wrote history plays.

I do not think that Seferis was essentially a political poet, it is just
that his honesty and his linguistic power, his young achievements as a
poet, put him in a unique position to write about the greatest events of
his lifetime, and he did so to the very end of his life. He never dried up
as a poet. But his last project in prose, which the national crisis and
then his death brought to nothing, was a translation of those charming
stories in the dialogues of Plato which philosophers call the myths,

being shy I suppose of the word fiction, which might make Plato sound like a writer. Anyone who never knew Seferis and wishes they did should read his diaries, some of them written in the form of letters. In those he is completely himself, with all his variety.

3 October 1932 [he was thirty-two]. The great mistake of my life has been that I was made for the sea and I became a landsman. It is a mark of the marine man that he is never satisfied anywhere.

Seferis was serving in England. He summed up that experience later (about 1948) in 'Letter to a Foreign Friend':

I remember the time – it now seems so long ago – when I was making my first faltering discovery of London, which I thought of as a gigantic sea-port, and of the English language, whose music sounded so much more fluid than that of our own tongue. Also, the shock I experienced at the sour taste of death in the fog, and the intensified circulation of fear in the arteries of the great city. Death, I kept thinking, is for us a sudden wound; here it is a slow poison.[26]

On 17 October 1932, he read in an English newspaper, 'Ten Snakes Free', and the note about one of them, 'They say that it cannot live long in the cold night air, and that although it is strong enough to kill a goat in its native country, it has no future in England.' Under December he writes only 'Kew Gardens. Paphiopedilum. Cypripedilum. 65°.' On 4 January he was in Folkestone on a gloomy evening. Next day he had flu with a temperature of 100°. 'Foreign fogs. I have not many words at my disposal. It seems to me that I spent all the courage I brought with me at the beginning. It was not a little.' On the 13th, 'The high spirits I brought with me to this place have been drained away. They lasted until last spring. Now they are gone and I need to make much more effort to hold out for as long as I must.' Then next day,

We must be sensible and keep to our small fields. The God who feeds the charming fish in the aquariums, and the squirrels in the royal parks of London, must have kept back at least a crumb for those who write, without any expectation from the past or from the future. It is raining. I woke when they brought me the papers, the letters, and a cup of tea. News from Greece: a moral purge. News from London. They have not yet caught Mr. Furnall the murderer. It goes on raining.'

But on 24 February he was considering Stratis the marine man or the mariner, Stratis Thalassinos, one of the personae of his poems to come. 'This business is going to make me spit blood. I remember the snakes in my "Love Story" [his first ambitious poem]; if you multiply by 1000, maybe you will get an idea. Stratis Thalassinos is a parallel or a triangle, as follows: El Greco. Bach: introduction to the Second Suite and tune of the Third. A rock in the sea, somewhere in Greece. I stretch it, I stretch it like strings. If it won't utter I shall burst.' He then discusses a quotation from Eliot, whom he loves more and more. 'The poet makes poetry, the metaphysician makes metaphysics, the bee makes honey.... you can hardly say that any of these agents believes, he simply does.'

Some of these notes represent simply a clever man clearing his head of cleverness in order to write. But the strings held. The sea-rock with the overtones of Bach and a touch of El Greco did utter. And in spring Seferis felt a bit better. He heard Stravinsky and saw an almond tree in blossom in Kew Gardens. The thoughts he wrote down are passionately intense and the observations extremely acute. The fragments of news and the stray conversations are already halfway to entering into poems. They drag atmospheres along with them as vivid to us as they were to their writer. Few poets have so rich a mixture to work on, so well recorded before they start to write poems. His professional life was lonely, he was far from home, and unable to marry at that time, and quite uncertain of his future: hence no doubt the intensity of his observations.

I suppose the most characteristic artist of the modern movement may be Picasso, a multiple artist of deliberately dazzling virtuosity and flaunting elegance, who incessantly sought to break through and remake the boundaries of his art, destruction and creation being for him one process. Picasso and Seferis have it in common that their new beginning, their freshness of technique, grew from the cracked shell of an earlier artform that had already dropped off the traditional tree, in Picasso's case *art nouveau* drawing, in that of Seferis the exaggerated *art nouveau* elegance of his early rhymed poems, the best of which was conceived as free verse before it was varnished into rhyme.[27] They both had enough contradictions in their early work for their later work to break open in unexpected ways. It could be said of Seferis and poetry as Picasso wrote of painting: poetry is stronger than I am, it makes me do what it wants. But Picasso's vitality lies in a constant dissatisfaction with definitions, a constant redefining of the pictures on the canvas or the page, an endless renewal of techniques. The vitality of Seferis in his poetry is not so technical: what he redefines is not so much the boundaries of the poem, though he does do that, as life, and the world, and the experience of life. The element of Bach in him is very strong. I imagine that he thought more of Stravinsky than Picasso as central to the modern movement, and more of French poetry than of English, except for Eliot.[28] What he sought out was freshness, in any source, from the simplicities of peasant speech to the lively directness of his friend Henry Miller; his classicism was instinctive, like Bach's geometric sense in music. Language is more a given thing than form and colour, and a true poet is not able to whizz about over the surface of the sea like a sailboard, he has to have a deeper keel. In modern Greek the recovery of the roots of the language, which are ancient, popular roots, is a symbol and a part of the revival of the Greek nation, the soul of Greekness, the sense of being Greek. To that revival a hundred years after its beginnings George Seferis contributed crucially. Like Solomos, the first great poet of the modern language, Byron's contemporary, Seferis had a wide European culture but a deeper inwardness with his own language, like Langland's or John Clare's with English. He was convinced that poetry is absolutely necessary to modern mankind – 'La poésie a ses racines dans la réspiration humaine'[29] – and he wrote in that spirit.

For years after the return from exile in October 1944 he wrestled with ways to express his greatest rediscovery, Greek light. 'Something of it', he writes, 'is caught in "The King of Asine", and something in "The Thrush". But I do not know if I shall ever be able to express this basic element, as I feel it is, this fundamental of life. The only thing I have come to understand here is that no problem is ever solved by a full stop, you have to go on further or burst.'[30] The need to express and the constant inadequacy of expressions are the lot of all habitual poets: Shakespeare and Donne suffered from them as badly as we do. It is poetry itself and the poem itself that drag the writer by the scruff of his neck into new techniques. In his work any novelty of technique is always a response to the particular subject, the particular poem. From the technical point of view his lifework is not exactly a progression, but more a long, slow consideration and a sifting backwards and forwards like the movement of the sea over its pebbles. The phases of the moon offer the parody of an explanation, the immense shifting of the earth's gravity comes closer. The movement of his poetry is the movement of his mind. It is deeply personal, and therefore both intimate and enigmatic.

Here are two poems from *Mythistorima*. It was published in 1935 when he came home from London. It was his second book and his first perfect poem or sequence of poems.

Mythistorima Part 5

We had not known them.
At bottom it was only hope that said
how we had known them all as little boys.
We saw them twice or so, then they took ship,
cargoes of coal, cargoes of grain, our friends
were lost beyond oceans and for ever.
Dawn finds us out beside the exhausted lamp
covering paper awkwardly, with effort,
with sailing ships and mermaids and seashells;
we go down to the river towards the sea,
we spend nights in cellars that smell of tar.

Our friends have left
maybe we never saw them, and maybe
we did encounter them when sleep had still
carried us close up to the breathing wave
maybe we seek them since we seek the other life
that lies beyond statues.

Mythistorima Part 6
M. R. [Maurice Ravel]

The garden with the fountains in the rain
you will see only from the low window
through clouded glass. Your room
will be lighted by nothing but firelight:
some distant lightning will at times show up
the wrinkles of your forehead, my old Friend.
The garden with the fountains in it was
in your hands rhythm of the other life
outside broken marbles, tragic columns,
it was a dance among the oleanders
near the new stone quarries,
clouded glass will have cut that from your hours.
You will not breathe; the soil and the tree-sap
will spring out of your memory to strike
against that window stricken by the rain
from the outside world.

The images are directly presented, they have no introduction, no
conclusion, they are poetry that has attained the condition of music. If

the images are metaphors for anything, then they are metaphors that have broken loose and have a life of their own. Their phrasing is perfect. The passion that they communicate is curiously pure but as real as something read in a newspaper. An earlier poem in this series (number four, 'The Argonauts') offers no explanations and somehow thereby is all the more compelling. It was the first poem by George Seferis I ever read, picking out the meaning with a French translation: in 1955, in that odd little office like a nest in a plane tree where they used to confine the Oxford Professor of Modern Greek. I still find it among my ideal poems.

> C'étaient de braves gars les compagnons ne se plaignant
> Ni de la fatigue, ni du soif, ni du gel,
> Ils faisaient comme les arbres et les vagues
> Qui acceptent le vent et la pluie, ...
>
> (Robert Levesque, 1945)

Mythistorima Part 4
The Argonauts

And the soul
if she will know herself
must look into a soul:[31]
we have looked into that mirror
and seen the stranger and the enemy.

They were good lads the companions, did not cry out,
neither from toil nor thirst nor from the frost,
they had the bearing of the trees and waves
which accept the wind and accept the rain
without altering among alteration.
They were good men, days on end
they sweated at the oar with eyes cast down
breathing in rhythm
and their blood reddened their disciplined skin.
Sometimes they sang, with eyes cast down
when we passed the desert island with the prickly pears
towards the west, beyond the cape of dogs barking.
If she will know herself, they said
she must look into a soul, they said
and the oars beat the gilt sea-surface in the sunset.
We passed by many capes, many islands, the sea

that opens into another sea, gulls and seals.
Sometimes unhappy women wailed
weeping for their children lost
and enraged women sought Great Alexander
and glories buried in the depths of Asia.
We put in at beaches full of nighttime smells
with birdsong, watersprings left on the hand
the memory of a great happiness.
Their souls became one with the oars and the rowlocks
with the face at the prow
with the rudder-wake.
The companions died in order,
with eyes cast down. Their oars
show the place where they rest on the seashore.

No one remembers them. Justice.

George Seferis said that the words from Plato about 'the soul if she will know herself' reminded him of some lines from Baudelaire, from 'Les morts des amants'.

Nos deux cœurs seront deux vastes flambeaux,
Qui réfléchiront leur doubles lumières
Dans nos deux esprits, ces miroirs jumeaux.

It is not possible to pin down the subjects and the boundaries of all these poems, any more than one can pin down the subject or the boundary of the soul. One of my favourite sayings of Seferis, as indicated in the preceding chapter on Dryden, was said to an enquiring young woman: 'I am no alchemist, my dear, I do not know where the body ends or where the soul begins.' What the poem leaves behind in the reader's mind is an image, images,[32] and some unforgettable phrases, and of course the last word, justice, δικαιοσύνη, hissing and rumbling at the end like a thunderbolt. A later poem about the ages of man throws some light on this one, I think. It is called 'Mr Stratis Thalassinos describes a man'.[33] I refer particularly to the fourth part, 'Palikari', 'Young Man'.

I travelled one year with Captain Dysseus
I was fine
in the good weather I settled in the prow beside the
    mermaid,
sang of her crimson lips watching the flying fish,

in storm I huddled in a corner in the hold with the
    ship's dog to keep me warm.
After a year saw minarets one morning,
the mate told me
'That's Hayia Sophia, this evening I'll take you to the
    women.'

The poem intensifies, and becomes like a short story: as a story
Graham Greene might have written it. It ends: 'On the ship that night
I could not bear to go near the mermaid, I was ashamed.' The fifth
part is called 'The Man'. It is mostly in prose but it contains these
verses:

They told us you will win when you submit.
We have submitted and have found ashes.
They told us you will win when you have loved.
We have loved and found ashes.
They told us you will live when you give up your life.
We gave our life up and we found ashes.

If this is Eliot, it is certainly Eliot with a difference. But I find
Mythistorima in some ways the most Greek of all Seferis' poems, at
least at an obvious level. The images of Greece were sharpened I
suppose by his exile in London, just at the memory of his beloved Paris
in the 'Ravel' poem was sharpened. The most perfect single poem in
this whole series is probably the one about the plane tree (number
fifteen). 'The Argonauts' is by an infinitesimal degree more rhetorical,
less purely a poem. But probably for that reason I can neither find nor
construct any translation of number fifteen that will bear reading
aloud. The poem begins 'Sleep folded you in green leaves like a tree,
you breathed as a tree does, in the quiet light.' After that I am lost. The
opening lines of all the poems are tempting to the translator, as the
first simple notes of a famous piece of music might be to a novice
pianist, but as they continue, as they build up, these poems are too
complex in their musical counterpoint and alterations of tone to be at
all easily translated.

Here are some of the openings of poems in *Mythistorima*:

What is it our souls seek for, travelling
on the decks of decayed ships....?
                              (No. 8)

The port is old, I can wait no longer
for the friend who left for the island of pines

or the friend who left for the island of plane trees
or the friend who left for the open sea....

(No. 9)

Three rocks, a few burnt pines, a lonely church
and above that
the same landscape begins over again,
three rocks shaped like a gateway and rusted....

(No. 12)

Dolphins banners and cannon shots
the sea so bitter....

(No. 13)

But the rhythms are more different than I have made them. The recorded voice of George Seferis reading his own poems makes it plain that their rhythms, and the undertow and momentum of their rhythms, differ more from poem to poem than one might realize from the printed page. In all his serious poems, and he seldom or never published any others in his lifetime, though he planned to do so, his voice is deadly serious, but the rhythms differ; the reader must ride them with a light rein until they assert themselves. They will not respond to heavy-handed intellectual or philosophic analysis either. He disliked 'people who try to express worldviews in writing poetry'.[34] A philosopher once asked him what his worldview was. He replied, 'My dear friend, I'm sorry to say that I have no worldview. I don't know, perhaps you find that scandalous, Sir, but may I ask you to tell me what Homer's worldview is?' Yet if I had to name two poets in all history who deeply considered the world and expressed in their work that depth of consideration, I think I would name Homer and Seferis. In something that I once wrote he singled out for approval the sentence, 'Poetry is the naked exercise of the whole man.'[35] It seems true of his poetry. Part of the technical strength of poetry is the amount it manages to leave out, but that can also be measured as a weakness; it is a question of the power or weakness of implication. In this matter Seferis was extremely strong.

Here end the works of the sea, the works of love.
Those that shall dwell one day here where we end
should the blood blacken in their memory, overbrim,
let them not forget us, powerless souls among the asphodels
let them turn the victims' head to Erebos.

We who had nothing will teach peace to them.

This is the end of *Mythistorima* (number twenty-four), written I assume in December 1934, in Athens. He dates the series 'December 33 to December 34'. But on 16 December 1934 he wrote: 'Last spring something better appeared, dimly at first: what I now call *Mythistorima*. Then it got lost, and then in the few days I spent at Spetsai it reappeared more clearly. Then it progressed stumbling into chasms of silence and curtains of sleep. Now that I have got halfway, what I foresee is once again the dark hole.' He was in fact nearly finished.[36] The poem is drawn from the past, but it is also a thrilling celebration of his return to Greece in the summer of 1934. One must not be deceived by translations into imagining that Greece and Greekness were less than essential to him as a poet and as a man.

Mythistorima was printed in an edition of only 150 copies. Seferis notes privately that his first book had had 200 copies. 'Progress.' The flint of the poem had thrown off stray sparks in his head. He recorded them in his papers as 'Useless sketches for *Mythistorima*'. He was right, I am sure, not to incorporate them, but they have some interest, because they underline the strength of feelings of his we had only divined in *Mythistorima*, though they belong to his lasting themes.

> Three thousand years
> we have been paying for this story,
> with every one of us it alters
> and remains the same....
> (26/11/34)

One of these sketches was a poem about the Furies of Aeschylus (finished in March 1935). The idea recurs in the *Three Secret Poems* and in prose in his famous public statement against the dictatorship of the Colonels.[37] Incidentally, it is worth noticing that his first intention was to take some words from the *Agamemnon* of Aeschylus[38] as the epigraph of *Mythistorima*: ominous words about the spirit within him self-taught, chanting the lamentation of the Furies without hope. But the physical presence of Greece overcame him and he chose from Rimbaud,

> Si j'ai du gout ce n'est guères
> Que pour la terre et les pierres.[39]

The Rimbaud was appropriate to his poem, the day of the Furies was to come, although in *Mythistorima* they already make their presence felt.

I know of no poet at all more honourable in his lifework than George Seferis, and of no modern poet I much or at all prefer to read. I like his stubbornness both of principle and of affection. I like his rooting into the rock. It was only after the Asia Minor disaster of his boyhood, with the vast migration that entailed of Greeks falling back on mainland Greece, some of whose families and whose towns had been established in Asia since 500 years before Christ, that his generation redefined what it was to be Greek. To that task he contributed what only a poet and a very honest poet can contribute. He really deserved to be a national hero, as much as the soul of man, with all the melodramas of its inwardness, deserves to be immortal.

The special home of his poetry was, as he wrote of Cyprus in the poem 'Engomi':

> in the despair of stone in power eroded,
> in the empty place with the thin grass and thorns
> where an unheeding snake slid away,
> where it takes them a long time to die.[40]

APPENDIX

In the translation of these poems, which are for children, I have altered only the place names.

Limericks

Ποιήματα μὲ ζωγραφιές σὲ μικρὰ παιδιά (Athens 1975).

1

A young girl in remote Samarkand
had buried one hand in the sand
stretched the other out far
and took hold of a star,
that young girl in remote Samarkand.

2

There was a young girl of Canton
who had thirty-one overcoats on,
when they said Why so many?
she replied There's not any
relief except this in Canton.

3

There was an old Duchess of Lawn
who cried out in her sleep through a yawn:

I've kicked over five eggs
in a line with my legs,
I have kicked them all night until dawn.

4

A Minister down in the Cape
whom a gadfly drove mad as an ape
waved a leek up and down
in a clergyman's gown
while he drummed his own head for a jape.

5

At Cairo one day an old priest
stole a chop in a tavern, the beast,
when they said what effrontery!
he replied For my country!
and I am not ashamed in the least.

6

There was a young lady of Kraak
whose hair was half ginger, half black,
she tied pretty strings
on some beetles with wings,
and she took them to graze around Kraak.

7

There was a young girl of Herat
who would say, Can I have some of that?
now she's swollen and yellow
as a violin cello
and the people lament in Herat.

8

There was an old woman of Wales
who carried a douche and two pails
full of eau de cologne,
and by rock, stock and stone
she went running, poor lady of Wales.

9

An assassin who stopped in Montrose
had asparagus tied to his nose,
and it swung and it swung
from his nose as it hung,
till it lulled him to sleep in Montrose.

10

There was an old woman of Crete
who at Easter had one bean to eat,
when she said I want double
there was terrible trouble,
and she died for her bean, poor old sweet.

11

A lady who lived in Hong Kong
had three husbands, all rich but not strong,
and one love sweet as honey
who stole all their money,
so their livelihood now is by song.

12

There was a young lady called Flo
who twirled round like a top on one toe,
when she tired of gyration
she made a sensation
eating fifty small fish in a row.

13

There was an old lady of Ham
who ate a whole dish of rose jam,
when it came on to rain
she ran home down the lane,
and at once she exploded in Ham.

14

There was a young housemaid of Fleet
who cried out, Try the water for heat,
I put plenty of mustard
in that bucket that's rusted,
for madam's hot bath for her feet.

15

There was a Grande Dame in a shop
who took out a dish and went chop,
because what could be coarser
than breaking her saucer
as she ate her ice-cream in a shop?

16

There was a young rotter called Pongo
who lost his poor wife in the Congo,
as she tried to get out
and to find him, the lout,
her finger bones played bongo bongo.

17

There was a young lady of Clun
who read Plutarch's *Lives* one by one,
as she ended she crowed,
flung one more in the road,
and rejoiced, that young scholar of Clun.

18

There was a young lady of Lima
who ran to get on to a steamer,
when she got to the shore
she had no money more,
so they had to return her to Lima.

19

There was a young lady of Graz
who fished with a trident for sprats,
when a pink-spotted sow
jumped in over the bow
and she drowned the young lady of Graz.

20

There was a small boy in a park
who spied a huge beast, what a lark,
with belly enormous
and ears like a dormouse,
which surprised that small boy in the park.

George Seferis (trans. P. L.)

W. H. Auden

I admire Auden extravagantly, but I am baffled what value to set on his poetry, so I find myself tinkering with the biography that underlies it. The critical biography in the tradition of Johnson's *Lives of the Poets*, Scott's *Life of Dryden* and Ellmann's lives of Joyce and Yeats is said to be an unreliable and a distracting instrument for analysing poetry, but other critical instruments often turn out to be more unreliable and more distracting. Auden in his day was a glamorous and a charismatic figure, and the glamour has not yet faded from the printed page. More than any poet since Byron he expressed not just himself or an age, but within that age and self a moment and a crisis: therefore once you know the skeleton outline of his biography, the intimate detail throws little further light on his poems, or on the extent or the failure of his talent or his genius, any more than the fascinating irrelevant details of Byron's life. Auden's moment was the 1930s, the age of anxiety, but the climax of the 1930s was the war, and after the London Blitz what Auden has to say pales into insignificance.

And yet he refuses to be confined into one stage of his life, practically into the process of growing up, which was what he was doing until 1939. He began as a poet of dense, suggestive phrases expressing the soul, as Louis MacNeice put it, in telegrams, but by 1936 the 'beautiful telegraphese' had withered away in the course of his development.[1] What survived the 1939 war was a brilliant intelligence, a crisp, generous essayist, a critic or rather an educator of genius, and at least a little more than the ghost of the poet he might have been. He was the poet as critic, the poet as entertainer, and a little less successfully the poet as psychiatrist or wise uncle. Year by year, he never ceased to astonish, any more than Byron did; in the 1950s and early 1960s we hung on his words as a poet more perhaps than on any others. That effect will diminish with time and already is diminishing: but Auden's relation at least to his 1930s audience enters into the centre of his poetry more than Lord Byron's and rather as Shakespeare's does into the centre of his. The lavish, casual squandering of Auden's lyric gift in so many unexpected ways and places is part of that relationship, and once again it recalls Byron. Tennyson can be imagined as hoarding his gift for solemn emotions and great poems. Shakespeare calculated every lyrical moment, but Auden meant to astonish us with his prodigality, and so he did. More than most poets, he fulfilled the ideal of Yeats[2] that every fresh poem should be a law unto itself, and the finish or polish of the poem 'should merely make plain that law'. When at last he turned to the attempt to write great poems on a solid scale, 'In Praise of Limestone' for instance, we feel an affection and an admiration for the result, but they are not great poems any more than Clough's 'Amours de Voyage'. On almost all occasions, his art simply refuses to be monumental.

When people talk about rejecting the modern movement I have the feeling that it was Auden, more than Pound or Eliot, who frightened them. So far as I know the first person to define modernism and to chart its progress as a movement with a beginning and an end, at least in poetry and in English, was Cyril Connolly in 1965. In his *Hundred Key Books of the Modern Movement (1880–1950)*[3] he included Auden's *Orators* (1932) and *Another Time* (1940) and *Collected Shorter Poems* (1950). As I have said, I think Auden's later poems overleap restrictive categories: nor am I convinced that the modern movement was quite dead and buried by 1950. But Cyril Connolly, who was an Auden fan,[4] makes the telling remark that *Another Time* was 'the last Auden which people learnt by heart'. With the exception of Betjeman and Larkin, and some lines of Bunting, it may be the last English poetry of any kind that people learnt by heart. As for the modern movement, the idea of modernity is essential to Auden's poetry. He and most of his friends were the children of pre-1914 liberal families, and the product of progressive schools founded around 1900. When he came back to Oxford as Professor of Poetry in the late 1950s, he was therefore a visitor from another world in more senses than one.

He had such authority then that to me at least his prestige still casts a glamour on the chair I hold, and of all Professors of Poetry it is in his steps I most fear to tread. That is not just because of his brilliant originality in lecturing, or his surprising personal conversation, glass in hand. He was not as easily available to undergraduates then as myth now maintains: his famous sessions in the Cadena Café in the summer terms were usually solitary; undergraduates sat at other

tables staring at him, mostly too awed to approach. His point was that
he was both a great poet and a figure from history.[5] If you were a poet,
you sought him out later in the day. Dom Moraes has recorded such a
moment in 'A Letter':[6]

> Of one dying poet I was not afraid,
> In conversation like an avalanche,
> Convincing mainly by the noise he made.
> He reinforced his views with gin-and-French.
> Wrinkled and heaving, tuskless elephant,
> He levelled a thick finger, grained with ink.
> 'To love somebody, that is what you want.'
> 'Yes,' I would say, accepting one more drink.

Love is the preoccupation of his poetry as of his life. It is sometimes
hidden by sketchy disguises, but always present. Perhaps in some very
wide sense of the word love there are no poems but love poems:
including love of life, love of country, love of peace, love of the dead,
love of self, *narcissus poeticus* being the flower of many poets, and
love of God, transcendent love. That is what is right or wrong with the
Aeneid, and what defeats and redeems Milton in *Paradise Lost*. Auden
is the least sentimental and yet warmest-hearted of poets, though we
may read him sentimentally or cold-heartedly. Or is there objectively
some touch of coldness, some confusion of sentiment, in his best
poems? In 'Lay your sleeping head, my love', 'Soul and body have no
bounds'?[7] The love he celebrates here, like the love in his political
poems and his purely friendly poems, is at least never superhuman.

> Wandering lost upon the mountains of our choice,
> Again and again we sigh for an ancient South,
> For the warm nude ages of instinctive poise,
> For the taste of joy in the innocent mouth....
> But we are articled to error; we
> Were never nude and calm like a great door,
>
> And never will be perfect like the fountains;
> We live in freedom by necessity....[8]

All the thoughts and the feelings of his pre-war poems are in some
way confused or imperfect, often inexcusably pretentious, and always
reflecting the typical, never the best consciousness of their decade,[9]
and yet they are touched with lyricism like the most powerful moonlight, their singing tones are true though their intellectual sources are a

chaotic miscellany, and their tendencies are sometimes infantile or dangerous. Auden is the best writer of first lines in the language. Reading the first lines of his poems makes one think of another Donne or Baudelaire, even another Shakespeare of the sonnets. He seemed in his day utterly to overshadow such fine and solid poets as Louis MacNeice and Stephen Spender, just because of the excitement, the continuous lyric drive, of so many of his poems. Eliot expressed the strange opinion that Auden's spiritual development outran his technical development: 'I think we shall have to be patient in waiting for the poetry, because I think his spiritual development has outstripped his technical development, while his technical virtuosity is such that it is able almost to deceive us (and himself) into thinking that it is adequate.'[10] Perhaps that is why one so often remembers Auden in fragments, so seldom on the whole in complete poems.

> Frantic the music of the violins
> To drown the song behind the guarded hill . . . [11]

> Taller today, we remember similar evenings,
> Walking together in the windless orchard
> Where the brook runs over the gravel far from the glacier . . . [12]

> On Sunday walks
> Past the shut gates of works
> The conquerors come
> And are handsome. . . . [13]

Sometimes after a wonderful beginning like a swallow-dive, Auden's poems land in muddy water with a splash. 'O Love, the interest itself in thoughtless heaven' degenerates into a prosing tone and recovers and then loses itself more than once: as if he scorned to write a perfect poem, although his ear was perfect. He relished his prosy element as he relished his private jokes and the German cabaret songs that link him against his will to Brecht, at first a less gifted but in the end a greater poet, and his film scripts, which link him to John Betjeman, who had an ear as perfect as his, but almost no other gift at all.

> Time that is intolerant
> Of the brave and innocent,
> And indifferent in a week
> To a beautiful physique,
>
> Worships language and forgives
> Everyone by whom it lives;

> Pardons cowardice, conceit,
> Lays its honours at their feet.
>
> Time that with this strange excuse
> Pardoned Kipling and his views,
> And will pardon Paul Claudel
> Pardons him for writing well.[14]

The lines that follow these famous stanzas on the death of Yeats read like a trial run for one of his few long, perfect poems, 'September 1, 1939'. He turned against that in later life, as he did against many of his most popular statements: not I think from eccentric petulance, but because his feelings were confused, and he was critical of his own thoughts. He glared at his old self with deliberate incomprehension, as he did at Yeats. 'Do you think he was telling the *truth*', he asked with a furious snorting laugh, 'when he said he wanted to be a mechanical bird when he was dead?'[15]

> Intellectual disgrace
> Stares from every human face,
> And the seas of pity lie
> Locked and frozen in each eye.
>
> Follow poet, follow right
> To the bottom of the night,
> With your unconstraining voice
> Still persuade us to rejoice;
>
> With the farming of a verse
> Make a vineyard of the curse,
> Sing of human unsuccess
> In a rapture of distress;
>
> In the deserts of the heart
> Let the healing fountain start,
> In the prison of his days
> Teach the free man how to praise.

This is a lofty statement of the poet's vocation, but 'September 1, 1939' demanded a tone that was deeper or more real, and something in Auden rose to the long-feared, long-expected occasion. Later he returned to aesthetic and private solutions, and step by step became a poet in a way *manqué*, a self-wounded veteran, a figure of tragedy. Sir Stephen Spender has suggested he was happiest as a prep school master, and surely nothing in Auden's criticism is more brilliant than his *Oxford Book of Light Verse* (1938). He wanted to be 'simple, clear and gay', a kind of poetry he oddly associated with modern democracy, although historically one must admit it is more normally to be found in aristocratic societies. Aeschylus is not simple, or clear, or gay. After 'September 1, 1939', he soon returned in *New Year Letter* (January 1, 1940), to building his clever, overclever nest of words, with Schubert, Mozart, 'Gluck and food and friendship', condemning England in stronger terms than Germany, since hypocrisy is worse than apathy, and invoking Christianity in unsuitably vague though admittedly moving terms. He was praying really not to God but to his own childhood.

> O Unicorn among the cedars,
> To whom no magic charm can lead us,
> White childhood moving like a sigh
> Through the green woods unharmed in thy
> Sophisticated innocence,
> To call thy true love to the dance,
> O Dove of science and of light,
> Upon the branches of the night,
> O Ichthus playful in the deep ... [and so on][16]

The peculiar inadequacy of this poem is observable as falsity of tone, but more deeply it has to do with date. Auden's intellectual musings and his charm are not serious enough for 1940, because we know what happened then, and his poems demand to be read in their historical context. The poets one likes to read about 1940 are Aragon,[17] Heinz Winfried Sabais, Bertolt Brecht or the young Roy Fuller, less mature as a poet and far less fluent than Auden, but genuine, real, our own. Auden was born in 1907. Peter Huchel was born in 1903.[18] He wrote a poem, or a series of three short poems, called 'Germany', which I have translated. It shows as Sabais shows that one did not have to be English or French to write genuine poetry about the events of those years.

> ### 1927
> There's enough hidden fire and hidden gold
> under the heavy roots of the forest.
> Germany is dark. Germany is cold.
> Where the flame rusted in a ring
> the salt of tears stuck on the pot,
> blood soaked through the shroud crying.

But never walked in the dawn dew
by strong, absolute voices led,
eyes crucified, beatified,
a Joan of Arc naked-footed.

1933

Do not pride yourselves my most late sons,
care for the light, my lonely sons.
Be spoken of in later times
and let that chain not clank that gleams,
on spirit let it softly chime.

1939

World of the wolf, world of the rat.
Blood and filth on the cold hearth.
But the shadows of the dead gods
still tread on earth.
Godlike remains man and has his peace.
And will again breathe out his breath free.
Though he is mocked now by the howling pack
they will go by.[19]

Morally, German poets like Huchel and Sabais may in 1940 stand higher than Wystan Auden, but not always, not everywhere. Sabais was a pilot in the German Air Force; his early poem 'Looping the loop over the West' conveys the illusion of freedom in flight very well. Only two of the twenty-two members of his squadron survived. 'After the war,' he writes, 'we all sat down and read T. S. Eliot.'[20] He ended his life defending moderate and responsible socialism against the extreme left; he was Mayor of Darmstadt; his best poem was about this whole life, written in the few months before his death in March 1981, when he knew that he was dying. He attained greatness as a poet, but I speak of him here only because it is high time to introduce some new characters into our discussions of the poetry of between the wars, and of the Second World War. And yet when all this is said, Wystan Auden's statement of 'September 1, 1939' remains classic. So is his poem 'The Fall of Rome'. So is his poem 'The Shield of Achilles'. Between these three poems he records the war and what followed the war in unforgettable words, with less depth than Eliot in the fourth *Quartet*, but more clearly.

September 1, 1939

I sit in one of the dives
On Fifty-Second Street

Uncertain and afraid
As the clever hopes expire
Of a low dishonest decade:
Waves of anger and fear
Circulate over the bright
And darkened lands of the earth,
Obsessing our private lives;
The unmentionable odour of death
Offends the September night.

Accurate scholarship can
Unearth the whole offence
From Luther until now
That has driven a culture mad,
Find what occurred at Linz,
What huge imago made
A psychopathic god:
I and the public know
What all schoolchildren learn,
Those to whom evil is done
Do evil in return.

Exiled Thucydides knew
All that a speech can say
About Democracy,
And what dictators do,
The elderly rubbish they talk
To an apathetic grave;
Analysed all in his book,
The enlightenment driven away,
The habit-forming pain,
Mismanagement and grief:
We must suffer them all again.

Into this neutral air
Where blind skyscrapers use
Their full height to proclaim
The strength of Collective Man,
Each language pours its vain
Competitive excuse:
But who can live for long
In an euphoric dream;
Out of the mirror they stare,

Imperialism's face
And the international wrong.

Faces along the bar
Cling to their average day:
The lights must never go out,
The music must always play,
All the conventions conspire
To make this fort assume
The furniture of home;
Lest we should see where we are,
Lost in a haunted wood,
Children afraid of the night
Who have never been happy or good.

The windiest militant trash
Important Persons shout
Is not so crude as our wish:
What mad Nijinsky wrote
About Diaghilev
Is true of the normal heart;
For the error bred in the bone
Of each woman and each man
Craves what it cannot have,
Not universal love
But to be loved alone.

From the conservative dark
Into the ethical life
The dense commuters come,
Repeating their morning vow,
'I will be true to the wife,
I'll concentrate more on my work,'
And helpless governors wake
To resume their compulsory game:
Who can release them now,
Who can reach the deaf,
Who can speak for the dumb?

All I have is a voice
To undo the folded lie,
The romantic lie in the brain
Of the sensual man-in-the-street

And the lie of Authority
Whose buildings grope the sky:
There is no such thing as the State
And no one exists alone;
Hunger allows no choice
To the citizen or the police:
We must love one another or die.

Defenceless under the night
Our world in stupor lies;
Yet, dotted everywhere,
Ironic points of light
Flash out wherever the Just
Exchange their messages:
May I, composed like them
Of Eros and of dust,
Beleaguered by the same
Negation and despair,
Show an affirming flame.

Auden's later objection to his own poem was an objection to the second last stanza about love, and yet in retrospect that conclusion appears intelligible enough and accepted enough.[21] Does the notion that 'Accurate scholarship can Unearth the whole offence' seem naive? The intellectual history of Europe that he actually offers us in numerous poems is often amusing, sometimes tiresome, mostly too dispersed. But the insights here are very sharp: the stanza about Thucydides, and the one about the faces along the bar, who cling to their average day, are excellent. At its deepest level, this is almost a Quaker poem. Did Auden inherit some rags and tatters of Quakerism through E. M. Forster? It seems the best side of him, as of so many others. His Marxism was boyish and shallow; it gave a didactic edge he was glad to have to his literary criticism before the war, nothing more than that. 'The Fall of Rome', which he dedicated to Cyril Connolly in 1947,[22] is both lighter and bleaker than 'September 1, 1939'. It takes a tone from satiric poems and ballads written years before, but it catches something perfectly, and as no other English or American poet can. He had already found the right tone in November 1937.

'Into many a green valley
    drifts the appalling snow;
Time breaks the threaded dances
And the diver's brilliant bow.

'O plunge your hands in water,
    Plunge them in up to the wrist;
Stare, stare in the basin
    And wonder what you've missed.

'The glacier knocks in the cupboard,
    The desert sighs in the bed,
And the crack in the tea-cup opens
    A lane to the land of the dead.'[23]

   John Bayley remarks that Auden's is 'an art which uses didacticism as a plaything'.[24] However earnest he became in later life, he was never humourless, and that was always true. The nearest he ever came to explaining it was in a letter to Ursula Niebuhr: 'Do you know the Spanish proverb, "God writes straight with crooked lines"? As far as art is concerned, he has no option, because the straight ones leave no mark on the paper.'[25] In an essay on Henry James, Auden noticed 'a style of metaphorical description of the emotions which is all his own, a kind of modern Góngorism'. Góngora is a fertile source for modern poetry, and what is said of James surely applies to Auden's own poetry, including 'his respect for the inalienable rights of every subject to its own form and treatment'. All the same it is worth noticing that, when 'The Fall of Rome' was printed in *Horizon*, Stephen Spender's *European Witness* was a new book. Cyril Connolly was writing in despair and disgust about London, 'now the largest, saddest and dirtiest of great cities with its miles of half-painted, uninhabited houses, its chopless chop-houses, its beerless pubs, its once vivid quarters losing all sense of personality, its squares bereft of elegance, its dandies in exile, its antiques in America, its shops full of junk ... '. Spender was criticized for enthusiastic vagueness in the stated aim of *European Witness*: 'Today we are confronted with the choice between making a heaven or a hell of the world in which we live, and the whole of civilization will be bound by whichever fate we choose.... The only answer to this past and this present is a conscious, deliberate and wholly responsible determination to make our society walk in paths of light.' Personally I still find these words inspiring, as I do Matthew Arnold's fog-eaten poem, 'Rugby Chapel'. But Auden's 'Fall of Rome' is intoxicating.

The Fall of Rome
(for Cyril Connolly)

The piers are pummelled by the waves;
    In a lonely field the rain

Lashes an abandoned train;
Outlaws fill the mountain caves.

Fantastic grow the evening gowns;
Agents of the Fisc pursue
Absconding tax-defaulters through
The sewers of provincial towns.

Private rites of magic send
The temple prostitutes to sleep;
All the literati keep
An imaginary friend.

Cerebrotonic Cato may
Extol the Ancient Disciplines,
But the muscle-bound Marines
Mutiny for food and pay.

Caesar's double-bed is warm
As an unimportant clerk
Writes I DO NOT LIKE MY WORK
On a pink official form.

Unendowed with wealth or pity,
Little birds with scarlet legs,
Sitting on their speckled eggs,
Eye each flu-infected city.

Altogether elsewhere, vast
Herds of reindeer move across
Miles and miles of golden moss,
Silently and very fast.

A number of Auden's best poems are extensions of the same theme, which revolves around the central political crisis of his lifetime, the 1939 war and its results. All he saw of that war was devastation when it was over, and that is what he best records, not only in 'The Fall of Rome', but later in the title poem of *The Shield of Achilles* (1955) and, with an irony which I think is unconscious, in 'Fleet Visit', a poem in which Auden has his happy holiday home on the island of Ischia, while the American fleet rides at anchor in the bay.[26] This is an exuberant, faintly ominous poem: it finds Auden happy for a moment with his new American, or rather New Yorkerish, personality. What a different momentum he would have given to the same images in 1938. The central phrase of his long pseudo-Horatian poem in praise of

Ischia to Brian Howard is about some hot springs which 'improve the venereal act'. Now he considers the American fleet, remaining intransigently himself.

Fleet Visit

The sailors come ashore
Out of their hollow ships,
Mild-looking middle-class boys
Who read the comic strips;
One baseball game is more
To them than fifty Troys.

They look a bit lost, set down
In this unamerican place
Where natives pass with laws
And futures of their own;
They are not here because
But only just-in-case.

The whore and ne'er-do-well
Who pester them with junk
In their grubby ways at least
Are serving the Social Beast;
They neither make nor sell –
No wonder they get drunk.

But their ships on the vehement blue
Of this harbour actually gain
From having nothing to do;
Without a human will
To tell them whom to kill
Their structures are humane

And, far from looking lost,
Look as if they were meant
To be pure abstract design
By some master of pattern and line,
Certainly worth every cent
Of the billions they must have cost.

In his later Christian poems Auden claims to have attained an invulnerable inward peace, but strangely limited. 'I know that I am, here, not alone, But with a world and rejoice Unvexed . . . ' because he is only waking up, he is still 'Adam previous to any act'. The poet no more knows 'whose Truth he will tell' than the hangman knows who he has to hang, or the judge what sentence he may pass. His view of human fraternity and faith is subtle but surprising. It recalls a sermon I heard Auden preach some years later in Westminster Abbey, in which he denounced the New English Bible set before him as a heretical document, and assured the congregation that his God was the God of the orthodox, but like Simone Weil he had not yet come to the point of believing in him. I am not prepared to claim that Auden's Christianity entered more deeply into his poetry, or generated as much in it, as his Marxism had done, but if it did enter more deeply into his personal life, it was his barrier against chaos and the only understanding he had of personal tragedy. The explanation of this may be that it coincided with middle age, and the unhappiness of an elderly lover. He was, as I used to be, heretical only in being a patripassionist: that is, he could not conceive that the Father did not suffer over the sufferings of Christ. Later, and more and more intensely, he turned for consolation and for expression to music. His 'Horae Canonicae' hardly summon up Gregorian chant; they do show a constant reverence for Eliot, whom as a poet he was not really able to abolish into his own style.

That was for him a recurring type of problem. His early ode in the style of Hopkins to the Repton School rugby fifteen was a regrettable enterprise. Among the fleeting influences on his verse technique at different times I notice Edward Lear, Harry Graham's *Ruthless Rhymes for Heartless Homes*, Emily Dickinson, Edwin Arlington Robinson, Marianne Moore, Bridges, Hardy, Housman, Edward Thomas, Winston Churchill, Beowulf, Tolkien, De la Mare, Shakespeare, Pope, Byron and the critic Saintsbury, who inspired in him the ambition 'to write a poem in every metre'. He was fertile in every translation and brilliant in pastiche. He solved the problems of rhyme as lesser men solve crossword puzzles. His multiplicity is one of the most overwhelming things about him. He disported himself in poetry like a whale in a bath tub. He would not abjure any aspect of himself. No joke was too bad for him to cherish it, but he made extremely good jokes as well. He was a magpie anthologist, but better than any other in this or the last century. He told Kenneth Rexroth that he learnt more about writing poems from writing an erotic narrative in thirty-four stanzas than from anything else he ever wrote, but the result is so repulsive that he never publicly acknowledged it. He clearly thought of the subject of those verses as just another literary challenge.[27] One might suspect some literary influence of Verlaine, but

Auden despised French poetry, and as Verlaine's translator Alistair Elliot remarks, 'that vocabulary of obscenity is not easy'. I doubt whether Auden in New York possessed the annotated version of Verlaine's filthy poems secretly printed at Metz in 1949, but who can tell? I suppose the obscenity arises from suppression, and that unsuppressed erotic poetry, the poetry of genuine love, had receded beyond his grasp: hence his concentration on the private group, the small circle of friends. There is no point in blaming that.

The nearest he came to true solution to these problems was musical, as one might expect from his 'Hymn to Cecilia'.

> Blonde Aphrodite rose up excited,
> Moved to delight by the melody.
> White as an orchid she rode quite naked
> In an oyster shell on top of the sea;
> At sounds so entrancing the angels dancing....

In *The Rake's Progress* he achieved his solution in 1951. That opens with formal and pastoral celebrations of love; the lovers are to be 'ever happy, ever fair'. But after all its transfigurations and allegories, the rake is in the churchyard with Shadow, who shows in this scene distinct traces of A. E. Housman and Oscar Wilde: 'Think not your soul to save.' 'Count eight. Too late.'

> Midnight is come: by rope or gun
>   Or medicine or knife
> On the stroke of twelve you shall slay yourself
>   For forfeit is your life.

The rake is saved by love. In the madness that overtakes him, he crowns himself with grass and sings in a childish voice.

> With roses crowned, I sit in the ground;
>   Adonis is my name,
> The only dear of Venus fair:
>   Methinks it is no shame.

In his madness, he becomes an artist devoted only to love. He is redeemed in Bedlam as he dies, with verses that return to the eighteenth-century convention of the opening scene. Anne in the epilogue points the moral:

> Not every rake is rescued
>   At the last by Love and Beauty:

W. H. Auden

> Not every man
> Is given an Anne
> To take the place of Duty.

The redemption happened through his vision of Anne coming to him as Venus, and recognizing him as Adonis: psychologically, from Auden's point of view, a significant choice of roles. That choice, and Stravinsky's music, released in him powers that lay deep: a vision of innocence restored by love, expressed in lyric verse.

> Gently, little boat
> Across the ocean float,
> The crystal waves dividing:
> > The sun in the west
> > Is going to rest;
> > > Glide, glide, glide
> Toward the Islands of the Blest.

> Orchards greenly grace
> That undisturbèd place,
> The weary soul recalling
> > To slumber and dream,
> > While many a stream
> > > Falls, falls, falls,
> Descanting on a childlike theme.

> Lion, lamb and deer,
> Untouched by greed or fear
> About the woods are straying:
> > And quietly now
> > The blossoming bough
> > > Sways, sways, sways
> Above the fair unclouded brow.

Wystan Auden was a tragic poet, and in spite of all his public attitudes essentially a private, intimate poet. He retained an innocence, however sophisticated his mind was; in old age he resembled some unlikely carthorse that might still frisk in a field or might nuzzle one's hand expecting sugar. The contradictions of his character are beyond my scope, except that the poems reveal the presence of many fascinating contradictions, some of the most important-looking being superficial but some deep. You can understand an artist's purpose in his work only if the work has successfully accomplished that purpose, but some of Auden's work is not successful and some of it, before the war at least, is too incoherent to be worth normal attention. At his best he seems simple but is not, seems dramatic and clear, but shelters a deeper moving stream of thoughts and of feeling, just as Louis MacNeice does in 'Bagpipe Music'. There was a decency about his somewhat crusty later attitudes. He hated Socratic bullies and never sought for disciples. If it is true as I conceive that his generation was the last to see the scorned title 'man of letters' as a modest, ironic boast, that is all the worse for us.

> I count myself a man of letters
> Who writes, or hopes to, for his betters.

It is a paradox that he was almost never content to be purely a poet, yet he never denied and never betrayed his vocation as a poet.

> Follow poet, follow right
> To the bottom of the night,
> With your unconstraining voice
> Still persuade us to rejoice.

The formulation is romantic, the programme apparently impossible, but he carried it out, I think. Few writers and almost no poets are so deeply interesting. Had he never lived, we could not possibly have imagined him: had he never written, I dread to think how dull English poetry would have become. He was a liberator and a magician in verse. As he wrote in 'Caliban's Address to the Audience', a long prose pastiche of Henry James which he claimed was the poem he was proudest to have written,[28]

> There is nothing to say. . . . There is no way out. There never was, – it is at this moment that for the first time in our lives we hear, not the sounds which, as born actors, we have hitherto condescended to use as an excellent vehicle for displaying our personalities and looks, but the real World which is our only *raison d'être* . . . that we may rejoice in the perfected Work which is not ours. . . . Its spaces greet us with all their grand old prospect of wonder and width; the working charm is the full bloom of the unbothered state, the sounded note is the restored relation.

This Christian view of things seems to me typical of a particular Oxford generation: it would have appealed to Tolkien and to C. S. Lewis. What a long time ago that seems today.

The roots of Auden's condition come to light in his vigorous anal-

ysis of A. E. Housman and of Edward Lear. The sonnet to Housman
is lethally unfair. Housman's life was better organized than Auden's
and on the whole happier; he did not 'timidly attack the life he led',
and his savage remarks about pretentious idiots have a basis in his
own difficult early career, not in homosexuality. But it may well be
that Auden viewed himself at some level with the same rigour and
bitterness, so that all the rest seemed to him sometimes a pose or a
poise. That is one of the roots of his performances as a poet. The other
side of him, the thing he longed to be, is expressed in the Edward Lear
sonnet: 'he wept to himself in the night. A dirty landscape-painter
who hated his nose.... affection was miles away. But guided by tears
he successfully reached his Regret. How prodigious the welcome
was....' Auden's hunger for affection was certainly as intense as
Lear's, but he was not always as successful, or as obviously desperate
in obtaining it, as Lear was with children. Of the three poets, Edward
Lear's life and art were the most sublimated, and he was the greatest
artist, but he was also the unhappiest. About Auden there can be no
complete verdict, his poetry is somehow embarrassing as well as
great; to select his few perfect poems that might resist all criticism
is to do him a disservice, because he exists in the messy sprawl of his
entire lifework, and the bigness of that presence is a crucial quality.
All the same one must seek him not in his poetry, but in his poems,
poem after poem, all different.

In Memory of Robert Lowell

In this century we have passed through a period, and it may not be over yet, when American poets have dominated British imaginations, those of young poets perhaps even more than those of whatever other readers poetry may have. I suppose the first internationally influential American poet was Walt Whitman. Hopkins and Bridges discussed him avidly, Tennyson admired him and so did Tolstoy. The admiration of the French for the poetry of E. A. Poe is another matter, since I think it derived from the inability to pronounce his verses properly; pronounced like French they take on fresh and mysterious qualities. I have heard something similar said of the influence of Byron on Pushkin, and one might well believe it. But between American and native English poetry the differences are subtle. They are not just a question of national characteristics, but they do include differences of subject matter, and to a slighter extent of traditional sensibility.

It is not just a matter of the modern movement either. That existed in many languages, and took a number of quite different, mutually contradictory forms. It meant one thing to Apollinaire, quite another to Pasternak and another again to Mayakovsky, quite another again to Ezra Pound, to Eliot, to Carlos Williams. In its second generation the modern movement in poetry affected a number of writers deeply on both sides of the Atlantic. To a young poet in the 1950s Eliot and Pound were already classics, and when Basil Bunting's *Briggflats* appeared in 1966, and when the later works of David Jones appeared, it seemed obvious that they had a classic greatness. With Eliot at Faber's, and Auden writing his best and most mind-opening criticism in the 1950s and 1960s, young poets learnt what they needed to know with speed and pleasure. But now that the modern movement is supposed to be over, though its corpse has not yet been convincingly dissected, American poetry seems to be further away. The British islands are more isolated, insularity is looking like a virtue, the level of blood sugar in our veins is low and still falling. There seem to be fewer great poets alive anywhere in the world. I believe a new poetry is coming, but I reserve that speculation for a later lecture. When it comes I think it will owe something to Seamus Heaney, and to lessons learnt from Robert Lowell.

Being alive in Robert Lowell's lifetime, and reading his poems as they appeared, was a fascinating privilege. It was like being a contemporary of Tennyson or of Donne: it was not only delightful, but he interpreted the world, he spoke about real things and one could understand him. At least that is what one felt at the time, but now with many rereadings I find his formidable power grows, though I become much less certain of what I understand from him. This lecture must therefore be to some extent autobiographical. Making up one's mind is a cumulative process; critics should reveal their working; it is proper for lecturers to contradict themselves. John Berryman spoke of Lowell's 'evergreen ingenuity'. That and his constant, extremely bold revisions and adaptations of old lines and old images in new contexts made it harder than it looks to interpret him. He was in much of his work more a man making something, putting together something out of materials, than he was a man saying something. He complained about this in himself:

> the revision, the consciousness that tinkers with the poem – that has something to do with teaching and criticism. . . . Poetry has become a craft, merely a craft, and there must be some breakthrough back into life. . . . The kind of poem I thought interesting and would work on became so cluttered and overdone that is wasn't really poetry. . . . Most poetry is very formal. . . . Somehow we've tried to make it look difficult.[1]

He was speaking there of his work as a very young man. He was brought up as he says in what was thought of as a great age of criticism. Young poets used to rush out to read the latest critical article as you and I might rush out to read a new poem by Philip Larkin. These critics were almost all American, but the same atmosphere had begun to blight the air even in amateurish Oxford, where poems sprouted like fritillaries and critics passed by like the clouds, as early as the 1950s. I recollect then being several times told that after Eliot poetry was going to be no good, this was an age of criticism and the critics were more worth reading than the poets. I take it to be an axiom we now share that no such age could exist.[2] The best critics usually are poets: Dryden, Johnson, Arnold, Eliot, Auden, Pound,

Lowell. But in Lowell's generation[3] of American poets, 'all the good ones taught', they all read a lot of criticism, they read very widely, they argued endlessly and competitively, like some hectic seminar; the meditation of literature which stands behind all poetry in every age came out very densely, under very high pressure, in their poems. They were far more professional than most English poets, both for better and for worse.

Robert Lowell never stopped thinking about poetry; his criticism was bold and fascinating. A few lines of his about Propertius are as good as any criticism of Eliot's. His vignette of his pupil Anthony Snodgrass has a sharpness that is almost rasping, but a remarkable justice. He understood Eliot, and Elizabeth Bishop, and John Berryman, and Pound in old age, with intense insight. But his own poetry clarified, I am not sure whether it simplified. Eileen Simpson, John Berryman's first wife, has written the best memoir[4] of that early group of friends. She says of Lowell in later life, 'Whereas in Maine he had looked younger than his years because of the "terrifying innocence" in his face, he now looked older because of the marks illness had etched around his eyes and mouth.' Certainly Lowell's greatest power as a poet was his communication of the experience of life. His illness and his fear of madness were part of that. So are his wistfulness, his affection, his acceptance of the real, his love of peace and the religious sense that sometimes seems so deep in his inspiration and at other times like a light that has gone out. This last very unusual quality he has in common with Shakespeare. It may be relevant that he once said the core of Shakespeare could best be sensed in *Macbeth*.

By religious sense, I do not mean to refer to the Catholic quality of his convert period, which of course came very early. John Berryman remarks in an essay[5] that 'The early poems writhed, crunched, spat against Satan, war, modern Boston, the Redcoats, Babel, Leviathan, Babylon, Sodom.' It did not occur to me when I first read them that they had anything to do with the low-toned Catholicism of the London suburbs in which I was brought up. I do now see that he must at the time have looked at least in America like the new poet of the Catholic subculture. But the cultural distance is still vast. To leave a family of Boston mandarins and join the Boston Irish must have seemed an enormous step to him, but somehow he carried Calvinism with him, and his inner rage about Calvinism. And his love–hate for America, which is just as intimate and as foreign to us as his feelings about his own family, had already begun to work itself out. He was anti-capitalist and anti-war, asking what had gone wrong with

America in its most honourable years since the War of Independence. And yet his stand is convincing. One understands America better for trying to understand Lowell's poetry.

I like 'Thanksgiving's Over', a guilty dream in Third Avenue about the suicide of a mad wife, which is the last poem in my edition of *The Mills of the Kavanaughs*. It ends like this:

> Winter had come on horseback, and the snow,
> Hostile and unattended, wrapped my feet
> In sheepskins. Where I'd stumbled from the street,
> A red cement Saint Francis fed a row
> Of toga'd boys with birds beneath a Child.
> His candles flamed in tumblers, and He smiled.
> 'Romans!' she whispered, 'look, these overblown
> And bootless Brothers tell us we must go
> Barefooted through the snow where birds recite:
> *Come unto us, our burden's light* – light, light,
> This burden that our marriage turned to stone!
> O Michael, must we join this deaf and dumb
> Breadline for children? Sit and listen.' So
> I sat. I counted to ten thousand, wound
> My cowhorn beads from Dublin on my thumb,
> and ground them. *Miserere*? Not a sound.

His poetry was always full of strange details no one else used or dared command, and his intonation is so personal, and his technical ability is so invigorating, that it seems there is nothing in the world that might not get said in his verse. And yet what does he choose to express? The boredom, the inadequacy of church to these people, conveyed with merciless fidelity. In his early poems even hell is burnt out. Otherwise, a reader unfamiliar with *Land of Unlikeness*, 1944, a limited edition from a small press cannibalized later, *Lord Weary's Castle*, which won him the Pulitzer Prize at thirty in 1947, and *The Mills of the Kavanaughs* will be surprised how many of the techniques, and how much of the material of his poetry, are already present in them. Of all these poems the greatest and one of the clearest, syntactically the least teasing and symbolically the least heavy going, had already appeared in an early version in *Partisan Review* in 1945. This is 'The Quaker Graveyard in Nantucket'.

It has a later, fuller version in the Faber *Poems 1938–49* which is also in *Lord Weary's Castle*, and a third version, made I am not sure when, but quite severely cut, which is to be found in the *New Oxford*

Book of American Verse and elsewhere. The swelling of the poem into its longest version was certainly an improvement. It gave us the third part and the seventh. The final cuts are an act of bold self-criticism. They remove an element of billowing symbolism and a heavy tidal flow as if the sea had been chewing mud. But they also remove part six, the extraordinary two stanzas about Walsingham. I suppose Lowell came to think their peculiar Catholic imagery irrelevant to the Quakers, and to the dead sailor, his cousin Warren Winslow. Before he added part seven in *Lord Weary's Castle*, they were the climax of the poem. By cutting them, and cutting the first half of part seven as well, he made the entire poem more formidable and more marine: that is, stronger. All the same I know of no other poem in English where so many exhilarating verses have been jettisoned wholesale, and no other poet who would have dared to do it. Auden in old age altered his poems, but that was only fiddling about with his opinions. This is one of the cleanest pieces of pruning in English literature.

That is only the beginning of Robert Lowell's vast achievement as a poet. Throughout his life he disciplined himself by verse translations. Not all his versions are to be dismissed as adaptations or imitations. Hie Propertius is remarkable, his Juvenal is masterly: it exactly conveys the spirit, tone, meaning and resonance of its original. His Dante is better still: it goes beyond what Eliot reproduced of Dante in memorable scattered lines. I assume that Seamus Heaney in 'Station Island' and elsewhere draws not only on Dante but on Lowell's Dante. A style is like an infection. Lowell caught his Dantesque style from Eliot, and I hope I may live to see it infect younger poets. Lowell's Dante and his Juvenal are both to be found in *Near the Ocean* (1967), which also includes two of the greatest poems of his maturity, 'Waking Early Sunday Morning' and 'Fourth of July in Maine'.

The translations were written in 1962, when he was forty-five. His Racine and the amazing collection called *Imitations* were both published in 1961, and it was in the early 1960s he began translating Aeschylus, and completed *Agamemnon* and *Orestes*. His *Prometheus* was produced in 1967, and his *Baudelaire* appeared in 1969. Since the same period saw *For the Union Dead* (1964), the first version of *Notebook* (1969) and the three short plays in *The Old Glory* (1965), it will be seen that the quantity as well as the quality of his work was remarkable. How odd then that his poem 'Tenth Muse', which is addressed to Sloth, should appear in *For the Union Dead*. It is not exclusively about sloth, it is a kind of farewell to organized religion, to be taken with 'Beyond the Alps' in the same collection, and 'Waking

Early' in the next. This is a new kind of verse, redeemed from rhetoric by an intricate descant and waterfall of interweaving tones. I do not think it was learnt from *Life Studies*, where the verse is supposed to be suddenly so free and the material so confessional. I think it may have been learnt from his own translations of Pasternak in *Imitations*.

It is never very easy to see the influence of foreign poetry on any generation of English readers. That depends on the changes of translation and on such freaks of chance as the Nobel prize or a famous novel, and it comes to us late, sometimes a generation late. Laforgue and Apollinaire were dead before they were much read in England: indeed most of us first knew Laforgue as the charming ghost that haunted Eliot's machinery. But I have the impression that between the wars and as late as the 1940s French poetry expressed the soul and the intellect of Europe; there was something central about it, and everyone read it who could. Today the influence of French comes from further back in time, Rimbaud and Baudelaire, perhaps even Racine. But for the last thirty years we have been overshadowed by Russian poetry. Most of that also has come to us late. In the summer of 1911, T. S. Eliot and Rupert Brooke were sitting in much the same cafés in Munich. Eliot was finishing 'Prufrock', and Brooke was conceiving 'Grantchester'. They never met. In the summer of 1914, when he was twenty-six, Eliot went to study philosophy at Marburg under Professor Cohen. The young star of the same seminar in 1912 was Pasternak; he gave up philosophy for a love affair and for poetry in that year. Eliot is an ominous and deadly poet; however great, he strikes with a dead sound on the final note of nine. Pasternak is inspiring, thrilling, life-giving. After reading Eliot you enter into his silence, but Pasternak and Robert Lowell make you want to write poetry of your own. It is as if your mind was being broken open with pickaxes of light. New technical possibilities flourish in every cranny of Lowell's versions of Pasternak.

> Summer says goodbye to the station.
> Running in its photographer's black hood,
> and blinding us with flash-bulbs, the thunder
> takes a hundred souvenir snap-shots....

Pasternak's poetry began as baroque fireworks, with a strong sense of the force of life. It simplified, perhaps as Lowell's did, under the weight of his experience of life. They both offer what Kafka complained of in modern books, 'mere wavering reflections of the present'. They both break through in the course of poems into vistas of terrible truth, and they mimic these breakthroughs, breaking down the taboos of life, by breaking down taboos of rhythm and of words. They are both formal masters, like pre-romantic poets, and yet they both treat formality with disrespect. To be free you have to break loose, there has to be something to break: that is as true of poetry as it is of life. And poetry has to be constantly surprising: the breakthrough to an appalling truth is an inheritance of the modern movement from romantic poetry. No modern poet is so full of life and surprise as Pasternak, even though his poems are terrible, awe-inspiring. Robert Lowell tries to extract his essence, and succeeds to a remarkable degree, by ramming two or three poems into one.

Hamlet in Russia, A Soliloquy

'My heart throbbed like a boat on the water.
My oars rested. The willows swayed through the summer,
licking my shoulders, elbows and rowlocks –
wait! this might happen,

when the music brought me the beat,
and the ash-gray water-lilies dragged, and a couple of
daisies blew,
and a hint of blue dotted a point off-shore –
lips to lips, stars to stars!

My sister, life!
the world has too many people for us,
the sycophant, the spineless –
politely, like snakes in the grass, they sting.

My sister!
embrace the sky and Hercules
who holds the world up forever
at ease, perhaps, and sleeps at night

thrilled by the nightingales crying . . .

The boat stops throbbing on the water . . .

The clapping stops. I walk into the lights
as Hamlet, lounge like a student against the door-frame,
and try to catch the far-off dissonance of life –
all that has happened, and must!

From the dark the audience leans its one hammering brow
against me –

ten thousand opera glasses, each set on the tripod!
Abba, Father, all things are possible with thee –
take away this cup!

I love the mulishness of Providence,
I am content to play the one part I was born for . . .
quite another play is running now . . .
take me off the hooks tonight!

The sequence of scenes was well thought out;
the last bow is in the cards, or the stars –
but I am alone, and there is none . . .
All's drowned in the sperm and spittle of the Pharisee –

To live a life is not to cross a field.'

We often judge a poem by the amount of reality the poet puts into
it, as if the ultimate aim of poetry were to capture and to represent the
whole of reality in the end, with all its grit and grime. It is pleasing and
surprising to encounter realities that never seem to have been inside a
poem before. But modern poetry succeeds rather in proportion to
what it leaves out. Hermetic poetry left out the plot, surrealist poetry
left out the meaning, a lot of modern poetry leaves out the plain logic
of prose, some poets deal high-handedly with syntax, Apollinaire
abandoned punctuation. All these devices dramatize and intensify,
and somewhere, to some degree, Robert Lowell uses all of them. But
his lines never quite lose the rigour of his classical translation and the
vigorous solidity he picked up from Villon and Rimbaud, and above
all from Pasternak.

He was for a time a public figure and he made gestures towards
public poetry. We used to think of him in the 1960s as a public poet,
an important public voice in a way that Auden had ceased to be in
1939. Auden was an amiable literary uncle with dazzling party tricks,
and a true poet, truer to his poetry and truer in it than most people yet
realize. But Lowell was important because he spoke for America, with
all its weight behind him. He was closer to us because he seemed to
have suffered the modern world, where Auden seemed to be playing
with it, seemed almost to have invented it. What we loved in Robert
Lowell's poetry was his sad and serious tones, and the touches of
humour.

O to break loose. All life's grandeur
is something with a girl in summer . . .

elated as the President
girdled by his establishment
this Sunday morning, free to chaff
his own thoughts with his bear-cuffed staff,
swimming nude, unbuttoned, sick
of his ghost-written rhetoric!

No weekends for the gods now. Wars
flicker, earth licks its open sores,
fresh breakage, fresh promotions, chance
assassinations, no advance.
Only man thinning out his kind
sounds through the Sabbath noon, the blind
swipe of the pruner and his knife
busy about the tree of life . . .

Pity the planet, all joy gone
from this sweet volcanic cone;
peace to our children when they fall
in small war on the heels of small
war – until the end of time
to police the earth, a ghost
orbiting forever lost
in our monotonous sublime.

There is a finality about that last sentence. The strong, baroque climax, as in the sonnets of John Donne, has dissolved away. The dying fall in so tight a form of stanza as this poem has shown an authority not achieved without long labour. It is crescendo in descant with diminuendo. A close study of the whole poem, which has fourteen stanzas and a strange, wandering momentum only revealed at the end, and the more powerful for that, would show a striking abundance of variations within the same stanza form. I mean variations of rhythm and syntax, making the successive stanzas almost more unlike than like one another. They correspond to changes of tone within the stanza as well as between stanzas. First in fact he sets up a form, then he breaks it, alters it, readapts it and transforms it. The opening lines 'O to break loose', 'Stop, back off' and 'Fierce, fireless mind, running downhill' are transmuted in the final stanzas, and those echoes are powerful. The break after 'war' in the last stanza of all corresponds to a series of similar breaks in early stanzas, which become more and more irregular, until this one, the first to occur in mid-line. It creates a memorable closure.

Robert Lowell's poetry was always peculiarly memorable. It is the function of poetry to be learnt by heart and recited. The most memorable poetry is the best. Our periodicals at present are full of shortish poems where you forget the beginning before you reach the end. Long, casual, informal rhythms without momentum are hard to remember, so Lowell has a head start; even his free verse has a memorable tensity. Metre is repeated rhythm, it has to be self-echoing, because we recognize rhythms only when they are repeated, then they may haunt our memories, and they may also stimulate our imaginations. The difference in *Life Studies* is as Lowell told the *Paris Review*'s interviewer, 'I couldn't get my experience into tight metrical forms.' But even Lowell's famous looser style in *Life Studies* is not very loose.

> The lobbed ball plops, then dribbles to the cup....
> (a birdie Fordie!) But it nearly killed
> the ministers. Lloyd George was holding up
> the flag. He gabbled, 'Hop-toad, hop-toad, hop-toad!'....

The rhymes and half-rhymes are essentially rhythmic devices, like punctuation marks. The diction, as usual with Lowell, has a peculiarly American, maybe a Bostonian precision. I used to think Eliot's prose style had an impersonal, absolute authority, and no doubt he strove for that, but now I am inclined to think of it as a personal variation on the style we encounter as Henry James; he has the same fastidious daring in prose and in verse, and I think Lowell shares it. Poetry always has some special relation to vernacular speech, though the relation varies between poets. Lowell's vernacular is grander and crisper than ours, but in *Life Studies* his relation to it is often close. I doubt whether 'confessional' is the right word for this poetry, except in the sense, as Richard Ellmann put it, that it was as if the universe was confessing. In his family poems, Lowell leaves out far more than he puts in. The most sexual poem, 'To Speak of the Woe that is in Marriage', which is an overflow from 'Man and Wife' on the page before it,[6] has the monotonous, brooding quality of *The Mills of the Kavanaughs*. It has the same almost impersonalized, ranting, chanting tone. 'The merciless Racinian *tirade*', or in the published version:

> your old-fashioned tirade —
> loving, rapid, merciless —
> breaks like the Atlantic Ocean on my head

Some poems in *Life Studies* are political, including the first version of 'Beyond the Alps', which was republished with a third stanza Lowell had cut, restored on John Berryman's advice, in *For the Union Dead*. In the second English edition of *Life Studies* in 1968, this stanza gets slightly revised. My own view is that Berryman was wrong. The stanza is fine enough, quite as good as what was cut from 'The Quaker Graveyard in Nantucket', but the poem is simpler, leaner and stronger without it. It is certainly a memorable poem: 'God herded his people to the *coup de grâce*.' In all these poems, in the three books, *Life Studies*, *For the Union Dead* and *Near the Ocean*, Lowell's themes are so closely interwoven that in a way they read like one poem: not cannibalized like his early verses, not a set of variations like the late sonnets, and not simply one man's mind or one man's story. They read like a continuous opus. Single poems are detachable only as single epigrams are detachable from the poems.

> and the Republic summons Ike,
> the mausoleum in her heart.

But at their best these poems are chamber music, played to be overheard of course, yet they have a musing privacy, a sadness which is the reverse of depressing. One of these, which is technically a foretaste of *Near the Ocean*, is 'Tenth Muse', in *For the Union Dead*. From where we stand now it occupies almost a central position in Robert Lowell's poetry. It has his best formality and his best informality. It is apparently made of nothing. It seems completely original. Its tone is wry and personal and highly convincing. It hardly deals with politics, though it has implications about power, yet it says as much about New England as Emerson's 'Concord Hymn'.

Tenth Muse

> Tenth Muse, Oh my heart-felt Sloth,
> how often now you come to my bed,
> thin as a canvas in your white and red
> check dresses like a table cloth,
> my Dearest, settling like my shroud!
>
> Yes, yes, I ought to remember Moses
> jogging down on his mule from the Mount
> with the old law, the old mistake,
> safe in his saddlebags, and chiselled
> on the stones we cannot bear or break.
>
> Here waiting, here waiting for an answer
> from this malignant surf of unopened letters,

always reaching land too late,
as fact and abstraction accumulate,
and the signature fades from the paper –
I like to imagine it must have been simpler
in the days of Lot,
or when Greek and Roman picturebook
gods sat combing their golden beards,
each on his private hill or mountain.

But I suppose even God was born
too late to trust the old religion –
all those settings out
that never left the ground,
beginning in wisdom, dying in doubt.

In the late 1960s and early 1970s, Robert Lowell wrote what seemed a never-ending series of unrhymed sonnets. Once he had spent a hundred hours on a stanza, now he wrote three or four of these poems a week, and at times more. They have been underestimated. They stand infinite rereadings. They have the same weight of reality and personality, but they have it almost more intensely with fewer strokes of the brush. Technically, they are marvellously abundant. He spoke of *Notebook* while he was writing it as a single long poem. He wrote to the critic A. Alvarez, 'I want this book to hit with a single impact: the parts are not meant to stand by themselves.' But *Notebook 1967–8* (first edition May 1969, second July 1969, expanded edition 1970) was not meant to be either a chronicle or a confession; he said it was not in a preface entitled 'Afterthought'.

He offers a list of public events of 1967–8, but he dealt with these realities only obliquely. 'I lean heavily on the rational,' he wrote, 'but am devoted to unrealism. . . . the true unreal is about something, and eats from the abundance of reality.' He claimed in fact no more than the usual licence of modern poetry. He referred to some of his own lines as 'hermetic', meaning I think that they contained private allusions. In the deeper sense he is certainly hermetic, in communicating feeling immediately with the barest network of words, and without full narrative explanations. Here again in fact he is leaving out more than he puts in. But he is in very close control of what he is doing. 'For the poet without direction, poetry is a way of not saying what he has to say.' Robert Lowell never fell into that trap, certainly never in the last ten years of his life. He has some interesting things to say about his unrhymed sonnet form or stanza form.

'My meter, fourteen line unrhymed blank verse sections, is fairly strict at first and elsewhere, but often corrupts in single lines to the freedom of prose. Even with this license, I fear I have failed to avoid the themes and gigantism of the sonnet.' He printed several hundred of these in the full version of *Notebook*, and eighty new ones and a massive revision of the rest in *History* in 1973. In a note to *History* he refers to *Notebook* not as a collection but as 'my last published poem', and he complains about its jumbled composition. *History* is to be a reworking, with less waste material and clearer lines. But in fact this problem of unity and this search for a perfectly adaptable stanza form go a long way back in his work. One is free to treat *Notebook* and *History* as collections of short poems or as two attempts at a long one. Lowell was particularly conscious even as a young man of the book, the short collection of poems, as something that ought to make a strong, single impression. Perhaps that arises from reviewing, or from the endless mutual criticism of his own generation of young poets attempting to launch their first books.

T. S. Eliot said to Roger Hinks that 'a poem is the result of an urgent need to make a whole out of things which have nothing to do with one another',[7] and there is some such feeling about *Notebook* and about *History*. In a profound way, these poems are an attempt to make sense of life, and they convey in all their divagations the seriousness of that attempt. It is interesting that Lowell once said in praise of Eliot, 'Eliot has done what he said Shakespeare had done: all his poems are one poem, a form of continuity that has grown and snowballed.'[8] In the brief compass of a lecture it is hardly possible to demonstrate the continuous force and the cumulative technique of Lowell's unrhymed sonnets, but one can at least defend the form itself. The fact that they are held together in no obvious way, by no rhyme scheme or metrical insistence, means that what does hold them invisibly in place, the syntax and the rhythmic impetus, and all their small devices, have to be very finely judged in order to do their work. And they do work; the constant reworking made them work. He reduces Rimbaud to a sonnet, his own translation of Horace to a sonnet, and his old poem 'In the Cage' (1944) to a sonnet. Technically these are the workshop chippings of a master, they are gleefully contrived, and no two are at all the same.

De Gaulle est Mort

'When the French public heard de Gaulle was dead,
they popped champagne on all the squares –

264

even for Latins it was somehow obscene.
Was he their great man? Three days later
they read in the American press he was . . .
I kept asking those student questions you hate;
I remember a Paris taxi-driver told me:
"I would have popped champagne myself. . . . At last
France has someone better than Churchill to bury;
now he's dead, we know he defied America –
or would we have ditched them anyway?"
His choirgirls were pure white angels at Notre Dame;
I felt the Egyptians really wanted to eat
Nasser – de Gaulle, much bigger, was digested.'

I chose this sonnet because the variations of how a phrase can sound,
how it can behave within the line, and how the line can behave within
the sonnet, are so elaborate. The punctuation is very careful: question-
marks, colon, semi-colon, different kinds of pauses, rows of dots, long
dashes, quotation within quotation, questions and pauses within the
line, nearly every way in which·syntax and the phrasing of speech can
enliven the texture of a poem. One feels the attempt to avoid 'the
themes and gigantism of the sonnet', and I think that succeeds. But
History has power, violence and the nature of greatness for its major
theme. Lowell never loses his head about violence in these poems, he
never worships it or glorifies it, and he never glorifies the modern
world, though he is obviously on terms with it. Some of the poems are
the journal of a great man who knows the life of his time. He writes
ironically about books, and warmly but often obliquely about writers.
Nowhere will you find literary anecdotes and vignettes of our time so
oblique and so telling. In very few places will you find the same
inwardness with public events, with a personal reaction expressed so
purely and strongly: the death of Che Guevara for example, and a five-
hour political rally. The secret of *History* in the final form of the book
is that he writes about the Bible, the Greeks, European history and his
own times, his own year and his memories, with just the same kind of
intensity, in just the same stanza form. Consider the obliqueness and
the intimacy of this portrait of Ezra Pound:

Horizontal on a deckchair in the ward
of the criminal mad. . . . A man without shoestrings clawing
the Social Credit broadsheet from your table, you saying,
' . . . here with a black suit and black briefcase; in the brief,
an abomination, Possum's *hommage* to Milton.'

Then sprung; Rapallo, and the decade gone;
and three years later, Eliot dead, you saying,
'Who's left alive to understand my jokes?
My old Brother in the arts ... besides, he was a smash of a poet.'
You showed me your blotched, bent hands, saying, 'Worms.
When I talked that nonsense about Jews on the Rome
wireless, Olga knew it was shit, and still loved me.'
And I, 'Who else has been in Purgatory?
You, 'I began with a swelled head and end with swelled feet.'

I like the tartness of his sympathy for Pound. He said elsewhere:

> Very ugly emotions perhaps make a poem.... Pound's social credit,
> his Fascism, all these various things, were a tremendous gain to him;
> he'd be a very Parnassian poet without them. Even if they're bad
> beliefs – and some were bad, some weren't, and some were just
> terrible, of course – they made him more human and more to do
> with life, more to do with the times. They served him. Taking what
> interested him in these things gave a kind of realism and life to this
> poetry that it wouldn't otherwise have had.[9]

These remarks were made in about 1960, soon after the publication of
Life Studies. In a sidelong way they perhaps illuminate the subject
matter of *Notebook* and *History*, and the degree of the poet's identification with that subject matter. Poets like this seldom take up with
any idea because it might be useful in poetry, though they can be
shown in retrospect instinctively to have sought out things in life, even
situations, which might nourish their art. Ted Hughes once said to me
when I had just gone through some vast personal earthquake, a
transformation of my life: 'I see, you sucked that dry, you used it up
and moved on.' I found that shocking at the time, but who knows
what the unconscious determines?

A poet's themes are passionate engagements, they are not flirtations
to be exploited. A poet does not consume the universe, he does not
even consume his own life, in order to nourish poems. But once he is
writing, then he uses up everything that comes to hand, everything
that his memory and perhaps his unconscious can lay hands on, that
might be fed into that poem. I think there is no doubt that in *Notebook* in its two stages, and finally in *History* with its cleaner line
of progression, Lowell like Milton at the same age, his party like
Milton's being in defeat, his health like Milton's terribly overshadowed, his time as a public figure like Milton's time being over, deli-

berately set out to write a great poem. *Notebook* even in its first form is the sketch of a mighty composition. Its greatest success and its only failure are that Robert Lowell had almost too much to say. But I take *Notebook* to be the last attempt of the modern movement at the great, impossible ideal of that movement, a modern epic poem.

As for Robert Lowell's ambition, John Berryman had already delivered a just verdict on that in a review of *Lord Weary's Castle* in 1947:[10] 'Without first-rate qualities, ambition is nothing, a personal disease; but given these qualities, the difference is partly one of ambition.' Those who hate the modern movement, and want to set up Thomas Hardy, Edward Thomas, Philip Larkin as an alternative tradition, will be interested to hear that Berryman went on somewhat to belittle Hardy for lack of ambition, wrongly in my view: 'notwithstanding a long and reverent love for Hardy, I think Eliot was right when he observed on the occasion of Yeats's seventieth birthday that Hardy now appeared, what he always was, a minor poet'. It may be that minor poetry can be more useful than major poetry, more itself, more authentic, it may be that there are necessary poets; I find Lowell and Hardy both necessary. It may just be that Eliot was flattering Yeats on his birthday. Certainly, Lowell's ambition is part of his generosity as a poet, the abundance of his inspiration.

The last phase of Robert Lowell's life seems to have taken the critics by surprise, like every other phase of it. It does take time to absorb poetry, it takes many readings. In youth we tear a book apart, we read it twice between midnight and four in the morning, we are hungry for poetry, and we are confident that we know the real thing as soon as we look at it. But critics are busy and professors are tired, and their minds are more cluttered than ours. Maybe it takes a poet to catch a poet. Every time Robert Lowell was idolized for a new style, and that process seems to have taken longer to occur after *Life Studies*, he proceeded to abandon the style and break the idol. *The Dolphin* and *For Lizzie and Harriet* were published together in 1973 and *Day by Day* in 1977, the year of his death. The best article about his late poetry I saw was by Helen Vendler.[11] She took the line that *Day by Day* was 'another swing of the pendulum toward the freedom that in Lowell was always being rebuked by a new imposition of metrical form'. That seems a particularly American view, that freedom is natural. I think Robert Lowell thought as we do, that it was attained. In his technique as a poet, it certainly was forced on him, and striven for, and attained. Metrical form in his verse was always being rebuked by a new imposition of freedom.

Those blessèd structures, plot and rhyme —
why are they no help to me now
I want to make
something imagined, not recalled?
I hear the noise of my own voice:
The painter's vision is not a lens,
it trembles to caress the light....[12]

This whole poem has a sensitivity, almost a fragility, though the lines are quite unbreakable, that one finds in lyrics by William Carlos Williams. It rehearses old themes with utter lack of aggression. It reflects, as much of his last poetry does, a few years of peace and affection, a rather quiet life for him, in which he and his wife nested like swans in an obscure part of Kent.

Pray for the grace of accuracy
Vermeer gave to the sun's illumination
stealing like the tide across a map
to his girl solid with yearning.
We are poor passing facts,
warned by that to give
each figure in the photograph
his living name.

These are not minor poems, but they are written in a minor key. They are undogmatic, and the human world is treated in them, as Helen Vendler says, like an arboretum or a Noah's ark. It is represented not criticized. The same peaceful, unsavage mood and almost the same beautiful looseness, the personal, vernacular, musing tone, are already to be found in *Lord Weary's Castle*, but most of Lowell is to be found there in one way or another; the last poems, more than was usual with him, directly reflect a particular time of his life. His constant revision and self-criticism show him in several instances crumbling away the clay feet of his own ferocity and grand rhetoric, his old self-image. He even did it in poems.

These are the tranquillized *Fifties*,
and I am forty. Ought I to regret my seedtime?
I was a fire-breathing Catholic C.O.,
and made my manic statement,
telling off the state and president, and then
sat waiting sentence in the bull pen
beside a Negro boy with curlicues
of marijuana in his hair.[13]

Now he was nearer sixty. There is a deeper truth to life in the last poems, I am inclined to think, but they read like a coda to his life's work; he could not possibly have written them without going through all the rest, and we would not so easily see all we do see in them, if our ears had not already got used to his personal tones. The relationships in *Day by Day* are not at all simple, and the last ones about an institution and about loneliness are intensely sad. The verbal music is correspondingly complex. *The Dolphin*, like *Lizzie and Harriet*, is more unrhymed sonnets, another journal, and perhaps it has been neglected for that reason. They mark the end of his sonnet habit, but now the surface is more subtly, more lightly incised than *History*, the pen hardly scratched the paper. They show the increase in personal delicacy, in a deep, personal truth about life, that was noticed with 'the change' of metre by critics of *Day by Day*. The poems are still hermetic, perhaps more so than ever, and the narrative more fragmentary than ever. These are not so much snapshots, photographs, as moments when one's eyes are stunned by the explosion of a flashbulb. The politics have gone, the dramas are on a personal scale, but the plot is still not revealed, though today one may know much of it. These poems are snatches of an intimate conversation.

> Any clear thing that blinds us with surprise,
> your wandering silences and bright trouvailles,
> dolphin let loose to catch the flashing fish....
> Poets die adolescents, their beat embalms them,
> the archetypal voices sing offkey;
> the old actor cannot read his friends,
> and nevertheless he reads himself aloud,
> genius hums the auditorium dead.
> The line must terminate.
> Yet my heart rises, I know I've gladdened a lifetime
> knotting, undoing a fishnet of tarred rope;
> the net will hang on the wall when the fish are eaten,
> nailed like illegible bronze on the futureless future.[14]

It was in his unrhymed sonnets, through the early ones and in the later ones, that Robert Lowell achieved a perfect control, an even speaking voice in a poem which is not the Spirit brooding over the face of the waters, but a style in which every line has room to breathe for itself. Probably no one but another poet will understand what a difficult achievement that is. Each poem perfectly fills its own space. The closure no longer needs to be a climax, though it can be. I find the increase in finesse in these stanzas or poems more astonishing now than when they were first printed. Nothing could make the early ones look crude, or look intoxicated with 'the themes and the gigantism of the sonnet', except these later ones. I am sure that *For Lizzie and Harriet* and *The Dolphin* are intended as long single poems, and they work wonderfully like that: far more easily than *History*, let alone *Notebook*. The tones and subjects are similar, they are simply different poems. *Lizzie and Harriet* contains rewriting; it begins with the same poems, only slightly revised, as *Notebook*.

I do not think we will ever sort out all Robert Lowell's revisions until we get a complete collected poems, with every collection he issued just as it appeared, and notes pointing out the history of every revision: almost a variorum edition, but one in which every revised publication is treated as a new creation. I would like to make a public plea for that. At present we have no Collected Poems of Robert Lowell, and some of his work is hard to come by. We also ought to have a full publication of the manuscript drafts for *Near the Ocean*, which are in the Houghton Library at Harvard, where Helen Vendler refers to them. Admittedly, in his Note to the second edition of *Notebook*, the poet wrote, 'I am loath to display a litter of variants, and hold up a target for the critic.' That is why I am not really suggesting a variorum edition, only a Collected Poems, a full replay of all his magnificent work.

Robert Lowell might once have held the Chair I now shamefacedly hold. If he had done he would have been its most distinguished holder since Matthew Arnold. My purpose this evening is to summon his mighty ghost. What he had to teach then, he still has to teach; it is all in his poems. But I am also speaking of him because I was so proud to know him: very few poets can have been so much loved as human beings. It is therefore a particular delight that he still can be known and loved in the modest, personal poetry he wrote at the end of his life, particularly I think some for his daughter Harriet. Poetry is a serious and a demanding art, and Robert Lowell's poetry never ceased to be that. Out of the strong come forth sweetness, that is all.

> I see the country where the lemon blossoms,
> and the pig-gold orange glows on its dark branch,
> and the south wind stutters from the blue hustings;
> I see it; it's behind us, love, behind us –

For Lizzie and Harriet is only 66 unrhymed sonnet stanzas, and *The Dolphin* is 104. Taken alone they would make Robert Lowell the most interesting poet that was writing then, or is now, in our language, except possibly for Philip Larkin. They skirt or deliberately avoid the semblance of greatness; there is a closing down of great themes, an increase of privacy and of pleasure, but these poems are built to last. They are the crown of his work, if only because they supply what it lacked. They offer to readers that intimacy, that entry into privacy and the soul, which great art so often promises and so seldom delivers.

Day by Day has a dying fall. It constitutes a portrait of the artist at the end, and the presence of death, the death of his friends and his own coming death, makes it poignant. It was published in New York a few weeks before he did die. Helen Vendler, reviewing it in the *New York Times Book Review*, seemed rather cross at the time that the poems left out the facts of his life that they alluded to. 'There is no denying these poems need footnoting.' Ian Hamilton calls some of the poems 'loose, chatty'. A year after that book review, Helen Vendler was arguing that '*Day by Day* tends to spoil a reader for early Lowell,' she liked it so much. Lowell certainly ended, as she said, 'as a writer of disarming openness', but he was always disarming; *Day by Day* does not want and could not stand footnoting; late Lowell does not spoil us for early Lowell. One should simply read the poem 'For John Berryman (After reading his last *Dream Song*)'. The saddest thing to be said about Robert Lowell is that he shared what John Berryman said of Gatsby, his 'extraordinary gift for hope, a romantic readiness', but he lived into a time when hope was over.

Philip Larkin

For all his lucidity, Philip Larkin's poetry is satisfyingly deep. It shimmers with ironies and tensions of feeling, his words are very carefully chosen, and he writes out of a core of privacy which it would in some way be indecent to try to penetrate. The man in his multiplicity is clearly enough revealed in his novels, his jazz criticism and his prose pieces and in the important collection of studies of him, *Larkin at Sixty*. My purpose is to stick as far as possible to his poems, and among those to his most memorable poems. There is no doubt about his greatness as a poet, it is too obvious to need to be defended. You can prove it to yourself by the simple test of ringing a few lines like metal on metal, or by observing the procedure and the movement of feeling and thought in any of fifty poems. He passes the further test that, for twenty years since the death of Eliot, he was the living poet most admired by living English poets, and among others by Robert Lowell. If a time comes when poets reject him, that will be because they will reject his century and his generation. Fashions like that are always temporary; his fame is secure. If Dr Johnson failed in the end to demolish Cowley, I do not think anyone will succeed in demolishing Philip Larkin.

There is no alternative tradition to his, unless you call David Jones a one-man alternative tradition. We shall have to discuss Larkin's dislike of the modern movement, in which I think his common sense came almost to philistinism. The modern movement in poetry was not really a movement at all, and it has not left us a tradition, only some amazing monuments. There is a sense in which English poetry in Larkin's time needed to be reinvented, and he really reinvented it, as Attlee reinvented British society. He liked to pose as a conservative curmudgeon, but it was a pose; Philip Larkin was a rather pure aesthete, and it was under his guidance that Hull University Library built up its fine manuscript collection of labour history, papers of the

National Council of Civil Liberties, the Socialist Medical Association and the Women's Co-operative Guild.[1] He was a grammar school boy brought up in the days of public school superiority, with an anguished affection for this country and a penetrating intelligence. One of the paradoxes of his poetry is how such withering common sense could be the basis of great poetry, and how such an intense vision of ordinary life could be the basis of such strongly individual criticism of life. I think the novels of Henry Green were once an influence on him. Another paradox is how such mastery, such authority in poetry, came to emerge from the ordinary promise of the poet of *The North Ship*.

His early verse really was promising, but as he said himself, the musical influence of Yeats predominated. 'In fairness to myself it must be admitted that it is a particularly potent music, pervasive as garlic, and has ruined many a better talent.' All the same there are themes, a dryness and a sad honesty that are foreign to Yeats, or at least to the early Yeats he then knew, which one can trace from *The North Ship* into the novels, and into the mature poetry. One sees them in retrospect. And even under Yeats' influence he wrote well, and somehow more purely than the Yeats who influenced him; he came late to Yeats' last poems.

> That stones would shine like gold
> Above each sodden grave,
> This, I had not foretold,
> Nor the birds' clamour, nor
> The image morning gave
> Of more and ever more,
> As some vast seven-piled wave,
> Mane-flinging, manifold,
> Streams at an endless shore.[2]

That sense of desolate and infinite freshness did not desert his poetry until the end; it can be felt in the title poem of *High Windows*. But his mature view of life was probably close to something he wrote about the novelist Barbara Pym:

I like to read about people who have done nothing spectacular, who aren't beautiful and lucky, who try to behave well in the limited field of activity they command, but who can see, in little autumnal moments of vision, that the so-called 'big' experiences of life are going to miss them; and I like to read about such things presented not with self pity or despair or romanticism, but with realistic firmness and even humour.... In all her writing I find a continual perceptive attention to detail which is a joy, and a steady background of rueful yet courageous acceptance of things.... I think 'development' is a bit of a myth; lots of writers don't develop, such as Thomas Hardy or P. G. Wodehouse, nor do we want them to.[3]

He himself did develop, but mostly in the period between *The North Ship* (1945) and that of *The Less Deceived* (1955), in the ten years between twenty-three and thirty-three. During that time he privately printed and distributed his pamphlet, *XX Poems*, in 1951, with very little response; his papers in the British Library suggest that he considered a second such pamphlet. Those ten years in which he was learning his trade as a poet and writing his two novels have not to my knowledge been thoroughly studied, but the poem written in the late 1940s that he added as a coda to *The North Ship* when that was reprinted in 1966 indicates that his style began to alter, to become tougher, purer and more flexible, very early on within the ten years.[4] The writing of his novels may have helped the process on. Beyond that one can speak only of stubborn intelligence and hard work.

The classic statement of his view of life, the distilled message he most deeply believed, and was proudest of stating so purely, was the end of 'Dockery and Son'.[5] He published that when he was forty-two.[6] The poem has to be taken whole; it is like a short story in a way, or like the best chapter in a novel. The verse technique is masterly, it goes beyond prose technique without losing the bite or the immediacy of prose. The last lines are just as memorable and cut just as deep as he intended.

> For Dockery a son, for me nothing.
> Nothing with all a son's harsh patronage.
> Life is first boredom, then fear.
> Whether or not we use it, it goes,
> And leaves what something hidden from us chose,
> And age, and then the only end of age.[7]

The only line in the poem I am not sure of understanding is 'Nothing with all a son's harsh patronage'. The only line where rhetoric perhaps outruns conviction is 'Life is first boredom, then fear.' For many people life is first fear, then boredom. For some life is neither boredom nor fear. It is possible that subliminally Larkin was remembering 'Old Man River', in which Paul Robeson is 'tired of living', and 'feared of dying'. But as a personal statement it works, and as an epigram it is unforgettable; all the closing lines of the poem are unforgettable.

The self, the first-person singular of a Larkin poem, is not always or completely identical with Philip Larkin. In 'Dockery and Son' it is, though the poem itself is lightly veiled as a fiction. In 'A Study of Reading Habits', the poem that ends 'Books are a load of crap', the speaker is not really Philip, but related to him at several points. He made it very clear in conversation that books were never to be preferred to life. His greatest strength as a poet was surely the sharpness of his observation and criticism of life. He came to feel hatred and shame for the poem about Chichester Cathedral, 'An Arundel Tomb',[8] mostly because of failing to spot that the petrified gesture that so moved him, the dead couple holding hands, was a piece of Victorian and sentimental restoration, but also because he came to think the last lines somehow untrue:

> Our almost-instinct almost true:
> What will survive of us is love.

He decided this was not even almost true, but what shamed him most was the slight scholarly inaccuracy. His honesty is rather unique among modern poets, his emotions and visions are intense, but he thinks the whole time, and with his whole intelligence. Sometimes a poem gets elaborately worked out like a rhetorical structure, the climax is often a throwaway sentence, but the poem gives it a deadly pungency. The 'I don't know' at the end of 'Mr Bleaney', the end of 'Toads Revisited', and the 'again' at the end of 'MCMXIV' are examples of this technique. He was a poet with all a writer's and some of a film-maker's skills.

Days

> What are days for?
> Days are where we live,
> They come, they wake us
> Time and time over.
> They are to be happy in:
> Where can we live but days?
>
> Ah, solving that question
> Brings the priest and the doctor
> In their long coats
> Running over the fields.[9]

This short poem is as disturbing as anything he wrote, and the more so of course because the question is unanswered. What he shared with

John Betjeman[10] was not just a love or a love-hatred of the provinces – he lived his life in Coventry, Oxford, Wellington, Leicester, Belfast and Hull – or musical clarity, or anti-modernism, or even humour; it was panic-stricken fear. He was complacent about nothing, not even about atheism. As a poet he was not obsessed by death, rather by the narrowness of life, and by every kind of serious question about life. I suppose it is roughly true that post-war continental philosophy was built on thoughts like his, while British philosophy was built to exclude them, but I do not expect this observation would have given him pleasure. The only psychologically strange thing about his thoughts and feelings, the 'emotional concept' which he said a poem is meant to perpetuate and arouse in others, is the near suppression of his childhood. You learn more about it in two pages of the introduction to *All What Jazz* than you do in the whole corpus of his poetry. In his brilliant poem 'I remember, I remember', he lets fantasy overgrow childhood, because 'Nothing, like something, happens anywhere.'[11] But he lets his feelings go in passionate regret over lost youth and historical change. he does so in a number of poems, and in prose most memorably at the end of that same introduction to *All What Jazz*, written in 1968 at the age of forty-six.

I would like to deal here with the daunting question of whether or why Philip Larkin dried up at an unnaturally early age; I think the critics who said he did were those who resented his supremacy over English poetry; they longed for ranker meat, sweeter, richer puddings, all the alcohols of Victorian religion and the romantic movement. They thought Larkin wrote austerity poetry and took a sour attitude to life. My own feeling is that his intellectual range was great, his austerity was admirable and his few mistakes occurred when he deserted it, as it may be argued that he did in the final, incantatory stanza of 'Church Going', and the last lines of 'An Arundel Tomb'. As a poet he was so nearly faultless as he was just because he wrote only when he needed to say something, and he said just that with beautiful precision. Some poets I could name are so wet they could never dry up. The last poems Philip printed, which were all reprinted in the Sunday papers the weekend after his death, are as deadly accurate and as beautiful as any he wrote. They have the same spring in them, so there was no decline, only a silence. He was never an abundant writer; nor do I see how any poet could be who wrote only the distilled truth of his experience of life. Shakespeare wrote little after the age of forty-six and so far as we know nothing after forty-nine. Larkin published *High Windows* at fifty-two, and went on writing prose into his sixties.

It may be that his drying up was a mellowing, an end of disturbance.

It was not the same as the setting hard of his taste: that happened early, in jazz as in twentieth-century poetry. He started to love jazz when he was twelve, and his jazz life flowered at Oxford, where of course he found friends. But after that he lived in lodgings, there was a break. He got back his records in 1948, but his taste stayed the same.[12] It is worth noting that in jazz as in poetry he was unenthusiastic about the revival movement which went on doing now what had once been done better. But he noticed his isolation only when he began to review jazz records in 1961, at the age of thirty-nine. He also noticed at once that it was then too late in the day to protest against the modernist movement in jazz, though in the end of course he did so, in *All What Jazz*. In poetry the case is a little different. I am old enough to remember the sensation in the 1940s and 1950s that any young poet must escape from the overwhelming shadow of Eliot, from all his unlearnable lessons and oracular axioms, or else perish. In the special group culture of Philip Larkin and his friends at Oxford, an element of mockery, of refusal to be duped or put off, was certainly one ingredient. The Professor of Poetry was Adam Fox, a harmless old clergyman who wrote an epic poem about Old King Cole in Spenserian stanzas. The essay by Kingsley Amis in *Larkin at Sixty* and the almost affected ignorance of country churches in Larkin's 'Church Going', suggest that the mockery almost amounted to a raw refusal to be educated.

Poets live how they can, how they must, in order to survive as poets. I have nothing against Larkin's generation in this matter.[13] It is just that his sobriety of public manner covers a robust individuality, an impertinence if you like, as spirited as Skelton's. Where there is jazz there is life. But the works of Pound, let alone Eliot, are not a pot of ink flung in the face of the public.[14] Outbreaks of ink-flinging, and paint-flinging as well, have increased lately, but the rule is still the same; Eddie Condon, quoted by Larkin, stated it for jazz, and it applies to poetry. 'As it enters the ear, does it come in like broken glass or does it come in like honey?' What Larkin disapproved of in Charlie Parker, in Henry Moore, in Picasso and in Ezra Pound, was 'the irresponsible exploitation of technique in contradiction to human life as we know it. . . . Modernism helps us neither to enjoy nor endure.' I can only reply that Moore, Picasso, Pound and above all Eliot have helped and do help me to enjoy, and if I must to endure. So does Philip Larkin, as much as any writer in this century. His poetry is not a sad path leading backward towards Hardy, it is not a gloomy stroll in a provincial town. He deals with love, death, time, art, modern life, modern history and the soul, the individual. He is as fresh as paint, his poetry is as fresh as paint, his poetry is as fresh and intense as Andrew Marvell's, of whom he wrote, 'What still compels attention to Marvell's work is the ease with which he manages the fundamental paradox of verse – the conflict of natural word usage with metre and rhyme – and marries it either to hallucinatory images within his own unique conventions or to sudden sincerities that are as convincing in our age as in his.'[15]

> A thrush sings,
> Laurel-surrounded
> In the deep bare garden,
> Its fresh-peeled voice
> Astonishing the brickwork....[16]

Those lines are from 'Coming', one of a number of poems expressing a joy and generosity with which Philip Larkin is not often credited. The joy is entangled in metaphysics of a kind, as it would be in Marvell, and there are jokes. For instance, the girl in the photograph album:

> In pigtails, clutching a reluctant cat;
> Or furred yourself, a sweet girl-graduate;
> Or lifting a heavy-headed rose
> Beneath a trellis, or in a trilby hat
>
> (Faintly disturbing, that, in several ways)....

The images really are as vivid as hallucinations, and they are hard to forget. That is because of the extreme precision of certain suggestive words, and the perfect matching of rhythms, with never a word wasted. Fresh-peeled. Heavy-headed. Larkin really is like the most brilliant photography, he is the Cartier-Bresson of poetry. He makes John Ashbery look like a helicopter spraying a prairie of thistles from the air. It is an essential to Larkin that he never uses too many words, and vagueness never pleases him. Whatever is suggestive in his poems, whether it is a vernacular aphorism or just an epithet, 'age, and then the only end of age', or 'fresh-peeled' or 'heavy-headed', is at the same time precise. That precision is what locks the image or the poem in place, as the brambles hold the mist of leaf in place.

> Green-shadowed people sit, or walk in rings,
> Their children finger the awakened grass,

Calmly a cloud stands, calmly a bird sings,
And, flashing like a dangled looking-glass,
Sun lights the balls that bounce, the dogs that bark,
The branch-arrested mist of leaf, and me,
Threading my pursed-up way across the park,
An indigestible sterility.

Spring, of all seasons most gratuitous,
Is fold of untaught flower, is race of water,
Is earth's most multiple, excited daughter;

And those she has least use for see her best,
Their paths grown craven and circuitous,
Their visions mountain-clear, their needs immodest.[17]

I find his sadness and honesty convincing though I do not take it to be an exact self-portrait, just a subject for which he had a particular feeling. 'Deprivation is for me', he said, 'what daffodils were for Wordsworth.' But what enthralled me about his poems, long before I was mature enough to test them against experience of life, was their movement, their courteous, unassertive progression like a formal piece of music, even through a long poem: the technique of the photograph album and, I remember, wooing the reader towards the unexpected blunt saying at the end, as the calm sea might woo a ship on to the rocks. Auden woos one sometimes on to a sandbank, and leaves the sea to do its worst; Yeats woos one on to the cardboard rocks of a baroque theatre, but Larkin wafts the reader on to a really rocky shore.

Horny dilemmas at the gate once more,
Come and choose wrong, they cry, *come and choose wrong*....[18]

As Larkin's poetry went on, the message of his aphorisms became more drastic, less aggressive, flatter, the truth and not a menace, something shared, something we must all admit. How much of that is distilled wisdom, and how much is personal feeling distant from ourselves, only the experience of life can teach us. The process is all the more difficult because poetry is part of the experience of life, it is a descant against life. I note only that some of Larkin's late poetry has a sadness and a stillness, a sunset quality of pure beauty and simple vision: it is not a different kind of wisdom or a new mood. The end of 'The Explosion', the last poem in *High Windows*, is a vision that exists for its own sake, but so in a way are the photographs in the album with our sudden distance from them, and so is the end of 'At Grass', the poem about old race-horses on the last page of *The Less Deceived*.

> Dusk brims the shadows.
> Summer by summer all stole away,
> The starting-gates, the crowds and cries –
> All but the unmolesting meadows.
> Almanacked, their names live; they
>
> Have slipped their names, and stand at ease,
> Or gallop for what must be joy,
> And not a fieldglass sees them home,
> Or curious stop-watch prophesies:
> Only the groom, and the groom's boy,
> With bridles in the evening come.

There are certain simple devices of older poetry that he never gives up using, in spite of his vernacular clarity and beautifully free breathing. He still uses rhyme for instance, and rhyme and punctuation, which of course includes syntax, are his principal devices to retard or accelerate rhythm. He has no mission to avoid even the most obvious rhymes and half-rhymes, shadows and meadows, boy and joy, but he knows the exact weight of every syllable he uses. He has Housman's sense of syllables, but he uses it for much more complex effects, because he has so much more to say. He uses puns, consciously or half-consciously, 'they have slipped their names' carries a half-suggestion about manes. Elsewhere we have 'a crowd of craps' instead of chaps, and 'stares' where you might expect 'stars'. He likes alliteration, 'the unmolesting meadows' and 'the shit in the shuttered château'. He is prepared to accept the inversion of natural word order, but only very deliberately, for particular purposes. 'A serious house on serious earth it is . . .'

> Only the groom, and the groom's boy,
> With bridles in the evening come.

All these are Georgian devices but Larkin is certainly not a Georgian poet. The difference is an urgency, a control of rhythm and a sense of reality. The bell-chimes of their poems stun you to sleep. Larkin stuns you awake. They are verbally soft at the edges, they are imprecise, and the forms and rhymes of their poems lead them by the nose. Larkin's diction is solidly weighted, he is to them as Tolstoy is to Kipling, he can lead the form of his poem by the nose, lead the noise by the nose, whenever he chooses. Georgian poems smell of weekends in the country, but Larkin's countryside in the first poem of *Whitsun Weddings*, 'Here', and in the railway landscape of the title poem of that book, is real and without falsity, like the sky.

> Fast-shadowed wheat-fields, running high as hedges,
> Isolated villages, where removed lives
>
> Loneliness clarifies. Here silence stands
> Like heat. Here leaves unnoticed thicken,
> Hidden weeds flower, neglected waters quicken,
> Luminously-peopled air ascends;
> And past the poppies bluish neutral distance
> Ends the land suddenly beyond a beach
> Of shapes and shingle. Here is unfenced existence:
> Facing the sun, untalkative, out of reach.

'Mr Bleaney', who follows this poem, is even further beyond the reach of Georgianism, I suppose. People in Larkin poems give deadly exact meaning to places, where in the poetry of Edward Thomas they give only a resonance to the woods of Surrey or Hampshire. Most of Larkin's landscapes are allegorized, that is why they are so alive. He has not had to stop thinking in order to let himself feel. His ideal poem, since I believe every poet has an ideal unwritten poem which never can be written, which alters throughout his life and leads him on, or if not his ideal poem then his ideal of art, is expressed in terms of jazz, in his poem 'For Sidney Bechet'.[19]

> On me your voice falls as they say love should,
> Like an enormous yes. My Crescent City
> Is where your speech alone is understood,
>
> And greeted as the natural noise of good,
> Scattering long-haired grief and scored pity.

There are two double meanings in the last line, whether intended or not. He may mean wild-haired grief, and the lined face of pity, but he might almost mean long-haired critics and written music that has to be played from a score. There is an immediacy about his poetry, and a complex, apparent informality, that may well be taken over from the ideal of jazz as jazz used to be when he was young. But it was not just his own youth that he regretted. It was a world, and one that ended before he was born. In his later poetry he regrets our world too,[20] but his generation like mine learnt in childhood that the greatest disaster and in a way the end of the world happened in 1914.[21] Never such innocence again.

In some ways, Philip Larkin's poetry records a view of life or a dialogue with life (like Job's dialogue with God only more humorous) with peculiar fullness. But there seems to be no doubt that for him the honesty belongs to the calling of a poet; poetry is not, as autobiography might be, a surgical instrument for achieving self-knowledge, or for breaking oneself up. A poem is a thing made, a thing perfectly constructed, an arrest of time, just as a piece of music or a jazz performance might be. I think the mythical loneliness of his life, which readers read into the poems, is only the artist's loneliness, not probably a fact of his biography. The truth is that few contemporary poets, if any, have so entered into the world, or so loved it, as Philip Larkin. But he gave his view of a poet's calling quite early, in 'Reasons for Attendance', connecting it with a view of youthful sex which ought to be taken into account by the way, in interpreting 'Sexual Liberty came about in 1963'. Since these two strands are interwined we ought to consider the complete poem.[22]

Reasons for Attendance

The trumpet's voice, loud and authoritative,
Draws me a moment to the lighted glass
To watch dancers – all under twenty-five –
Shifting intently, face to flushed face,
Solemnly on the beat of happiness.

– Or so I fancy, sensing the smoke and sweat,
The wonderful feel of girls. Why be out here?
But then, why be in there? Sex, yes, but what
Is sex? Surely, to think the lion's share
Of happiness is found by couples – sheer

Inaccuracy, as far as I'm concerned.
What calls me is that lifted, rough-tongued bell
(Art, if you like) whose individual sound
Insists I too am individual.
It speaks; I hear; others may hear as well,

But not for me, nor I for them; and so
With happiness. Therefore I stay outside,
Believing this; and they maul to and fro,

> Believing that; and both are satisfied,
> If no one has misjudged himself. Or lied.

This is comparatively early Larkin, it has the sharp edge and the metaphysical bony structure typical of *The Less Deceived*. In that volume he so controlled and reinvented his poetry that he seems almost to have reinvented a personality. The later poetry is often much more dashing in its movement, and swifter in its effects. But before considering this poem it was necessary to lay down some of Philip Larkin's particular themes and the novelist's persona through which he often treated them.

> What calls me is that lifted, rough-tongued bell
> (Art, if you like) whose individual sound
> Insists I too am individual.

That lies at the root of all his poetry and perhaps of all poetry. The other day I quoted it on a television discussion programme, and Melvyn Bragg answered that art insisted to him he was one of many. No doubt both are true, but of art as a calling, art as a constant preoccupation, what Philip Larkin says is truer and goes deeper, I think. As a reader one is alone with the poem. As a poet, Philip Larkin is particularly alone with his subject, even when that subject is universal. The sadness of his poetry is the same aesthetic sadness to be felt in the paintings of Watteau; it is because the sun will go down, it is the passage of time. Some of his poems are so quiet you can hear it, in others he builds it into the practical, everyday world and the limitedness of the detail of human life, but you can still hear it.

> I listen to money singing. It's like looking down
>   From long french windows at a provincial town,
> The slums, the canal, the churches ornate and mad
>   In the evening sun. It is intensely sad.[23]

The poem that follows this is the shortest and most insubstantial of all his lyrics. It says almost nothing except by implication what every work of pure aestheticism must say.

> Cut grass lies frail:
> Brief is the breath
> Mown stalks exhale.
> Long, long the death
>
> It dies in the white hours
> Of young-leafed June

With chestnut flowers,
With hedges snowlike strewn,

White lilac bowed,
Lost lanes of Queen Anne's lace,
And that high-builded cloud
Moving at summer's pace.

At first sight this is almost a defiantly minor poem, but it is not Georgian. No emotion has been inflated, indeed they have scarcely been summoned. The language has not been made to tintinnabulate with lyricism, nothing has been forced. We are simply made conscious of a season, but since the observations are so accurate, the poem is curiously original, as if there had never been quite this June, never quite this poem. This poem taken on its own would hardly substantiate Philip Larkin's greatness, but it would his mastery and authenticity as a poet. It would put him on a level with Ivor Gurney, though the details he deploys might suggest he was more modern, and the limitations of this little poem are obviously self-chosen. He wrote a number of poems about spring, far more powerful than this, some of a visionary intensity and meaning: 'The Trees', for instance, whose 'greenness is a kind of grief'.

Yet still the unresting castles thresh
In fullgrown thickness every May.
Last year is dead, they seem to say,
Begin afresh, afresh, afresh.

The wind is like the 'Wedding-wind' in *The Less Deceived*. But the trees, like unresting castles as year by year they age, express a rather pure sorrow that belongs to a later time of life, a sorrow at leaving the sun. The image is hard to forget, and the words attach themselves to the reality whenever one sees it. It is very rare for a poet to achieve this, though Tennyson did it frequently in *In Memoriam*: 'the trees Layed their dark arms around the field', and 'Only through the chestnut leaf The chestnut pattering to the ground', for example. Eliot achieved it here and there in the *Four Quartets*. I had thought it impossible nowadays for any poet so to impose himself on nature, to make his words so right, so economic and so unforgettable, that whenever you see some simple, natural thing you think of that one poem. Philip Larkin has done this more than once, not always about nature, but always in images of great intensity. One occasion is the ending of the title poem, 'High Windows'.

And immediately

Rather than words comes the thought of high windows:
The sun-comprehending glass,
And beyond it, the deep blue air, that shows
Nothing, and is nowhere, and is endless.[24]

Sometimes Philip Larkin gives such hallucinations of reality in his poems, such intensity of vision if you like, that he seems the only possible kind of poet. But in fact he has few followers who can be taken seriously. They lack his faultless rhythms, his vernacular strength of speech, and his visionary quality. They lack the turnings and processes of his poems. They lack his intelligence, as we all do. What he opened up for later generations was a few principles, which he stated quite clearly, and his courage to get rid of clutter and to carve life open to the bone. Beyond that he left only the inspiring, invigorating example of his own complex poems. They are as simple as jazz and as complex; they teach us to take pleasure, and to endure. He is fortunately almost impossible to imitate, though he may well from an early age have educated his own contemporaries among poets, according to their capabilities. Even where he chooses to drop his own persona and to write sheer fiction in verse, as he does in 'Livings', he carries it off with arrogant brilliance.[25] His persona may be missing but his personality is not.

Poem one is an agricultural merchant, 'I deal with farmers, things like dips and feed.' He operates in provincial towns and stays at the unreformed provincial hotels of 1929; there is no *Good Food Guide*, and he is just a middling kind of businessman, not very high up the social ladder, though higher than Mr Bleaney. In all these poems we hear of preoccupations, jobs and ambitions, but they all end in mystery and in the night. Philip Larkin knows his characters better, resents them less, gets more inside their worlds, than John Betjeman does with the businessmen he so hates. The first character talks in the bar about:

Who makes ends meet, who's taking the knock,
Government tariffs, wages, price of stock.
Smoke hangs under the light. The pictures on
The walls are comic – hunting, the trenches, stuff
Nobody minds or notices. . . .

The character does rather hate and despise this world all the same. It is not a good sign for the persona of any Larkin poem if he feels shallowly about essential England, or about the First World War. This man's last words make him ridiculous, and perhaps abominable. 'It's time for change, in nineteen twenty-nine.'

The second poem is more mysterious altogether. It is the monologue of someone who lives near the sea, by a great port, perhaps on a cliff above it. 'Seventy feet down The sea explodes upwards, Relapsing, to slaver Off landing-stage steps – Running suds, rejoice!' He or she likes the tenacity of mussels and limpets that the sea fails to move. They watch the sky by day building up grape-dark over the sea, and hear of bad weather on the radio,

> Fires in humped inns
> Kippering sea-pictures –
>
> Keep it all off!

At night it snows, and a slight obscurity disturbs this verse:

> By night, snow swerves
> (O loose moth world)
> Through the stare travelling
> Leather-black waters.

Either 'stare' is a word Yeats used for a bird, as I think Craig Raine as a publisher believes, or the snow travels through the eyesight of someone staring at night, as John Wain suggested the other day,[26] or else, as I once conjectured, 'stare' is a misprint for 'star',[27] but by improving the weather so that stars are visible my conjecture decreases the power of this stanza, so John Wain's interpretation is at least more convincing than that. Leave the solution in suspense for a moment. In the final stanza:

> Guarded by brilliance
> I set plate and spoon,
> And after, divining-cards.
> Lit shelved liners
> Grope like mad worlds westward.

This poem is very strong on fear of the sea, but not strong on answering questions like who and why.[28] Is it about a lighthouse keeper, and are we supposed to know that from the first line, 'Seventy feet down'? Can it be about someone who makes a living by divining with cards, and therefore only at night?[29] Some half-mad old woman? Is it set on the Irish coast, which the poet certainly visited? Is the fourth stanza of 'Church Going' any help?

Or, after dark, will dubious women come
To make their children touch a particular stone;
Pick simples for a cancer; or on some
Advised night see walking a dead one? . . .

Plate and spoon suggest southern or western Ireland, I think, as well as the liners groping westward, and the divining-cards, and the almost surreal terror of the sea and snow. But if I am right about Ireland, then 'stare' is simply the Irish word for a kind of bird that Yeats used. The cricket-like noise of the wireless – 'Radio rubs its legs, Telling me of elsewhere' – may refer to Morse code, which favours a lighthouse keeper. At any rate, the mysteriousness of this entire poem belongs to its character and its passionate fear. As a poem on its own it would be very unusual for Larkin. As a contrast with the other two poems of 'Livings', I find it thrilling and chilling. Philip Larkin once said in a television interview that the main reason he felt suited to Hull was that he liked being 'on the edge of things'.[30] The second poem of 'Livings' is even more on the edge of things.

The first and third poems of 'Livings' are social. The farmers' merchant is a lonely man, he dines alone, and at night he lies alone worrying, but after dinner he drinks whiskey with the local characters in the Smoking Room, then he hears dominoes in the bar, so he goes to the bar and stands a round. The second poem begins in frightening isolation, and somehow the last stanza makes it worse. 'Lit shelved liners Grope like mad worlds westward.' The watcher on the cliff or in the lighthouse is freezing with loneliness. In the first poem 'a big sky Drains down the estuary like the bed Of a gold river'. In the second the weather gets worse, grape-dark by day and snowing by night. The third poem is dinner in a Cambridge college, but it dissolves into the world outside, cold fields, silent cobbled streets, a cat, a bell chiming, a student shivering, a college room.

Above, Chaldean constellations
Sparkle over crowded roofs.

No novelist and no historian has ever conveyed the life of a college in the seventeenth or early eighteenth century so powerfully or so well. Philip Larkin does it through the conversation after dinner. It touches on livings, and therefore on essential England. Advowsons are important, because these men can only afford to marry and leave the college when their turn comes for a college living as a parson. (Advowson is the right to present a clergyman to a parish in the

Church of England, and these fellows of an eighteenth-century college are all clergymen.) They are not very pious, but the poet relishes them. In fact he once said to me he had thought of a country vicar's life quite seriously; it seemed to him an almost ideal solution for a poet. It would I suppose be a way of being 'on the edge of things', and it would satisfy the passionate identification I think he felt with English provincial life. Perhaps without that passion one could scarcely be an English poet of any importance. I think that these apparently fictional poems, all of them about other lives, and one of them set in another century, express something that lay deep in him. The title poem of *The Whitsun Weddings*, and 'Show Saturday' in *High Windows*, express the same. You could call it love of life. It includes a very vivid sense of the sap of life in what might seem a narrow world, and an amazing power to convey that life. No poet in our times has thought so deeply about other people's lives, or about how they make their livings.[31] His fit of horror about Mr Bleaney, and his sudden astonishment at the thought of Dockery, are only part of this aspect of Philip Larkin.

So we find him among seventeenth- or eighteenth-century college fellows. The end of this poem is as lonely as the other two. The night is as mysterious as that in the second poem; the effect of loneliness is cumulative. The wood from Snape and the position of sizar, a student working his way through college on a scholarship, place the poem in Cambridge.[32] Why did he choose Cambridge? I suppose because it was a cold, unfamiliar, deeply provincial place. The conversation recalls John Aubrey but port circulates; the date is uncertain and the scene is more or less ageless. As a parody of senior common room conversation it comes very close to reality. Only regicide is now an unlikely subject, and in some colleges *pudendum mulieris*. The poem itself is another monologue, but nothing is said particular to the first person. He just records an evening. The scene dissolves as it might do in a film. As he crosses the quadrangle (or should I speak of a combination room and a college court?) he is conscious at once of the cold air of the fens, and the silence of the streets. One lonely sizar shivers over his books.

The first person of the poem goes to his own dull room. The stars glitter. Why Chaldean? Cold, strange and distant, like Cambridge, with some added hint of seventeenth-century astrology, obscure prophecy, the apocryphal Book of Daniel. Remember the divining-cards, and 'time for change in nineteen twenty-nine'. In each of these poems we enter a small, vivid world unconscious of its future. Nineteen twenty-nine surely recalls 1939. The war was just far

enough off to cast no shadow. The world of the third poem survived in
its essentials into the second half of the nineteenth century. The older
members of the University today remember old men in their own
youth who might almost be called survivors of it: Canon Jenkins, for
example. In a way I am sorry this poem is not about Oxford, but in a
way of course it is. Of the poets Oxford has bred or nourished in the
last hundred years, none is closer to us than Philip Larkin. From our
point of view he nearly never sounds a false note. Auden revisited us
in later life like a favourite great-aunt with foreign laurels and exotic
decorations on his hat. Matthew Arnold operated in Oxford like an
aesthetic missionary. But Philip Larkin slipped in and out as he chose,
as if he had never left. We understand his jokes and most of us feel
very strongly for his feelings about life. I suppose we are proud of
nearly every word he ever wrote, which is more than we can quite say
of the others. In the third poem of 'Livings', he scores a bullseye. No
words are wasted, no tone is wrong, but the college is suddenly
distant, lonely, terrible. He begins smoothly and warmly, like C. P.
Snow only better; the second stanza increases pace and adds to the
jokes, but the third is splendid.

Tonight we dine without the Master
(Nocturnal vapours do not please);
The port goes round so much the faster,
Topics are raised with no less ease —
Which advowson looks the fairest,
What the wood from Snape will fetch,
Names for *pudendum mulieris*,
Why is Judas like Jack Ketch?

The candleflames grow thin, then broaden:
Our butler Starveling piles the logs
And sets behind the screen a jordan
(Quicker than going to the bogs).
The wine heats temper and complexion:
Oath-enforced assertions fly
On rheumy fevers, resurrection,
Regicide and rabbit pie.

The fields around are cold and muddy,
The cobbled streets close by are still,
A sizar shivers at his study,
The kitchen cat has made a kill;

> The bells discuss the hour's gradations,
> Dusty shelves hold prayers and proofs:
> Above, Chaldean constellations
> Sparkle over crowded roofs.

The critic Eric Homberger wrote of Philip Larkin as 'representative of the modern English condition: a poetry of lowered sights and diminished expectations'. I think the opposite is the truth: he by no means represented the condition of England, though he spoke passionately about that, but often without resignation. His poetry set its sights on a wide range of subject matter, and on the technical mastery of Yeats, which I suggest that he achieved. He thereby and in other ways raised the expectations we have of a poem or a poet very high, painfully so for the rest of us. He increased the number of things one can do inside a poem. His jokes, his snarls and growls and his suave parodies are by no means all of the same kind. He recaptured ground from the novel; he wrote with Crabbe's realism and Clare's purity. He warbled native woodnotes wild. If his poetry was as John Bayley said of it, inwardly 'like a Vermeer interior, both wholly accessible and completely mysterious',[33] that is because great poetry, perfectly successful poetry, always is mysterious. It is so simple that one can scarcely believe it. As for the 'poetry of lowered sights and diminished expectations', I am old enough to remember the same being said of Eliot.

The critical tools that are being used at the moment to analyse Philip Larkin's works seem to me the wrong ones. Technically, they need to be much more subtle. The words we use for analysing poetry are so often the wrong ones. A technical description of his work ought to show how utterly unlike anyone else's it is. A historical description of it ought to be very much fuller than anything we have been offered. It is no use discussing his opinions, for example, without a close watch on the comings and goings of persona and personality in his poems. And we must attune ourselves to his ear, which is better than ours. It has at least been realized[34] that Larkin's aborted career as a novelist – he began a third novel as soon as he finished the second, but never finished the third – had a crucial influence on his poetry. John Bayley has noticed the unique tranquillity of his changes of key, and the innocent absence of knowingness in his writing. But it will take critics a long time to catch up with Philip Larkin. His poems must be measured, like all the best poems and with whatever awkwardness, against one's own experience of life. By that test they ring sound. 'The brevity of his poems, as of Hardy's,' (John Bayley again), 'is an aspect of their robust variety.' But he found his theme, the theme that belongs to him alone, and his unique tones. He will always be remembered for that theme and those tones.

I have the uneasy feeling that Philip Larkin would prefer to be more closely scrutinized by what he called 'the normal standards of criticism', though I am never quite certain what those are. In the opening salvo of his attack on Charley Parker in 1965 he points to the popular view that every one of Parker's performances was perfectly and equally brilliant, producing records 'to which we can only go down on our knees'. It would be useful, says Larkin, 'to know whether Parker got better, or changed, and, if so, in what direction'. I think Larkin's poetry did change, and did get better. The shorter poems increased in speed and intensity. The vernacular became more vernacular, the rhythms of the sardonic, lighter-looking pieces became faster and smoother. At the same time in *High Windows* Larkin wrote more expansively, he showed more private emotion, and even his grief where it showed was less constricted. In poems like 'Show Saturday' and 'The Explosion', he dwelt more lovingly on details than he usually had done in the past. *The Less Deceived* is masterly and classical, with a tendency to severity. Its few moments of liberated emotion are more 'poetical' than they would be in later poems. *The Whitsun Weddings* has a handful of his finest poems: it is deeply stamped with humanism and with sadness. But in *High Windows*, anger, irony, affection and every other emotion are unleashed. His technique makes everything memorable. A high concentration of his greatest poems is in this book. The precision of his descriptions and his rhythms reaches an absolute.

> Down stucco sidestreets,
> Where light is pewter
> And afternoon mist
> Brings lights on in shops
> Above race-guides and rosaries,
> A funeral passes.[35]

The three poems he printed after *High Windows*, written in the next few years, are meditations on old themes. 'Aubade' is a full, thorough statement of a philosophy of life and the fear of death. 'I work all day and get half-drunk at night.' He considers death extremely plainly, and the persona of the poem is certainly his own. Earlier in life he might have used some masking figure such as Mr Bleaney. The second of these three poems is called 'The Life with a Hole in It'. It is about his wishes in life and how one never gets one's wishes and what it is that determines what one does get. He describes the rich, successful

novelist he would have wished to be and the poor schoolmaster he
feared to be in memorable terms.

> So the shit in the shuttered château
> Who does his five hundred words
> Then parts out the rest of the day
> Between bathing and booze and birds
> Is far off as ever, but so
> Is that spectacled schoolteaching sod
> (Six kids, and the wife in pod,
> And her parents coming to stay). . . .

In the end we are destined, as he said in 'Dockery and Son', to 'what
something hidden from us chose'. Understanding at last what that
mechanism has been in one's own life is little consolation to a dying
man. That is the subject of 'Continuing to Live'. It is about a man who
comes to know his limits.

> Anything else must not, for you, be thought
> To exist.

> And what's the profit? Only that, in time,
> We half-identify the blind impress
> All our behavings bear, may trace it home.
> But to confess,

> On that green evening when our death begins,
> Just what it was, is hardly satisfying,
> Since it applied only to one man once,
> And that one dying.

The mystery ingredient of 'Continuing to Live' is its skilful transition of tones. Larkin is an empiricist: he knows Freud, he questions
traditional values. Some kind of logical positivism was the dominant
philosophy of his youth; his poetry must have survived a severe drench
of criticism, and indeed self-criticism. But he speaks as directly and
musically as some marvellous jazz solo, once heard and never forgotten. Consider the extraordinary effect of the simple word 'green'
in the last stanza. His final tone depends on that one word, and on
a rhythm that comes to rest in the last line. One of Philip Larkin's
most neglected qualities, which runs through phrase after phrase,
phrasing after musical phrasing of his poems, is their unusual beauty,
either with or without the *vox humana* of this sad stanza.

Goodbye to the Art of Poetry

Robert Graves said there can be no long poem
and that Virgil and Milton who wrote them
were tying short poems together with string.
How long after all does any bird sing?
The machine of a poem is not natural:
the mysterious bird-call, the apple's fall
reach out from earth and the sun towards death,
a perfect poem is a dying breath:
and yet it lives as long as music can,
say three days of the chanting of a blind man,
holding within it an image of time:
the god sleeps and the bell may never chime.
Leningrad, its heart of snow and railways,
one star of violet trembling in that haze,
spreads from one stanza into many days.
Pax Britannica, wild roses, coal:
Milton ebbing and thundering in the soul,
poems longer than a wax light can burn,
poems it takes a human life to learn.
Yet it remains true the genuine sign
of greatness in a poem is one line.
   What poetry and what greatness may be
bothers all professors of poetry:
there is something ridiculous I confess
in sharp-eyed connoisseurship of greatness:
better to seek for what is genuine:
a world spacious enough to wander in,
the truth live in the ear as truth of tone,
a line that rings like stone ringing on stone
or a line like the sea heard in a shell,

never again so clearly or so well
as it was in the beginning, in childhood,
when poetry was the untrodden wood:
Seasons return, but not to me returns
Day, or the sweet approach of Ev'n or Morn,
Or sight of vernal bloom, or Summers Rose,
Or flocks, or herds, or human face divine . . .[1]
Milton, poet of the spirit's expense,
youthful intellect and sharpness of sense,
truth to age, truth to experience,
in whom all learning, rhetoric and belief
have been drowned out in the knowledge of life,
sea-pebbles, sea-coarsened and sea-refined,
long rhythms of a man lonely and blind
whose paradise might not be lingered in:
he felt death in his eyes, dawn on his skin,
cold, wild poetry like the Atlantic,
archangelic construction of music:
intellectual myth, necromancy:
this is greatness and truth in poetry.
Milton's age was like Raleigh's in the Tower,
a man defeated, high on love of power.
In the dark seed of poetry is pride:
remember Mayakovsky's suicide,
then call to mind the dark God of Milton
and the bread that his blindness was fed on:
the long and sweet procedures of his breath,
The rigid satisfaction, death for death.[2]
So godlike and so dark in poetry,
he lies beyond what we can choose to be,
poets cannot choose their own tragedy.
    Yet what the poet is, chooses to be,
is the momentum of all poetry,
the momentum of life, the dying breath,
in which life is the transcendence of death,
an unearthly and unnatural bread
and earthly resurrection of the dead.
τοῖς μὲν γὰρ παιδαρίοισιν
ἐστὶ διδάσκαλος ὅστις Φράζει,
τοῖσιν δ' ἡβῶσι ποιηταί.[3]
It is schoolmasters who discourse to boys,

but it is poets mature time employs.
A poet is not all that he will be:
his way of changing is his poetry:
his virtues are in nature, and by them
nature's resurrection is his poem.
   Or that is what the old poets believed;
the poem and the self that they conceived
begins with the *Symposium* of Plato:
eros is still the most that poets know.
The realist groan and the secular hymn
are lost from *eros*, and still seeking him.
The river-mists of verse that cling and soak,
the last wild honey dripping down the oak,
the boughs of fresh leaf on the dying tree,
bird tunes of Tennysonian poetry
haunting us, lost in us, as we are lost,
wither in frost. Poetry is that frost.
Because we have said what we had to say
and our beliefs yellow and fall away.
The faith of poets is the last bird-call,
uncouth, neglected, individual.
It is rooted much deeper than the mind
in the language of birds and of mankind
falling like light in the most silent wood.
It is what Mayakovsky understood.
I know the strength of words, I know the beat of words
never applauded from the theatre boxes
but they break coffins loose, they walk away
on their four wooden legs. They let you rot,
they will not print you or publish you,
you lighten girth, gallop, and your hooves ring
down centuries, and iron expresses
creep up to kiss your calloused hands,
poetry. I know the strength of words.
They look like nothing, like a flower dropped
and shattered under the tread of a dancer.
But a man in his soul, in his lips, in his bones . . .[4]
   Thinking of my title I am not sure
whether you came expecting a lecture
rather than all these impassioned sayings,
bits of old poems and workshop chippings,

or whether linking the title with Horace
(whose *Ars Poetica* Fraenkel could not face,
it is an intellectual disgrace)
you expected poetry cold in the
aspic of neo-classic theory.
The English poem is a sun that sets.
Observation of poems and poets
reveals death in them and death of belief,
and resurrection in them, the fresh leaf,
that sprouts living out of the dead poem:
poems consume life as the rose his stem.
Philip Larkin's poetry made such sense
that you could rest in complete confidence
whatever he said would be genuine:
and as lively as jazz, as clean as gin.
There are no mysteries, only our lives,
and death, and something in us that deprives
the self of the old self it was wound in:
this is a poem balanced on a pin,
a dazzle of Marvellian mysteries,
a nettle against spring, as our life is.
The trees are coming into leaf
Like something almost being said;
The recent buds relax and spread,
Their greenness is a kind of grief.

Is it that they are born again
And we grow old? No, they die too.
Their yearly trick of looking new
Is written down in rings of grain.

Yet still the unresting castles thresh
In fullgrown thickness every May.
Last year is dead, they seem to say,
Begin afresh, afresh, afresh.[5]
   The msyteries of life were in language
when reason shone supreme in its own age,
when faith withered and was disquieted
and only faith in reason was not dead,
in the deep woods there was no smell of smoke,
honey of wild bees dripped in the green oak.
It was in Dryden Hopkins found his wish

for 'naked thew and sinew of English',
and 'my style tends always towards him.'
It is still proper to wander through those dim
mysterious woodlands and clear parklands:
the sea whispers and glitters on those sands.
Since Dryden's age we find less breathing-space,
the lovers are all untrue, and our chase
has nothing now in view. The gods return
to see the crop shaved and the stubble burn
where salt crackled and nightingales complained,
and their lawns were sheep-whitened and moon-stained.
Dryden is most lucid, most reasoning,
most embittered, hungry and life-giving,
each poem is a long philosophy,
a place to walk about, to muse, to be.
From Land a gentle Breeze arose by Night,
Serenely shone the stars, the Moon was bright,
And the Sea trembled with her Silver Light.
... Now when the rosie Morn began to rise,
And wav'd her Saffron Streamer thro' the Skies;
When Thetis blush'd in Purple, not her own,
And from her Face the breathing Winds were blown:
A sudden Silence sate upon the Sea,
And sweeping Oars, with Struggling, urge their Way.
The Trojan, from the Main beheld a Wood,
Which thick with Shades, and a brown Horror, stood:
Betwixt the Trees the Tyber took his Course,
With Whirlpools dimpl'd; and with downward Force
That drove the Sand along, he took his Way,
And rowl'd his yellow Billows to the Sea.
About him, and above, and round the Wood,
The Birds that haunt the Borders of his Flood:
That bath'd within, or bask'd upon his side,
To tuneful Songs their narrow Throats apply'd.
The Captain gives Command, the joyful Train
Glide thro' the gloomy Shade, and leave the Main.[6]
   How long and slow the movement of it is,
quicker of course than William Morris
and magical without romantic cheat:
with trumpet descant and a thin drum-beat.
How far it is from Homer's poetry,

the banks of flowers and the nodding tree,
personal death, impersonal poetry,
and far from the cold passions of Virgil,
the indignant soul that rushes and is still;
the hero dies and we are left alone,
the dream of Rome is as cold as a stone.
　　It was sex that revived the classic age,
sexual passion and ironic rage;
sexual intimacy and sexual dance
are the innocent part of the Renaissance,
which by the way never occurred in Wales,
barely touches the *Canterbury Tales*,
but in English is first heard of in Gower
and in Chaucer's *Troilus* comes to its power.
The early books are tense but in book three
love's powerful, pliable intimacy
creates entangled rhythms, fresh language,
a beacon-light to Wyatt and his age:
surf and waves that the sea combs and refines
as Shakespeare in his sonnets combs his lines.
Book by book, Chaucer's *Troilus* changes gear
(the epilogue is an ice-age I fear),
but this is our first recorded affair,
briar roses but with snow in the air,
in verse perfect, in construction unfree,
the first serious English love story:
small wonder poetry arose from it,
and variations of verse and sense and wit,
because our life was still the Atlantic,
intimate passion was still dramatic,
poetry was more than chamber music.
　　But poetry seeks out its own extremes,
those drowsy poems that proceed like dreams,
or Marlowe's hollow thunders and fresh rain,
or dying woods and Agamemnon's pain:
or Shakespeare flashing fires in a half-line,
the creamy vein, the yellow celandine.
A poem of one line expires in one,
having done more than most poems have done:
been pungent, modest, memorable, singing,
one with the earth and air, self-echoing,

it is the gravestone set at its own head
to mark the resurrection of the dead.
Though thou the wolf hoar had to priest
though thou him to school set, psalms to learn,
ever be his gears to the grove green.[7]
There are true poems, short, real lines like these
hidden in all natural languages:
poetry in its first natural state
is Homeric, tragic, illiterate,
the shortest and the longest of verses
cluster together where the firelight is,
and what they have in common is one thing,
a long line suitable for chanting:
a line we lost with *Beowulf* and *Gawain*,
a horn-blast we shall never hear again.
Our ears are trained to the Latin iambic,
where we once waved a wand, we beat a stick.
Heroic poetry closer to the sun
takes two lines of our ballads to make one:
In Scarlet town when I was young there was a fair maid dwelling.
That all the youths cried lack a day, her name was Barbara Allen.[8]
ζάχαρι εἶν' τὸ χέρι του, καὶ τὸ σπαθί του χάρος.[9]
In English the same line is short of breath,
'His hand was sugar, and his sword was death.'
Yet that Latin metre set Shakespeare free,
dramatic verse is our best poetry:
if you reread the sonnets you will find
they are dramatic verses of a kind,
only Shakespeare wrote them or could have done,
of shady poets the best, shadiest one.
Dramatic verse is dead, with all it brings.
The nightingale sings that all the wood rings,
She singeth in her song that the night is too long.[10]
Now our blood has run weak which once ran strong,
we have lost what underlay poetry,
a simple, sensuous intensity
that in the Sixties it used to be said
revolution revives, but now that's dead.
What lives will survive in another form,
like the ghost of a calm after the storm.
Smouldering revolutionary wars

drip like blood-dawns from bullet-holes like stars:[11]
the single word Liberty repeated
crows like a cock in the dark over the dead.
   Poetry is a dead horse, it's a mess,
a competition in the weekly press.
Yet Shakespeare's seeds are sleeping in that ground,
fatal and poisonous, and to be found
by who chooses, who searches and who needs,
with resurrection sleeping in his seeds.
We foolish old men have passed our lives long
fiddling with the echoes of a harsh song
in the secure knowledge it will be found:
the bones of Baudelaire lie in that ground.
And as it was surely in Chaucer's day
and in Shakespeare's, so now in our own day
our best hope lies in foreign poetry
and we reroot in foreign poetry.
The old daylight we needed to forget
has withdrawn from our coast: *the violet
has made its home now in the deepening shade,
the final refuge of the exiled soul.*[12]
Poets are exiles: poems are made whole.
In the last century Gautier decreed
writing poems is a gratuitous deed,
useless, non-moral and unnatural
(the view of half our uncles after all),
yet poems cannot be categorized,
they are primitive, they are not civilized,
poems are like a bird's song, natural,
being human they tend to be moral,
they have their use, they linger in the mind,
their spark of *eros* remains undefined
in all ages, ranks and societies:
eros is more than the mind can quite seize.
Take Jaccottet again, 'Daybreak' again:
*You are the light rising on cold rivers
the lark sprung from the field.* What simple verse,
and the thought is as primitive as sunrise,
the small skills of poets are mysteries
which like birdsong cannot be fully stated,
the very earth is laid bare and elated.[13]

True poetry never sates, never cloys,
is primitive because it is a noise,
an intricate string of minute noises
expressing what man thinks and feels and is
and civilized society represses.
When the two meet they will conflict headlong
in the most thrilling outburst of pure song,
in Virgil's images, Miltonic verse,
delighted and delightful and perverse.
    Pope in his rustic palace makes a stand,
but the world moves, the rope slips in the hand,
holding that verse the civilized hand burns:
poetry must forget all that it learns,
the rhymes, the couplets, the whole bag of tricks:
ancient poetry lies beyond the Styx.
Things come back only when they are unlearnt,
and the hand tingles where it had been burnt,
the noise dies out, the poets rearrange,
it is the noises change and never change.
What lives or dies? The scholar is a drudge,
the hungry poet is the only judge,
yet he longs for the scholar's curious ear:
how Chaucer sounds, what accent had Shakespeare?
When the free bird in the thin bramble sings
his song is learnt by ear: we learn such things,
poet from poet. I could only wish
I saw hope in departments of English.
    Oxford English can offer this defence:
since it was founded its vast influence
has extended through English poetry
and left it on the whole sober and free,
because it has been individual
and curious, with no dogmas at all,
and the canon is always altering:
the result has not been a silent spring.
Elsewhere I warn you these are heady days,
the canon does not alter, it decays.
Old libraries are sold now and not bought,
I hear it said, 'Spenser cannot be taught,
Milton is dodgy' – dodgy was the word,
that is the theatre of the absurd.

What fools abandon lingers in the mind,
it is what I worked all my life to find.
The man who said it moves between great cities
and sits (he said) on twenty-six committees.
Well, we must hop like sparrows for the grain
in the horse-dung, and cycle it again.
The dawn is cold, it takes another tone,
poetry is consumed to the bare bone.
   Ancient Gower brooded in *Pericles*
over a pantomime of mysteries,
Cerimon's resurrection of the dead,
love's long triumph, and God's justice sated.
And years before the Elizabethan stage
Gower's Pygmalion: *the cold image*
he feeleth warm / of flesh and bone and full of life.[14]
Poetry is like Lear on Dover cliff,
all lies, all truth, because wandering Lear
never stood on that edge, never fell there.
And the curse of Timon that brought plague on
Athens was Shakespeare's curse over London.
Let me look back upon thee. O thou wall,
That girdles in those wolves, dive in the earth
And fence not Athens! Matrons, turn incontinent!
Obedience fail in children! Slaves and fools
Pluck the grave wrinkled Senate from the bench
And minister in their steads! To general filths
Convert i'th'instant, green Virginity –
Do't in your parents' eyes! Bankrupts, hold fast,
Rather than render back, out with your knives
And cut your trusters' throats! Bound servants, steal!
Large-handed robbers your grave masters are,
And pill by law! Maid, to thy master's bed,
Thy mistress is o'th'brothel. Son of sixteen,
Pluck the lined crutch from thy old limping sire,
With it beat out his brains! Piety and fear,
Religion to the gods, peace, justice, truth,
Domestic awe, night-rest and neighbourhood,
Instruction, manners, mysteries, and trades,
Degrees, observances, customs and laws,
Decline to your confounding contraries,
Confusion live! – Plagues incident to men,

Your potent and infectious fevers heap
On Athens, ripe for stroke! Thou cold sciatica,
Cripple our senators, that their limbs may halt
As lamely as their manners. Lust and liberty
Creep in the minds and marrows of our youth,
That 'gainst the stream of virtue they may strive
And drown themselves in riot. Itches, blains
Sow all the Athenian bosoms, and their crop
Be general leprosy! Breath infect breath,
That their society as their friendship may
Be merely poison! . . . Timon will to the woods.[15]

Has this curse not a very modern sound?
The seeds of Shakespeare's curse sleep in our ground.
But poetry remains itself alone,
fresh as snow, cold as water, hard as stone;
and only poetry can colonize
the island or the untrodden paradise;
language roots in the mouth of the first dead
under the new crops in their shallow bed,
the illiterate and the anonymous,
feeds on provincial words and the green forest:
rising or dipping sun mean east and west.
Homer had no word for the north or south,
ice in the mouth or desert in the mouth,
yet for the wind he had a hundred names.

Poetry is still playing the same games,
ten thousand generations from Adam,
and the core of the poem is *I am.*
Of all definitions of poetry
what it is or has been or can be
I think Pasternak's is the most sublime:
'eternity's hostage in the hands of time.'[16]
Aristotle the old philosopher
says the end of philosophy is wonder,
and eternity's hostage is wonderful,
time's hand shapes it, we watch the poem cool
till we can handle it, expatriates
of that wonder which poetry creates.
Plato glibly overshadows us: we
have trouble with the word eternity,
we are not citizens of wonderland.

I know only what I hold in my hand,
poetry is godlike, not absolute good,
if God did not exist, poetry would.
What is caught in the margins of language
trapped in chance words like a bird in a cage,
has no status in being or logic:
poetry is a kind of cheap magic:
but poems have a right to speak and be,
and I love them and their cheap mystery.
They comfort me with their familiar chime,
eternity's hostage in the hand of time.
   We may be the last Europeans you see
to take eternity so seriously.
Time is really a new idea of ours,
hence the English obsession with clock-towers
(Russian eternity consumes all hours).
Only inside a poem can time play
and still be perfect, die and live and stay,
and there time is eternal in a way.
A timelessness hangs around verse-endings
and within poems time may fold his wings.
Waller's best poem holds time in its hands,
being *Battle of the Summer Islands,*
fought between the islanders and two whales.
He longs to be there and away he sails
over the always blue, spice-breathing seas
and like a native settles down: *palm trees*
Under the shadow of whose friendly boughs
They sit, carousing where their liquor grows.
... Such is the mould, that the bless'd tenant feeds
On precious fruits, and pays his rent in weeds.
With candied plantains, and the juicy pine,
On choicest melons, and sweet grapes, they dine,
And with potatoes fat their wanton swine.[17]
There is eternity in timeless time,
locked in an old verse, summoned in a rhyme,
drifting to life again out of its dust,
and all the halleluiahs of the just
will not disturb that black man from his tree,
ruffle the surface of the baroque sea
or make time run back from reality.

Poems are real and poems are impure,
in their beginning as in their closure,
heaven is what poems cannot endure.
Paradise is a bag of monkey-tricks,
a vision of Italian politics,
and love is not pure love if it can rhyme,
it is a hostage in the hands of time.
The human heart, that impure origin,
alone determines what is genuine,
and can discern it in tones of the voice:
the slurred rhythm, the small, particular noise
of music's innocent complexities,
bright eyes, pink cheeks, transparent mysteries.
Eternity sings in a bed of sands
when Cotton's *floods do clap their liquid hands*.[18]
Eternity applauded the baroque,
poetry shook with the delightful shock,
when heavy fancies of the court and stage
cut crisp in words brought in a golden age.
Gold never tarnishes but melts away,
it is most prodigal with dying day:
the old colour of honey and the sun
that names a golden age cannot make one,
darkness and green remained our mysteries,
there was no honey dripping down the trees.
  Poetry is vision and is truth,
grass crown of age, maturity of youth:
because the imagination is truthful
and Blake truthfully wrote that heaven is full
of angels in their thousands at sunrise.
If grace grant thee to go in this wise,
Thou shalt see in thyself Truth sit in thy heart,
In a chain of charity, as thou a child were.
... The light followed the Lord into the low earth.[19]
Poetry is to this degree faith
that it cannot be abolished by death,
the limits of its language are more clear
than the stars are, but also mistier.
A wise man wrestles where a child will know
how the world goes or things in poems go.
Thou shalt see in thyself Truth sit in thy heart[20]

by William Langland's art and by Blake's art:
the vision is the visionary's part
by whose pleased spirit and at whose hand we
take some of our beliefs from poetry,
from Christian or pagan equally,
poetry being natural to man,
and the soul being by nature pagan.
So in the death of Christ as in his birth,
light followed the Lord into the low earth.

   Of all arts and in all its mystery
poetry is the most deeply earthly.
Do you believe that grieving of the mind
left Tennyson purified or refined
in his long fit of deathly thoughts, or worse,
unequalled majesty of personal verse?
Many thoughts flocked round him when Hallam died,
In Memoriam is unrarefied,
it is individual, true poetry
with textures that we feel and smell and see.
And yet this is poetry of spirit
with a full-grown Victorian soul in it,
stoical and luxuriant and ill-starred
as an angel of stone in a churchyard.
Calm is the morn without a sound,
   Calm as to suit a calmer grief,
   And only through the faded leaf
The chestnut pattering to the ground:

Calm and deep peace on this high wold,
   And on these dews that drench the furze
   And all the silvery gossamers
That twinkle into green and gold:

Calm and still light on you great plain
   That sweeps with all its autumn bowers,
   And crowded farms and lessening towers,
To mingle with the bounding main:

Calm and deep peace in this wide air
   These leaves that redden to the fall:
   And in my heart, if calm at all,
If any calm, a calm despair:

Goodbye to the Art of Poetry

Calm on the seas, and silver sleep,
  And waves that sway themselves in rest,
  And dead calm in that noble breast
Which heaves but with the heaving deep.[21]
One kind of grief was never better stated,
one landscape never better celebrated:
no world so hung round one departed friend,
no sentence so mused to its deadly end,
deadly and physical and dramatic,
motionless end of motion: all one trick:
a trick of the heart though, as of the poem.
Notebooks fill up but poems empty them,
the poet shivered backwards to belief
and in one poem emptied years of grief,
years of controlled thought, of uncontrolled sense,
of landscape and the downs and their silence.
   The greatest poets of our century
in English make us deeply uneasy,
because for better and also for worse
they wrote their own lives raw into their verse:
Pound died as mad as dying Hercules,
Yeats in desire and rage, and both of these
half in love with political violence,
folly of proud minds, madness of proud sense.
Tom Eliot, among these three greatest,
declined into his gentlemanly west,
then woke one day in love, married, and then
scarcely wrote anything ever again.
I have the greatest sympathy with him,
I even love his late verse and the dim
and Christian capers he wrote for the stage,
verse theatre is a therapy for old age:
if it could be more he'd have made it so.
The hardest thing for poets is to let go:
the rope still burns and the hand is still burnt.
From Pound you can still learn as I have learnt
the ABC of the whole modern movement,
forget how he arrived or where he went,
he was a poet by the hardest test:
Eliot's letters to and from Pound are best.
I have feared William Yeats as Larkin did,

those hollow thunders and those raw cries hid
more madness than he knew, more that was false,
thrills by hindsight at the Waterloo waltz,
all the exaggerations of Byron
without the honesty, face painted on
(almost) for a senate of assassins,
bumpkins and sly fellows, a phoney prince.
   And yet Yeats is a great, great poet
whom I admit I never can forget.
Still, he is wit's and scarcely nature's child
and about as honest as Oscar Wilde:
but that he lived into his serious age
and that his verses burn the dusty stage.
Of these three poets it was only he
who touched the last limits of poetry,
as that had been physically defined
in his time by the ear and voice and mind.
Stress metres ended and down Kipling went,
but Yeats was saved by his Irish accent.
It was the language altered: one forgets
such a change is first noticed by poets.
   As for the modern, that began in France,
and to its music we have danced our dance.
By one of history's spectacular twists,
two at least of the greatest modernists
were anti-modernist founding fathers
by the majestic sweep of their great verse:
New England Lowell, Russian Pasternak
had heard the river heave and the ice crack
and lived to see all nature musical
as it had been, yet transformed after all,
because language first transforms in the ear,
then the poem descants on what we hear.
But there is also personal progress:
the condition of success is unsuccess,
and the change of a language in a life-span
may be less than the changes in a man.
Lowell's *Notebook* of 1970
and *History* of 1973
differ by vigorous muscular strength
exercised in poems of the same length,

the unrhymed sonnet or the quatorzaine;
it was his vice to do things over again.
It was his vice, maybe it was his craze
just as Picasso's was in his last days,
endless, prodigal creativity:
but I feel the loose muscle in *History*.
Notebook was one long poem he did say,
and the revision like cutting away
the marble from the figure in the rock.
What I liked was the metronomic clock
controlling history as the dead soul
in the live poems swayed their barcarole,
their dying notes, their individual tone,
their seagulls' cries ripped open to the bone.
And poetry is as history is,
the consequences sleep in their causes,
the world to come hangs on a poet's rhyme
but we are not aesthetes of future time,
Blake's head is nothing but a dreaming bone,
his angel lay sleeping in a stone;
something in him quarried to set it free:
cutting away that rock is poetry,
the truth of poetry is history.

   And all the old aesthetes wasted their days
refining down the world into a phrase,
in love with ghosts of roses, scents of doubt,
finding the world too coarse to write about:
Narcissus drowned in one long wavering note,
nothing to say, no birdsong in his throat.
Yet there arises one compelling ghost,
one trumpet voice, the art's father almost,
the aesthete Yeats, a voice that carries still
when the horsemen have vanished from the hill.
... At Mooneen he had leaped a place
So perilous that half the astonished meet
Had shut their eyes; and where was it
He rode a race without a bit?
And yet his mind outran the horses' feet.

We dreamed that a great painter had been born
To cold Clare rock and Galway rock and thorn,

To that stern colour and that delicate line
That are our secret discipline
Wherein the gazing heart doubles her might.[22]
The poem goes off there, as poetry,
it is not tied down to reality.
The only painter I know Irish-born
is Francis Bacon, hates hunting, and is torn
by deeper stresses than that idiot zoo
of national bogies Yeats admitted to.
   It is something to cut deep, to cut new,
we need unlikely medicines, pursue
the truth and true passion and true courage.
The pleasant verse of a complacent age
is claustrophobic and means death to us:
Sir John Denham's best poem is 'To Morpheus'.
The poetry of the possession of heaven
is merely charming to unburied men.
We are not in that chorus which was picked
to chant with Francis or with Benedict,
we mope in ruined cloisters, and our Christ
is what Ulysses looked for in the west:
the gilded waves and the sea-monster's hum,
the islands of the blest, the Christ to come.
He did not lead the Russian revolution;
he does not guard the British constitution.
Tennyson's patriotism is stinking air,
Blake was half mad, and Blok died in despair.
The truth of poetry is a dying breath.
Pasternak says the fresh air smelt of death
in our days, and to open a window
was to open a vein.
               It has been so,
and now of our tormented century
what will live longer than his poetry?
We all live, we are immortal spirit,
we nest in our poem, we live in it,
yet when poets die and their work is done
the greatest poem is the unwritten one.
In our fresh May, in our leafless November,
it is the unanswered question we remember,
the unwritten poem is the eternal muse,

poems like fallen leaves drift and confuse
and we lie down in languorous sunsets:
the sun falls out of heaven and forgets
all the music of poetry and its pains,
only the unwritten poem remains,
thrilling in Andrew Marvell, close in Donne,
unattained, always nearly the next one.
If the poet turns from it, it comes near,
soars in seasons, lives in the dying year,
speaking in ragged birds' voices maybe
or nightingales of the last century.
The poet's truth is what the poet can,
there is no expression of the whole man.
In his bones lives a wind-torn loud something:
Destroyer and creator, Shelley said,
the spirit of a wind raising the dead.
Only the herdsman crying to the herds
demystifying unpretentious words
which are somehow immediate to the heart
utters mere life, which is the poet's art.
A child can exercise it, shepherds can,
or some illiterate imprisoned man;
we sift through old poems as gardeners
gather dead leaves that the wind hardly stirs.
This is our service, because immortal
spirit is trees that live by leaves that fall.
We are religious at life's funeral.
    I fear the time when this will not be so,
when poetry's occasions seem to grow
into one complex intellectual act,
but the occasions of spirit contract
into the carving of a cherry-stone,
and poetry dies back into the bone:
when poetry belongs to colleges,
a subject only for remarks like these,
and one by one the great examples go,
too difficult to read, too hard to know,
when poems illustrate old politics
and new critics and all such monkey-tricks,
books crumble and the reprints cost too much
being made just for colleges and such.

Poets like Gower are doomed I assume
(he's out of print, Bodley's lost a volume).
Once the transmission of the poet's art
was in the ear, through poems learnt by heart.
That skill is running out into the sand.
Against this withering I take my stand.
Look back at Matthew Arnold whose complaint
was against all things marginal and quaint,
and yet he loved the Afghans and the Irish,
complained there were not critics in English
like the critical community in France.
How happy those days seem from a distance.
Leavis laboured for the truly central,
Eliot's centre was not there at all.
What is central? The individual
as Larkin saw: art, whose *rough-tongued bell* . . .
Insists I too am individual.[23]
The one centre of English poetry
and the one centre there can ever be
is the individual, obstinate soul:
poetry is poems, never the whole
nation, the whole tradition, the whole man,
but snail-sensitive, antiquarian,
bathed in fire, making things, breaking them,
spirit, dry bones, blind eyes of the poem.
Rumi said, *You see through each cloak I wear*
Know if I speak without mouth or language.
The world is drunk on its desire for words:
I am the slave of the Master of silence.[24]
There is a silence beyond poetry,
and poetry reaches to that silence
or poetry punctuates a silence,
or it is punctuated with silence.
Poetry is the silence between lines,
it is a gesture of quite silent signs.
It is wingbeats, the white swan's dissolution,
unknown to schools of earthly elocution:
the imprisoned spirit echoing on bone,
the flight of the alone from the alone.
When that withers, poetry is undone:
the world hovers round it with kind advice,
but poetry's as lost as paradise.

Notes and References

INTRODUCTION

1. Cf. Th. Klauser, *Die Cathedra im Totenkult der heidn. und christl. Antike.*

THE LAMENTATION OF THE DEAD

1. Federico Garcia Lorca, *Obras Completas* (1972), pp. 1171–1272.
2. Paul Éluard, *Oeuvres Complètes*, Pléiade edition (1968), p. 1262. This poem, 'Gabriel Péri', was printed in the collection *Liberté* in 1944.
3. *Lycidas*, ll. 142–50.
4. Cf. Margaret Alexiou, *The Ritual Lament in Greek Tradition* (1974), p. 212, n. 107.
5. Second Book of Samuel, 1, 17–27.
6. C. M. Bowra, *Heroic Poetry* (1951).
7. *Odyssey* XXIV, 58–62.
8. *Iliad* XXIV, 720f.
9. C. W. MacLeod, *Iliad Book XXIV* (1982).
10. It is interesting that the lamentation of Achilles for Patroklos in Book XVIII echoes the style of women's laments, and women arm him for his vengeance. In the wake for Patroklos in Book XIX, Briseis begins the lamentation. Its resonance overflows into the prophecy of the death of Achilles at the end of the book.
11. Cf. Patrick Leigh Fermor, *Mani* (1958), ch. 5, 'Lamentation'.
12. Alexiou, *Ritual Lament in Greek Tradition*, p. 13.
13. Cf. Jasper Griffin, *Homer on Life and Death* (1980), ch. 4.
14. *The Poetic Edda*, vol. I, text and translation ed. Ursula Dronke (1969), p. 98.
15. *Marko the Prince*, tr. Anne Pennington and Peter Levi (1984). p. 145.
16. Cf. Svetozar Koljevic, *The Epic in the Making* (1980), pp. 252–3.
17. *Marko the Prince*, p. 24.
18. Arnold Passow, *Popularia Carmina Graeciae Recentioris* (1860), recently reprinted in Athens.
19. Ibid., p. 288, no. 406.
20. The *Tachydromos* collection, *Ta Demotika Mas Tragoudia* (1966), p. 327, no. 218.
21. Mrs Hall came across traces of the lament during her Irish travels. See *Hall's Ireland* (1842).
22. Eilís Dillon, 'The Lament for Arthur O'Leary', *Irish University Review*, vol. I, no. 2 (1971), pp. 198ff. Thomas Kinsella

in *An Duanaire 1600–1900: Poems of the Dispossessed*, Ó Tuama and Kinsella (1981), follows Eilís Dillon rather closely; his albeit extracted version is almost never an improvement. K. H. Jackson in his Penguin *A Celtic Miscellany* (1971) prints a prose version with useful notes, bibliography and comparative material. John Montague printed a part of the Lament in his *Faber Book of Irish Verse* (1974).

23. There has been some dispute over conflicting versions and the order of stanzas. For example stanza XVIII might fit best after XIII. Eilís Dillon follows Dr Seán Ó Tuama's edition of 1961, but in *An Duanaire* (1981) the father's two stanzas XIII and XIV disappear altogether. This change favours a smoother run, but I think it is for the worse. K. H. Jackson gives these two stanzas to Eileen herself, which must be wrong. The *An Duanaire* text also leaves out stanzas XXXI to XXXIV inclusive: in them XXV is answered, the women are thanked (although in stanza VIII as in stanza XXVII it was only one old woman, stanza XXI has more than one), and John Cooney and Eileen's brother-in-law Mr Baldwin are cursed. I do not think these stanzas are false or intrusive, since the poem is intended to be dramatic and various, not a pure, performed lament. Stanza XXXII is a matter of taste. It seems to me a turning point of the poem.

24. Eileen's twin sister Máire was married to Baldwin, and Eileen first saw Arthur O'Leary from the window of their house in Macroom. Baldwin handed over the disputed horse to Morris.

FROM AESCHYLUS TO JAMES FENTON

1. Miletos fell in 494 BC, and the play was probably in 492. Cf. Herodotos, 6,21.
2. Cf. Oliver Taplin, *The Stagecraft of Aeschylus* (1977), pp. 304ff.
3. Ibid., pp. 11 and 15–16.
4. Ag. 810–54. Trans. P. L.
5. James Fenton, *London Review of Books*, 10 November 1988.
6. Perhaps this unity is artificial, but it is discernible. The messenger's speech in the text begins earlier, with the avenging ghost or evil god that tricked Xerxes, and ends later with Xerxes crying out and taking flight.
7. Taplin, *Stagecraft of Aeschylus*, pp. 1ff.
8. *Essay on the Original Genius and Writings of Homer* (reprint 1972), p. 286.
9. Taplin, *Stagecraft of Aeschylus*, app. D, pp. 460ff.
10. In *Have You Anything to Declare?* (1936), an anthology collected by Maurice Baring, who also notices Aeschylean lines in Ronsard:

   Je te salue, heureuse et
      profitable mort,
   des extrèmes douleurs médecin
      et confort.

11. 'In a Notebook', *A Vacant Possession* (1978), and *The Memory of War* (1982), now in *The Memory of War and Children in Exile: Poems 1968–83* (1983).
12. Cf. Eric Sams, 'The Myth of Memorial Reconstruction', *Encounter*, December 1988.
13. I could say this because I was speaking to an Oxford audience.
14. 'In Memoriam Günter Eich', *Die Neunte Stunde* (1979). Trans. P. L.

15. 'Deutschland (i) 1927', *Gedichte* (1948). Trans. P. L.
16. 'Warschauer Gedenktafel', *Chausseen Chausseen* (1963). Trans. P. L.
17. Trans. P. L.
18. 1968. Reprinted in *Terminal Moraine* (1972), no. 7 of Part 1.
19. Cf. Peter Levi, *History of Greek Literature* (1985), pp. 408–10.
20. *Seven against Thebes*, 709–11. Trans. P. L.
21. Ibid., 1054ff. Trans. P. L.

HORACE

1. The most succinct and the best-argued introduction to Horace is in Nisbet and Hubbard, *Commentary on the Odes* (1981), vol. 1.
2. Only Denham's three lyric stanzas to Morpheus, which typically of Denham are his best poem, almost rise to Horace's style.
3. *Milton's Shorter Poems*, ed. J. Carey (1971), no. 33. One should abolish Carey's question-mark in line 12.
4. 'Exegi monumentum' and Sonnet 55, 'Not marble, nor the gilded monuments . . .'.
5. The high tide of the modern view of Horace is well stated by Nisbet and Hubbard, *Commentary on the Odes*, vol. 1, p. xxvi.
6. Housman, *More Poems* (1936), V, Horace, *Odes* 4,7. First published in *Quarto*, vol. 3, 1897, when he was professor at University College, London.
7. Gray's closest adaptation of Horace is in Latin, not in English verse. It belongs as closely to his own time and his own personality as Housman's translations: 'O lacrymarum fons,

tenero sacros / ducentium ortus ex animo quater / felix in imo qui scatentem / pectore te pia nympha sensit.'
8. Dedication of *Manilius* to M. J. Jackson (1903), vol. 1.
9. His translation of the 'Regulus' ode is notable: *A Diversity of Creatures* (1917), and *Complete Stalky Stories* (1929).
10. Nor is it his fault that Kipling's *Horace*, as it was called, was posthumously published about fifteen years ago, for the ridiculous price of £63. It deserves to be issued in a more normal commercial edition.
11. Horace in the odes is not classical, in the formal sense of Burckhardt and Wolfflin 'that a classical work is that which embodies a technical or formal process which has reached its maximum of development according to its own laws', because the laws have scarcely been formulated, the contradictions are still vigorous. For 'classicality', see Roger Hinks, *The Gymnasium of the Mind* (1980), p. 34.
12. Ep. 1,20, 17 to the end.
13. Odes 4,1, 28 to the end.
14. I.e. 'sub trabe citrea': I take *trabs* to be the bough of a tree not the beam of a temple. Venus is a modest-sized marble statue in an orchard in the open air.
15. Odes 4,7, 13–16, reading 'pater' for 'pius', a traditional not a Virgilian phrase.
16. 'As if', says Housman, 'the secret of the classical spirit is open to anyone who has a fervent admiration for the second-best parts of Tennyson' (Cambridge Inaugural Lecture, 1911).
17. Fraenkel wrote eloquently on a fragment of Naevius in *Kleine Beobachtungen*.

18. Odes 3,5.
19. Not badly translated by way of D'Annunzio by G. S. Fraser.
20. What can be learnt from Ovid is simple, though it is capable of infinite exploitation: by Marlowe for example, by Shakespeare and by Tennyson. There are many subtle lessons in Virgil's *Eclogues*, and a kind of perfection in the *Georgics*. Horace has the rhythmic undertone and the concreteness of the Chinese 'Lament for the South', and many of the virtues of Japanese Basho.
21. See Venosa in the 1904 Baedeker Guide. Modern guides have much less of the local atmosphere. Odes 1,1, 2; 2,3, 9.
22. 'On First Looking into Loeb's Horace', *Collected Poems* (1980), p. 109.
23. Bunting's version of this poem (privately printed, 1972) says:

    We must let earth go and home,
    wives too, and your trim trees,
    yours for a moment, save one
    sprig of black cypress.

24. Issued in fifty copies by the Pelican Press in 1923. He died in 1848 at the age of thirty-one. Brother of the famous novelists.
25. Last part of Odes 1,17.
26. In simple phrases like 'Neu desint epulis rosae, neu vivax apium neu breve lilium' (1,36, 15), the word 'vivax' is the mystery. Without it the lily's brevity would be sentimental.
27. Odes 4,4. James Michie, *Odes of Horace* (1963, 1987).
28. The victory of Claudius Nero was nearly 200 years old, in 208/9 BC, in the north-east of Italy. The Claudian and Julian families were closely allied, so this was an ancestor.
29. Eduard Fraenkel, *Horace* (1957, finished 1955).
30. Odes 1,22, 9f. His house at Tibur was above the waterfall and the valley of nightingales. V. Aen. 7, 81ff.: beside the ilex grave and the pure water-springs where Virgil's king Latinus consulted the prophetic god Faunus. Both houses were in their different ways thought suitable for him as a poet; when Virgil died, Horace was the national poet (v. Aen. 8, 81ff.).
31. Michie, *Odes of Horace*.
32. Ep. 1,16, 78–9. On slavery and death. The poem refers to the *Bacchai* of Euripides, where the god in prison in disguise tells the tyrant, 'The god himself will free me when I will.'
33. 3,29, 21f.

DRYDEN'S VIRGIL

1. The poem on the death of Lord Hastings shows how; cf. lecture on Milton. Cf. also his dedication to Busby and the note on the third satire of Persius.
2. J. M. Osborn, *John Dryden: Some Biographical Facts* (revised edn., 1965)
3. His income by 1670 was good but precarious. His salary was not always paid.
4. In return he agreed to provide three plays a year, which he failed to do.
5. Dennis, quoted by Malone, remembers that Dryden admired Milton in 1694 twice as much as he had in 1674 (when *The State of Innocence* was published).
6. James Osborn doubts it, but the circumstantial evidence is strong, and Dryden's dedication of the *Aeneid* begins with a similar foolish ring: 'A Heroick

Poem, truly such, is undoubtedly the greatest Work which the Soul of Man is able to perform.'

7. As a critic he stood on Dr Johnson's shoulders, and as a biographer of Dryden, on Malone's.
8. He calls the frigid excesses of wit Clevelandisms.
9. Saintsbury's 1881 *Dryden*, p. 139, followed in 1882 by his revision of Scott's *Dramatic Works of Dryden* (1808).
10. The first edition of Virgil has a list of subscribers, but the important subscriptions were to the plates. They do not really indicate his readers.
11. In the Dedication of the *Aeneid*, he seeks like Virgil for 'Souls of the highest Rank, and truest Understanding'.
12. The concluding section of 'New England Poets and Further', posthumously published in the *London Review of Books*, vol. 27, no. 2, 21 February 1980.
13. Saintsbury, *Dryden*, p. 147.
14. Dryden revels in royal compliments; cf. Aen. 8, 882–902.
15. Tillyard suggested that Dryden added a burlesque element to serious subjects and even epic, but that existed already. It is better to say his verse is always a sparkling performance.
16. His Virgil was magnificently published by subscription in 1697, as *Paradise Lost* had been in 1688.
17. *Deus nobis haec otia non dedit.*
18. 'To His Sacred Majesty, a Panegyrick on his Coronation', 11. 53ff.
19. Ll. 73 ff. and 19–20.
20. Scott discovers a strain of coarseness in Dryden's *Aeneid*. Today one would say the poem gains by it. It exists in Virgil, but not in

the same places. In his treatment of Christian epic in *Discourse on Satire*, Dryden implicitly condemns Milton.

21. H. M. Hooker, *Huntingdon Library Quarterly*, 1945, and L. Proudfoot, *Dryden's Aeneid and its Seventeenth-Century Predecessors* (1960), make a case for obscurer versions, including an anonymous one (1672), but I am not convinced the influence is important.
22. Aen. 6, 362–3.
23. Dedication of Virgil's *Pastorals*.
24. Ec. 2, 7ff.
25. Geo. 3, 13.
26. Geo. 2, 11–12.
27. Geo. 4, 189ff.
28. It is instructive to compare the brilliant modern verse translation of this passage by Robert Wells (*Georgics*, 1984), his verse technique being equally faultless, but more frugal than Dryden's.
29. On Latium's happy Shore you shall be cast:
    Where gentle *Tiber* from his Bed beholds
    The flow'ry Meadows, and the feeding Folds.
30. Dryden liked an introduction to a French version of the *Aeneid* by Segrais.
31. Cf. Preface to *Sylvae*, the 1685 second part of *Miscellanies*. It is curious that Dryden's Theocritus is far smoother than his Virgil *Eclogues*, and less alive, although he loved Theocritus.
32. Cf. Aen. 6, 953–61.

VISIONARY POETS

1. *Required Writing* (1983), p. 79 (written 1955).
2. Ibid., p. 83 (written 1964).
3. Cf. also Stephen Spender, *Jour-*

nals (1985), pp. 346–7, 438, 462.

4. Cf. Robert Alter, *Art of Biblical Poetry* (1985), ch. 1.

5. Job 38, 3: 'Gird up now thy loins like a man; for I will demand of thee, and answer thou me.'

6. Job 42, 5: 'but now mine eye seeth thee'.

7. There is even a Christian visionary poem in Greek hexameters, possibly by Quintus of Smyrna, recently found on papyrus, but I think still unpublished in 1986.

8. See Appendix 1.

9. Cf. Spender, *Journals*, January–February 1953.

10. N. K. Sandars, *Poems of Heaven and Hell* (Penguin, 1971); N. K. Sandars, *Gilgamesh* (Penguin, 1960 and 1972).

11. Ed. G. R. Driver (1956). I have slightly modified his version.

12. Cf. G. Holmes, *Dante* (1980), pp. 72f.

13. Trans. P. L.

14. Trans. P. L.

15. Canto 28, 19–21.

16. The poems of Garcilaso de la Vega (d. 1536) and his friend Juan Boscán (d. 1542) were first printed in 1543. Cf. in general Gerald Brenan, *St John of the Cross* (Cambridge University Press, 1973), which contains the poems with facing translation.

17. I am in two minds about his prose. It can be extremely exciting, his aphorisms are gripping, and a streak of the Renaissance runs through his prose as well as his verse: a sense of adventure and of the power of reason, 'some to the studious universities, some to discover islands far away'. For his scholasticism, cf. *Obras* (1630), p. 764; for 'gubernarse en todo per razon',

cf. p. 215; for the islands far away, cf. *Obras*, Cancion 33.

18. The Sanlucar and Jaén versions; the second is a revision of the poem made to suit the prose explanation he was then writing. It plainly violates the natural flow and impetus of the poem.

19. Trans. P. L.

20. 'Spiritual Canticle', Brenan, *St John of the Cross*, p. 152.

21. T. Carmi's anthology of Hebrew poems: Judah Halevi, p. 350, and Samuel Haganid, p. 298.

22. In K. Muir and S. Schoenbaum (eds), *A New Companion to Shakespeare Studies* (1971), pp. 104–5.

23. It is based on chastity, on the kind of love that Simone Weil discusses in her 'En quoi consiste l'inspiration occitanienne?', in *Écrits historiques et politiques*, trans. Richard Rees as 'The Romanesque Renaissance' (*Twentieth Century*, September 1960).

24. This is confirmed by his unforgettable adaptation of an extremely physical ghost poem by Propertius ('The Apparition').

25. *Divine Meditations*, 7.

26. John Carey, *Donne* (1981), pp. 127ff.

27. Introduction to *The Oxford Book of Christian Verse* (1940), p. xix.

28. Said by his editor Tulloch to be the most worthwhile and least readable of the Cambridge Platonists. He spent three years late in life translating his own works into Latin. There are several strange visionary poems among the occasional verses of the Cambridge Platonists. Vaughan was born and died eight years later than More.

29. 'The Song of Hylobaris' concerning Divine Providence.

30. 'The World'.
31. 'Religion'.
32. When his poems were first discovered in the nineteenth century, Grosart attributed them to Henry Vaughan.
33. 'Nature', *Works*, ed. A. Ridler (1966), p. 32.
34. 'The Odour', ibid., pp. 109–11.
35. *Centuries of Meditations* (1908), 4,71.
36. 'The God in the Tree (Early Irish Nature Poetry)', in *Preoccupations (1968–78)* (1980), p. 181.
37. The eighteenth-century Oxford Professor of Poetry Robert Lowth was an important influence on Smart's idea of scriptural versification, and also on Blake's prophetic books, but he drove neither of them mad and made neither of them visionaries.
38. Blake's *Island in the Moon* (1787) is a clue to much that comes later. It has something in common with Peacock.
39. On Stukeley, Stuart Piggott is the authority in *William Stukeley* (1950 and 1985). But Blake's vision of England is in many ways Shakespearean; cf. the final stanzas of Minstrel's Song in his *Edward III*, written as a boy.
40. Composed and etched 1804–20.
41. But he was not utterly neglected. When he died one of the royal princesses sent £200 to his widow, who returned it saying others were in more need.
42. 'The Everlasting Gospel' (c. 1818).
43. 14 September 1800.
44. 'Hölderlin's Madness' (1938), reprinted in *Collected Verse Translations*, ed. A. Clodd and R. Skelton (1970).
45. The Inquisition arrested Luis de Leon, a professor at Salamanca in the student days of John of the Cross, for translating the Song of Songs into Spanish.
46. Friedrich Hölderlin, *Poems and Fragments*, ed. M. Hamburger (bilingual edition, 1966), p. 370.
47. Trans. P. L.
48. *Horace* (1957), pp. 199–200. Cf. pp. 258ff.
49. Trans. P. L.

ANON.

1. I. and P. Opie, *The Oxford Dictionary of English Nursery Rhymes* (1980), 132.
2. James Fenton's essay 'No Nonsense' (*New Statesman*, Christmas 1977) throws much light in a brief space on nonsense poetry.
3. Opie, *Oxford Dictionary of English Nursery Rhymes*, 110.
4. Most execution was by hanging, and the bell for it was St Sepulchre's. Chopper for axe sounds unlike the beheading of a nobleman.
5. F. J. Child, *English and Scottish Popular Ballads* (1900), no. 113. Cf. Alan Brilford in E. B. Lyle (ed.), *Ballad Studies* (1976).
6. D. C. Fowler, *A Literary History of the Popular Ballad* (1968), pp. 10ff.
7. *The Oxford Book of Ballads* (1969), no. 17.
8. Lajos Vargyas, *Researches into the Medieval History of Folk Ballad* (Budapest, 1967), p. 275.
9. S. Koljevic, *The Epic in the Making* (Oxford, 1980). Also Fowler on 'Mrs Brown of Falkland', *Literary History of the Popular Ballad*, p. 294.
10. Canto LII.
11. 'A Poacher', from *The Parliament of the Three Ages*, ed.

M. Y. Offord (Early English Text Society, 1959), p. 246.

12. Analysis can of course teach a great deal: J. J. Duggan (ed.), *Oral Literature* (1975); Fowler, *Literary History of the Popular Ballad.*

13. 'Birmingham Song', from an Irishwoman in Dublin. Cf. Hugh Shields, 'The Grey Cock', in Lyle (ed.), *Ballad Studies.*

14. Among these are 'Clerk Saunders' (Child, *English and Scottish Popular Ballads*, nos. 69A and 77B) and 'Sweet William's Ghost' (ibid., no. 77). The lover in the 'Birmingham Song' is distinctly unearthly: one feels the chill in him. The burning Thames, the mysterious desperation, the wetness and the girl's disturbance reinforce this feeling. So of course does the music.

15. Cf. *The Oxford Book of Local Verses* (1987), 293.

16. *Letters of E. FitzGerald* (1894), vol. 2, p. 345.

SHAKESPEARE'S SONNETS

1. *R.E.S.*, vol. 34, no. 134, May 1983, pp. 151f.

2. Very early for an English sonnet in print. Cf. F. Yates, *Renaissance and Reform* (1983), p. 179.

3. The other claimant, a genuine W. H., is William Herbert, born 1580. He came to London in 1597 delighted at the prospect of marrying Bridget Vere, Burghley's grand-daughter, who was thirteen, but it fell through. He was a lifelong womanizer and had a bastard in 1601. Married in November 1604. Date and character are wrong for the sonnets.

4. Chastity sets up a special tension, and homosexual love was to Elizabethans inevitably chaste. Simone Weil makes this important point, which she extends to the poetry of Languedoc and to Plato, in 'The Romanesque Renaissance', *Twentieth Century*, September 1960. See Appendix 1.

5. The last line, like Donne's 'Death thou shalt die', is scriptural and a commonplace. The ballad by John Phillips lamenting Southampton's father ends, 'Yet death in him lies dead no doubt, by means of noble fame'.

6. Shakespeare cannot have known that the bodies of the Earls of Southampton were preserved in honey. If he had done, what a sonnet he might have written about it.

7. For example, Luigi Tansillo (1510–68), born in the same town as Horace: 'Amor m'impenna ...'.

8. 'Choice of Valentines', in Nashe, *The Unfortunate Traveller* (Penguin, 1972), p. 458.

9. Sidney in a sonnet makes it plain he has no mystical or hidden meaning: his love means what it says. But then why is the warning necessary? And does it go for all Sidney's sonnets?

10. *Palladis Tamia.*

11. Sidney's sonnets become passionate only when the girl marries; when he marries himself, they cease.

12. Based on Catullus, 'Vivamus mea Lesbia atque amemus'.

13. Milton uses the scheme abba, abba, cd, cd, cd ('Methought I saw my late espoused saint').

14. Shakespeare's schoolfriend Thomas Combe's moral emblems are like truncated sonnets, ending in the same way with an

emphatic couplet. His verses are adapted from the French.

15. Some editors do print full stops.
16. On pictorial art (Gombrich), 'lifelike' is defined not against life but against other pictorial images of life, that is, against our expectations of art.
17. I take the obscenities noted by Kerrigan to be a fantasy of lecherous scholars.
18. 'Immortalia ne speres, monet annus' (Hor. c 4,7).
19. *Spectator*, 24 January 1987.
20. *More Letters of E. FitzGerald* (1902).

MILTON'S EARLY VERSE

1. Guillaume de Salluste, seigneur du Bartas (which is near Auch), 1544–91. 'La Semaine: Seconde Semaine, Le Premier Jour'. He wrote other poetry in Gascon dialect, which may well be less insipid than his vastly influential epic-scale poem on the Creation.
2. Ps 114, 7–9 (I have emended v. 7).
3. Ps 136, 29–30 and 33–4.
4. Anne Barton, *Ben Jonson* (1984), shows his influence on the late Jonson. It is strong in Herrick and Cowley among others. For Milton himself, cf. R. Trickett in *Essays and Studies* (1978). Milton's punctuation in poetry, which was rhythmical rather than logical, was a tribute to Spenser; cf. M. Treip, *Milton's Punctuation* (1970).
5. Trans. P. L. On a stray leaf found with Milton's Commonplace Book in 1874 with a Latin lyric poem and a prose piece, all three about early rising: surely an imposition for being late for school. The page is headed 'Carmina elegiaca'.

6. Ovid, *Fasti*, 4, 428.
7. 'On the Death of a Fair Infant Dying of a Cough', 2 and 19.
8. The same kind of liberal unorthodoxy appears in l. 139 of 'Christ's Nativity': 'and hell itself will pass away'.
9. 88–9.
10. 96.
11. Eleg. 1 ad C. D., 49 ff. Trans. P. L.
12. 53–61. Trans. P. L.
13. Eleg. 5, 69.
14. Eleg. 5, 131–2. Trans. P. L.
15. Trans. P. L.
16. Trans. P. L.
17. Bishop Corbett's 'Elegy on Lady Haddington' is in the same vile taste:

> Thou that of faces honey-combs dost make,
> And of two breasts two cullenders....

18. Trans. P. L.
19. Trans. P. L.
20. Jonson had an honorary degree from Oxford (1619) and so ranked as an Oxford poet. It was not unprecedented to commemorate a mere poet or learned man in such a book: cf. *Camdeni Insignia*, 1624, and *Justa Funebria Ptolemaei Oxoniensis Thomae Bodleii*, 1613–14.
21. Mary Crum dismisses this possibility with little discussion: *Poems of H. King* (1965).
22. The vogue for English sonnets was over thirty years before. Some early Milton sonnets are in Italian. 'The Nightingale' was his first (?1629) and begins from 'Bembo's Rime': 'O rosignuol che'n queste verdi fronde ...'. Cf. *Milton's Shorter Poems*, ed. J. Carey (1971), pp. 88–90.

23. 'To the Reader', Preface to 'Christ's Victory'.
24. Trans. P. L.
25. 47–8.
26. 'Hence, all you vain delights', in Fletcher's *Nice Valour*, and Strode's reply to the song.
27. On this scandal, cf. John Wain, *Professing Poetry* (1977), pp. 192–212.
28. 30–3. Trans. P. L.
29. Is it 'rabido sub sole' or 'rapido' (V. Ec. 2, 10–12)?
30. 37–49. Trans. P. L.
31. Canon King's father was Bishop of London; Milton's grandfather had worked at Christ Church as a singer.
32. Cf. R. Michell, *Orationes Crewianne* (1878), pp. 168–9.

EDWARD LEAR

1. Quoted by Sir E. Strachey in the introduction to *Lear's Nonsense*, reprinted as *Edward Lear's Nonsense Omnibus* (Penguin, 1986).
2. Chichester Fortescue, later Lord Carlingford.
3. Part 1, canto 1, 279–84.
4. He would extend his powers on the simplest occasion, just for a joke, as in 'O! Mimber for the County Louth'.
5. The 1852 edition of Tennyson's poems was copiously illustrated by pre-Raphaelite artists Lear knew and admired: it must have been his model, but it offers none of Lear's grasp of landscape, and Tennyson hated it, though he liked Lear's efforts.
6. Cf. *Tennyson*, ed. C. Ricks (1969), pp. 736–40.
7. 'So all day long the noise of battle rolled / Among the mountains by the winter sea' is magnificent, but it sounds like the last echo of the Napoleonic wars. (Written 1833–4, *Morte d'Arthur*.) Reality returns with every reference to the lake, as the picture of it is slowly built up.
8. *New Tale of a Tub*. Other books in the series include *Jo: Miller for Rail and River* (with comic borders), and *A Shilling's Worth of Nonsense*, by the editors of *Punch*.
9. Introduction to *Selected Poems of W. M. Barnes*, ed. T. Hardy (1908).
10. Review of *Lear's Letters* (1907), reprinted in his *Punch and Judy* (1924).
11. There was an old woman called Towl
    Who went to sea with her Owl,
    But the Owl was seasick
    And screamed for physic,
    Which sadly annoyed Mistress Towl.
12. This recurs in 'Mrs Spiky Sparrow' as 'Many thoughts of trouble come, Like to flies upon a plum, As last night, among the trees, I heard you cough, I heard you sneeze....'
13. R. J. E. Tiddy, *The Mummer's Play* (1923).
14. There was also an unfinished sequel to 'The Owl and the Pussycat': Davidson, *E. Lear* (1933), pp. 247–8. Going to sea in a sieve is what the witches do to stop James I from crossing the sea to claim his bride (*News from Scotland*, c.1596). Congreve refers to this. I am grateful for the explanation to Richard Greene and Sally Purcell.
15. 1938.
16. Knowsley, where Lear's humour first flourished, was an enormous house where a swarm of children, grandchildren and

cousins ran about together. It was not a suburban nursery, but a whole world of children.

17. In an early version (Davidson, *E. Lear*, pp. 241–3), one does believe it; the ending is happy.
18. Ricks (ed.), *Tennyson*, pp. 228 and 284.

BORIS PASTERNAK

1. Published in 1990.
2. 'I Would Go Home Again', *New Statesman*, 27 December 1958, p. 903. Mr Kayden had previously published this in *The New Republic*; he was in correspondence with the poet.
3. *Poems by Boris Pasternak*, trans. L. Slater (1958, improved with additions 1959). (*Fifty Poems [1963]* reprinted in *Poems 1984*.)
4. 1925–7. First *1905*, then *Lt. Schmidt*, which belongs as part of *1905*.
5. R. Lowell, *Imitations* (1962), pp. 137–40. The feeling expressed in the poem existed in Pasternak at least since the death of Mayakovsky in 1930, when he suddenly found himself billed as *the* great poet of the revolution and of Communism.
6. A. Gladkov, *Meetings with Pasternak* (1977).
7. *Zemnoe Prostor* (1945), including poems from *Early Trains* (1940), which was unobtainable by the end of the war.
8. Quoted by E. Crankshaw, Introduction to *An Essay in Autobiography* (1959).
9. Trans. Lydia Pasternak Slater. For M. Harari's version, cf. *Poems and Essay in Autobiography* (Collins, 1990), p. 93.
10. His dramatic free-handedness with nature owes something to Lermontov, to whom his first important collection, *My Sister, Life*, is dedicated.
11. *Tratto di Apelle* (Allison & Busby, 1982), section 2, para. 4, p. 69.
12. 'Thunderstorm, Instantaneous Forever'. Trans. L. Pasternak Slater.
13. In *Safe Conduct*.
14. Trans. M. Rudman and B. Boychuk (1983).
15. 'Mary Magdalen'. Trans. L. Slater.
16. 'Evil Days', *Dr Zhivago*, last stanza, trans. M. Harati.
17. *Selected Poems*, trans. J. Stallworthy and P. France (Penguin, 1984), p. 143.
18. Trans. P. L.
19. 1886, on the funeral of his friend Barnes.
20. Trans. P. L.
21. This interesting relationship is well discussed by Sasha, Boris Pasternak's brother, who was in Mayakovsky's class at school, in his memoir *A Vanished Present* (1984).
22. Bokstein, 'In Memory of Leonid Aranzon', trans. R. McKane, *The Shalford Book of Twentieth-Century Russian Poetry* (1985).
23. In a letter to Martin Browne: Peter Ackroyd, *T. S. Eliot* (Hamish Hamilton, 1984), p. 266.
24. Trans. Rudman and Boychuk, *My Sister – Life and A Sublime Malady* (1983).
25. *From Gorky to Pasternak* (1961), pp. 382ff.

GEORGE SEFERIS

1. Odcomb's Complaints, 1613, Taylor.
2. 'In the Manner of G. S.', in *The King of Asine* (John Lehmann, 1948), pp. 57–9.

3. Seferis was a close friend of Tsirkas, who wrote the pioneering study *The Political Kavafis*. During the war in Egypt, Seferis copied out by hand all the poems of Kavafis (Cavafy), and annotated them; the notebook survives, and he used it in writing later essays. He found that his notes agreed substantially with Tsirkas, who was an ex-Communist.

4. Some of his English critics used to resent poems of his about Cyprus. I never shared that view. I have just reread all his Cyprus poems and find them admirable, torn and sad.

5. Rex Warner, Introduction to *The King of Asine*.

6. 'The Nutcracker and the Sugartongs', in *Tetradio 2* (1976), p. 123. He owned fine Lear watercolours of Crete and of Athens. Cf. E. Lear, *Cretan Journal* (1984), pp. 25 and 48.

7. 'Piazza San Nicolo' (1937), 'Les Anges sont Blancs (To Henry Miller)' (1939), 'Stratis Thalassinos among the Agapanthi' (January 1942).

8. Seferis and Eliot were close friends. Seferis came across 'Marina' in a London bookshop in the early 1930s when he was Vice-Consul (1931–4). 'Marina' first appeared as an *Ariel* poem, printed by itself (1930), and that was the edition he picked up. His translation of it is masterly.

9. 'An Old Man on the Riverbank' (Cairo, June 1942).

10. 'Stratis Thalassinos on the Dead Sea'.

11. New York, June 1965 – Princeton, winter 1968.

12. Trans. P. L.

13. *Writers at Work (Paris Review* interviews, 4th series) (Penguin, 1976).

14. Essay of November 1966, 'Conversation with Fabrice'.

15. He says so in 'Conversation with Fabrice'.

16. Three-volume Temple Classics.

17. *Spectator*, 20 September 1986. Robert Frost said it was what does not survive.

18. Ἀντιγραφές (1963).

19. That the translation may in virtue of its rhythm and seriousness (just *may*) be better than the original appears from Baudelaire (pre–1853):

M'aimez vous, dit Fanny, l'autre jour,
Sérieusement, m'aimez vous, commes vous dites?

This is a version of Mr Walmisley (d. 1866):

Do you, said Fanny t'other day, In earnest love me, as you say?

20. Private conversation.

21. With notes by George Savidis (1976).

22. Cf. also 'Chorus from Seferis Vinctus', a parody of 'Under the Bam under the Yan under the Bamyan Tree' (1944), p. 82 of the same collection.

23. Theotokas and Seferis, *Correspondence 1930–1966* (1975), p. 49.

24. Eliot's 'to purify the dialect of the tribe' (not quite equivalent) was written later. The line about blank paper lies behind a stanza of the third of *Three Secret Poems*.

25. Trans. P. L.

26. *On the Greek Style*, ed. Rex Warner (1966), p. 163.

27. *Paris Review* interview with Seferis.

28. Cf. *A Poet's Journal: Days of 1931–34*, 13 March 1933.
29. *Allocution, Stockholm* (*Discours de Stockholm*, 1963), p. 13.
30. *Days of 1945–51*, 26 November 1946.
31. Plato, *Alcibiades*, 133B.
32. I once pointed out to the poet that the line about accepting the wind and the rain came from Homer; he agreed, yet his memory of Homer's line had been quite unconscious.
33. Written in London in 1932.
34. *Paris Review* interview with Seferis.
35. 'Pancakes for the Queen of Babylon'.
36. *Days of 1934–40*, 1 April 1935.
37. Cf. Peter Levi, *The Hill of Kronos* (1980), pp. 152–3.
38. Aesch. Ag. 990ff.
39. 'Fêtes de la Faim', ll. 3–4.
40. Trans. P. L.

W. H. AUDEN

1. MacNeice, *Selected Literary Criticism*, reviewing *Poems* in 1931 and *Look, Stranger* in 1936.
2. Letter to K. Tynan, 28 September 1888.
3. Dedicated to Maurice Bowra. Reprinted in 1986.
4. He first heard about Auden in a newspaper article by Tom Driberg ('These Names Make News') called 'Awareness of Auden', in the *Express*. They first met in Spain in the Civil War.
5. John Fuller, reviewing a new edition of *The Orators* in 1966, agreed with the estimate of *The Orators* delivered by J. Hayward in the *Criterion* on its first publication: that it had been the best contribution to English poetry

since *The Waste Land*.
6. To Dorothy Tutin, in *Poems* (1960).
7. January 1937, from *Another Time* (1940).
8. ?Autumn 1938.
9. The two men of action he admired were Lenin and T. E. Lawrence.
10. Letter to the Niebuhrs quoted in *W. H. Auden*, ed. S. Spender (1975), p. 114.
11. Remembered by Basil Boothby; I am unable to trace it.
12. March 1928.
13. August 1929.
14. From 'In Memory of W.B. Yeats (d. Jan. 1939)'.
15. Reported by Basil Boothby in Spender (ed.), *W. H. Auden*.
16. Helen Gardner chose this passage for an anthology of religious verse.
17. Some Aragon, trans. L. MacNeice, is to be found at the end of his *Collected Poems*, ed. E. R. Dodds, (1966).
18. Peter Huchel, *The Garden of Theophrastus and Other Poems*, German text with translations by Michael Hamburger (1983).
19. Trans. P. L.
20. Heinz Winfried Sabais, *The People and the Stones: Selected Poems*, trans. Ruth and Mary Mead (1983).
21. All the same, 'Fifty-Second Street' is a lie. That street had no dives. He was really sitting in Forty-Second Street, I imagine, which was a low bohemian street full of homosexual dives.
22. *Horizon*, April 1947.
23. 'As I Walked Out'.
24. Spender (ed.), *W. H. Auden*.
25. Introduction to Henry James, *The American Scene* (1946).
26. The sailors were good-looking

not mild-looking, in the first version of the poem.
27. *The Platonic Blow*, long circulated in typescript, printed in New York in 1965.
28. *Writers at Work* (*Paris Review* interviews, 4th series) (Penguin, 1976).

IN MEMORY OF ROBERT LOWELL

1. Cf. Ian Hamilton, *Robert Lowell* (1982), pp. 338, 341–3.
2. The theorists have dismantled criticism just as the critics dismantled poetry.
3. *Writers at Work II* (*Paris Review* interviews) (Penguin, 1977).
4. *Poets in Their Youth* (1982).
5. *The Freedom of the Poet* (1976).
6. For an early version cf. Ian Hamilton's *Robert Lowell*, pp. 265–6.
7. R. Hinks, *Journal*, p. 84.
8. *Paris Review* interview with Lowell.
9. Ibid.
10. 'Robert Lowell and Others', reprinted in *The Freedom of the Poet*.
11. *Parnassus*, Spring/Summer 1978, pp. 75–100.
12. Epilogue, *Day by Day*.
13. 'Memories of West Street and Lepke', in *Life Studies*.
14. 'Fishnet', in *The Dolphin*.

PHILIP LARKIN

1. Cf. B. C. Bloomfield on 'Larkin the Librarian', in *Larkin at Sixty* (1982), p. 51.
2. XVII, *The North Ship* (1945).
3. In letters to Charles Monteith, quoted in *Larkin at Sixty*, pp. 42–3.

4. This view is now confirmed by his *Collected Poems* (1988).
5. He said so more than once to A. N. Wilson, whose *Spectator* obituary in December 1985 contains much important information about him.
6. *The Less Deceived* (1955), p. 31.
7. *The Whitsun Weddings* (1964), p. 37.
8. Ibid., p. 45.
9. Ibid., p. 27.
10. John Wain (in *Oxford Magazine*, 4th Week Hilary Term 1986) states this well.
11. *The Less Deceived*, pp. 38–9.
12. *All What Jazz* (1970), pp. 17–18.
13. A footnote to the 2nd edition (1984) of *All What Jazz* makes the point that 'If I haven't been proved right, I haven't been proved wrong either. In any case, my views haven't changed.'
14. He would not have attacked Eliot.
15. *Required Writing* (1978), p. 253.
16. 'Coming', in *The Less Deceived*, p. 17.
17. 'Spring', ibid., p. 36.
18. 'Arrivals, Departures', ibid., p. 44.
19. *High Windows* (1974), p. 16.
20. In ibid.: 'Going, Going', p. 21; 'Homage to a Government' (1969), p. 29; 'Show Saturday', p. 37; 'The Explosion', p. 42.
21. *The Whitsun Weddings*, p. 28.
22. *The Less Deceived*, p. 18.
23. *High Windows*, p. 40.
24. The poem is about sex and youth 'and everyone young going down the long slide. To happiness, endlessly.' But the ending, provoked perhaps by the word happiness, gives it pause.
25. *High Windows*, pp. 13ff.
26. John Wain, 'Philip Larkin's

Poetry', *American Scholar*, Summer 1986.

27. This would not be the only misprint in *High Windows*.

28. John Fuller thought the subject might be Yeats in his tower.

29. George Hartley, who reviewed *High Windows* in the thirteenth and last issue of Harry Chambers' magazine *Phoenix* (Spring 1975), confirms the lighthouse solution. I have only just come across this (September 1986).

30. *Monitor*; cf. *Times Literary Supplement*, 24 January 1986.

31. *The Whitsun Weddings*, pp. 10 and 37.

32. In Oxford a sizar was called a servitor. Trinity Dublin also had sizars. Philip Larkin liked such peculiar nouns, e.g. losels, loblolly-men, in 'Toads', *The Less Deceived*, p. 32.

33. *London Review of Books*, 5–18 May 1983.

34. By Andrew Motion in *Philip Larkin* (1983) and Alan Brownjohn in *Larkin at Sixty*, for example.

35. 'Dublinesque', *High Windows*, p. 28.

GOODBYE TO THE ART OF POETRY

1. Milton, *Paradise Lost*, 3, 41–4.
2. Ibid., 3, 212.
3. Aristophanes, *Frogs*, 1054–5.
4. Vladimir Mayakovsky, last section of his final poem.
5. Philip Larkin, 'The Trees', in *High Windows* (1974).
6. Dryden's Virgil: *Aeneid*, 7, 9ff.

7. *Oxford Book of Medieval English Verse*, no. 278. 'Gears' means instinct and habit and inclination.

8. 'Barbara Allen', anonymous English ballad.

9. *Erotokritos* of Kornaros, Book 1.

10. *Oxford Book of Medieval English Verse*, no. 333.

11. Bei Dao, 'Declaration'. See his *The August Sleepwalker* (Anvil, 1989).

12. Philippe Jaccottet, 'Au petit jour', from *Ignorance* (1957). See the bilingual *Selected Poems* translated by Derek Mahon (Penguin, 1988).

13. Jaccottet, 'Au petit jour'.

14. John Gower, *Confessio Amantis*, 4, 422–3. Cf. Christopher Ricks, *The Force of Poetry*, pp. 27–9.

15. Shakespeare, *Timon of Athens*, Act Four, scene 1.

16. 'eternity's hostage...': from Boris Pasternak's poem 'When the Weather Clears'.

17. Edmund Waller, as on p. 304.

18. Charles Cotton, 'Christmas Day, 1659'.

19. Langland, *Piers Plowman*, 5, 615.

20. Ibid., 18, 239.

21. Tennyson, *In Memoriam*, XI.

22. W.B. Yeats, 'In Memory of Major Robert Gregory'.

23. Philip Larkin, 'Reasons for Attendance', in *The Less Deceived* (1955).

24. Andrew Harvey, from *Love's Fire – Recreations of Rumi* (1988).

Index

Index